W9-BAQ-647

FIVE
MINUTE
FIXES

FIVE MINUTE FIXES

Instant Answers
for Hundreds of
Everyday Hassles

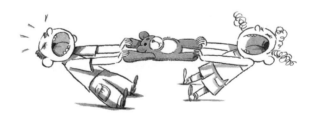

Reader's Digest

The Reader's Digest Association, Inc.
Pleasantville, New York/Montreal

Project Staff

Editor
Don Earnest

Designer
Rich Kershner

Contributing Editors
Joseph Gonzalez
Nancy Shuker

Contributing Copy Editor
Susan Ball

Contributing Indexer
Ellen Brennan

Contributing Illustrators
Harry Bates (how-to)
Travis Foster (humor)

Reader's Digest Home & Health Publishing

Editor in Chief and Publishing Director
Neil Wertheimer

Managing Editor
Suzanne G. Beason

Art Director
Michele Laseau

Production Technology Manager
Douglas A. Croll

Manufacturing Manager
John L. Cassidy

Marketing Director
Dawn Nelson

Vice President and General Manager
Keira Krausz

Reader's Digest Association, Inc.

President, North America and Global Editor-in-Chief
Eric W. Schrier

Library of Congress Cataloging-in-Publication Data

Five minute fixes / Reader's Digest.-- 1st ed.
    p. cm.
  Includes index.
  ISBN 0-7621-0509-7 (hdcvr)
  1. Home economics. I. Reader's Digest Association.
  TX145.F565 2004
  640--dc22

                                        2004020057

Address any comments about *Five Minute Fixes* to:
The Reader's Digest Association, Inc.
Editor-in-Chief, Home & Health Books
Reader's Digest Road
Pleasantville, NY 10570-7000

To order copies of *Five Minute Fixes*, call 1-800-846-2100.

Visit our Web site at **rd.com**

Printed in the United States of America
3 5 7 9 10 8 6 4 2
US4535/G

Acknowledgments

The author wishes to thank Jeff Edelstein, Kelly Garrett, Dougald MacDonald, Arden Moore, Eric Metcalf, Logan Ward, and Dave Warner for their invaluable contributions to the text. Yacht rigger Brion Toss and illustrator Margie McDonald were a particular help with knot-tying information. A grateful tip of the hat also goes to Alexandra Benwell for her I-can-find-out-anything research talents, and to the hundreds of experts who divulged their trade secrets.

To our readers

About This Book

Solving a Knotty Problem

I love discovering clever, better ways of doing things. My family laughs when I announce that I've found a "sneaky back way" to the local food market that detours traffic lights and jammed roads. I can browse a hardware store for hours, finding gizmos that solve problems I didn't realize I had. I've never been prouder than the day I whittled a plastic milk jug into a convenient, handled paint carrier to dip my brush into while standing on a ladder.

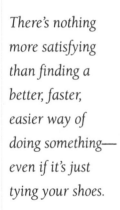

So you can imagine how my eyebrows rose the day an acquaintance told me that he knew a superior way of tying shoes. No more kneeling on the sidewalk to bind up errant laces. This technique, my friend assured me, was easy to learn (because it's similar to the conventional knot you learned in kindergarten), never comes unbound, and lets you quickly untie the laces the same old way—by tugging on one of the ends. I won't go into detail on how the knot is tied, because you'll find that information, with illustrations, on page 137 of this book. But I tried the technique then and there. It worked beautifully, and I've been using it ever since. I am now the master of shoelaces that once were wild and wanton and prone to coming undone at the worst possible times.

There's nothing more satisfying than finding a better, faster, easier way of doing something—even if it's just tying your shoes.

Going to Unexpected Experts

Perhaps I'm crazy, but I consider that knowledge of a better way to tie shoes a great gift. Just a morsel of information, passed from one person to another—at zero cost—and one more distraction has been erased from my life. I've thrown big money at lesser problems.

I hope you have a similar experience, several hundred times over, as you browse through and read *Five Minute Fixes*. To put this book together, my team of how-to writers scoured the countryside for the handiest people we could find in all walks of life. We talked with builders, painters, mechanics, nurses, forest rangers, scoutmasters—people whose expertise you would expect to find in a book like this. But we didn't leave it at that. We also grilled a fashion show manager, a lion tamer, a butler, an odor scientist, a TV "robot wars" show champion, Antarctic explorers, a rafting guide, a movie set builder, and other intriguing people. Our quest was to provide a fresh approach to problems you confront every day, such as a nicked windshield, water rings on antique furniture, and a torrent of spam e-mail. And you'll find solutions to a few problems we hope you never encounter, such as what to do if you find yourself face to face with a grizzly.

Covering a Wide Range of Problems

We've tried to make the scope of this book as extensive as everyday life itself. Of course, you'll find fast solutions to hundreds of problems related to your home. There are housecleaning and home-repair challenges that range from cleaning grimy carpets and filmy shower doors to fixing holes in walls, stopping trickling toilets, and getting rid of recalcitrant doors and aggravating pests. You'll also find solutions to problems related to organizing and decorating your home and dealing with clutter and storage. And the fixes extend to the exterior of the house and into the yard and garden. There are even answers on how to deal with blackouts, rebellious plumbing, and other household emergencies.

The array of subjects covered here, however, stretches far beyond your house and property. You'll learn quick ways to handle unexpected food mishaps, such as burned roasts, oversalted or overspiced stews, and crumbling cakes. And you'll discover how to deal with problems concerning your clothing—popped buttons and stains, for example—and appearance, such as frizzy hair. There are solutions to problems related to parties and weddings, such as handling difficult or unexpected guests, and awkward social situations, such as who you should introduce to whom and how to offer condolences. You'll find ways to tackle situations that pop up every day in our modern times—what to do when you lose a wallet or when a credit card won't swipe, how to deal with telemarketers, how to find a cheap flight, and how to deal with road hazards. There are even solutions to common health problems, including queasiness, rashes, and a paper cut, as well as dangerous outdoor situations, such as getting lost in the woods.

The result of all this, my team believes, is the largest and best collection of solutions to everyday problems ever put to paper. So gather up your duct tape, baling wire, and baking soda, start leafing through these pages, and watch your daily hassles melt away. You can do it. It's as easy as tying your shoes!
—*Jeff Bredenberg*

Contents

PART ONE
Home Care and Repair

■ Housecleaning

■ Tools and Workshop

■ Furniture

■ Walls and Ceilings

■ Floors

■ Doors and Windows

■ Electrical Problems

■ Plumbing Problems

■ Emergencies and Home Safety

■ Pests

PART THREE

Kitchen and Cooking

Manners and Social Obligations

PART SEVEN
Everyday Life

Modern Living

Electronic Life

Family Life

On the Road

PART EIGHT
Everyday Health and Hygiene

Common Discomforts

Minor health emergencies

The Five Minute Philosophy

The joy of fixing things

A toy train breaks. A child's tears flow. You grab the glue, and that evening the engine is as good as new. Total cost of the repair: pennies. The hug you get in return: priceless.

Your toilet runs, even when you jiggle the handle. After lifting the tank lid, you spy the mangled rubber stopper at the bottom. Snap in the $1.29 replacement part, and the toilet stops on cue. But the feeling of satisfaction, for plugging the leak without paying a plumber, keeps flowing all afternoon.

It feels good to fix things.

Despite the forces working to turn ours into a disposable culture— ever busier schedules, ever available cheap consumer goods—the fix-it philosophy remains deeply embedded in the human psyche. Whether it's gluing a child's toy or rescuing a burned roast or mending a broken chair leg, it not only feels good to fix things, it is good—responsible, ethical, economical—to fix things.

Coping with the daily flood of problems

Fixing things was once part of everyday life. We had fewer things, and part of being a good homeowner, parent, or grandparent was the ability to run a sound household and keep things clean and working right. But times have changed. We're busier than ever, we own more stuff, the stuff we own is more complicated. As a result, problems bombard us daily in every corner of our lives. Maybe it's the car (you locked the keys inside), the house (the floor squeaks), your feet (they stink), or a party guest (she just won't leave). Having the know-how necessary to solve each and every dilemma is impossible. That's the nature of trouble, the nature of life.

And yet the problems keep coming. Many are trivial, many are humorous, and some sap the spirit right out of you. When we launched the writing of this book, we sat in a room and brainstormed all the things that could go wrong in a typical day: around the house, in the garden, in the kitchen, with the clothing, and on and on. At first, it was great fun. Like kids in a mud puddle, we came up with lots of easy ways to make a mess.

But as we got past 200 things, then 300 things, then much beyond, the laughter died down. Not just because of the big number, but also because so many of the problems on the list had actually *happened* to each of us. We may be an incredibly diverse bunch of folks, but who among us hasn't had to deal with a popped button, hardened candle wax on the table, an unwanted visitor, or a stuck window?

The search for fast and easy solutions

Five Minute Fixes was created to quickly put the smile back on your face whenever such annoyances emerge. In the pages that follow, you will encounter an extraordinary assortment of remedies to hundreds of everyday problems we are sure you have faced or will likely face sometime soon. Some of the solutions are absolutely ingenious. Some will strike you as basic common sense. (But remember: It is exactly when trouble happens that common sense is in shortest supply!) And all are tested and proven to work.

The Mother of Invention

Every problem can be an opportunity to learn something new. And every so often problems inspire true innovation, not to mention fame and fortune. Here are a couple of not-so-big grievances that positive thinkers spun into gold.

- In the 1890s, the Kellogg brothers of Battle Creek, Michigan, were on a quest to create new grain-based products. They succeeded, creating a coffee substitute and a kind of granola. But the Kelloggs' most important innovation came about by mistake. One day, the brothers goofed, letting some cooked wheat germ go stale. Instead of tossing it, they forced it through the rollers that they used to press their oat dough into granola. Each wheat berry came out as a separate flake. They baked the flakes and decided they tasted good. At some point, someone added milk. The rest is breakfast-cereal history.

- One day in 1948, when Swiss amateur mountaineer George de Mestral arrived home from walking his dog through a field, he noticed burrs clinging to his clothes and the dog's fur. Studying a burr under his microscope, he realized that tiny hooks made the seedpod stick to the loops in his pants fabric. This gave him the idea of developing a two-part nylon fastener, one part made up of burrlike hooks and the other part composed of soft loops. Combining the words *velour* and *crochet*, he called his invention Velcro. It stuck.

Just as important, all the solutions are fast and easy. Although we didn't take a stopwatch to each task to determine whether it could be done in under five minutes, we've tried to maintained the spirit of this book's title throughout.

That includes how we've organized the book. We've tried to make it as easy as possible to locate problems and their solutions. Our goal was to let you know your problem's remedy within 60 seconds of picking up the book. A fast look at the table of contents should get you to within a few pages of your destination, and a quick scanning of the headings should get you to the precise answer. Once there, we've written each solution to be succinct and clear. No windy discourses on tools and materials here!

Of course, you needn't wait for problems to occur to read further. We're sure you'll find this book wonderful to browse through and read at your leisure. Not only will you learn all about fast, simple fixes, but you'll also be amused at our tales of world-class goofs, world-class fixes, and secret tricks of the trade that some people with very interesting jobs have divulged.

Getting in the right mind-set

Not sure you're ready for this? You're in good company. Many people claim they are lousy at fixing things and are easily intimidated by tools, instructions, or the risk of doing further damage. We commiserate. As we said before, the modern-day world is so complicated, so diverse that no one can possibly be master of every common skill.

But guess what? You don't need to be. More important than expertise is attitude. To become truly savvy at fixing mechanical as well as health, kitchen, social, and other vexations, what you really need is the right mind-set. As you'll see, you almost never need expertise with a particular tool or in a special subject area to fix something. All you need is some confidence and the willingness to give it a try.

We polled some highly resourceful people to find out just what it is they all have in common. We didn't ask about specific skills; among the dozen or so contacted, one is a knot expert, another a salvager of architectural treasures, two more form an adventure photography team. Instead, we probed them for insight into their philosophy. As savvy fixers, what makes them tick? We've distilled the results into a set of easily digestible principles. Read them. Learn them. Keep them handy, as you would a kit of tools.

■ THE NINE RULES OF
HIGHLY EFFECTIVE FIXERS

#1 Be positive

You've seen the bumper sticker. *Stuff* happens. Minor frustrations are the norm, not the exception. Trying to pin blame on someone is usually a waste of time. Negativity clouds the mind. Got it? Good. Because avoiding the victim trap is an essential component of the fixer philosophy. If you drop and break a china cup, you can think "unfair," or you can marvel at how long you and that cup defied gravity, a force powerful enough to sling planets through the solar system. Then you can zero in on a solution.

You must get over that initial emotional response to a problem. Only then you will start to think of solutions. If you assume there is a way to deal with a problem, you'll probably find one. Think self-fulfilling prophecy.

#2 Have a sense of humor

If looking on the bright side is an indispensable fix-it trait, sometimes it's also necessary to get downright silly, especially when things are so bad (a backed-up toilet is flooding the hall, a downpour drenches your business suit before an important meeting) that the alternative is tears. If negativity clouds the mind, acute stress shackles bright ideas. Break those chains with a little laughter.

#3 Think fast, but take your time

Sounds like some impossible Zen paradox, right? Like "What is the sound of one hand clapping?" Well, there's an important distinction between thinking fast and acting fast without thinking. The latter is called panicking, and panic has no place in the Five Minute Philosophy.

Say your son loses a tooth in a backyard ball game. He's screaming, his friends are screaming, blood is everywhere. What do you do? Rush him to the hospital? Yes, but... thinking fast, you search for the tooth and find it lying in the grass. Sure enough, as the fix on page 364 confirms, that dislodged tooth might be reimplanted. Rinse the tooth with water (touching the crown only) and slip it back into the socket (or into a cup of cold milk) to prevent it from drying out. Now you can drive your son—carefully—to the emergency room. A well thought-out fix is more effective than a botched attempt at a speedy fix.

#4 Be prepared

You might think being prepared means stocking the world's most complete set of tools: a different gadget for every loose nut, leaky pipe, or scratched antique credenza. Not true, as you'll find out in the next section, "The Five Minute Toolbox." A garage-load of tools is expensive and mentally burdensome. (Where is that three-tined, chrome-plated thingamabob?) Not being able to put your hands on a tool can turn a five minute job into a two-month-and-five-minute job.

Along with the "Toolbox" section's specific list of versatile tools for your Five Minute Toolbox, here are some ideas on how to generally prepare yourself for the problems that punctuate our daily lives.

• **EXERCISE YOUR HANDS.** You may take them for granted, but your hands are your best tools, whether used alone or in conjunction with a screwdriver, pot scrubber, or garden rake. Practice fine motor skills with detailed work such as needlepoint or piano playing. Build strength by squeezing a tennis ball while watching television. Hone hand-eye coordination through art projects, such as sculpting, whittling, or calligraphy.

• **EXERCISE YOUR MIND.** It's like a computer database of past experience. Make a mental note every time a problem arises and you attempt a solution, whether you're successful or not. The database will build on itself, improving your effectiveness.

• **HAVE TOOLS AT THE READY.** OK, you can get only so far using your hands and mind. Here's a good general tip for being tool-ready for most household fixes. As we suggest later, keep two tool totes handy—one filled with what you need for light repairs (claw hammer, small ruler, cordless screwdriver with two-way bit, locking-style pliers, brads, finish nails, flashlight, pencil, stud finder) and the other empty. When a special project arises, load the empty one with the right tools, and you're ready.

#5 Think out of the box

Some fixes are straightforward. Others demand creativity. Say your window screen has a small hole. The most straightforward approach would be to replace the screen. But that's overkill, both time-consuming and expensive. You could, of course, patch it with a piece of screen, but the patch would be an ugly blemish on the otherwise uniform screen. After a little creative thinking, you dab clear nail polish over the hole, which invisibly seals it. Voila! That's thinking outside the box.

Another example: What do you do if the drawstring comes out of your pajamas? Do you toss them and buy another pair? Of course not. And yet you'll find no special pajama-stringing tool at your local hardware or fabric store. Thinking creatively, you tie the end of the drawstring to a pencil and poke that through the pajama waist, bunching and smoothing the fabric until the tip pokes through the other hole. No pencil or other tool to tie the string to? Wet one end of the drawstring and place the string in the freezer. Once it has hardened, use the stiff end to work through the waistband. The true five minute fixer knows that anything is a potential tool.

#6 Know thine enemy

Trying to tackle a problem that you don't fully understand can make matters worse. Let's say you've got ants in your house. Your first response might be to grab a can of bug spray and start blasting. But if those ants happen to be Pharaoh ants, then the queen will splinter the colony, creating new queens to lay more eggs for survival. Instead of conquering the ants, you may have unwittingly doubled or tripled the colony's size.

So study a problem. Analyze it. Break it down into its most elemental parts: ants, house, access point between the two. Do your homework. (Maybe your local cooperative extension agency can identify the ants.) And then choose a solution. In this case, sealing up the entry point will likely halt the migration of ants into the house.

There simply isn't a ready-made solution for every one of life's little problems. But with a little creativity, anything, even frozen string, can become a tool.

#7 Be flexible

A necessary ingredient for the aforementioned creativity is flexibility: the ability to adapt to new situations. Being flexible means keeping an open mind, whether that involves the tools you use or the results you seek. The key to flexibility when it comes to tools is to step back from the name of an object, which limits how it can be used. Take a bread pan, for example. If you view it as a deep-sided rectangular metal tray rather than merely as a pan for bread, a world of uses may open up.

#8 Start simple

If the simplest solution doesn't work, move on to more involved ones. If your car won't start, you would first check the battery and maybe try jump-starting it. If that doesn't work, check the spark plugs. If it's not the spark plugs, try the carburetor. There's no reason to expend time, effort, and resources if the simplest possible solution solves the problem. Besides, a step-by-step approach—from simplest to most involved—gives you a problem-solving structure to follow.

#9 Think it through

Guided imagery. Cancer patients use it to overcome pain. World-class athletes depend on it for success. Author Dale Carnegie espoused it as a way to win friends and influence people. Also known as visualization, guided imagery is the practice of mentally mapping out a sequence of desired results, such as a golfer visualizing her swing, the arc of the ball, and where it will land on a fairway. Practicing guided imagery can help the savvy fixer anticipate goof-ups and achieve greater problem-solving success.

Here's how visualization might apply to a five minute fix. Once you've settled on a solution but before you dive in and start gluing that ladder-back chair back together, take a few minutes to walk through the sequence of events in your mind. See each step. Feel it. Try to experience it before you actually do it. Layer on any details, such as the fit of the chair rungs and the dripping of the glue, to fill out the picture. Relax. Don't rush. Finally, linger on the most important image: the end result. Your goal is to start with success clearly imprinted in the mind.

The Five Minute Toolbox

Tools are the intermediaries between you and your environment. They allow you to turn a nut when your hands don't have the gripping power; to move a mountain of compost when you don't have the muscles or stamina to carry that much stuff all at once; and to cut materials that are too tough to break with your hands.

To make many of the fixes in this book, it is important that you have a good set of conventional tools, such as hammers, saws, screwdrivers, and pliers, and you'll find a description of these tools in the special feature starting on page 26. But in this section, we want to draw your attention to some often-overlooked tools and supplies that are versatile, inexpensive, and durable time-savers. We surveyed some of the handiest people we know about the unexpectedly useful tools and other supplies that a person should have on hand to handle the kinds of problems covered in this book. And the results are given below. If you put these items on your shopping list and stock your home, car, and workplace with them, 99 percent of life's everyday fix-its will roll aside like, well, water off duct tape.

A first-rate fixer like you always has a good set of tools handy. But is there baking soda and vinegar in your workshop?

■ SOME UNEXPECTEDLY USEFUL TOOLS AND SUPPLIES

✔ Duct tape

What's not to love about duct tape? It's strong, flexible, and waterproof. You can cut it to any length your task calls for. And when its job is done, chances are the same piece will still be perfectly good. Just wrap it around the outside of the original roll, and you can use it again. Duct tape comes in a variety of colors, the most common being silver.

We know a photographer who improvised a dental cap for himself with duct tape when he broke a molar during an Antarctic expedition. This supertape seems to hold much of the rest of his life together, too.

TRICKS OF THE TRADE

Impromptu Tools at Your Fingertips

Not every tool has to be bought off the rack at your home improvement store. Scores of everyday objects around you will fill in nicely when "official" tools are not available. Colin Wallace, a Toronto Scout leader and consultant on organizational effectiveness, offers these ideas for improvised tools:

• Use a coin as a screwdriver for slotted screws.

• Use a belt buckle as a bottle opener.

• A credit card will scrape ice off your windshield.

• Use a necktie as a sling for an injured arm.

• A quarter makes a good measuring tool. Its diameter is 1 inch (2.5 centimeters). And a dollar bill is 6 inches (15 centimeters) long.

• Extend your arms out parallel to the ground at shoulder level. That distance, fingertip to fingertip, is equal to your height.

He uses it to keep the little rubber caps from popping off his tripod, to cover his wrists and ankles when mosquitoes attack, to fix a leaky canoe, and to restore a split paddle. He has even repaired a pair of torn work pants with a half dozen strips of red duct tape.

✔ Dental floss

Dental floss is string on steroids. It's superstrong and comes in a compact case. When you travel, chances are you take some with you in your toiletries kit, so all you need to do is remember that floss can do more than just clean teeth. Travelers swear by it for repairing torn tote bag straps and backpacks. (It helps if you've also packed a big sewing needle.) Dental floss is much stronger than thread, and its slippery surface allows it to slide more easily through tough fabrics. You can also use it to tie a package closed or as a clothesline when you're on the road.

One Peace Corps volunteer we interviewed used floss to repair a broken necklace. She just threaded the loose beads onto a piece of floss and knotted the ends, which sufficed until she got the necklace home for a permanent repair.

Dental floss has culinary uses, too. For instance, you can use it to slice a cake by holding the floss taut across the top of the cake, pushing down, and then sliding it out the side. It can be used to slice cheese as well (unwaxed for soft cheese, waxed for hard).

✔ Sewing kit

Keep a compact sewing kit near at hand. Not only is it handy for stitching up your split pants in a jiffy, but the needles are also useful for extracting thorns, glass, splinters, and the like from your skin. (Remember to sterilize the needle with a match first.) At a minimum, include black and white thread in your kit; throw in a few other colors for versatility. Stock the kit with three needles—small, medium, and large (for tough fabrics).

✔ Multitools

Going out and about with a case of tools is impractical. That's what makes the Swiss Army Knife, the Leatherman, and other multitools so popular. These fold-up, many-tools-in-one gizmos are lightweight and compact. They come in a variety of models, so you can select the array of tools you'll be most likely to need.

For example, one model of Swiss Army Knife sports two screw-drivers (flat head and Phillips), durable scissors, a bottle and can opener, a corkscrew, a nail file, a magnifying glass (to help you read small print or start a fire with no matches), and two knife blades (one with a ruler on the blade). Other models offer such unexpected items as tweezers, wire strippers, and toothpicks. Some even have clocks, alarms, and mini-flashlights.

Leatherman and its competitors are essentially a pair of pliers with a host of additional tools that swing out of the handles when needed. They tend to be a little more bulky than the Swiss Army Knife and can include heavier-duty tools, such as miniature wire cutters, files, and saws. When you're contemplating your choice, here are a few things to think about besides the variety of models:

- Do the sharp tools lock in place, so they won't close on your hand while you're using them?
- Do several tools tend to swing out of the handle when you're trying to pull out only one of them?
- Does the frame come in a high-visibility color? Multitools are easily lost in the woods (one park ranger has collected a buck-etful), so picking one in a bright color is a good idea.

✔ Zip ties

Some people never go anywhere without zip ties, also known as cable ties. These strong nylon bands consist of a head (something like a belt buckle) and a slotted band. Wrap the band around two or more objects, slip the tapered end through the locking head, and tighten. The objects are bound fast.

Zip ties are great for holding car parts in place, bundling wires, binding newspapers, repairing fences, substituting for shoestrings, securing ponytails, and more. You typically have to snip the tie to release the objects you've bound together, although some ties feature a release mechanism. Zip ties are sold in a variety of colors, range in length from 4 inches to 11 inches (10 to 28 centimeters), and are available at home improvement stores.

✔ Galvanized wire

Galvanized wire (also known as baling or bale wire) is a great way to affix one object to another. And unlike duct tape and zip ties (see above), galvanized wire can stand up to extreme heat, which means you can use it to secure a wobbly muffler on your car or a loose carburetor on your lawn mower. This wire, which is $\frac{1}{16}$ inch (1.6 millimeters) thick, comes on a roll and can be purchased at hardware and home improvement stores. It can be twisted and snipped with pliers. Among its myriad uses:

- When you've stripped the threads on a screw on an appliance, run some galvanized wire through the screw hole and twist it to hold things together until you can make a permanent fix.
- Galvanized wire can be used to mend fences in a variety of ways; for instance, you can use it to splice broken wires, fasten wire fencing to a post, or reinforce a post that has cracked or broken.
- Use it to hang things up, such as pictures in your house, bird-houses, wind chimes, or seasonal items stored in the garage.
- String some galvanized wire between two trees and throw a blanket over it to make a play tent for the kids.

✔ Staple gun

Which would you rather do: spend an hour tapping tacks or brads with a hammer, or accomplish the same task in a few minutes with a spring-loaded staple gun? On this planet, most people would opt for the latter. With the squeeze of a handle, a staple gun will fire a hefty two-pronged staple into wood and other hard but penetrable surfaces. Use it to put up holiday decorations in just moments, to hold speaker wires in place, to secure a broken window screen, or to tack down plastic sheeting before a storm arrives. Some people use their staple guns for creating elegant window treatments, draping and securing fabric, and reupholstering furniture.

If you're going to do a lot of stapling, consider a model that will allow you to adjust the firing strength of the gun, or even consider an electric unit. If the stapling you're doing is meant to be temporary, wrap a hefty rubber band around the staple gun so that it's right next to where the staple shoots out. This will act as a "spacer," leaving the top of the staple protruding so it can be removed easily.

✔ Spray lubricant

Life is full of things that don't slide and glide as easily as they ought to—hinges, lug nuts, zippers, and pruning shears, just to name a few. For that reason alone, it's worth keeping cans of spray lubricant in your car, toolshed, office, and kitchen cabinet. You can buy this stuff just about anywhere, including supermarkets, hardware stores, discount stores, auto stores, and home improvement stores. The most famous brand is WD-40, but other brands are available, too.

Aside from straightforward lubrication, there are scores of other inventive uses for spray lubricant, including these:

- Coat garden tools with it to prevent rust.
- Spray it on your snow shovel to keep slush from sticking to it.
- For crayon marks on hard surfaces such as tile, counters, wood furniture, and painted walls, just spray the lubricant on and wipe the marks away.
- Spray it on building ledges and eaves to repel pigeons.

✔ Compressed air

For some cleaning tasks, you need a blast of wind—and nothing more. Cleaning fluids will wreck some delicate items (such as dried flowers). And you might think that just puffing up your cheeks and blowing onto that electronic game cartridge will do fine for dislodging dust, but you'd be running a risk: Your breath carries tiny water droplets, which can damage electronic parts. The solution is compressed air. Pick up several cans at a computer store or photo shop and station them in your toolbox, office, kitchen, entertainment center, and garage.

Here's just a sampling of other things you can clean with compressed air: cable ports on computers, cameras, CD and DVD players, computer screens, electric shavers, keyboards, power tools, sewing machines, slides and negatives, smoke alarms, and typewriters. Cans of compressed air also are handy for cleaning in hard-to-reach places—the blades of a tabletop fan, for instance. Many brands of compressed air come with a little extender tube that can get the blast of air closer to hard-to-reach spots.

When you're using cans of compressed air, hold the can upright. Otherwise, you might get some of the propellant mixed in with the air, dampening something you didn't want to get wet. Also remember that the air is rushing out with considerable force and could damage delicate objects. You can reduce the force, of course, by moving the can farther away from the object being cleaned. And make sure your compressed air doesn't drive dust into the housing of your electronic equipment—say, through the vents on the side of your computer monitor. For that kind of cleaning, a handheld vacuum would be a better choice.

TRICKS OF THE TRADE

Make Instant Wind from a Squeeze Bottle
If you don't have a can of compressed air handy, Don Morin, president of the Canadian Professional Sewing Association in Toronto, offers a clever way to improvise: Thoroughly clean out an old plastic squeeze bottle (for example, one that contained dishwashing liquid) and squeeze the bottle to make compressed air. The air blast won't be as strong or prolonged as what you get from a can of compressed air, but it will do a nice job of puffing debris out of sewing machines, keyboards, appliances, or other intricate objects. And you can't beat the cost!

✔ Baking soda

Sodium bicarbonate, also known as good old baking soda, is the multitool of the chemical world. You can use this nontoxic, mild alkali for scores of chores around the house, including cleaning, scouring, polishing, and removing stains. But aside from cooking uses, baking soda is probably most famous for deodorizing refrigerators. Open a box and stash it in the back of the fridge, and it will absorb odors, keeping your milk from tasting like your leftover Chinese food. Here's just a sampling of its other uses:

- Sprinkle some baking soda on a damp sponge and use it as a gentle scouring powder.
- Smother a grease fire with it on the stovetop.
- Brush your teeth with it.
- To remove a musty smell from carpeting, sprinkle the carpet with baking soda, let it sit for three or four hours, and vacuum it up.
- Mix 2 tablespoons in 1 quart (1 liter) of warm water and use it to clean hard surfaces, such as tile, counters, and stainless steel.

✔ White vinegar

White vinegar is another inexpensive and versatile household substance. Buy this mild acid by the jug at your supermarket or wholesale club. Mix ¼ cup in 1 quart (1 liter) of water for cleaning hard surfaces, including windows. Vinegar kills germs and mold. It also removes stains, grease, and wax buildup and does a super job of breaking down mineral deposits on faucets and showerheads.

Vinegar can even be used to remove soil from the hems of pants. Use a cloth to dab the vinegar on until the mark is wet, let it dry, and brush off the loosened soil.

More jobs for white vinegar:

- Use white vinegar as a hair rinse to neutralize alkaline residue left by shampoos.
- If glassware comes out of the dishwasher looking filmy, bathe each glass for a minute or two in vinegar, wipe with a scrubber sponge, and rinse.
- To clean your coffeemaker, fill the tank with a half-and-half mixture of water and vinegar, put a new filter in the basket to catch loosened debris, and turn the machine on. Let the coffeemaker run through its entire cycle, then run it through two more cycles with fresh water.

✔ Rubbing alcohol

Rubbing alcohol is a top-notch cleaner, stain remover, and disinfectant. It's inexpensive and versatile. It also dries quickly, so it makes a great streak-free window cleaner and is good for removing dirt from electronic gear that could be damaged by water, such as calculators, remote controls, and keyboards.

- To make your own glass cleaner, mix ½ cup of rubbing alcohol, 2 squirts of dishwashing liquid, and a gallon of warm water.
- To kill germs on your child's toys and furniture, moisten a cleaning cloth with rubbing alcohol and wipe.
- To remove a lipstick stain from fabric, pretreat it by blotting on rubbing alcohol. Then launder as usual.
- To remove an ink stain from fabric, pour some rubbing alcohol on a cleaning cloth and blot (don't rub) at the stain. Let the moistened stain sit for half an hour, then blot at the stain with a fresh cloth, adding more alcohol as needed. Keep moving to new sections of the cleaning cloth, drawing out more ink as you go. Rinse the stain with ¼ cup of white vinegar mixed with 1 quart (1 liter) of water, and rinse again with straight water.
- To remove hair spray buildup on your bathroom mirror, pour some rubbing alcohol on a cleaning cloth and wipe.

Some warnings: Don't get rubbing alcohol confused with drinkable alcohol: Rubbing alcohol is poisonous and is also highly flammable. Keep it away from kids.

Basic Household Tools

Ninety percent of being a good five minute fixer is being prepared for most common problems. So make sure that your toolbox is stocked with these essential tools:

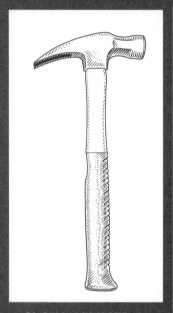

■ CLAW HAMMER

Every toolbox should have an average-weight (16-ounce or .45 kilogram) claw hammer, with a two-pronged claw opposite the face, for driving and pulling nails and for light demolition work, such as busting sheetrock. Make sure the head is drop-forged steel (and not cast iron, which will chip). Whether it is wood, fiberglass, or steel, the handle should feel comfortable when you swing the hammer.

■ ELECTRIC DRILL/DRIVER

For drilling and driving screws, a good electric drill/driver is a must, and given today's battery technology, it does not need a cord. For all-purpose use, choose a T-handled tool, which balances the battery weight better than one with a pistol grip. One with variable speeds allows you to use a low-rpm setting for driving screws and a higher one for drilling. Buy a basic set of drill bits and a couple of driver bits. (For driver bit sizes, follow the advice about screw-driver sizes opposite.) Buy a brand you trust, and don't pay more for packaged extras, such as flashlights and small circular saws, that you won't need. If you own two batteries, you can always keep a charged one on hand when the other dies.

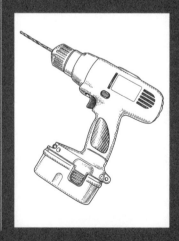

■ WRENCH

The most common and useful type of wrench, the adjustable (or Crescent) wrench, is great for turning square and hex nuts and bolts. A thumbscrew opens and closes its parallel jaws, allowing for quick and easy adjusting. For maximum versatility, buy a medium-sized wrench.

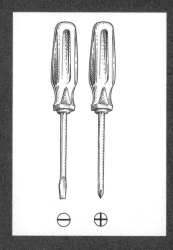

■ SCREWDRIVERS

Keep a handful of screw-drivers in your tool kit—at least two sizes of regular slotted screwdrivers ($^3/_{16}$ inch and $^1/_4$ inch or 4.7 and 6.3 millimeters) and two sizes of Phillips screwdrivers (#1 and #2). In Canada, you'll need a Robertson square-drive screwdriver. Buy good-quality screwdrivers, which are still relatively inexpensive. Keep a cheap slotted screwdriver around for prying and chiseling.

■ TAPE MEASURE

Tape measures feature spring-loaded, retractable steel tapes, or "blades." They come in different blade widths and lengths.

For around-the-house use, a 16-foot (5-meter) tape measure with a $^3/_4$-inch (2 centimeter) blade is a good, compact choice.

■ PLIERS

Pliers are handheld levers (the joint being the fulcrum) that help you get a grip on what you're doing. There are many types—some that lock, others with cutters near the pivot—but for the basic toolbox, all you really need are medium-sized slip-joint

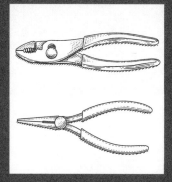

pliers and needle-nose pliers. The former, made to fit the palm comfortably, are highly versatile. They have both flat and curved sets of teeth in their jaws, for gripping objects of different shapes, and feature an adjustable (or slip-joint) pivot, allowing you to grip both large and small objects. Needle-nose pliers, which often feature wire cutters, are not adjustable

but come in many sizes. These long, pointed pliers are useful for twisting and looping wire, fishing out dropped screws, and delicate work, such as small-appliance repair.

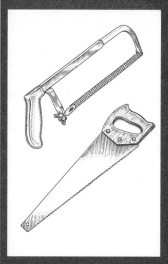

■ SAWS

Two handsaws that will cover most of your needs are a crosscut saw and a hacksaw. Tapering from heel (near the handle) to toe, crosscut saws, used for cutting across the grain of wood, vary in both length and teeth per inch. The longer the saw, the fewer strokes needed to finish the job. The more teeth on the saw, the smoother the cut. A 12-tooth per inch tempered-steel crosscut saw that is 22 inches (56 centimeters) long is a good all-purpose saw. Hacksaws

continued

continued from 27

are for cutting metal. They come with replaceable blades, which also vary in tooth count (14 to 32 teeth per inch) and length (8 to 16 inches or 20 to 40 centimeters long). The thicker the metal, the fewer teeth the blade should have. A good all-purpose hacksaw has an adjustable frame that adapts to both blade lengths.

■ CARPENTER'S SQUARE

The simplest carpenter's square is an L-shaped steel ruler used to mark straight lines perpendicular to a board's edge. The combination square is a versatile variant with a base that features a level and allows you to mark both 90- and 45-degree angles.

■ PUTTY KNIFE

Whether you're filling nail holes with spackling or scraping old paint from windowsills, a putty knife is a must for any toolbox. These come in various blade widths. A 2-inch (5-centimeter) knife is not too wide for scraping paint or old caulk, nor is it too narrow for spreading fillers.

■ LEVEL

A carpenter's level, which has a bubble of air inside a tube of liquid, can tell you if a surface is perfectly horizontal (level) or vertical (plumb). Levels come in different lengths. A 2-foot (60-centimeter) level is practical for household use.

■ CLAMPS

Clamps are helpful for holding surfaces together while gluing or when you need a third hand for securing that piece of wood you're working on. They come in many styles and sizes. Common household clamps are C-clamps, which have an adjustable threaded jaw that closes on a fixed jaw, and spring clamps, which can be opened and closed quickly by squeezing the handles.

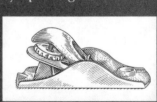

■ PLANE

Handheld planes, such as a block plane or bench plane, contain razor-sharp blades that lock in at adjustable angles. By drawing a plane evenly across wood, you can smooth and trim the surface or clean up the edges.

Safety Gear

No matter how fast you can do a job, always wear safety gear appropriate to the job you are doing. Here are some tips on selecting what you need:

- **Safety goggles.** Don't rely on ordinary eyeglasses to guard your eyes when particles may be flying. Wear special protective safety glasses with side shields (you can get them for your prescription) or safety goggles that can be worn over your regular eyeglasses.
- **Earmuffs.** Wear ear protection when decibel levels start to rise. Earmuffs are easier to take off and put on than earplugs and are harder to misplace. But both protect equally well if their noise reduction rating (NRR) is at least 25.

- **Dust masks.** For ordinary dust and paint fumes, use disposable dust masks labeled "NIOSH-approved," indicating approval by the National Institute of Occupational Safety and Health. They are thicker than cheaper masks and have two straps for a tighter seal. If you need more protection, look for a respirator with changeable dual cartridges that are color-coded to filter out the particular types of toxic dust or fumes you are working with.
- **Work gloves.** Protect your hands from abrasive materials with sturdy cloth-and-leather work gloves. Protect your hands from toxic or irritating liquids with heavy rubber gloves.

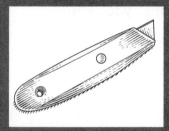

■ UTILITY KNIFE

Even if you're just using it to slice up cardboard for recycling, a utility knife can be a handy tool to keep around. For safety's sake, choose a model with a retractable blade. Standard blades are double-ended (reversible), and extras can often be stored safely and conveniently in the knife's handle.

■ WOOD CHISEL

A chisel is a sharp, precisely beveled tool used for deep-cutting or shaving wood. If you needed to mortise (or recess) a hinge in a doorjamb, you would tap on a chisel with a mallet. A ½-inch (1.25-centimeter) chisel is a good general-purpose tool.

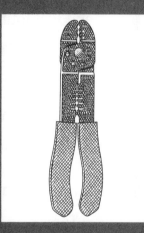

■ ELECTRICIAN'S TOOL

An electrician's multipurpose tool has many uses, including cutting, stripping, and crimping wire. Small pliers on the nose also allow you to grip and twist wire.

PART ONE

Home Care and Repair

The key is stuck in your door, and the lightbulb broke off in its socket. You lost your Phillips screwdriver, and you found a ring—a white one, marring your antique table. The baby threw up on the carpet, and the dog has fleas. (Or is it the other way around?) Sound like a bad day? Read on, and these dilemmas will roll right off your back.

Housecleaning

PROBLEM STOPPER

Keeping Candles from Dripping

Removing wax from a candelabra is one thing, but getting it off fine furniture or tablecloths can be a chore. You can prevent the wax from dripping in the first place by putting your candles in the freezer for at least 24 hours before lighting them.

■ HARD-TO-CLEAN ITEMS

My ceiling is so high, I can't reach the cobwebs

TAPE A FEATHER DUSTER TO A POLE Pulling out the extension ladder is not a practical option here; you'd never get around to it. The trick is to attach a feather duster to the end of the kind of extension pole that painters use to roll paint on ceilings. Attach the duster using duct tape (for a more permanent connection) or a couple of twist ties (if you don't want to commit the pole or the duster to full-time cobweb duty). Then simply brush away the webs.

How do I clean my chandelier without making a mess?

USE AN UMBRELLA TO CATCH DRIPS You can quickly clean a crystal chandelier without taking it apart by using an umbrella as you spritz with an alcohol cleaning solution. Mix 2 teaspoons of rubbing alcohol and a pint of warm water in a spray bottle. Hang an opened umbrella upside down, attaching the handle to the bottom of the chandelier. Cover the bulbs and sockets with sandwich bags secured with twist ties. As you spray the cleaner on, the umbrella catches the dirty drips. Because the umbrella is closer to the source, it catches a lot more drips than would newspapers or a drop cloth spread out on the floor.

My candelabra is covered with wax

PEEL AND THEN MELT THE REST WITH HOT WATER One popular trick for removing wax from candlesticks is to put them in the freezer and then peel off the hardened wax. But candelabras and menorahs are often too big to fit into a freezer. And if they contain dissimilar metals that freeze at different rates, freezing could harm them. Instead, try the following technique, which is faster and works like a charm: First, remove as much of the wax as possible with your fingers. Then run hot water over the candelabra in the kitchen sink. Hot water won't hurt silver, but it will melt the wax right off.

Candle wax dripped onto my woodwork

USE ICE CUBES TO HARDEN IT To remove wax drippings, use the cold treatment. Carefully peel off the biggest chunks with your fingernails or a plastic kitchen scraper and chill the remaining wax with ice cubes in a plastic bag. Once chilled, the wax will be easier to break up and remove. Wipe off any remaining bits with a cloth moistened with mineral spirits (paint thinner). Some people recommend warming candle wax to wipe it off, but try this only as a last resort, since the wax could melt and penetrate deeper into the wood's pores.

Dusting my plants is tedious work

SHOWER THEM INSTEAD Quit dusting your indoor plants—just give them a shower once in a while. Place the dusty plants on the floor of your shower. Set your showerhead on mist and spritz the plants. If you're afraid of overwatering them, wrap each pot in a plastic bag, covering as much of the top of the dirt as possible. Let the plants dry before returning them to their normal locations.

WORLD-CLASS FIX

Old-Fashioned Cleaning Methods

Before the days of powerful cleaning products, people had some ingenious ways of cleaning. At Virginia's Frontier Culture Museum in Staunton, costumed staff members demonstrate some of those techniques. Here are just a few:

- To clean feather mattresses, they lay the mattresses on the grass on a rainy day. When the mattresses are soaked through, they're hauled to the barn to dry.

- They scrub wooden floors and worktables with water and sand. After much elbow grease, they rinse the floors, let them dry, and sweep up the sand. In a way, it's like sanding off the top layer of wood.

- They "sweeten," or remove mold or mildew, from wooden buckets by rubbing them with water and ashes, which are mildly abrasive and caustic. The insides of the buckets are then exposed to the sun's ultraviolet rays. Sunning the buckets sterilizes them, destroying any bacteria growing inside.

- To wash wool blankets, they dunk them in soapy, near-boiling water. Then they remove them and, without rinsing, hang them to dry. The hot water does not damage the preshrunk wool. And the old lye soaps aren't sudsy and don't leave much of a residue. What little residue remains acts as a natural insect repellent.

- They scrub iron cooking pots with ashes and then season them with beef tallow.

My louvered doors are a pain to dust

USE A CLOTH-WRAPPED RULER Louvered doors can be dust magnets and a challenge to clean. Here's an easy way to clean them: Wrap a clean cotton cloth around a wooden ruler. Spray the cloth with your dusting cleaner. Then slowly run the flat end across each louver to pull up the dust easily and completely.

My baseboard heaters are clogged with dust

USE A HAIR DRYER TO BLOW THE DUST OUT Some baseboard heaters have hundreds of little crevices—quite a pain when it comes to dusting. Here's a quick and easy way to dislodge all the dust that can collect in them: Aim the nozzle of a hair dryer (set on Cool) at the dust-clogged baseboard heater, just as you might do with a leaf blower on a sidewalk. By aiming in one direction along the top of the baseboard, you'll be able to blow the dust to the floor. After a quick sweep with the vacuum cleaner, the dust will be gone.

Vacuuming my ceiling fan is a pain

USE AN OLD SOCK ON YOUR HAND TO CLEAN IT Ceiling fan blades are notorious for collecting mounds of dust. Here's a remedy that's faster and easier than trying to vacuum the blades: Place a sturdy stepladder under the fan. Pour a quart of water into a plastic bowl and add a squirt of dishwashing liquid. Dip an orphaned tube sock in the solution and wring it out. Slip the sock over your hand, climb the ladder, and run your socked hand lightly over the fan's blades, making sure to clean both the top and bottom.

■ WINDOWS

A sticker on my window left a mess

REMOVE LEFTOVER ADHESIVE WITH WD-40 You can spend hours trying to scrape sticker residue off window glass. Even razor blades don't always get off all the goop. And since leftover adhesive collects dirt, soon you're looking at an ugly splotch. Try this: Remove as much of a sticker as you can using your fingernail or a razor blade and then spray a little penetrating lubricant, such as WD-40, on the adhesive that remains. Wipe with a paper towel or rag, and the goop will come right off.

TRICKS OF THE TRADE

Erase Those Smudges
Are your patio doors covered with finger smudges and pet paw prints? Erase them in a jiff with this solution from a kindergarten teacher in Florida. When she's in a hurry, she rubs a clean blackboard eraser over her glass doors to "erase" the smudges without the need for a commercial glass-cleaning product.

Secondhand smoke is killing my windows

WASH WITH AMMONIA SOLUTION To remove nicotine film or other grime from windows, you need ammonia. Mix 1 cup of lemon-scented ammonia in 2½ gallons (9.5 liters) of water and use this solution to clean the windows. The ammonia will cut through the grime, and the lemon scent will leave your house habitable.

My windows get dirty too fast

CHANGE YOUR HEATING AND COOLING SYSTEM'S FILTER If the interior glass surface of your windows gets dirty unusually fast, you may need to change the filters on your furnace or air conditioner. Modern airtight homes trap more dust, pollen, dander, and other particles inside than ever before. Furnace and air-conditioner filters help trap that dirt and also extend the life of your appliances. Filters should be changed every month or two or anytime you can't see light through the filter when you hold it up to a light.

My windows always streak after washing

Washing windows is a tiresome chore, but it's even worse when your labors leave streaks on the windows. Here's how the pros avoid streaking when they wipe off their windows:

- Use a window-washing squeegee with a smooth, soft rubber edge. (Or use crumpled-up black-and-white newspaper—avoid the color sections.)
- Dry a 1-inch (2.5 centimeter) strip at the top or side of each window and always start your squeegee there—starting on dry glass is one key to avoiding streaks.
- Don't wash windows in direct sunlight, because quickly dried glass is more susceptible to streaking. Evenings or cloudy days are the times for window washing.

My shades are filthy

DUST OR WASH THE SHADES Dust shades regularly with a soft cloth, a duster such as the Swiffer, or the dusting brush on your vacuum. (Be sure to dust both sides of the shades.) If they're stained or spotted, it's time for a real cleaning. Though you can wash them in place (with a drop cloth over the floor and furniture), it's best to remove the shades. Place one shade at a time across a worktable covered with a plastic

TRICKS OF THE TRADE

Telling Which Side of the Glass the Streaks Are On
Can't figure out whether those ugly streaks are on the inside or outside of your windows? When you clean your windows, wipe the inside of the windows in a side-to-side direction and the outside in an up-and-down direction. This way, you can step back and easily see which side the streak is on, so you won't waste time recleaning the side that doesn't need it—and running the risk of introducing new streaks.

PROBLEM STOPPER

Keep Venetian Blinds Clean

Here's an easy way to keep the grime from air pollution or household activity from building up on the metal slats of venetian blinds: Wipe a thin coat of clear appliance or automobile wax on the blinds. The coating will keep dirt and dust from sticking, making it easier to clean with your duster or vacuum.

sheet or shower curtain. Wash vinyl shades using a sponge and a solution of ¼ cup white vinegar in 1 quart (1 liter) of warm water. Washing them in the bathtub is even easier. Run some warm water in the tub, add a squirt of dishwashing liquid, and wipe each side with a large sponge. To rise, dunk them in clean water or hold them under the shower. Then wipe with a clean, soft cloth.

Many fabric shades can also be washed, but take a close look at the care instructions before washing them. It's best not to leave them in the water for more than a minute or so.

My blinds are dust magnets!

USE AN ANTISTATIC SPRAY To keep dust from piling up quickly, use an antistatic spray, such as Static Guard, on the window blinds right after you clean them.

There's mildew on my window frames

WASH WITH A BLEACH-DETERGENT SOLUTION Black or gray mildew spots on wooden frames can be cleaned for good with a solution of 2 ounces (60 milliliters) of household bleach and 1 ounce (30 milliliters) of laundry detergent in a quart of water. Wearing rubber gloves to protect your hands, sponge the solution on the spots, let it sit for ten minutes, and then rinse thoroughly with clean water.

My screens are filthy

REMOVE AND WASH The best way to clean window screens is to remove them from the window and wash them outside. Using a broad, soft-bristled brush, scrub both sides of the screens with warm to hot water and lemon-scented dishwashing detergent. Pick up the screen by its edges, hold it at an angle so most of the screen surface is facing the ground, and rap one edge lightly against a firm surface. This will shake loose any dirt. Rinse with a hose and air-dry thoroughly before reinstalling.

My outside windowsills get dirty so quickly

APPLY A COAT OF FLOOR WAX Because your exterior windows are exposed to the elements, they are subject to collecting a lot of dirt. But there is a simple way to keep your sills clean: Wipe on a coat of clear floor wax to protect them.

■ BATHROOMS

My bathroom grout is grungy with mildew

SPRAY IT WITH VINEGAR Mildew on grout is no match for that miracle household cleaning dynamo called vinegar. Just pour some white vinegar into a container, dip in an old toothbrush, and scrub away at the mildew. Or pour the vinegar into a spray bottle, squirt it on the mildew, and let it sit for ten minutes. Rinse with water and apply the old toothbrush if necessary.

SPRAY IT WITH A BLEACH SOLUTION Bleach is also effective in removing mildew from tile grout. Fill a spray bottle with equal parts of household chloride bleach and water. Spray the grout, let it sit a few minutes, and then wipe with a clean white cotton cloth. You can also use commercial-quality paste grout cleaners, but avoid pumice stones—using them takes far too much time and removes far too little mildew from the grout.

If you find it impossible to remove the stains in grout, you might want to consider staining the seams a dark color. (See "My tile grout just won't come clean," page 71.)

The mirror fogs up when I shower

COAT THE MIRROR WITH GLYCERIN After a warm shower, you wipe off the bathroom mirror with a towel, but it just fogs up again within seconds. Try this quick solution: When you clean your bathroom, wipe a little glycerin (available at drugstores and some hardware stores) on the bathroom mirror. Buff it lightly with a soft cloth. The thin coating of glycerin will prevent the glass from fogging and will last about a week; less, if you have a lot of people taking showers.

Bathroom mirror fogging up? A quick coating of glycerin will keep the steam off.

Hair spray has hazed my mirror

WIPE IT OFF WITH ALCOHOL You probably have a fast, easy solution for hair spray haze right there in your medicine cabinet. Rubbing alcohol will cut right through the stubborn spray that's mucking up your bathroom mirror. Pour a little alcohol on a cleaning cloth or paper towel and give the mirror a rubdown.

PROBLEM STOPPER

How to Have a Lint-Free Mirror
A lot of the materials people use to clean bathroom mirrors—such as cloths and paper towels—tend to leave lint behind. Try paper coffee filters instead. They make dandy cleaners for glass surfaces and mirrors because they leave no streaks or smudges.

My shower curtain is crawling with mildew

WASH IT OFF WITH A BLEACH SOLUTION Shower curtains can be tricky to clean because they are big and cumbersome. Getting rid of mildew, especially during damp weather, can be especially challenging. Here's a solution that's quick, easy, and low-cost: Pour 1 gallon (3.7 liters) of warm water and ½ cup of household bleach into a plastic bucket. With plastic gloves on, soak a sponge in this cleaning solution, give it a squeeze to avoid drips, and wipe. The mildew will vanish. Rinse using the showerhead.

I'm ready to toss this filthy shower curtain liner

TOSS IT IN THE WASHER Don't throw away your liner just because of mildew and dirt buildup. Extend its life by cleaning it in your washing machine. Set the machine on the gentle cycle with warm water and 1 cup of regular laundry detergent or ½ cup of vinegar. Afterward, whirl it in your drier, set on Low Heat or Fluff, for about 20 minutes. Your liner will come out clean and wrinkle-free. Rehang it immediately.

My glass shower doors are filmy

CLEAN THEM WITH VINEGAR, BAKING SODA, AND SALT Stubborn mineral buildup on glass shower doors is no competition for a few common household ingredients—white vinegar, baking soda, and

Bathroom of the Future

In 1936, famed architect and futurist Buckminster Fuller presented a prototype of "the bathroom of the future." Designed to be inexpensive, compact, efficient, and a breeze to clean, the Dymaxion Bathroom consisted of four precast metal or plastic sections that bolted together into a single unit. Curved walls with smooth surfaces and large-radius corners eliminated germ-harboring nooks and crannies and grime-collecting grout lines and made cleaning with disinfectants a snap. The Fog Gun, a hyperefficient hot-water vapor shower, used only a cupful of water per shower and cleaned without soap. The waterless Packaging Toilet shrink-wrapped human waste for composting. And downdraft vents swiftly drew steam away. The superefficient design even kept the mirror from steaming up and the sink from splattering.

Alas, the Dymaxion Bathroom never caught on—although visitors can still see the prototype at the Henry Ford Museum in Dearborn, Michigan.

salt. Spray vinegar on the door and let it sit for a few minutes. Next, create a paste with equal amounts of baking soda and salt. Use a damp sponge to rub this paste over the door; then rinse well.

My laundry hamper stinks

PUT A FABRIC SOFTENER SHEET IN THE HAMPER The solution is simple: Place a sheet of fabric softener in the bottom of your laundry hamper and change it every week. Or sprinkle some baking soda in the bottom of the basket.

Those nonslip bathtub stickers won't peel off

LOOSEN THEM WITH LAUNDRY PRESOAK You know the ones: They're shaped like flowers and fish and are stuck on with industrial-strength adhesive. Instead of ruining the smooth surface of your tub trying to scrape them off, follow these simple steps for removing them:

1. Carefully lift corners on each sticker using your fingernail or a plastic scraper. (Metal will scratch most tubs.)
2. Spray the stickers with a good dose of laundry pretreatment product, such as Shout or Spray 'n Wash. Let the stickers soak in the spray for a few hours. This should loosen the stickers and allow you to peel them off.
3. Wipe up any adhesive residue and the laundry spray. Clean and rinse the tub thoroughly.

My brass fixtures look dull

POLISH THEM WITH BAKING SODA AND LEMON JUICE Don't rush out to buy an expensive brass cleaner. Save time and money by making a paste with equal amounts of baking soda and lemon juice. Dip an old toothbrush in the mix and lightly scrub the fixtures. Let the solution dry a few minutes and then buff the fixtures with a clean cloth. They'll look brand new.

The nooks and crannies in my bathroom are hard to clean

USE AN OLD TOOTHBRUSH An old toothbrush is the perfect time-saving bathroom-cleaning tool. For example, you can use it to clean the tracks of your bathtub's sliding glass doors. Simply spray bath-

TRICKS OF THE TRADE

Keep Your Shower Tile Sparkling
If you have little time for housekeeping, here's an easy way to keep your shower tile free of mildew. On the shower caddy next to your shampoo, keep a spray bottle of household bleach mixed with water (1 cup of bleach to 4 cups of water). Once a week, take a few extra moments after your shower to spray the tiles with the bleach solution. Then aim the showerhead all around for a thorough rinse. For just a few seconds' investment, you'll keep your tile looking brand new. But be sure to keep the bleach solution out of the reach of kids.

room cleaner on a paper towel and wrap the towel around the bristle end of the toothbrush. Then scoot the brush along the tracks to dislodge dirt. Or put the little bristles to work on the grime that collects around the rim of a bathroom sink. Once the bristles have loosened the dirt, just mop it up with a damp sponge.

I hate those mineral deposits on my bathroom faucet

USE AN OVERNIGHT VINEGAR WRAP No one likes crusty white deposits on a faucet. Try this easy solution: Before you go to bed one night, head to your kitchen for a bottle of white vinegar and three paper towels. Saturate the towels in the white vinegar and wrap them around the faucet like a cocoon. In the morning, remove the towels. Fill the basin with warm water, plus a squirt of dishwashing liquid. Dip an old toothbrush in the solution and scrub the faucet to remove the final bits of mineral deposit.

■ KITCHEN CLEANUP

There's a burn mark on my laminate countertop

TRY BAKING SODA ON LIGHT BURNS If the burn mark on your laminate countertop is light brown, you may be able to remove it by covering it with a thick paste of baking soda and water. Let the mixture sit for 20 minutes, then scrub it off. If the burn has eaten through the laminate, you may want to install a drop-in insert (see page 61).

My laminate countertop is scratched

HIDE THE SCRATCHES WITH CAR POLISH If the scratches aren't deep, you can hide them with a car polish, such as NU Finish. Apply the product according to the directions. Buff with a soft cotton rag.

My expensive stone countertop has a stain

REMOVE WATER-BASED STAINS WITH HOT WATER Most stone stains result from liquids that seep into the stone's pores and then evaporate, leaving colored solids. To remove the stain, you need to put those solids back into solution and extract them. To remove a water-based stain, such as fruit juice, pour hot (but not boiling) water on the stain. Let the water stand for a few minutes and then soak up the excess. Lay a handful of paper towels on the stain, cover that with a piece of plastic wrap, and lay something heavy on top, like a pot of water. Let this stand overnight. In the morning, the paper towels should have drawn out the stain.

REMOVE OILY STAINS WITH ACETONE For oil-based stains, such as olive oil, follow the same procedure but instead of hot water, use (unheated) acetone. You can buy acetone at the hardware store, or you can use most nail polish removers, which are acetone. Next morning, remove the towels and wash the spot with warm, soapy water. In either case, if the stain is still there, repeat the process.

The carpets near my kitchen are grimy

USE A SPECIAL GREASE-REMOVING COMPOUND That dingy film on the carpet near your kitchen is grease. When you cook, minute particles of airborne grease land on the kitchen floor, get picked up by your feet, and are tracked onto the carpet. Vacuuming won't help. Unless you remove the grease, it will sink deeper into the fibers, turning darker and darker as it collects more dirt.

There is an easy solution: Carpet stores sell a product, called Capture, specifically designed to combat this stubborn grease. It looks like moist baking soda and comes in a plastic tub. Here's how to use it:

1. Using water in a spray bottle, mist the high-traffic areas of the carpet where the grease has collected.
2. Sprinkle the product on the dark spots and let it sit for half an hour to absorb the grease.
3. Vacuum up the powder.

When kitchen grease gets tracked onto carpets, there's a fast solution: a grease-absorber called Capture.

My big family gathering left a big mess

CLEAR UP THE WORST RIGHT AWAY There's no need to wear yourself out by tackling the *entire* mess immediately. Spend just a few minutes whipping the aftermath into shape, and then do the detail work in the morning. Assuming you have already put perishable foods away, here are the steps to follow:

1. Collect bottles, cups, and glasses. Look for spills and deal with them right away.

2. Empty half-filled glasses and cups in the kitchen sink. Toss out plastic and paper. Set the glasses on the counter. Do the same with plates and utensils.

3. Fill the dishwasher with as many dishes as you can fit in and start it when it's fully loaded.

4. Gather up the garbage in plastic bags, starting in outer rooms and working your way toward the kitchen, so that you centralize the clutter there. Take garbage out as soon as bags are filled and tied, to prevent accidental leaks and odors.

5. In the morning, after a good night's sleep, finish up by dusting and vacuuming, again working your way toward the kitchen. Clean the kitchen last.

■ ACCIDENTS

Glass just shattered all over my floor

PUT THE PIECES IN A BOX, NOT A BAG Whether it was a wineglass, a lightbulb, or a mirror that got smashed to smithereens, here's how to quickly and safely handle shattered glass. Watch your step and warn others away.

1. Wearing thick work gloves, pick up the large pieces first. Put them in a box or bucket, since a bag may tear, and the shards inside can still stab you.

2. If the breakage was on a carpet, keep picking. Vacuum up only the smallest bits.

3. If the spill was on a hard floor, such as wood or tile, sweep up the fragments and then wipe the area with damp paper towels. Those near-invisible but still-dangerous slivers will stick to the moist paper. Toss the towel after one or two swipes and grab a fresh one, repeating until you have wiped up the entire area.

4. When you've finished, seal the box, write "Broken Glass" on the outside, and set it out with your trash. That way your garbage collector won't get cut.

A garbage bag broke on my carpet

PICK UP THE SOLIDS Quick! Grab a new bag to stash all the solids in. Don't be squeamish about the garbage. You can wash your hands as soon as you've finished. Just watch out for broken glass or sharp metal can lids.

BLOT UP THE LIQUID AND VACUUM Next, blot up any liquids with paper towels. Contain large spills by blotting from the outer edge to the center. Grab the hand vac (or full-size) and suction up the small stuff, such as crumbs and coffee grounds.

MIST AND BLOT REMAINING STAIN To prevent staining, lift the residue of any spilled liquid before it dries. The simplest stain-lifting technique is this: Mist water on the stain with a spray bottle. Blot with a clean, dry paper towel. Repeat until the stain is gone. Dry by laying a thin stack of paper towels on the spot with a weight, such as a brick, on top. (Put the brick in a plastic bag or on top of a piece of foil.) Brush the carpet pile to restore a consistent texture.

Since most carpets and rugs have pads under them, don't soak the stains. Carpet pads soaked with leftover cleaning solution can attract more dirt and lead to problems such as mildew and glue deterioration. Avoid rubbing the stain, which could push it deeper into the pile. Don't make a circular motion. That can destroy a carpet's texture.

I spilled coffee on my sofa

USE A CARBONATED BEVERAGE TO GET IT OUT Quickly use a cloth or paper towel to blot up the liquid. Then pour a little seltzer water, Sprite, or 7 Up on the stain and dab that up. The carbonation helps

Clean with Pantry Products

In your zeal to keep your bathroom clean, have you amassed a lot of pricey cleaning products? Do you have one product to clean your sink, another for the ceramic tile, and another to oust mildew from your shower curtain? Enough. Make your own cleaners for pennies. Keep a supply of baking soda, white vinegar, and rubbing alcohol on hand to conquer your dirty bathroom. Here are some tips:

- For those sticky spots on bathroom countertops, dampen a cotton ball with rubbing alcohol and dab away the spots.

- To keep your toilet bowl clean, pour ¼ cup of baking soda into the water and let it bubble for a few minutes before using your toilet brush and flushing.

- Other ways to clean a toilet: Sprinkle a packet of an unsweetened Kool-Aid into the bowl and let it sit for a few minutes. Then swish it with a brush and flush. Or try a denture-cleaning tablet (let it dissolve before flushing) or a can of cola (wait a few minutes before flushing).

- Mop a tile bathroom floor using a mixture of 1 cup of vinegar and 4 cups of warm water.

- To clean windows, mix equal amounts of distilled water and white vinegar in a plastic spray bottle. Spray the glass with the solution and follow by wiping with a clean cloth or paper towel.

bring the spilled coffee to the surface. Keep blotting the stain with an absorbent cloth to remove any liquid. Then rinse by dabbing it with fresh water.

I dripped candle wax on the carpet

IRON IT OUT ONTO PAPER To get candle wax out of fabric or carpeting, you basically need to reheat the wax and soak it up with paper. First, pick out whatever wax you can with your fingers. Then place newspaper over the wax and apply a hot, dry iron to the newspaper. The wax will melt, and the paper will soak it up. If your carpet is light colored, use white computer paper or a white paper towel instead to make sure no ink transfers to the carpet.

■ CHILDREN'S MESSES

My kid scribbled on the wall with a felt-tip marker

TRY INCREASINGLY STRONG MEASURES First try the simplest fix, which will be least harmful to the wall, and then use tougher methods if that doesn't work:

- Wipe with a dry paper towel. If the mark is still wet or the surface is smooth and nonporous, the paper towel may remove the mark.
- If wiping with paper alone doesn't do it, try moistening the towel with rubbing alcohol.
- It's still there? Go for the hard stuff—mineral spirits or kerosene. These are flammable, so be careful. They can also alter wall finishes, so test them first in an inconspicuous area of the same surface.

Unwanted felt-tip masterpiece on the wall? Get it off quickly with a paper towel—and perhaps rubbing alcohol or spirits.

The baby spit up on the carpet

SPRAY WITH WATER AND BLOT Vomit is a protein-based stain, so avoid using warm or hot water, which can fix the stain in the fibers of a carpet.

1. First remove any solids using paper towels.
2. Next, spray the area with cold water and blot. Repeat until the stain is gone.

3. If residue remains, soak the accident site in an enzymatic cleaner, the kind you buy at pet stores to remove odors. Wash and rinse according to product directions.

My son got chewing gum on my carpet

FREEZE IT WITH ICE AND SCRAPE OFF Grab some ice, put it in a plastic bag (to prevent leaking), and rub the ice on the gum until the gum freezes and hardens. Scrape away the hardened gum with a dull knife. If residue remains, remove it by blotting with a dry-cleaning solvent, such as Carbona. Be sure to test the solvent first, however, in an inconspicuous spot to make sure that it won't damage the carpet. This procedure also works with upholstery.

My kids got crayon marks on the kitchen table

USE TOOTHPASTE OR MAYO TO REMOVE THE MARKS Two common household items help remove crayon marks.

- For painted surfaces, put a dab of nongel toothpaste on an old toothbrush or dry rag and rub.
- For stained or untreated wood, rub real mayonnaise on the marks with a rag, let it sit a minute or two, and then wipe it off with a damp cloth.

■ PET CLEANUP

My pet pooped on the carpet

USE AN ODOR-CONTROLLING CLEANER Accidents will happen, not just with puppies or older pets that are losing control. Even the best-trained pets can have a mishap. Follow these steps to clean up:

1. Carefully remove the solid part of the poop using an inside-out plastic bag over your hand, which you then turn right side out to enclose the contents.
2. Blot up any liquid content with paper towels.
3. Soak the accident site with an enzymatic odor-removing cleaner, such as Nature's Way, available at pet stores.
4. Rinse residue with plain water to avoid leaving any scent that might draw the pet back to use the same spot.

TRICKS OF THE TRADE

Removing Kids' Pencil Art from Wallpaper
Your young child is playing in his room—perhaps too quietly. You walk in and discover that the budding artist has doodled on his wallpaper with a pencil. Don't panic. Instead, head for the kitchen for a slice of fresh bread. Rub the bread across the penciled area, and you'll erase the marks without marring the wallpaper.

BE READY FOR THE NEXT TIME For the next pet-poop accident, be prepared: Store a pet-cleanup kit in your broom closet or utility room. In it keep paper towels, plastic grocery bags (for disposing of solids and used paper towels), a sponge, and the enzymatic cleaner.

My pet wet the rug

SOAK IT UP WITH PAPER TOWELS If it's fresh, soak up the liquid with a paper towel. Then lay a thick layer of paper towels on the spot. Cover the paper towels with newspaper, being careful not to let the newsprint rub off on the carpet. Stand on the padding for a couple of minutes. The pressure will help the toweling draw up the liquid. Do this again with fresh paper towels.

THEN USE AN ODOR-REMOVING CLEANER Next, saturate the spot with an enzymatic odor-removing cleaner, such as Nature's Way, available at pet stores. This type of cleaner even works on old, dried urine stains. Rinse the area by spraying it with clean water and blotting up the water with paper towels. Avoid using fragrant cleaners, such as shampoos, soaps, or vinegar, to clean the rug. The scents, like the scent of the pet's own urine, might draw the pet back to the same spot to urinate again.

I smell pet urine, but I can't find it

USE A BLACK LIGHT TO FIND THE SPOT You don't always find the puddle when it's fresh. Often a pet will sneak into a room, relieve itself, and sneak back out again. You may know nothing about it until you follow your nose, and by then the puddle may be dry and—if it's a dark rug—invisible. To stop your pet from repeating this behavior, you'll need to remove the old urine, which means you must know where it is. To find it, try this trick. Turn out all the lights in the

Something Fishy

Star Burr, office manager of the Weyers Cave, Virginia, Merry Maids, knows of a woman who was so angry at her ex-husband for cheating on her that she hid raw shrimp in the curtain rods of his house just before she packed up and moved out. Soon after, the girlfriend moved in. Together, the couple searched and searched for the source of the foul smell. They looked in the refrigerator, in closets, under sofa and chairs. Nothing. The stench finally forced the two to find a new house. When they moved, they took the curtains—and curtain rods—with them. Burr never found out what happened to the pair. "Maybe they're living unhappily ever after," she laughs.

room. Then use a black light to illuminate the old urine stains. A black light, sold by hardware stores, is an ultraviolet light that makes some compounds, including some in urine, glow in the dark. Outline the stains with chalk or string, so you can locate them when you turn the lights back on. Then clean the area as you would a fresh stain. (See the previous answer.)

My pet keeps urinating on the same carpet spot

CLEAN WELL AND TRY RETRAINING Dogs and cats are territorial, but they don't post signs or hang surveyor's tape to mark a spot as their own. They pee on it. They'll do this outside on a tree—or inside, where they can ruin floors and carpets and create foul odors. There are several things you can do to stop them. The most basic is to completely remove all traces of urine from the spot they've chosen to mark. (See "My pet wet the rug," opposite.) After you've soaked up fresh urine using paper towels, take the paper towels to your pet's designated bathroom area, such as a litter box or an area of the yard outside. Take your pet to the spot and let it smell the urine there.

SPRINKLE WITH A DETERRENT COMPOUND If the pet continues its habit, consider using a deterrent, available at pet stores. These are usually strong-smelling substances that you sprinkle on the area a pet is marking. Some are stronger—and more offensive to humans in the house—than others. If it's your cat, and it suddenly won't use the litter box, it may be that it is reacting to change. Did you recently buy a new brand of litter? If so, switch back to the familiar brand. Is the box dirtier than usual? Clean it. Do you have a new cat that is sharing the litter box? Consider getting another litter box.

Pet hair is all over my furniture

VACUUM IT UP Pet hair can drive you mad. It turns up on sofa cushions and chairs, and then it winds up on you. And it is the devil to remove. First, try the vacuum cleaner, but use a lint-brush attachment. These pry up even those short, wiry hairs that embed themselves in your upholstery.

WIPE IT OFF WITH A RUBBER GLOVE You can also wear a damp rubber glove and rub your hand across the cushions. This clumps the hair for easy removal.

Tools and Workshop

Quit Splitting

To avoid splitting wood when you're driving a nail, try blunting the point of the nail with a light hammer blow. Sharp nails spread wood fibers apart as they're driven in; blunt nails crush the wood fibers. Another option is to try nailing into the lighter part of the wood, not the grain lines. The darker grain lines are harder and are more likely to start a split.

The best solution, however, is to drill a pilot hole for the nail. To do this, select a drill bit that's slightly smaller in diameter than the nail. (An old-time trick is to clip the head off a finishing nail and use it as a drill bit. Finishing nails tend to get dull rather quickly, so for big jobs use a drill bit.)

■ FASTENERS

I can't nail and hold boards together at the same time

USE SUPERGLUE TO HOLD THE PIECES An extra hand sure would help when you're working alone in an awkward position—up a ladder, say, or down on your hands and knees. But here's a fast, practical solution that some experts use: Keep a tube of woodworker's superglue, sold in woodworking shops and hardware stores, handy in your pocket or tool belt. When you need to nail or screw two pieces of wood together and can't hold both pieces at the same time, dab a little of the superglue between them, hold them in place until the glue dries (a matter of seconds), and then drive your nail in. Make sure you use fast-setting superglue, whose main ingredient is cyanoacrylate. This trick can also work for plastic, metal, and other materials. It's the best solution—hands down.

Finishing nails in my trim keep popping up

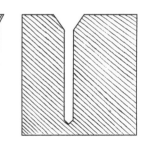

USE TRIM SCREWS A simple change of fastener is the answer. Trim screws draw pieces together better than nails. They have a thin shank and a tiny (3/16 inch or 4.7 millimeters diameter) head that you can easily hide with putty. Drill a 1/16 inch (1.6 millimeter) pilot hole and a 3/16 inch countersink (a shallow depression) for the screw head, then drive in the screw.

I dropped brads all over the floor

PICK THEM UP WITH A MAGNET This isn't a mess you can sweep under the carpet! If you have scores of brads, small nails, or tacks scattered about the floor, it will take eons to pick them up one at a time. The quick solution is to head for the refrigerator. Not for a beer, silly, for a magnet—the kind you use to put notes on the refrigerator door! If you drag a magnet across the spilled brads, you'll be able to scoop up a dozen or more at once and be finished in no time. The bigger the magnet, the better, of course.

I keep dropping nails all over the yard

MAKE A HOLDER FROM A TENNIS BALL If you don't feel like lugging a heavy toolbox all around to keep the little fasteners contained, try this container instead: Cut a slit in a tennis ball. Give it a squeeze and the slit will widen. Drop your screws or nails in and relax your squeeze to close it. Tuck the ball into your pocket and head out to your project. Squeeze the ball again to open the slit and shake out fasteners as you need them.

A slit tennis ball, if left empty, can serve another function: If you need to tap some delicate woodwork into place, slip the ball over the head of your hammer. It'll give the hammer taps a gentler impact.

We Share Borders, Not Toolboxes

Canada and the United States may have a lot in common, but they go their separate ways when it comes to tools. So says home-maintenance celebrity author Jon Eakes, who is from California, lives in Quebec, and speaks both English and French.

Take screws, for example. A Canadian street vendor named Peter Robertson decided in 1908 that the world needed a better type of screw than the kind with a single slot across the head. So he came up with a screw with a *square* indention in the head and a screwdriver with a square tip that fits neatly in the hole. (His screwdriver can even hold a screw in midair, allowing one-handed driving of a screw.) It is also hard to damage the square hole while driving the screw. More than 80 percent of screws used in Canada are now Robertson screws.

In the United States, in the mid 1930s, Henry Phillips developed the screw that bears his name—one with a cross-shaped indentation in the head. Canadians kept the Robertson screws, the United States kept the Phillips screws.

Canadians also have been adopting the metric system in fits and starts since the 1970s. Americans have tended to resist the idea more strenuously than Canadians and generally continue to use the old foot-inch system of measurement. "No kid under 20 knows what an inch is, and no adult over 30 knows what a millimeter is," Eakes quips.

By the way, sheets of plywood in Canada are measured in feet, for length and width, and in millimeters for thickness. In the United States, thickness is measured in fractions of an inch.

TRICKS OF THE TRADE

When Good Glues Go Bad

Glued-on caps can turn a simple task into a frustrating one. To keep a lid on this problem, store a little container of petroleum jelly in the same place where you keep your glue. When you replace the glue container's cap, dab a little petroleum jelly on the threads, and it will come free easily the next time.

I keep whacking my fingers when I hammer little nails

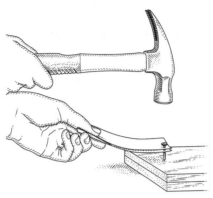

HOLD THE NAIL WITH A PIECE OF PAPER Gardeners get a green thumb; carpenters get a red thumb—the swollen kind. To keep your fingertips out of harm's way when you're hammering a small nail or brad, stick the nail through one end of a folded sheet of stiff paper. (A brad is a thin nail with a slight projection at the top of one side instead of a head.) Using the paper as a holder, drive in the nail. Before finally seating the nail, tear the paper away. The teeth of a comb, tweezers, or needle-nose pliers can also serve as nail holders.

I can't reach the place where I need to drive a screw

MAGNETIZE YOUR SCREWDRIVER The problem with driving a screw in tight places is that you can't get a hand in there to steady the screw while you get started. But you won't need to steady the screw if a magnetized screwdriver is holding it in place. You can quickly magnetize a screwdriver by dragging its blade over a magnet several times in one direction. Need a magnet? Check the refrigerator door.

A screwdriver that you've magnetized should hold its charge for about a week. To prevent the charge from draining out of it, keep it away from other metal objects. To demagnetize it, just drag the blade over the magnet in the opposite direction. If you're faced with this problem often, consider buying a factory-magnetized screwdriver, which will keep its charge permanently.

TAPE THE SCREW TO THE SCREWDRIVER If the magnet trick isn't feasible for you, a bit of adhesive tape will do the job. Tear off about 3 inches (7.5 centimeters) of tape and push the screw through the center of the sticky side of the tape. Insert the

TAPE

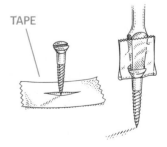

screwdriver in the slot of the screw and wrap the tape around the blade of the screwdriver.

USE RUBBER CEMENT TO HOLD THE SCREW Yet another alternative: Dab some rubber cement on the slot of the screw and then insert the blade of the screwdriver in the slot.

I've torn up the slot in this screw

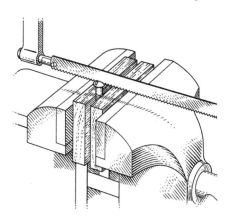

DEEPEN THE SLOT WITH A HACKSAW When you need to remove a screw and then drive it back in again, it's easy to chew up the screw's slot, especially if the blade of your screwdriver doesn't fit the slot. If you don't have a replacement screw on hand, a quick way to restore the old screw is to deepen the slot by running a hacksaw along it. In the case of a Phillips-head screw, do both slots. If you're repairing a screw out of its hole, don't hold the screw in your fingers. Put it in a vise between two scraps of wood, so you won't hurt yourself and can protect the screw threads.

■ TOOL PROBLEMS

My wrench is too big for the nut

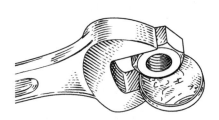

FILL THE GAP WITH A COIN Usually, bigger is better, but not when you need to remove a nut with an open-end wrench that is a tad too large for it. The solution is jingling in your pocket. Simply insert a nickel, dime, or penny between the wrench and the nut. The coin will serve as a wedge, making it possible to turn the nut. You'll have to experiment to determine which coin best fills the gap. A washer will also work.

I can't drill perfectly perpendicular holes

MAKE A SIMPLE DRILLING GUIDE For drilling down into a horizontal surface with a regular twist bit, make a drilling guide from two pieces of ¾ inch (19 millimeters) plywood, 1½ inches high and 2 inches wide (38 by 51 millimeters). Glue and nail the pieces together with finishing nails to form a corner. To use this guide, simply run your drill bit along the inside corner.

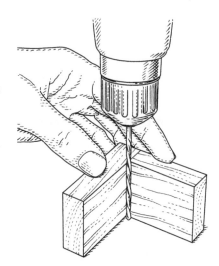

PUT A WASHER ON THE BIT SHANK When drilling a hole in a vertical surface, you can use the same guide block. But if you're using one of

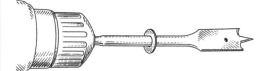

those wide spade bits, you'll need a different approach. Slip a washer over the shank of the bit before you put the bit in the drill. If the washer slides forward or backward as you drill, you're tilting the drill up or down. You'll still have to use your eye to keep the drill straight side to side.

I can't turn this bolt with my wrench

EXTEND THE HANDLE WITH A PIPE What you need is a longer handle on your wrench to give you more leverage. So find a small piece of pipe, slide it over the handle of your wrench, and use that to turn your stubborn bolt.

I don't have a Phillips screwdriver

CUT A SLOT FOR A REGULAR SCREWDRIVER It's a frustrating case of incompatibility: You need to drive or remove a Phillips-head screw and all you have on hand is a conventional slotted screwdriver. As in the problem on page 51, a hacksaw provides a quick solution to this dilemma. Use the hacksaw to extend one of the slots in the screw head so that it goes all the way across the screw's top. Then you can use your conventional screwdriver. If the screw is out of its hole, protect your fingers by holding it steady in a vise between two scraps of wood while you saw.

My saw is all gummed up with resin

REMOVE IT WITH OVEN CLEANER When sawing soft, resinous wood like pine, you're bound to get a gummy buildup that will make your saw blade seem dull. To remove the resin, spray the saw blade with oven cleaner, scrub with an old toothbrush, and rinse with water. (Wear rubber gloves and safety goggles when you do this.)

■ TOOL AND SUPPLY ORGANIZATION

I can't keep my screws and nuts straight

USE OLD FILM CANISTERS You could, of course, buy one of those plastic cabinets for nuts and bolts, but sometimes it's nice to have a smaller, more portable organizer. And wouldn't it be nice to have something you could access with one hand? An inexpensive, handy solution is old camera film canisters. They make great containers for small screws, nuts, tacks, and pushpins. And for those times when you're holding fast to a ladder, or you don't want to put down your cordless driver, you can pop the top off a film canister with one hand. Label the canisters with masking tape and a marker. Or color-code each canister with electrical tape, which comes in a rainbow of hues other than traditional black. But save your canisters now. With the popularity of digital cameras, film may soon be obsolete.

WORLD-CLASS GOOF

Know the Drill

It happens without fail, says Aaron Purvis, floor manager at Strosniders Hardware in Bethesda, Maryland. Every few months, a customer will come into the store to ask for a refund on a brand-new drill that does not work. The bit spins, they say, but nothing happens. No sawdust, no hole. Just smoke and the smell of burning wood. They're completely baffled—until Purvis explains that they've had the drill's switch set to reverse.

I keep losing my cordless driver bits

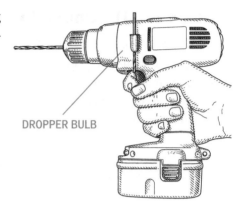

DROPPER BULB

MAKE A MINI HOLDER FOR THE BITS One of the best tools to hit hardware store shelves in recent decades is the cordless drill/driver. But those little bits are a chore to keep up with, especially when you find yourself in an awkward spot—on a branch building a tree house, for example—trying to alternate between two different bits. Yes, there are store-bought holders. But you can make a bit holder yourself using recycled materials. Pull the rubber squeeze bulb off the dropper of an old medicine bottle. Tape the squeeze bulb, open side up, to the side of your cordless driver or tool belt or ladder—wherever it's handiest. Slip your bit in there when it's not in use. Just make sure it fits snugly, so it won't fall out.

Ladder Safety, Step-by-Step

If you're a homeowner, chances are that at some point you'll need to unfold a stepladder or lean an extension ladder against the house for a routine repair. Read these safety tips so that you can avoid becoming a ladder-injury statistic:

• Use a ladder of the proper length. Your extension ladder should extend at least 3 feet over the roofline or similar working surface.

• Never stand on the three top rungs of a straight ladder. Never stand on the top step of a stepladder.

• Set straight ladders up at approximately a 75-degree angle.

• Don't exceed a ladder's weight limit (user plus materials), which should be posted somewhere on the ladder. And never have more than one person on a ladder at a time.

• Since metal conducts electricity, use a wooden or fiberglass ladder when working near power lines or electrical equipment. Regardless of the material, never let your ladder touch a live wire.

• Position the ladder on firm, level ground. Use large flat boards to make adjustments for uneven or soft ground. Have a buddy hold the bottom to steady the ladder, if possible.

• Before mounting a ladder, make sure all ladder locks are properly engaged.

• Do not set up a ladder in front of a door that is not locked, blocked, or guarded.

• When working on a ladder, keep your body centered between the rails. Do not lean to one side.

• Never leave a raised ladder unattended.

I can't keep track of my tools

GET ORGANIZED WITH TOOL TOTES Do you sometimes make half a dozen trips to the utility room to find the right tool? Or, worse, you can't find the right tool at all because your tools are scattered all over the house. Our favorite handyman has a solution. Get two tool totes, those heavy-duty plastic tool carriers with the side-by-side, lidless compartments. Always return the totes to the tool room when the job is finished.

USE ONE TOTE FOR LIGHT REPAIRS Keep one tote filled with what you need for light repairs. Here's what to keep in it:

- *16-ounce claw hammer*
- *locking pliers*
- *brads*
- *flashlight*
- *stud finder*
- *small ruler*
- *finishing nails*
- *pencil*
- *cordless screwdriver with two-way bit*

USE THE OTHER TOTE FOR PROJECTS Keep the other tool tote empty. When a special project arises, load it with the appropriate tools, and you're ready. Be sure to unload the special-project tools before you hang up your handyman hat. That way, you'll always know where your tools are.

I need a funnel right now

MAKE ONE FROM A PLASTIC BOTTLE If you don't have a funnel when you need one, you can make one fast from an old plastic soda or juice bottle. Just use a sharp utility knife to cut the bottle in half. Then use the spout end as a funnel.

Tools keep falling off my stepladder

USE LARGE RUBBER BANDS TO HOLD THE TOOLS To save yourself numerous trips up and down the stepladder to retrieve tools that keep leaping off the little folding tool shelf on your ladder, stretch two extra-large rubber bands around the shelf. Slide your tools under the rubber bands, and they'll still be there when you need them.

TRICKS OF THE TRADE

How to Save Trips Up and Down a Ladder

When you use a metal stepladder to hang pictures or change lightbulbs, a few easy tricks can save you from going up and down the ladder several times to retrieve the tools and materials you need. First, place an empty tuna can on top of the ladder and drop a small magnet from the refrigerator door into it to keep the can from moving. Or, if the ladder is aluminum, stick the can on with a doubled-over piece of duct tape. You can then put the nails and screws you need in the can. Next, take a souvenir plastic drinking cup—the kind you get at sporting events—and use duct tape to attach it to the side of the ladder at the top. Such cups are the perfect size for holding hammers, pliers, and screwdrivers. A second cup on the other side of the ladder can hold the fresh lightbulb and the used bulb.

My extension cord is a tangled mess

KEEP IT COILED IN A BUCKET Not only is your cord tangled, but every time you use it, you have to walk the cord out and re-coil the entire thing, even if you need to extend your reach by only a few feet. Here's a quick way to solve both problems:

1. Near the bottom of a plastic 5-gallon (19 liter) bucket, drill a hole large enough for the cord's plug to fit through.
2. Feed the plug end of the cord through the hole from the inside of the bucket, leaving a tail of a foot or so long hanging out.
3. Coil the rest of the cord in the bucket.

When you need to use the cord, draw out as much cord as necessary from the bucket. When you've finished, simply coil it back into the bucket. An added bonus: You can also use the bucket to carry tools to a job site.

My shop vac isn't powerful enough

WEATHER-STRIP THE LID If your shop vacuum cleaner isn't doing as good a job as you want, use this quick trick to increase its suction: Apply self-adhesive weather stripping to the inside of the lid at the point where it joins the tank edge. Use weather stripping that is ⅜ inch (9.5 millimeters) wide and ¼ inch (6.5 millimeters) thick.

■ SANDING PROBLEMS

My sandpaper is clogged with dust

SAND IT WITH ANOTHER PIECE OF SANDPAPER It's frustrating—and wasteful—when the gritty surface of the sandpaper you're using quickly fills with dust. But there's a fast solution to this problem: Instead of discarding the piece for a new one, lightly sand it with another piece of sandpaper. That will clear the dust and allow you to continue.

My workshop fills the basement with dust

CAPTURE THE DUST WITH A FILTER FAN Airborne dust is not just an annoyance—it can also ruin bearings and electrical switches. First, try catching the dust at the source. One easy way to do this is by attaching a furnace filter to a large box fan. To do this, screw two L-shaped metal brackets to the top of the fan and two to the bottom of the fan, positioning the brackets so they form a slide-in filter holder across the back of the fan. The fan will pull air through the filter, leaving the sawdust on the filter's out-

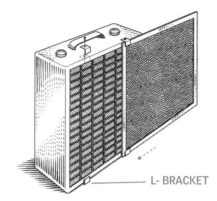

L- BRACKET

side surface. Put the makeshift filter fan on your bench when you're working so it can catch the dust before it becomes an airborne cloud. When the filter is full, vacuum it to remove the dust.

BLOW IT OUT WITH A WINDOW FAN Consider improving your shop's ventilation by installing a window fan. Reverse the fan's direction so that it pulls the dust-laden air outside.

Sanding grooves on trim takes forever

MAKE A MOLDED SANDING BLOCK If you'd rather not be "in the groove" any longer than necessary—especially if you have a lot to do—make a customized sanding block that exactly fits the pattern of the contoured wood trim you're working with. Here's how:

1. Mix water putty (or plastic auto-body filler) in a plastic bag.
2. Press the bag against the wood trim before the putty hardens so that the mix conforms to the surface.
3. When the putty hardens, remove the plastic bag and shape the sides of the hard-putty block with a saw or rasp for easy gripping.

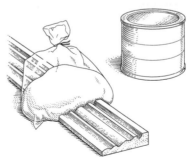

Now wrap a piece of sandpaper around the block and get to work.

Furniture

■ SCRATCHES AND DENTS

There's a dent in my sideboard

USE STEAM TO SWELL THE WOOD FIBERS Small dents can often be fixed with a bit of steam. First make sure that moisture can penetrate the wood. Remove the finish from the dented area by sanding the area or using a solvent, such as nail polish remover. Or just prick the area several times with a fine pin. Then cover the dented surface with a pad made by folding a wet cloth, put a metal bottle cap on the pad to spread the heat, and press the front tip of an iron on a high setting to the bottle top for a few minutes. The resulting steam will make the wood fibers swell. Repeat until the dent has disappeared. Sand the area and repaint or refinish. Don't try this on veneers or near the joints of furniture, because the steam can damage glues.

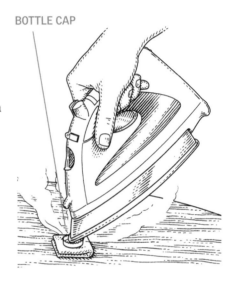

BOTTLE CAP

There's a scratch in my dining-room table

USE IODINE OR A NUT KERNEL, OR SHOE POLISH For a scratch that goes deep enough to expose the raw wood below the finish, here are some ready remedies that you can find around your house:

- For cherry or mahogany pieces, try using iodine to color the exposed wood.
- You can hide a small scratch on wood by rubbing it with the meat of a pecan or other oily nut, or even some peanut butter. Olive or vegetable oil also works. Buff with a clean cloth.
- Use a cotton swab to apply a paste shoe polish that matches the color of the wood.

Furniture's Enemies

Many people wait until it's too late to face the forces bent on damaging their fine furniture finishes. Once a surface is scratched, stained, or cracked, it may be costly to fix—or not fixable at all. Charles Sutton, publisher of *Furniture Review* and founder of Sutton Reproductions, a maker of high-quality period furniture replicas, says there are seven major enemies of wood finishes (not including young children). Know them. Avoid them.

- **Liquids** One of the most common problems stems from sweaty glasses left on tabletops. Water and other liquids penetrate a finish film and damage the wood underneath, causing cloudy or chalky stains that are hard to remove. Use coasters, and wipe up spills right away.

- **Heat** A hot cup of coffee placed on an antique finish can create a white ring, much like a watermark. Likewise, indirect heat, such as that in an attic, can damage wood finishes. Use coasters for hot drinks. Keep furniture at least 2 feet (60 centimeters) from radiators, furnace registers, and other heat sources. Use caution when storing wood furniture.

- **Dust** If you don't have dust in your home, raise your hand. Just as expected—no hands. Dust can dull finishes by filling crevices and causing microscopic scratches. Dust at least every two weeks using a soft, lint-free cloth (an old T-shirt or diaper will work great), neither wet nor dry but lightly dampened. Every three months or so, use a spray-on furniture polish (but not if you previously waxed your furniture), or once a year or so, reapply a paste wax.

- **Chemicals** Coasters can prevent water and heat marks, but be careful which kind of coaster you use. Those made of synthetic materials, such as artificial rubber, can soften and dull hard surface finishes. The same goes for plastic covers and pads. Avoid the use of such pads and coasters.

- **Acids** Body oils and perspiration contain lactic acid and salts that can break down wood finishes, leaving sticky, dirt-attracting areas. Plant and flower nectar can do the same thing. Place plants away from fine wood furniture. Regular dusting and polishing will remove body oils. Periodically clean "high-touch" areas, such as the arms of chairs, with a solution of a wood cleaner, such as Murphy Oil Soap, and water, following the dilution directions on the container.

- **Abrasions** Believe it or not, many furniture scratches and gouges had nothing to do with your kids. Unlikely suspects, such as lamps, ceramics, and other accessories with hard bottoms, are often the culprits. Place protective padding, such as stick-on felt sold in hardware stores, on the bottoms of all such accessories.

- **Sunlight** We all know how dangerous the sun's ultraviolet rays can be to human skin. Those same rays can wreak havoc on wood finishes, causing cracking, checking, and fading. The simple answer to preventing sun damage is not to place your furniture in direct sunlight. But that's not always easy. You can use shades, drapes, and blinds, as well as UV-screening films, on windows to block out the sun. You can plant shrubs in front of windows to block the sun. You can also rotate lamps and accessories on wood furniture that is exposed to sunlight to avoid noticeable dark spots where the sun never shines.

USE A FURNITURE TOUCH-UP PEN OR CRAYON Furniture stores and home improvement stores sell touch-up pens and "crayons" for scratches in wooden furniture. Match the wood as closely as possible, color in the scratch, and buff it with a cloth. You can also color a scratch to match the wood using a cotton swab and a furniture stain kit, available at hardware stores.

■ STAINS

My antique sideboard has water rings

RUB THEM OFF WITH MILD ABRASIVE Water rings only look perma-nent. Gentle scrubbing with a mild abrasive will usually remove the ring or white blemish caused when someone leaves a damp coffee cup or glass on a wood surface. Here are three quick solutions:

- Rub paste wax into the area using superfine (0000) steel wool.
- Apply a dab of white (nongel) toothpaste with a clean cloth.
- Mix cigarette ashes with mayonnaise and rub the mixture in with a clean cloth.

Whichever method you use, rub gently in the direction of the grain and be patient—it takes slow-motion elbow grease to remove the stain without harming the piece's finish.

My wood furniture has a dark stain

BLEACH IT OUT WITH OXALIC ACID Dark stains on wood furniture can be removed the same way they're eliminated on wood floors. (See "My wood floor has a dark stain," page 80.) But you have one advantage. Since furniture is usually portable, you can take your piece outside to a sunny area and let sunlight activate the oxalic acid, instead of using the halogen lamp recommended for floors. As with the floor, be sure to first test this procedure in an inconspic-uous area on the piece of furniture.

■ BURNS

My table has a bad cigarette burn

SCRAPE AND COAT WITH NAIL POLISH A permanent scar? Not nec-essarily. Here's a nifty fix for burn marks in wood or veneer.

1. Start by dabbing the burned spot with nail polish remover to dissolve the finish.
2. Using a small, sharp blade—a pocketknife blade, for instance—scrape away the charred wood, holding the blade perpendicular to the table surface and being careful not to gouge the wood.
3. If the fresh wood is lighter than the rest of the table, stain it to match using a cotton swab and a furniture stain kit, available at hardware stores. In a pinch, you can use a matching paste shoe polish to color the wood.
4. When the stain dries, thin two drops of clear nail polish with two drops of nail polish remover, mixing them with a toothpick. Use a small, cheap artist's brush to apply two or three coats of the thinned polish over the burned spot. Let each coat dry before applying the next one. After a few hours, polish the spot with superfine (0000) steel wool.

If the table has an oil-based finish (meaning it's not varnished), skip the first and last steps, which involve nail polish remover and nail polish. Do Steps 2 and 3 and then rub the entire surface with a clean rag dipped in a wood finisher's oil, such as tung oil or boiled linseed oil.

TRICKS OF THE TRADE

Removing a Faint Cigarette Burn
To touch up superficial cigarette burns on wooden furniture, make a paste of cigarette ashes and linseed oil and rub it on the burn mark, moving in the direction of the wood grain. Wipe off the residue with a rag moistened with linseed oil.

I have a deep burn on my kitchen countertop

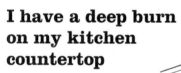

TILE

COVER IT WITH A TILE
If a burn has eaten through the laminate, the easiest solution is to hide the burned spot with a glazed tile. Glue the tile over the damaged area and use it as a countertop trivet. Use an epoxy or PVC (polyvinyl chloride) glue to secure the tile.

INSTALL A DROP-IN INSERT You can also cut out the burned part of the counter and replace it with a heat-resistant drop-in insert (available in various sizes at home improvement and kitchen supply stores). The replacement insert will provide a safe space to put hot pans and can also be used for cutting foods. Be sure to get an insert with a retaining rim, which will make the insert easier to install.

TRICKS OF THE TRADE

Fixing a Burn in Leather Upholstery
You may be able to fix small burn holes in leather upholstery by melting a little wax from a crayon of the same color. Use a lighted match or candle to carefully melt and drip the crayon wax into the hole. Then use the back of a spoon to smooth the hot wax before it dries.

First, trace the insert's outline on the counter in the area of the burned surface. Check the underside of the counter to make sure there are no obstructions. You'll probably have to remove a drawer. Then drill some starter holes and cut out the traced section with a jigsaw.

Follow the instructions that come with the insert to install it.

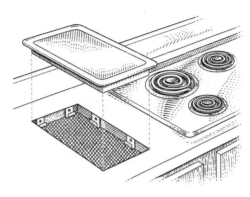

■ VENEER AND INLAYS

The brass inlay on my table is loose

RESET IT WITH HIDE GLUE Natural hide glue is the glue of choice for bonding brass to wood. Available from specialty woodworking dealers, this glue dries slowly and bonds well to metal. Here's how the experts do it:

1. Carefully pull up the loose inlay, making sure not to bend or twist the metal. (You may need an assistant or a prop to hold up the metal while you work.)
2. Cut a clove of garlic in half and rub the glue side of the brass with the cut side—this, according to woodworkers, etches tiny grooves in the metal.
3. Apply a bead of hide glue and press the inlay back into place.
4. Clamp or weight the repair for at least 48 hours.

There's a blister in the veneer on my 20-year-old sideboard

Small blisters on most veneered furniture can be repaired with yellow carpenter's glue and a few simple tools. Here's how:

1. Using the tip of a small, very sharp craft knife, cut a slit in the blister, following the wood grain.
2. Hold the slit open with the knife and use an eyedropper or needle-type glue applicator (available at woodworking stores) to

fill the blister with warm white vinegar. Let it sit for a few hours to dissolve the glue around the blister. Let the area dry completely.

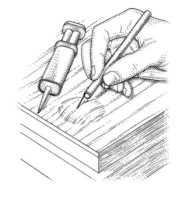

3. Now use a thin knife or a needle applicator (rinse the vinegar out and let the needle dry first) to insert a thin layer of glue across the surface of the wood beneath the veneer. Don't apply it to the veneer itself.

4. Slowly flatten the blister with a block of wood and put a weight, such as a couple of heavy books, on it until the glue dries.

My antique cabinet's veneer has a blister

IRON THE BLISTER If you have an older piece with veneer that has bubbled up away from the edge, there may be a very quick solution. Try ironing it with a warm iron. Put a dry washcloth or towel on the surface to protect the veneer. The heat from the iron should reactivate the hide glue that was commonly used on furniture until the early part of the last century. Weigh the area down with some heavy books after ironing it.

The veneer on my table has lifted

REGLUE THE LIFTED EDGE Veneer will sometimes peel, especially around the edges. The trick to repairing veneer is to remove the old glue and replace it with new glue.

1. If you can get under an edge, use a dull knife or letter opener to raise the loose veneer. But be careful. Wood veneer is thin and brittle. If you try to peel it back too far, it may crack. If it's too rigid to lift, sprinkle a little warm water on it to make it more flexible. Lift it and gently scrape the underside with a utility or craft knife or some other thin, sharp blade. Also scrape away glue from the base surface. Vacuum the dust and dried glue.

2. Once both surfaces are clean, use a small artist's paintbrush or the edge of the blade to cover as much of both surfaces as possible with yellow carpenter's glue. Press out as much of the excess glue as possible, wiping it away with a rag or paper towel.

PROBLEM STOPPER

Coping with a Spill
When someone spills a liquid on a wood surface, the quicker you soak up the liquid, the better. Chances are the piece has some sort of coating, either wax or varnish, which should protect the wood from brief contact with water. You can't beat paper towels for absorbency. Grab a handful, lay them out flat, and let them do their thing. Contain the spill by working from the outside toward the center. Remove towels as they become saturated and replace them with dry ones until the moisture is completely gone. Finally, rub the spot with a cloth moistened with furniture polish.

3. Lay a smooth piece of paper (no dyes or inks) on top of the veneer and weigh it down with a stack of books or something else heavy and flat.

4. When the glue has dried, remove the weight and paper and carefully scrape away any bits of stuck paper with the blade.

I can't get the glue under the veneer

BLOW IT IN If you have trouble getting glue under old, brittle veneer, try this trick: Cut a length of plastic drinking straw and flatten it somewhat. Then fold it in half and very slowly and patiently drip glue into one half. Slip the filled half under the veneer and gently blow in the glue.

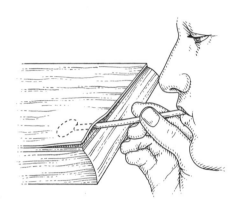

■ WEAR AND TEAR

My dresser drawer sticks

LUBRICATE THE RUNNERS You probably need to lubricate the sliding parts. If the drawer is on wooden runners, the quick fix is to remove the drawer (and everything in it), turn it upside down, and rub a white candle back and forth on the runners. Make sure there is no debris on the wooden tracks that hold the runners. If possible, rub wax on those as well. You could also use a dry spray lubricant, such as Elmer's Slide-All, available at hardware stores. Either one should solve the problem. If the drawer is on metal runners and uses some sort of ball bearing slide mechanism, a quick blast of WD-40 should get it sliding again.

My butcher block is dried out

APPLY OIL TO MAPLE Found in kitchens, bathrooms, and work-shops, a butcher block is one of those hardworking, unappreciated surfaces. Rarely is it finished with a surface coat, such as polyurethane. That means it tends to dry out, and when wood dries, it cracks, splits, and warps. Conditioning a butcher block, however, is easy. Most butcher blocks are made of maple, which has tight grains and pores. First, clean the surface with a mild solution of water and a squirt of dishwashing liquid and then blot it dry. Next, spread a liberal amount of mineral oil (available at hardware stores) evenly over the wood's surface using paper towels or a clean white cloth. For best results, warm the oil for a few minutes beforehand by setting the container of oil in a bowl of hot tap water. Once you have spread the oil, let it stand on the surface overnight (or, if that's not possible, for at least 15 minutes). Wipe away the excess oil with a clean cloth.

APPLY AN OIL-WAX MIX TO OAK Butcher blocks made of oak, a much "thirstier" wood because of its open grain, absorb oil and dry out at a quicker rate than maple. Here's a trick for quenching oak's thirst: Add a bit of wax to the mineral oil. (Use the kind of wax meant for canning or candle making; avoid colored waxes.) Carefully warm the oil in a disposable container and then gradually shave the wax into the oil, being sure not to use more than about 1 part wax to 10 parts oil. Spread the mixture over the butcher block and let it stand. Wipe away the excess after 15 minutes or more. If the surface is blotchy from the wax, scrape the surface with a plastic edge—an old credit card, for instance, or a windshield ice scraper—to remove the waxy lumps.

My side table's legs are loose

WRAP THE SCREW WITH FABRIC Legs on tables or desks that screw directly into the wood on the underside of the table can be fixed by filling the hole with a thin piece of cloth so that the screw fits more snuggly. First, unscrew the loose legs. Then cut a 1-inch (2.5-centimeter)-wide strip of old panty hose and drape it over the threaded end of the leg. Now screw the leg and its cloth shim back into the table and trim away any cloth that shows. If it's still not snug, try the same process with a thicker piece of cloth, such as a strip from an old sheet.

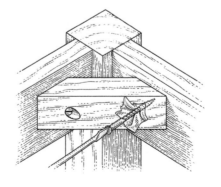

Smooth-Moving Drawers
To keep two-handled drawers sliding smoothly, never yank them open with one hand. If you pull repeatedly on one side, the drawer will eventually begin to bind. If you (or your kids) can't break the one-handed habit, install pulls in the center of drawers to ensure consistently smooth action.

The rung on my chair is loose

REGLUE AND SHIM THE JOINT If a chair joint is shaky, you can often reinforce it quickly without having to undertake the tricky task of disassembling the chair. Pull the joint apart slightly and scrape off as much of the old glue as you can, using a utility or craft knife. Then squirt white or yellow carpenter's glue around the rung, wiggling the pieces to work the glue into the joint. If the socket is enlarged, jam toothpicks (or wood matchsticks) into the fresh glue around the edges. Trim the toothpicks and wipe off 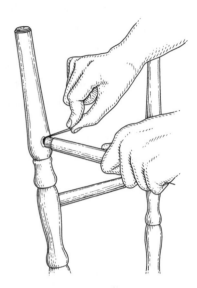 the excess glue with a damp cloth. After the glue dries, the rung will be secure, and no one will ever notice the toothpick shims.

A strand broke in my wicker chair

REJOIN THE STRAND WITH TAPE It's funny how that one little broken strand on a wicker piece can draw the eye. Suddenly, a pristine love seat is one step down the path toward dilapidation—in the eye of the beholder, anyway. The break is a breeze to mask, thank goodness. Using your fingers, push the two sides of the broken strand back into place so that the ends meet. Then bandage the two ends together by wrapping a thin layer of masking tape tightly around the break—two wraps will probably do it. Depending on how the wicker is woven, you may need to narrow the width of your masking tape by cutting it with scissors. Paint over the tape with the same color as the piece. If the wicker has a natural finish, you may need to darken the tape or alter its hue with a brown or orange marker.

A corner broke off my picture frame

MOLD A REPLACEMENT PIECE Ornate picture frames, especially old ones, are fragile. When part of the molding breaks off and is lost, you might think that fixing the frame would be impossible. Think again. You don't need to hire an expensive frame restorer (although if the frame is valuable enough, you might want to). Instead, mold a replacement piece using an oil-based modeling clay (sold in art supply stores) and a powdered water putty, such as Durham's Rock Hard Water Putty (sold in hardware and paint stores). Here's what you do:

1. Find a similar section or detail on the frame (most frames are symmetrical, with many repeated details) and cover it with modeling clay. It's important that the clay be oil based so that it doesn't stick to the frame or to the water putty.
2. Carefully remove the clay, which now has an impression of the section to be molded.
3. Mix up some water putty into the consistency of heavy cream. Fill the clay mold with the putty. Let the putty harden and then remove the clay. If you need to fine-tune the replacement piece in order to make it fit, remove the clay before the water putty hardens completely—when the putty is the consistency of bar soap—and carve it with a sharp knife.
4. Once the putty has hardened, glue the piece in place using yellow carpenter's glue. Paint it to match the rest of the frame. Or, if the frame has a natural wood finish, stain it to match using a wood stain.

My wooden drawer knobs keep coming off

USE WATER PUTTY TO HOLD THEM Knobs come off wooden cabinets as well as drawers. No matter. Whether the knobs are attached with screws or dowels, the following fix will take only minutes but will last and last.

Remove the knob. Fill the hole in the drawer or cabinet with water putty, such as Durham's Rock Hard Water Putty, sold in hardware and paint stores, and replace the knob while the putty is still wet. Scrape away the excess putty with a wooden matchstick. The putty will harden, expand slightly, and form a bond that will be even tighter than before. Don't use the knobs until the putty has completely hardened. (Note: If the wooden knobs are threaded, put the putty in the threaded knob hole.)

Use water putty for a fast fix when the knobs pop off your dresser drawers.

Walls and Ceilings

TRICKS OF THE TRADE

Fixing a Small Hole in the Wall

To quickly fix a small hole in the wall, tear a few facial tissues or paper towels into tiny pieces. Put the pieces in a plastic container. Mix in just enough yellow carpenter's glue to make a thick paste the consistency of peanut butter. Stuff the paste into the hole in the wall and smooth it flush with the rest of the wall. The patch will dry within two hours. Disguise the patch with a dab of paint.

■ WALL TROUBLES

There's a good-size hole in my wall

CREATE A CARDBOARD BACKING BEFORE FILLING Repairing large holes in wallboard can be tricky, since there is usually no backing behind them. Your patching compound just falls through the hole when you're trying to fill it in. Here's a technique that works well for holes up to about 2 inches (50 millimeters) wide:

1. Cut a piece of firm cardboard slightly larger than the hole. Thread a piece of strong string through the cardboard and knot it at the back. Push the cardboard through the hole in the wall and pull it toward you to form a tight backing that will support your patching material.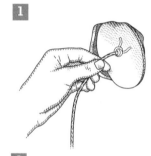

2. Apply fast-drying joint compound or spackling to the hole, filling it almost level with the wall surface. When the patch dries, cut the string flush against the wall. Score the surface of the patch. Apply more compound to make your patch level with the wall surface, and smooth it. Then sand and paint.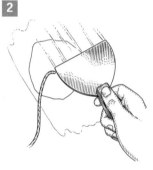

The nails in my drywall cause bumps and dimples

Those little mosquito-bite bumps are called nail pops. Nail pops are spots where vibration, temperature changes, or settling has caused movement in either the drywall or the nails that hold it up. Sometimes nail pops are not bumps but dimples. To fix them for good, follow these instructions:

DRIVE A SCREW NEXT TO A DIMPLE If the nail pop is concave (a dimple), drive a 1¼ inch (32 millimeter) drywall screw through the same piece of drywall and into the same framing member (the wall stud or ceiling joist) a couple of inches away from the dimple. Sink the head of the screw slightly without breaking the paper on the surface of the drywall. The screw will keep that nail from popping again. Spackle over both nail and screw heads; then paint.

PULL A PROTRUDING NAIL If the nail pop is convex (a bump), pull out the nail with a pair of pliers. It's not doing its job anymore. No need to drive in a new screw. Just spackle over the hole and paint.

Cracks in my plaster keep coming back

COVER THEM WITH FIBERGLASS TAPE If you've got an old house with plaster walls, you know how hard it is to get rid of stress cracks. Stress cracks occur when your house moves because of settling or seasonal swelling and shrinking. Even if you dig them out and apply a thick patch, these cracks will eventually resurface. The trick, say plaster experts, is to bridge these cracks with fiberglass tape, the kind used by plasterers and drywall specialists. (Avoid paper tape, which blisters.) Here's the procedure, which goes very quickly:

1. Apply a thin layer of setting compound to the crack, preferably a powdered, mix-with-water variety. Use a wide putty knife or a trowel.

WORLD-CLASS GOOF

When the Walls Come Tumblin' Down

The shift from plaster to drywall has made the once common plastering contractor an endangered species. So Bill Simantel, a Virginia plastering contractor, now specializing in historic restoration, secretly felt a tad of satisfaction when he heard about a friend's drywall dilemma. The friend's house rattled at night because of poorly installed drywall.

"The drywall people had not hit the nails that last lick like they should have," Simantel says.

The friend went around the entire house pounding the walls with the flat of his hand to check for loose sections. To stop the rattling—and secure his walls—he then hammered every loose sheet, one nail at a time.

For Spackling that Won't Crack

Our favorite plaster-and-historic-preservation specialist says that "wet," or premixed, spackling is notorious for shrinking and cracking. Such products are fine for nail holes. But when you're filling larger holes, you're better off using a powdered setting compound, which requires mixing with water. The powdered compounds harden without shrinking or cracking. They're sold by hardware and paint supply stores.

2. Press the mesh tape into the wet compound and apply more compound on top.
3. Spread, or "feather," the compound out on each side of the crack so that it blends in with the rest of the wall.
4. Once the compound has set, sand it smooth to match the existing finish. Then paint the wall.

There's a hole in my concrete block wall

PATCH IT WITH WATER PUTTY You're not going to knock a hole in a block wall as easily as in a sheetrock wall, but it can happen, especially in a garage, where a runaway riding lawn mower could punch a hole in a concrete block. There's an easy fix for this. Patch it as you would a hole in drywall, only use water putty, such as Durham's Rock Hard Water Putty, instead of spackling. Here are the steps:

1. To prevent the putty from falling into the hollow space inside the block, cut a thin piece of wood (a paint-stirring stick, for instance) slightly longer than the diameter of the hole.
2. Put a dab of fast-drying glue, such as a woodworker's superglue, on each end of the stick. Insert it in the hole and pull toward you so that the glue fastens the stick to the inside of the block. You may have to use two or more sticks to cover the space.
3. Mix the water putty as directed (usually 3 parts powder to 1 part water) and fill the hole. For the best results, make two or three applications, letting the filler dry between layers.
4. To make the finish blend in with the concrete block, dab the final layer with a washrag or rough sponge. Finally, touch up the spot with paint. (Use gray paint, if the block is unpainted.)

Cracks keep appearing in my wood trim

FILL THE CRACKS WITH CAULK Whether it's a windowsill, door casing, or crown molding, movement due to seasonal temperature changes will create cracks. Some cracks come and go. Others are permanent. Either way, the fast way to put a stop to these unsightly seams is to fill the gap with caulk and then touch up with paint. But make sure to choose the right caulk. Latex caulk is paintable, but it doesn't flex and won't hide cracks. Silicone caulk, like the stuff you apply around bathtubs, has plenty of flex but won't hold paint. So look for an acrylic latex siliconized caulk, a relatively recent addition to the growing shelf of caulks. It offers both flexibility and paintability.

Now for the proper application:

1. Cut off only the very tip of the caulk nozzle, giving you the thinnest bead possible.
2. Carefully squirt a thin bead into the hairline cracks. Wipe the surface smooth with a damp cloth.
3. Let the caulk dry. Then apply another coat to make up for any shrinking. Again, wipe with a cloth. The crack will be gone, and the trim will be ready for the touch-up paint as soon as the caulk dries again.

My drywall has blisters

CUT OUT THE BLISTER AND REFINISH Bubbles, or blisters, in drywall are spots where all the plaster compound was forced out from under the paper tape that covers drywall joints. With no compound to hold it down, the paper forms air bubbles. Time to play the surgeon. Using a sharp blade, such as a utility knife, carefully cut the blister out, trying not to gouge the wall. Spackle over the hole. Sand and touch up the paint.

My tile grout just won't come clean

STAIN THE GROUT A DARK COLOR Old white grout that has turned brown is nearly impossible to clean. Even bleach won't remove all

WORLD-CLASS FIX

Putty Good Stuff

If there were a Fix-It Hall of Fame for products, all-stars such as duct tape and WD-40 would certainly be asked to join. You might also see Durham's Rock Hard Water Putty, which comes in a red-and-yellow can with the muscle-bound mascot, Rocky Rock Hard, on the label. Sold at hardware stores since 1932, Durham's putty is a gypsum-based powder that you mix with water. It is moldable, castable, spreadable, and paintable. And as the name says, when it dries, it gets rock hard. Over the years, customers have come up with all sorts of uses for Durham's putty. In addition to its household repair uses, such as filling nail holes in wood, patching concrete block, and restoring ornate frames, artists have used it for sculpting, paleontologists for rebuilding fossilized dinosaur bones, and model train enthusiasts for constructing train sets. One of the most popular uses is casting parts for model rockets—a use the company does not endorse.

the soaked-in grunge. And regrouting the joints is messy, labor-intensive work. The time-saving solution is to stain the grout a dark color. A popular charcoal-colored stain will not only mask the dirt but will also give your tile a new look. Here's how to apply grout stain, available at tile stores:

1. Mix 1 cup of bleach with 2½ quarts (2.5 liters) of water and, wearing rubber gloves, scrub the grout with the solution to remove as much surface grime as possible.
2. Apply the grout stain as the label directs using a stiff-bristled artist's brush. If your tiles are not glazed, be careful not to get the stain on them, because it will stain them, too. If the tiles are glazed, you can wipe away stray marks.
3. Let the stain dry as directed before letting the grout get wet.

My fireplace wall has black stains

REPLACE THE FIREPLACE DOOR GASKETS These stains, usually finger-shaped, are a sign that smoke is seeping out around the doors. You can clean the stains by scrubbing them with a solution of ½ cup of washing soda in 1 gallon (3.7 liters) of warm water. But they will return unless you fix the source of the problem. First, open the fireplace doors. You should see a fiberglass gasket, much like the gasket on a refrigerator door, between the frame and the masonry surface. When these gaskets wear out, the seal is broken and smoke can escape. Buy a replacement fiberglass gasket, along with a heat-resistant adhesive to apply it with, at a store that sells fireplace supplies. Remove the old gasket and replace it with a new one, and your problem is solved.

■ WALL ATTACHMENTS

I can't find a wall stud to nail to

USE A MAGNET ON A STRING Finding studs with those expensive store-bought gadgets is a bit like using a divining rod to sniff out groundwater. It's hit or miss at best. For a better way that's also much cheaper, start with a small, strong magnet. (Suppository-shaped cow magnets, sold at farm supply stores and by large-animal vets, work exceptionally well.) Attach a couple of feet of string to one end using tape or glue. Dangle the magnet alongside the wall at about the height you want to drive your nail. Slowly move your hand along the wall, raising it up and down if you get no response. The magnet should be drawn to either a framing nail or a sheetrock screw in a stud. Mark the spot and use a level to project a line straight up or down to the height you want. Then drive the nail home. This works well on walls covered with drywall but may be less successful on walls covered with plaster. It won't work at all if the plaster is on metal lath.

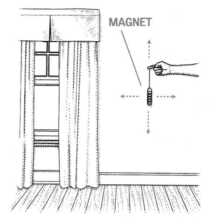

(In case you're wondering, cow magnets are for cows suspected of swallowing a nail or piece of wire. A veterinarian will administer the magnet like a pill. Once it's in the stomach, the magnet stays there, attracting stray metal to keep it from passing through the cow's entire digestive system.)

I get plaster dust all over when I drill holes in the wall

USE A COFFEE CAN LID ON THE CEILING Drilling into the ceiling is tricky, because the dust can sprinkle into your face. (Talk about an eyesore!) To contain the dust, drill through the center of a plastic coffee can lid and leave the lid on the drill bit. Then, holding the lid steady with your free hand, drill the hole in your ceiling. The lid will catch that troublesome dust. Clear lids work better than solid-colored ones because you can see the bit as you drill.

CATCH THE DUST IN A PAPER BAG Drilling into plaster or drywall often leaves an annoying sprinkling of white powder on the floor. Drilling can also chip the surface of the wall around the hole you're making. To avoid both problems, tape an open paper bag (or a coffee filter) under the location for the new hole, with the tape covering the spot you intend to drill into. The tape will ensure that the drill bit doesn't chip away any more of the wall than you want it to, and the

TRICKS OF THE TRADE

Clues that Help You Find Wall Studs
In most homes the distance from the center of one stud to the center of the next is 16 inches (40.64 centimeters), but sometimes it's 24 or some other interval. In older buildings, spacing may be irregular.

• Look for wallboard seams, especially when light hits at an angle.

• Look for a stud that is centered 14½ inches (36.8 centimeters) from a major corner.

• Look for a stud next to an electrical outlet; the box is nailed to a stud.

• Look for a stud next to a window or door edge.

• Look for nails in baseboards that go into studs.

bag will catch the plaster dust. When you've finished drilling, carefully peel off the tape and empty and reuse the dust catcher.

I can't hang pictures on my plaster walls

USE HOOKS DESIGNED FOR PLASTER Real plaster walls, found in nearly all homes until drywall became popular a few decades ago, are either hard as a rock or as crumbly as day-old corn bread. That makes driving picture hangers difficult. Instead of standard picture hooks, which bend when you try to drive them into plaster, or drill-and-insert anchors, which are overkill (and messy), look for hangers specially made for plaster. The hook part 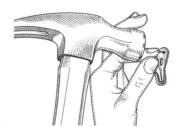 isn't all that different from normal picture hooks. The secret is in the nails, which are thin, needle-sharp, and made from hardened steel that won't bend when driven into hard plaster.

■ PAINTING PROBLEMS

I always spill paint when I stir it

MIX PAINT BY POURING IT BETWEEN CONTAINERS According to many painting pros, paint cans were never meant to be stirred or dipped into with a paintbrush. Cans are only for transporting paint from the manufacturer to the retail store and then to your home. To stir paint, they suggest a method that they call "boxing." Take two clean plastic containers that will each hold more than the amount of paint you'll be mixing. Pour the paint into one of the containers, scraping as much of the thick stuff off the inside of the can and into the container as possible. Now pour the paint back and forth between containers several times, as a method of stirring. If you'll be using more than one can of paint, box all your paint together to achieve a uniform color. Even the color of factory-mixed paint can differ between cans.

Whenever I paint or caulk, I wind up smeared with the stuff

KEEP A BUCKET OF WATER NEARBY Not only is this messy for you, but chances are the paint and caulk are also landing on other things you don't want them on, such as floors and furniture. You can use a rag to clean up the paint and caulk, but rags soon get coated themselves and wind up smearing everything. If you are using water-soluble latex paint, a better approach is to start your painting job with a rag in a bucket of water. Keep the bucket near you. When your fingertips get caked with caulk or coated with paint, dip them in the bucket and wash them. If paint drips on the floor, grab the rag, wring it out, and wipe up the paint before it has a chance to begin drying. With this method, the paint or caulk dissolves in the water, giving you a fresh wipe for every spill.

My paint touch-ups always stick out like a sore thumb

DAB PAINT ON WITH AN ARTIST'S BRUSH The trick to a good touch-up is in the touch. Say you've spackled over a nail hole in drywall. Instead of brushing paint on the white spot—a perfectly natural impulse when you've got a brush in your hand—lightly dot the spot with the paint-dipped tip of your brush. Repeat: Make dots, not brush strokes. Use the smallest brush possible. An artist's brush is best. If the paint job (and leftover paint) is no more than a year or two old, it should blend right in.

Painting cabinet doors and shelves gets paint everywhere

TAP NAILS IN AT TOP AND BOTTOM TO REST THEM ON WHILE DRYING You've removed a door or shelf from a cabinet to paint it. The problem is where to put the wet piece once you've brushed on the paint. Lay it across a pair of sawhorses, and you mar the paint job. Lean it against the wall, and you leave a thin line of paint on the wall and floor. The sure way is to paint one side at a time, but if you're painting several coats, this could take forever. Try this clever trick to speed up the job. Tap a couple of finishing

TRICKS OF THE TRADE

Better Masking
When you're using masking tape to protect wood trim during a painting project, firmly press down the edge of the masking tape with the edge of a flexible putty knife. This seal will prevent paint from seeping behind the tape.

nails—the size of the nail depends on the size and weight of what you're painting—into the ends of each shelf or into the tops and bottoms of each cabinet door before you paint it. Drive them firmly into the wood, but not too firmly, since you'll be removing them later. Leave them sticking out an inch or two. Paint the shelf or door. Lay a drop cloth or newspaper alongside a wall, stand the freshly painted shelf or door on one set of nails, and then lean it at an angle so that the top set of nails is against the wall, with only the nails touching. Once the paint has completely dried, carefully pull the nails out using a pair of pliers or a nail puller. If you use a nail puller (or the back side of a hammer), lay a cloth under the tool so that it doesn't damage the painted surface. Now you can quickly putty the holes and touch them up with a dab of paint.

■ PAINT CLEANUP

I can't get my paint rollers clean

It's essential to use good roller covers and to keep them clean. But too often, the paint soaks deep into the thick nap of the covers. Assuming you're using water-based paint, the trick for getting a roller cover clean is this:

1. Scrape excess paint off the roller cover using the semicircular blade on a 5-in-1 paint tool.
2. Fill a 5-gallon (19-liter) bucket with clean water and soak the roller cover overnight to loosen the remaining paint.
3. Using a roller cover spinner, spin the paint and water off the cover inside an empty 5-gallon bucket. The bucket will be tall enough to contain the spattering paint. Rinse with water and repeat.

You can buy a 5-in-1 paint tool and a roller cover spinner at a home center or at a hardware or paint supply store. If you need a 5-gallon bucket, ask at a supermarket deli section or a fast-food outlet; most discard several of them a day. Just take it home and wash it out well.

I hate cleaning paintbrushes each day

WRAP THEM AND FREEZE THEM OVERNIGHT If you're in the midst of a multiday painting job, you sure don't want those expensive paintbrushes drying out overnight. The labor-intensive answer is to thoroughly clean the brushes at the end of each day so they won't turn cardboard-stiff by morning. But there's a much easier method: Just wrap the brushes in plastic wrap and stick them in the freezer overnight, say painting pros. The cold and the plastic will prevent the brush from drying out. They may need to thaw a little when you retrieve them, but they'll be fresh and limber in just a few minutes.

My leftover paint always goes bad

You spackled the hole your son made in the sheetrock while playing Bob the Builder, and now it's time to touch up the paint. But wait: The paint cans in the basement are all mixed up, they're rusty, and the paint in them has dried up. Here's an easy, effective way to store leftover paint so that it will last up to three years:

USE THE RIGHT SIZE CONTAINER, SEALED TIGHTLY First and foremost, you want a tight seal. Air dries paint out and leaves a thick, leathery skin on top. Some people wrongly think that all you have to do is remove that skin. But do that and you remove some of the "top driers," ingredients that help the paint dry properly, and your next paint job will stay tacky for a week. The best way to keep air out is to use a container of the right size for your paint. Some pros suggest mason jars—a quart jar for a quart of leftover paint or slightly less, a pint jar for a pint or less, and so on. If you prefer to store the paint in the original can (which in some cases is OK and more convenient), tap the lid on with a rubber mallet or by placing a block of wood on the lid and hitting it with a hammer. If you hammer the lid directly with something metal, you risk denting the lid and damaging the seal. And if you keep the grooved can rim paint-free, the lid will seal better. (Paint stores sell plastic rim covers that snap over rims to keep them clean when pouring paint.)

STORE PAINT UPSIDE DOWN Next, store the paint upside down. That way, the paint forms an airtight seal. Keep it in a relatively cool place. Put the cans on cardboard, in case they leak (although if you've sealed them tightly, they should not). Make sure the paint does not freeze or get too hot. Both extremes can ruin it.

PROBLEM STOPPER

Killing the Odor of Fresh Paint
There's no need to assault your senses with the odor of fresh paint when you've been doing some redecorating around the house. As soon as you've put your painting equipment away, cut an onion in half and place the two halves in different parts of the room. Within a day or two, the onion will have absorbed the paint smell.

NOTE KEY DATA ON THE CONTAINER Record as much information about the paint as possible using masking tape and a permanent felt marker. Include date of purchase (and/or when applied), brand of paint, type of finish, the manufacturer's color code, and which part of which room it was used for. Write this on the bottom of the jar or can so that it is easy to read. If you put it on the side, it might get covered with dripping paint. (Anyway, the bottom will be facing up if you store the paint upside down.)

It's a hassle to dispose of old paint

LET THE PAINT SOLIDIFY In most places, it's unlawful to throw away liquid paint. Some landfills won't take it. So how do you get rid of that leftover paint that's gone bad? Here are two suggestions from the pros. Both let the paint solidify so that you *can* leave it at the curb.

- Let it stand in the can without the lid in an open place. The solvents will evaporate, the driers will dry up, and the paint will harden. But this method is only good for small amounts, and still it takes a while and could turn messy if you have curious children or cats.
- The other way is to use a commercial product, such as Waste Paint Hardener, available in paint and hardware stores. Toss these crystals into latex paint, acrylic paint, or wood stains, and the liquid quickly solidifies. The crystals and the hardened paint are both nontoxic and landfill acceptable.

Paint cleanup takes too much time

USE A PAPER PLATE AND MASKING TAPE You may consider yourself a Monet when it comes to selecting the right color to paint your room, but you dread cleaning up because of all the spills and the time it takes to clean your brushes. Here are two tips that will help you keep cleanup to a minimum:

- Place a large paper plate under the opened paint can to catch any over-the-side drips.
- Wrap 2-inch (5-centimeter) masking tape around the brush handle, making sure that it covers ½ inch (1.25 centimeter) of the bristles at the base of the brush. After you've called it a day, unwrap the tape and you'll discover that the tape prevented a lot of extra paint from soaking into the bristles. Your cleanup time will be much shorter.

Floors

■ WOOD FLOORS

My hardwood floor is scuffed up

RUB WITH EXTRA FINE STEEL WOOL A floor that's
thoroughly marred by scuff marks, shoe polish,
and paint splatters will give a room that
dreaded "tawdry old house" look in no time. But
hold on—there's no need to refinish that floor
just yet. Pick up some extra-fine steel wool (grade
000) at the hardware store and give the scuffs a very light
rubbing with it, taking care not to damage the floor's finish. You'll be
surprised at what a gleaming, like-new floor you had under there.

*Your wood floors
can get their
gleam back fast
with extra-fine
steel wool.*

My hardwood floor is scratched

STAIN AND VARNISH THE SCRATCHES The quickest way to fix small
scratches in your hardwood floor is to use furniture touch-up
markers, available at hardware and home improvement stores. Find
a stain marker that matches the color of your floor. (Stain from a can
will work, too.) After the stain dries, use an artist's brush to cover
the repair with polyurethane varnish, applying two or more layers to
build the area up flush with the existing finish.

There's a dent in my wood floor

STEAM THE DENT OUT Here's how to make the dent in your floor—
or in a piece of furniture—disappear like magic. The fix works only
if the dented wood fibers are not severed.

1. Remove any finish from the dented area. Sand off a top-coat
    finish, such as polyurethane. Remove a wax finish by rubbing
    with mineral spirits.
2. Fold a thin cotton cloth into a neat square that is larger than
    the dent. Soak the cloth in water and wring it lightly.
3. Lay the cloth over the dent and place a clothing iron, set on the
    hottest setting, on top of the cloth. The iron will heat the cloth,
    forcing steam into the dent and raising the grain of the wood.

Controlling Floor Squeaks

Many floor squeaks are seasonal. Boards shrink in the dry winter air, and gaps form between them, causing that annoying sound of wood rubbing on wood. You can often prevent squeaking by keeping your home's humidity levels more constant. Install a humidifier in areas with wood floors, and enjoy the sound of silence.

4. When the wood has dried, sand it flush and reapply the finish, if necessary.

My wood floor has a dark stain

BLEACH IT OUT WITH OXALIC ACID If you think those dark stains caused by sink leaks or pet urine are impossible to remove, think again. Here's an easy way to remove them:

1. Remove the wood's finish by rubbing with sandpaper.
2. Wearing protective rubber gloves, mix 1 cup of oxalic acid, available at paint and hardware stores, with 1 gallon (3.7 liters) of warm water. Then saturate the dark area with the solution.
3. Illuminate the area with a strong halogen light (such as the portable halogen construction lamps for sale at building supply stores or for rent at equipment rental shops). The halogen light, like sunlight, will react with the oxalic acid to erase the dark stain. Depending on the stain, it may take anywhere from 20 minutes to six hours.
4. When the stain is gone, remove the lamp and neutralize the area by rinsing with a fresh cloth and water. Once the section of floor has completely dried, sand it smooth and refinish.

Before you use this method, test the oxalic acid and halogen treatment on a small, inconspicuous part of the floor, such as a spot inside a closet.

Furniture polish has clouded my hardwood floor

REMOVE THE POLISH WITH WINDOW CLEANER The silicone in furniture polish can damage a polyurethane finish, leaving it cloudy or peeling. Similarly, hair spray can damage a floor's finish, softening or wrinkling it. If either of these has landed on your hardwood floor, begin by wiping with a damp cloth. If the blemishes remain, try removing them with an ammonia-free window cleaner.

My satin varnish turned out glossy

MIX THE VARNISH THOROUGHLY Even clear coatings, such as varnish and polyurethane, contain pigments, called stearated pigments. The less glossy finishes have more pigment, which is what makes the finish satin. But the stearated pigments are thick and stick to the bottom of a can of varnish like chocolate syrup in a glass of cold milk. For good chocolate milk, you've got to stir the syrup. For a true satin, you've got to stir the pigment. But don't shake the varnish, because you'll just get air bubbles that will ruin the surface of your floor or furniture. Instead, mix the varnish by "boxing" it as you would with paint. (See "I always spill paint when I stir it" on page 74.)

■ FLOOR SQUEAKS AND BOUNCE

My hardwood floor squeaks

SPRINKLE TALCUM BETWEEN CRACKS Wood floors squeak for different reasons. Sometimes the floor wasn't attached well enough to the subfloor. Other times a seasonal cycle of swelling and shrinking causes the floorboards to rub together. If the squeak is caused by a surface gap between boards, try a dry lubrication. Pinpoint the noisy boards and sprinkle talcum powder or graphite liberally in the crack. Lay an old towel over the powder and work it into the gaps with your foot. Wipe up the excess. If your floor has a wax finish, as opposed to a top coat finish such as polyurethane or varnish, try pouring liquid floor wax, the same kind you'd use to refinish the surface, between the boards.

SHIM BETWEEN THE FLOOR AND JOIST The problem may be a space between floor and subfloor. (A telltale sign is a floor that "gives" underfoot, as if there were an air bubble beneath it.) If you can access the floor from below, try this: Go below with a flashlight. Locate the squeak by having someone walk on the floor above. Carefully hammer a wide shim, or thin piece of filler wood, into the space between the subfloor and joist, pushing the subfloor up to remove the bubble. To keep the shim in place, spread construction adhesive or wood glue on the upward-facing side before hammering it.

SHIM

SCREW THE SUBFLOOR TO THE FLOOR If there is a gap between floor boards and subfloor, and you can access the floor from below, drive screws up through the subfloor and into (but not through) the

Roll with It

Prevent dents on floors by using barrel casters instead of ball casters on furniture legs. Use rubber casters instead of plastic or metal ones to prevent scuffing and streaking.

floor boards. Before you drive the screws, have someone stand on the floor above to make sure you get a tight fit. Be sure to use screws that are not more than 1¼ inches (3 centimeters) long. Also, it's a good idea to use washers on the screws to prevent them from overdriving, which can force the floor up or, worse, allow the screw tip to pierce the floor's surface.

SCREW THE FLOOR TO THE SUBFLOOR If you cannot get below the subfloor, screw trim screws—about 2½ inches (6 centimeters) long—into the floorboards from above to hold them snugly to the subfloor. To prevent the floorboard from splitting, drill pilot holes slightly smaller than your trim screws into the floorboard only (not the subfloor). Angle the drill toward the center of the floorboard. That angle helps hold the floor down. Once the hole is drilled, have someone stand on the loose board to push it tight against the subfloor, and then drive the screws into the predrilled holes. Countersink them (that is, drive the heads slightly below the surface of the floor). Fill the holes with a wood putty, trying to match the color as closely as possible. Try to choose a spot in the lighter colored, open-grain part of the floorboard, as the puttied screw hole will be less conspicuous there. Hide it even more by scratching the surface of the putty with a sharp blade to mimic the grain lines.

My floor bounces when I walk across it

REINFORCE THE JOISTS WITH PLYWOOD If your floor is springy, chances are your floor joists are not doing their job. There is an easy solution, however, as long as you have access to the underlying joists via a crawl space or basement. Measure the height and length of your floor joists.

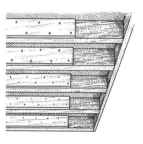

Cut strips of ¾-inch (19-millimeter) plywood to match. (If the joists are 10 inches [25 centimeters] high, then cut 10-inch strips of plywood.) Nail the strips along one side of each joist to give it additional support and to keep it from sagging. Nail in a diagonal line along the strip, from the top to the bottom and then back up to the top again, in a sawtooth pattern. If the problem persists, nail similar strips of plywood on the other side of each joist.

■ VINYL FLOORING

One of my vinyl floor tiles is damaged

USE A HEAT GUN TO REMOVE AND REPLACE IT The beauty of vinyl tiles is that they come in individual pieces. If one gets burned, stained, or scratched, you can easily replace it. The trick is in getting the sticky adhesive unstuck. And the quick solution is to carefully warm the tile with a heat gun, the kind used to strip paint. (If you don't have a heat gun, use a hair dryer or a clothing iron on a moderate setting.) Lift a corner with a putty knife. The tile should come right up. Soften the adhesive left on the floor with the heat gun and remove it with the putty knife. Apply new multipurpose floor tile adhesive, soften the replacement tile with the heat gun, and insert it.

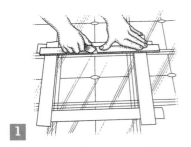
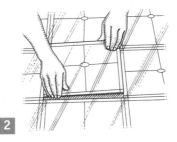

My sheet vinyl floor has a gash in it

PATCH THE BURNED AREA Here's a trick that makes repairing blemishes in sheet vinyl a snap:

1. Lay some extra vinyl over the gash. Match the design on the replacement piece with the design on the floor. Tape down the replacement vinyl piece to make sure it does not move during the cutting. Using a sharp utility knife and a straightedge, slice through both layers, cutting both your replacement piece and the piece to be replaced simultaneously. If possible, make your cut along a line in the design. Take your time. Now you will have an exact fit for the piece you will remove. Remove the burned piece, scrape up as much old glue as possible, and then apply a new coat of vinyl floor adhesive.
2. Insert the replacement piece and press it firmly in place. Cover the seams with a seam sealer, available at stores that sell vinyl flooring. Make sure the sealer matches your floor's finish (high gloss or low gloss, for instance).

There's an air bubble in my vinyl floor

SLIT IT AND SLIDE GLUE UNDER IT It's hard to keep air bubbles out of sheet vinyl flooring. They pop up and stand out as broad, flat,

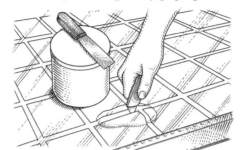

light-reflecting surfaces. Here's the quick fix: Use a utility knife to make a slit along the length of the bubble in an inconspicuous place, such as a dark line in the floor's pattern. Use a putty knife to spread a thin layer of vinyl floor adhesive under the bubble on both sides of the slit. Push up and down on the bubble to distribute the glue as widely as possible. Wipe up any excess glue and place a heavy object on the area to flatten it. Leave the weight in place overnight. The glue should be dry and the bubble flat in the morning.

I have a damaged vinyl tile but no leftovers to match

REPLACE IT WITH A HIDDEN TILE You can usually find a vinyl tile that won't be missed in a closet or under an appliance or permanent piece of furniture. Remove the tile by heating it with a hair dryer to soften the adhesive. Pry it up carefully with a putty knife. (Pick up a replacement for the hidden tile at a home improvement store. It doesn't have to be a perfect match.) Remove the damaged tile the same way—by heating and prying—and discard it. Scrape away as much excess adhesive as possible, using the hair dryer to soften it. Apply new adhesive and install the replacement tile.

■ CERAMIC TILE

There's a chip in one of my ceramic tiles

TOUCH IT UP WITH PAINT Even in large ceramic tile floors, your eye will zero in on the smallest chip or crack. The quick fix is to mask the defect with a little appliance touch-up paint so that your eye will overlook it. If the chip is deep, fill it before painting it. Use a woodworker's epoxy. It is sold by woodworking supply stores and mixes to a workable consistency, bonds tightly, and holds paint.

I have a damaged ceramic floor tile but no leftovers to match

REPLACE IT WITH ONE FROM A HIDDEN AREA If you don't have left-over tiles but need one to replace a conspicuous broken tile, look for a replacement in a closet or under a refrigerator or stove. Then don your safety goggles and take these steps:

1. To remove your chosen replacement tile, try to chip away the grout surrounding it by lightly tapping with a screwdriver or chisel and a hammer. You may, however, have to sacrifice an adjacent tile to get access to the underside of the replacement.
2. Once you can get under the tile with a firm, flat blade, gently tap and pry, tap and pry, until the tile pops up.
3. Pry up the broken tile or even pulverize it with a hammer. Go easy on this, too. Even though you don't need to preserve it, you can accidentally crack an adjacent tile. And flying tile particles can scratch or dent wood cabinets and sheetrock walls.
4. Remove as much as possible of the old adhesive bonding the tile to the floor, using a putty knife.
5. Spread new adhesive in the area and lay the replacement tile in it. Once it's dry, regrout the surrounding joints.
6. To replace the tile (or tiles) you removed from the hidden area, buy one of similar size and color, using a shard of the broken tile to guide you. Out of sight like this, "close enough" is fine. Install it the same way.

■ STAIRS

One of my stair balusters is broken

GLUE IT TOGETHER Balusters (the supporting posts for a banister) not only add character to a house but also protect pets and little ones from falls. A broken one is bad news. If a baluster is not badly splintered, the best and fastest solution is to glue it back together. Put yellow carpenter's glue on both sides of the break and clamp the pieces together, using squares of cardboard under the clamp jaws to protect the wood. If the baluster is round or if you don't have clamps, use a

PROBLEM STOPPER

Check Your Mat

Did you know that the chemicals in many synthetic throw rugs will yellow vinyl flooring? Most people learn the hard way—once the floor is yellow—and then there's no solution short of replacing the vinyl. If you want to put a doormat or small area rug in your kitchen or bath (or anywhere else you've got vinyl flooring), make sure it's made from natural fibers, such as sisal.

tight spiral of masking tape to secure the glued pieces. After the glue dries, fill any holes with wood putty; then sand and refinish.

My stair baluster is completely smashed

REPLACE THE BALUSTER To find a replacement for a badly damaged baluster, take the old baluster (or a neighboring one) to building supply stores and lumberyards until you come up with a match. If necessary, have a cabinetmaker turn a new baluster on a lathe. It's usually easiest to paint or finish a new baluster before you install it.

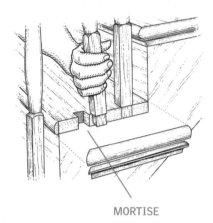

MORTISE

To replace a baluster, first check to see how it fits into the stair tread. If it goes into a slot (a mortise), here's how to proceed:

1. Carefully pry the trim off the end of the stair tread with a stiff putty knife or thin pry bar. Then pry out the bottom of the baluster.
2. Gently work the top of the baluster out of the handrail. If it is nailed, gently tap it out using a rubber mallet. Scrape out all the old glue at the top and bottom.
3. Test-fit the new baluster and cut it as needed to fit. Then put glue on both ends. Slip it in place, and nail as before. Use finishing nails, and to avoid splitting, drill holes for the nails slightly smaller in diameter than the nails.

If the broken baluster has a doweled lower end, follow these steps:

1. Saw the old baluster in half to remove it. Give each half a sharp twist with a wrench to break its glue seal. Clean out the old glue in the holes at both ends.
2. Cut the new baluster's upper end to fit into the handrail's hole with a ⅜-inch space above.
3. Trim the dowel on the baluster's lower end to a ¼-inch stump. Test-fit the baluster by pushing it up into the handrail and letting it drop into the tread hole. You may need to trim the upper end more and bevel its edge.
4. Put glue on both ends and set it in place.

■ CARPET

There's a small cigarette burn on my dining room carpet

GIVE IT A TRIM WITH SCISSORS When you get a small burn on your carpet, give it a haircut. Get a pair of sharp scissors and remove the surface burns by snipping off the charred tips of the carpet fibers. If the carpet is plush, it helps to feather out the area by lightly tapering the nap in a circle a little wider than the damaged area. If the burn didn't go too deep, the charring will disappear.

My carpet has a ragged edge

SECURE IT WITH GLUE Don't let that ragged edge run, or your problem will be harder to fix. Try this solution: Trim the excess fibers and smear regular white glue, such as Elmer's or any easy-to-apply glue that dries clear, liberally along the bottom of the ragged edge, where the tufts are joined. When the glue dries it will be invisible and will lock in the fibers, preventing further fraying.

My loop rug has a tuft poking out

TRIM IT OFF Whatever you do, don't pull the tuft. Loop rugs, such as Berbers, will run like nylon stockings, and it will become almost impossible to make the rug look normal again. Instead, get a pair of sharp scissors. Lie flat on the carpet and cut the tuft as close to the rug surface as you can. Do this the minute you notice an errant tuft. Otherwise, your vacuum cleaner's beater bar may catch it and cause it to run.

WORLD-CLASS GOOF

Wired for Trouble

Longtime carpet installers see it time and time again—husbands who are so eager to run speaker wire throughout the house that they ruin a rug. How? With drill in hand and daydreaming of their new stereos, they head to the basement and begin drilling holes up into floors for threading wire from room to room. Oops. They only remember the rug that's on the floor when their bits wind to a halt in a tangle of fibers.

TRICKS OF THE TRADE

Closet Carpet Keeper
If you're installing wall-to-wall carpet in a room, always carpet the inside of the room's closets, even if it seems unnecessary. The extra expense will be minimal. And if you ever need a carpet patch because of a stain, a burn, or a tear, you can cut it out of the closet. Yes, it's easy enough to save a remnant for patches, but remnants often turn moldy in basements or get inadvertently thrown out during spring cleaning. The closet carpet will always be there for you.

The seam in my carpet has torn open

SEW THE TEAR SHUT Most carpet tears occur along seams where two pieces of carpet were glued or sewn together. To fix such a tear, pull the carpet edges together and hold them in place with nails driven about 6 inches (15 centimeters) from the tear. Then use a curved upholstery needle and heavy fishing line to sew the pieces together. Make the stitch holes about ½ inch (1.2 centimeters) out from each edge and space them about

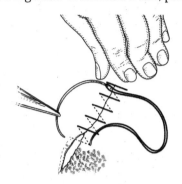

¾ inch (2 centimeters) apart along the seam. For the least visibility, make the top of the stitch perpendicular to the tear, and the underside diagonal. If you're rejoining a seam that was glued together, you'll find that the old glue tape underneath is tough to work the needle through. Use needle-nose pliers to help push the needle.

There's a permanent stain in my carpet

PATCH THE BURNED AREA For permanent stains and large burn marks in a wall-to-wall carpet, the only solution is to cut out the damaged section and patch it. The procedure is basically the same as illustrated for vinyl flooring. (See "My sheet vinyl floor has a gash in it," page 83.) Here's how to go about it:

1. Find a clean patch. If you have extra carpet, that's great. If not, take some from a closet or from under an appliance or a large piece of permanent furniture.
2. Cut the patch slightly larger than the marred piece you'll be removing. (Cut just the carpet, not the carpet padding.)
3. Place the patch over the burn mark or stain and use a utility knife to cut though both pieces at once, ensuring a perfect fit. To make sure the patch stays in place, put double-sided carpet tape on the pad under the seams and then set in the patch. Don't use staples or tacks. They'll pull down the padding, making the patch obvious.

If the new patch doesn't match the burned carpet in cleanliness and texture, consider making a double-switch. Take a matching patch from a pass-through area, such as a hallway, where people are much less likely to notice a patch. Then replace the hallway hole with the clean patch. (Ask a carpet store for a piece to patch a closet hole. It doesn't have to be an exact match, since no one will ever see it.)

Trying to cut carpet for the bathroom is too scary

MAKE A TEMPLATE TO GUIDE YOU When it comes to cutting new carpet, the trial and error approach is costly. You need to get it right the first time. Cutting carpet for a bathroom is particularly tricky because of the curved shape of the toilet base and the odd zigs and zags of cabinetry. The secret, say carpet installers, is to make a paper template first.

Buy a large roll of paper from a home improvement store or paint store and gather up scissors, a ruler, cellophane tape, and a pencil. Basically, you're going to piece together your template from smaller sheets of paper.

1. Start by placing a sheet of paper on the trickiest part of the floor. Trace and cut the paper to fit that area. Leave it there.
2. Go on to other sections of the bathroom floor until you've covered it all.
3. With all the paper sections in place on the floor, tape them together and check that the fit is perfect.
4. Remove the entire template and lay it over the carpet as a guide for cutting.

My floors are cold

INSULATE WITH CARPET PADDING In many older houses, the floors above the crawl space or basement are not insulated. In winter, cold air pools under the floors, cooling your feet and forcing your furnace to pump out more heat. The best long-term solution is to insulate the floor. For a fast fix, however, consider upgrading your carpet padding. Carpet padding gets an R-value rating—a measure of resistance to heat loss—just as wall and floor insulations do. Depending on the thickness and the material, a good quality padding can have an R-2 rating. While this is a long way from the R-11 to R-22 protection that insulation can provide, it will still do a lot to keep your feet warm in winter.

Doors and Windows

■ STORMS AND SCREENS

My window screen has a little hole in it

FILL IT WITH EPOXY GLUE A tiny hole in your window screen is a wide-open gateway to little bugs you want to keep outside. Repair small holes and tears with clear epoxy glue or clear nail polish. First straighten the torn strands with a toothpick, then apply the epoxy or polish to the area and spread it with a cotton swab. Open clogged mesh by pricking the cells with a clean toothpick before the epoxy or polish hardens. Repeat several times if necessary to build up a thick layer.

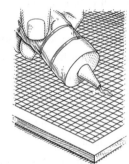

Patching a screen on a flat surface is easier than mending it in place. Working with a horizontal screen, you can reach both sides with your hands and can avoid unsightly runs when applying epoxy or nail polish.

My storm windows don't slide

CLEAN AND LUBRICATE THE TRACKS Modern combination storm and screen windows are a blessing, but grime and debris can accumulate in the tracks. Every couple of years, it's wise to clean them.

Remove each sash from the frame and set it aside. Wipe the tracks with a cloth and vacuum away dust, cobwebs, and debris. Use a damp foam-rubber edging paintbrush to scrub the interior of the tracks. Then work the narrowest slots with a stiff wet toothbrush or a rag draped over the tip of a screwdriver. While the tracks dry, wipe off the exterior sill with a sponge dipped in a solution of water and dishwashing liquid. Use a toothpick or awl to clear any dirt from the weep holes at the bottom of the window frame. (Weep holes let water drain away from the sill.) Finally, use a Teflon-based spray, such as Tri-Flow, to lubricate the tracks. (Don't use WD-40 or household oils, because they may attract dirt.) Spray the lubricant on a clean rag and apply a very thin coat on the tracks before reinstalling the sashes.

■ WINDOWS

I'm afraid that my windows aren't secure

LOCK THE SASHES WITH REMOVABLE NAILS It's a breeze for burglars to open most latched windows. They smash a single pane, reach in, and open the latch. Of course, you could install key-lock latches, but that's expensive (about $14 per window) and time-consuming. Here's a quick, low-cost solu-

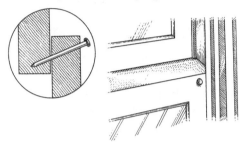

tion for securing your double-hung windows: Where the upper and lower window sashes overlap (when they are closed), drill a hole at an angle through the top of the lower window and extending about halfway into the bottom of the upper window. Drill the hole slightly larger than the nail you're going to insert in the hole you've drilled. (The nail should fit loosely so that it won't stick if the window wood swells.) Now insert a nail so that its flat head is flush against the frame. Paint the head to match the window color. When you want to remove the nail, draw it out with a magnet.

My windowpane got broken

REPLACE THE PANE Newer homes have double-glazed windows; to fix them, contact the manufacturer or your retailer and replace the entire sash. (The sash is the framed unit that you move up and down.) But many older houses still have windows with single-thickness panes that you can replace. Before you start, go to a glazier, a hardware shop, or a home center and have a new pane cut, about $\frac{3}{16}$ of an inch (4.7 millimeters) smaller in each direction than the opening that the pane fits into. Also buy glazing putty and a box of glazing points (tiny bits of metal that hold the glass in place). Then follow these steps to replace the broken pane:

1. Wearing thick work gloves and goggles, remove as much of the broken glass as possible.
2. Working on the outside of the window, use a stiff putty knife or a wire brush to scrape the old putty and glass fragments out of the groove that the pane fits into. If the putty has hardened, use a hair dryer or a soldering iron to warm and soften it. Use

TRICKS OF THE TRADE

Fixing a Cracked or Scratched Window
You can temporarily seal a small crack in window glass in a flash by brushing the breach with clear shellac or nail polish. (This is not recommended for car windows.)

To erase shallow scratches on glass, dab them with a little toothpaste and then polish the area vigorously for a minute or two. "Extra-whitening" brands work best because they contain more abrasives.

When you remove storm windows or screens for cleaning or storage, use a fine-tipped permanent marker to unobtrusively write a different number on each window frame and the same number on each matching sash that you remove. Store any fasteners in a small self-sealing sandwich bag and write the same number on this bag.

needle-nose pliers to pull out the old glazing points. Use a brush to coat the groove with linseed oil or thinned oil paint to prevent the wood from absorbing the oil in the putty.

3. Knead some glazing putty as if it were dough to soften it. Then smooth a thin layer on the inside edge of the groove. Insert the new pane and press it gently against the putty until the putty is about $\frac{1}{16}$ inch (1.6 millimeters) thick all around.

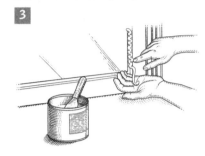

4. Insert new glazing points in the frame to hold the pane in place. One or two points per side will do with smaller panes; place the points every 6 inches (15 centimeters) with a larger pane.

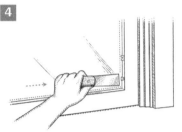

5. Roll more putty into a rope about $\frac{3}{8}$ inch (9.5 millimeters) in diameter and pack it into the groove over the edge of the glass. Use a clean putty knife to bevel and smooth the putty. Let the putty set for a week before painting it.

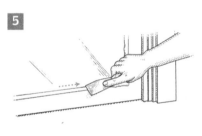

My window is painted shut

WORK A THIN KNIFE AROUND THE EDGES When you need ventilation in the summer, a sloppy paint job will come back to haunt you. Find a razor craft knife, a thin but hard spatula, or a butter knife. Slide it along the crack between the window and frame, breaking the seal created by the paint. For stubborn cases, brush turpentine along the seal first; then work your thin-edged tool along the crack.

My windowsills are rotting

USE AN EPOXY WOOD FILLER The grain splits, or entire sections of wood rot and crumble. These are common maladies in old houses with wooden sills. Instead of replacing the entire sill, try this simple fix: Use an epoxy wood-filling product, available at hardware stores. These epoxy products, which are different from epoxy glue, are easy to use and water resistant, and they hold paint well. And you can make the repairs without dismantling the window.

For splits in the wood grain, mix the epoxy to a pourable consistency and apply it to the cracks. Wipe away the excess. Let it soak in and dry. Next, mix up a thicker batch and spread it over the splits with a putty knife. Fill only the cracks and remove the excess. (Don't coat the entire sill surface, since that can trap water and lead to more problems.) Tip: Make sure the sill is dry before applying epoxy.

For deeper sections of rot, scrape out the rotted wood until you reach sound wood. Making sure the sill is dry, fill the space with a pastelike mixture of the epoxy. Fill the gap full enough that you can sand the patch level with the rest of the sill surface.

My window sash joints are sagging

STRAIGHTEN THE CORNER AND REINFORCE IT It's common for the lower corners of wooden window sashes to absorb water and eventually rot and sag. But you can prolong the life of your window for years with this quick fix.

1. Thoroughly clean the area around the joint in the sagging corner. (Work on the exterior side of the window.) Scrape with a wire brush and rub with sandpaper to remove peeling paint and rotted wood.

2. If you are working on an upper sash, cut a stick about 1 inch (2.5 centimeters) longer than the distance from the sill to the bottom of the upper sash. Wedge the stick under the corner of the sash and tap the side of the stick to gently raise the sagging corner. (Protect the sill by placing a thin piece of wood under the stick.) If  it's the lower sash you're working on, raise the sash as far as it will go and use the same trick to straighten it. Fill any cracks or gaps in the wood with silicone caulk. Let it dry.

3. Attach a metal L- bracket to the exterior of the corner. (Use a galvanized bracket and screws so that it won't rust.) Do the other corner the same way, if necessary. Finish by repainting.

My window sash cord broke

REPLACE THE CORD Until the middle of the 20th century, most double-hung windows relied on counterweights to raise and lower the sashes (that is, the frame and panes that form the movable part of a window). If you live in an older house, you know that the cords to these counterweights have a finite life span. When one breaks, the weight drops out of sight, and the window won't work properly. When this happens, many homeowners get so frustrated that they install brand-new windows. You can save money—and save those solid old windows—with the following repair:

1. Remove the sash stop. That's the narrow strip of vertical wooden molding that holds the window sash in place. It's probably attached with thin finish nails. Carefully pry it off with a stiff putty knife and a pry bar.
2. Remove the lower sash. If the sash cord on the opposite side is intact, remove it from the sash and tie the end to something (such as a pencil) to prevent the cord from slipping over the pulley and into the counterweight pocket. Set the sash aside.

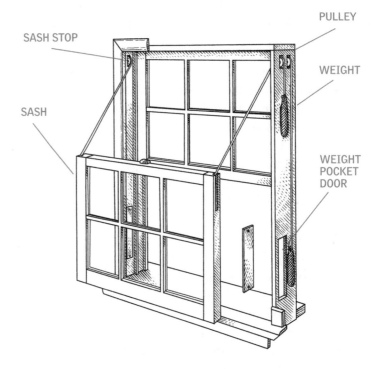

3. Open the counterweight pocket door (on the side with the broken cord). This door is typically held on with screws.
4. Remove the counterweight. Untie the broken cord.

5. Thread a new cord over the pulley. Do this by dropping a small chain—¼ inch (6 millimeters) long—over the pulley and into the pocket. (A chain is easier to thread through the pulley than a lightweight cord would be.) Tape a new sash cord (available at hardware stores) to the end of the chain, and pull the cord back over the pulley.

6. Attach the counterweight. Tie it to the appropriate end of the cord. Slip the weight back into the counterweight pocket.

7. Reconnect the other end of the sash cord to the sash. Adjust the length so that when the sash is sitting on the sill, the weight is drawn up close to the pulley. Knot the cord and slip it into the sash channel. Finish by putting the sash in place and nailing the stop back on.

TRICKS OF THE TRADE

Quick Fix for a Window Crack
You can seal cracked window glass temporarily or plug up a small hole in a flash by brushing the breach with clear shellac or nail polish. (Not recommended for windows on your car.)

My windows leak around the edges during driving storms

REPLACE THE CAULKING A good window should stop water even when rain is traveling horizontally. If your windows are leaking, most likely they need caulking. Inspect the caulk around the outer edges of the windows, between the window frame and the siding. Fill any gaps with caulk. Check to see whether the old caulk is still good: push it with your finger. If it gives a little, it's still good. If not, it needs to be replaced. For caulking, buy a tube of 1-part polyurethane mixture caulk and, if you don't have one, a caulking gun. Here's how to proceed:

1. Scrape off the old caulk completely to ensure a proper seal for the new caulk.

2. Insert the tube in the gun and tighten the plunger against the tube. Then cut off the tip of the tube's nozzle at a 45-degree angle with a utility knife.

3. Place the nozzle against the seam angled in the direction it will travel, and squeeze the trigger gently for an even flow of caulk as you move along the seam.

4. Smooth the fresh caulk with the tip of a Popsicle stick or an old spoon handle.

My casement window crank is balky

CLEAN THE TRACKS AND CRANK MECHANISM If a casement window crank just spins without moving the window, chances are its gears are stripped and the crank mechanism needs to be replaced. However, if it's just balky, the crank mechanism and the window's tracks probably need cleaning. Open the window until its extension arm lines up with a small slot in the track that allows the arm to be popped out of the track. Use a stiff toothbrush or a rag over the tip of a screwdriver to dislodge any dirt from inside the track and then wipe the track, extension arm, and all hinges with a rag. Lubricate the track, hinges, and crank assembly with a Teflon-based spray, such as Tri-Flow, and reassemble the window. Crank away!

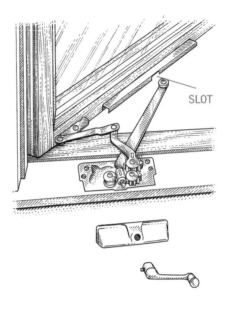

My window shade won't roll up

REWIND THE SPRING INSIDE THE ROLLER Rejuvenating a lazy window shade is a snap—the spring just needs to be reloaded. First, remove the shade from its brackets. You'll notice that the metal pins protruding from the sides of the shade are different: One end is rounded and the other end is flat like the tip of a conventional screwdriver. The flat end will slide easily out of its slot-shaped bracket hole, and then

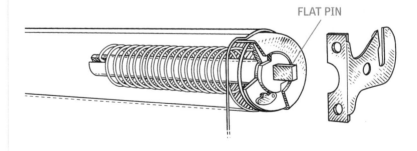

the round-pin end will come free. Hand-roll the shade all the way up around the shade cylinder and then replace the shade in its brackets—round-pin end first. Now when you pull the shade down, you will feel the reloaded spring inside the cylinder engage, ready to lock the shade into place at your bidding.

■ DOORS

The hinges on my door are loose

PACK THE SCREW HOLES WITH TOOTHPICKS When door hinges come loose, the cause is screws that have torn through the wood that was holding them in place. You don't need to find new screws; you just need to repair the wood. First, determine which hinge is coming loose and on which side—the door or the door frame. Then follow these steps:

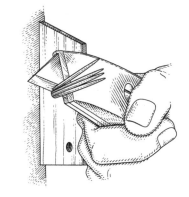

1. Open the door all the way and prop it into correct position by tucking a book, folded towel, wooden wedge, or some other object under its lower edge.
2. Using a screwdriver, remove the screws from the loose side of the malfunctioning hinge.
3. Take wooden toothpicks, dip them one at a time in yellow carpenter's glue, and insert them in the screw holes in the wood until you can pack no more in.
4. Using a utility knife, cut the toothpicks flush with the wood. Let the glue dry.
5. Drive the screws back into their original holes, where they will now hold snugly.

PLUG THE SCREW HOLES WITH DOWELS An alternative to the tooth-pick method: Use a drill to make a clean, round hole where each screw had been. Buy a wooden dowel (available at hardware, home improvement, and hobby stores) of the same diameter as the drill bit you used. Slide the dowel into the hole to measure how deep it will go into the wood. Pull the dowel out and saw it off so it will fit flush with the surface. Slather the dowel with yellow carpenter's glue and slide it into place. Repeat for each hole. Let the glue dry before you drive the screws back in. You may need to drill a pilot hole for the screws in the dowels, depending on how hard the dowel is.

My wooden door is sticking in the frame

RUB THE DOOR EDGE WITH SOAP If the weather has caused a wooden door to swell up and stick in its door frame, an instant solution is as close at hand as your bathroom sink. Grab a bar of hand soap and rub it along the edge of your door to give it a thin coating. Now your lubricated door will slide into place with ease.

The doors in my house close on their own

BEND THE HINGE PINS Your problem isn't ghosts. The house has settled, and the door frames are out of plumb. That means the hinges are no longer in line with each other. You could rehang the problematic doors, but there's an easier solution: Remove the hinge pins (the rods that hold the two parts of the hinge together) one at a time. If a hinge pin won't pull out easily, use a screwdriver with a hammer against the cap of the pin to drive it up and out. Lay each pin on its side and give it a whack with a hammer, then set it back in the hinge. The idea is to bend the pin slightly so that the hinges are tight enough to prevent the door from swinging by itself.

INSTALL A MAGNETIC CATCH Here's another way to solve the problem: Use a magnetic catch, the kind you find in kitchen cabinets, to hold the door open. Screw a magnetic cabinet-door catch to the floor on the spot where you want the door to stand open, and screw its strike plate to the back of the door. Make sure the catch is far enough out from the baseboard so that the doorknob won't hit the wall. If necessary, mount the catch on a small block of wood to raise it high enough to contact the bottom of the door.

CATCH

My doorstop is loose

REMOUNT IT USING WATER PUTTY Doorstops project from baseboards to prevent doorknobs from denting walls. All someone has to do is accidentally kick or step on it, and the doorstop will jiggle loose. The solution is to unscrew the doorstop, fill the hole with some water putty, such as Durham's Rock Hard Water Putty, and replace the device while the putty is still wet. Scrape away the excess putty with a wooden matchstick. Use tape to hold the doorstop in the correct position until the putty hardens. When the putty does harden, it will expand slightly and form a bond that will be even tighter than before.

I can't paint the bottom edge of the door

APPLY PAINT WITH A CARPET SCRAP
You'd like to protect the door's wood, but removing the door from its hinges is a lot of trouble just for the sake of painting that inaccessible bottom edge. So find a scrap of carpet that's several inches wide. Apply a generous swath of paint to the carpet. Then slide it under the door and rub it back and forth to coat the bottom edge.

There's a big, ugly dent in my metal door

FILL IT WITH AUTO-BODY FILLER You can quickly fix a dent, or even a hole, in a metal door with auto-body filler, available at home improvement and auto supply stores. Here's how:

1. Sand the damaged area down to bare metal with medium-grit sandpaper.
2. Mix up and spread on some auto-body filler with your fingers (wear gloves). This stuff hardens fast, so mix up only as much as you can use in five minutes or so.
3. Sand the patch with medium, then fine, sandpaper. If you have a raised panel door, shape the patch to match its contours.
4. Prime the patch and paint the door.

There's a hole in my hollow-core door

FILL IT WITH WOOD FILLER Don't think you have to buy a new door. There's an easy way to patch a hole in a wooden hollow-core door, as long as it has a painted finish or you're willing to paint it. First, carefully remove the splintered wood from around the hole. If it's a small hole, you can pack it with wadded up aluminum foil and

TRICKS OF THE TRADE

Quieting Noisy Weather Stripping
Bronze weather stripping on a doorjamb can make an annoying scraping noise when the door brushes against it. The instant fix is to rub a white candle on the strip to silence it and keep it operating smoothly. If you find any gaps between the strip and the door where air is sneaking into the house, use a screwdriver to pry the flap out to fill the gaps.

then fill in the remaining space with powdered wood filler, such as Durham's Rock Hard Water Putty. Smooth the patch with a putty knife. When the putty has dried, sand it smooth. Depending on the size of the patch, prime and paint the patch area or the entire door.

MAKE A BACKING FOR A LARGER HOLE If the hole is more than a couple of inches wide, you can create a "paint-stick lath" using a flat wooden paint-stirring stick. Saw (or break) the stick so that it is about an inch longer than the hole. Put a couple of drops of superglue on either end, insert the stick in the hole, and pull it back against the inside of the door so that the glue hardens and holds it in place. If the hole is really big, you may have to use more than one paint-stick lath to build up the backing. Next, apply the putty as before, smoothing it with a putty knife. When the putty is dry, sand it smooth. Wipe away all dust from the door. Paint the entire door with a coat of stain-killing primer and then apply your finish coats of paint to the door.

■ LOCKS AND LATCHES

My bedroom door won't latch

The cause is simple: The latch bolt on the door is not being caught by the strike plate on the door frame. But finding a solution requires a little detective work, because the latch bolt and strike plate can be out of sync in a few different ways. Start by checking the strike plate for wear marks, and observe how the latch bolt hits the plate as the door closes. If you can't see how it hits, put a little lipstick on the end of the bolt and check the mark it leaves on the strike plate.

SHIM OUT THE STRIKE PLATE If the bolt doesn't extend far enough to go into the plate—usually because the plate is recessed too much—you will need to put a thin piece of material, such as cardboard, as a shim under the plate. To do this, take out the two screws holding the plate and use the plate as a template to cut a shim, complete with bolt and screw holes, from shirt cardboard. Put the shim

STRIKE PLATE

under the plate and screw it back into place. You may need more than one shim.

TLC: Tender Lock Care

• Never oil a lock. The oil will gum up the sensitive pins inside. Every few months, spray the keyholes with a cleaning lubricant, such as WD-40. Hold a cloth beneath the lock to catch the runoff. It will be black with grime. Keep spraying until the runoff is clear.

• If you're going to paint a door, always remove the lock beforehand. Paint can ruin a lock.

• Be careful about installing weather stripping between the door and the frame. Locks are meant to have a little play to allow for expansion and contraction. Take away that play with weather stripping, and you can put pressure on the lock, causing it to malfunction. It's better to install weather stripping around the frame, but do it with the door closed, so that it won't extend too far into the door-closing space, causing the door to fit too tightly.

NUDGE THE DOOR FRAME STOP BACK Sometimes the stop—the strip of wood that the door hits against on the frame—is too far forward, preventing the bolt from going into the strike plate. This can happen because the stop has swollen or shifted position with settling. Whatever the reason, you can usually use a block of wood with a hammer to nudge the stop back slightly. If necessary, you may need to pry off the stop and renail it, or use a plane or utility knife to trim it down.

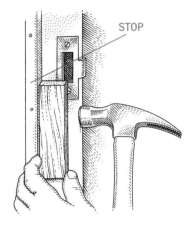

STOP

ENLARGE THE STRIKE PLATE OPENING If the bolt and strike plate are only slightly out of alignment vertically, it's usually easiest to enlarge the opening in the plate a bit with a file. To do this, remove the two screws in the strike plate with a screwdriver. Then saw a slot in a heavy piece of scrap wood and set an edge of the strike plate in the slot to hold it steady while you file. After filing, screw the plate back onto the door frame.

MOVE THE STRIKE PLATE If the bolt and strike plate are more out of alignment vertically, you'll have to reposition the strike plate up or

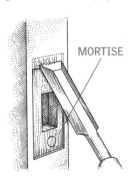

MORTISE

down a bit to a position where it can do its job. (This is the last resort because it involves more work.) Remove the strike plate and use a chisel to extend its mortise (the recess cut into the frame in which the plate sits) and to enlarge the hole behind the plate that the latch goes into. Then plug the old screw holes with toothpicks, matchsticks, or a dowel coated with glue. After the glue dries, drill new pilot holes for the screws and screw the strike plate into its new position. Fill the old mortise area with wood filler.

INSTALL A LARGER STRIKE PLATE If the old plate and frame are worn or damaged, buy a slightly larger strike plate from a hardware store and install it in place of the old one. It will look best if it completely covers the damaged area.

My lock just spins when I turn the key

GET THE TAILPIECE REPLACED A
spinning lock is a sign that the
lock's tailpiece, an interior part that
activates the latch, is broken. You
probably don't need an expensive
new lock, but you will likely need a
locksmith to make the inexpensive
repair. Remove the cylinder and
take it to a locksmith. While you're
at it, fix the problem that caused
the tailpiece to break (see "My door
lock is getting really hard to turn," below), or you'll end up with
another broken tailpiece.

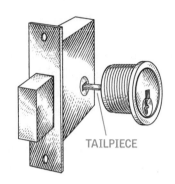

TAILPIECE

I bent my door key

STRAIGHTEN IT IN A VISE A bent key is a weakened key. This
means that at any time, it could snap off in your lock, creating an
even bigger problem than you already have. So the best fix for this
situation is a preventive one—get a new key. But if you simply have
no alternative but to use the bent key, squash it flat in a vise. You
may have one in your garage. If you don't, try flattening the key by
placing it between two pieces of wood and hitting it with a hammer.
If the key is not too badly damaged, it will still slide home nicely
into the keyhole and will allow you to open your door. But once
you've gotten into the house, get out your backup key and throw
away the bent one. If you don't have a backup, go straight to a locksmith, hardware store, or home improvement store to have two
copies made (one for use and one to keep in reserve).

My door lock is getting really hard to turn

CLEAN THE LOCK OR GET A NEW KEY If your lock is not operating
properly, take the following simple steps to isolate—and fix—the
problem. Operate the lock with the door open. If the lock is stiff,
clean and lubricate the lock. Spray the keyhole with a cleaning lubricant, such as WD-40. The runoff will be black, so hold a cloth
underneath to catch it. Otherwise, the runoff will stain your door.
Spray until the runoff is clear.

If lubricating and cleaning the lock doesn't cure the stiffness, you
may have a poorly cut key and need to have a new key made. If at all

possible, find one of the original keys that came with the lock and try it in the lock. If it works, get it duplicated.

MOVE THE STRIKE PLATE If the lock functions properly while the door is open but is stiff when the door is closed, the problem is in the strike plate on the door frame. If you must pull on the door to make the lock engage, move the plate toward you slightly. If you must push to engage the lock, move the plate in the other direction. Unscrew the plate, fill the holes with glue-coated wooden matchsticks, and drill new pilot holes for the screws in the right spots. You will need to slightly enlarge the recessed mortise in the door frame that the plate fits in.

My door lock is frozen

SPRAY IT WITH WD-40 If your lock freezes up in cold weather, spray a little penetrating lubricant/degreaser, such as WD-40, into the lock to loosen the mechanism. Don't use oil, a mistake that locksmiths see all the time. People put motor oil, cooking oil, or household oil in their locks, all of which only gum up the works and makes matters worse.

HEAT YOUR KEY If you don't have any WD-40 handy, heat your key with a match (be sure to hold it with a glove or cloth to keep from burning your fingers) and insert it in the lock. The heat will thaw the frozen mechanism.

WORLD-CLASS GOOF

If I Ever Get Outta Here

Believe it or not, Ron Gregory of Beaver Lock and Key, in Etobicoke, Ontario, gets calls all the time from panicked homeowners whose spouses are stuck in the bathroom. The door is locked, they say, and there is no key. There's not even a keyhole.

Most bathroom knob sets have what is known as a privacy lock. Instead of a keyhole, there is simply a small hole in the center of the knob. Poke a rod into that hole and push—or insert a flat-head rod in the hole, push, twist—and the lock will pop open. "I can't even tell them over the phone what to do because they're in such a panic," Gregory says. "So I rush over, stick a small screwdriver in the lock, and the door opens." Not counting travel, he clocks maybe two minutes on the job. "I don't charge them," he says.

My key is stuck in the door lock

GIVE IT A SHOT OF WD-40 This is usually a sign of an old lock, one whose pins are not aligning properly because the lubrication has dried out. Shoot some penetrating lubricant, such as WD-40, into the lock and then rotate and jiggle the key. Now try to remove the key. It should come right out. If not, pinch the key so that your fingertips touch the lock and then work it out slowly. This pinching motion straightens the key and gives you leverage. Your next step should be to replace the lock's cylinder.

I can't find the keyhole at night

MAKE IT GLOW IN THE DARK If you have trouble finding the door lock in the dark, dab a few drops of luminous paint around the keyhole for increased visibility.

My kids keep forgetting their house keys

INSTALL A KEY BOX Hiding a spare key outside for use by forgetful family members isn't a good idea. Soon the entire neighborhood will know it's under the third stone from the doorstep in the front garden. Instead, install a key box, like the ones that real estate agents use, somewhere outside your house. Key boxes are small safes for keys, with a combination dial on the front. Mount yours in a visible location to discourage tampering, and secure it to solid framing with the long screws provided. Change the combination periodically if you give it to cleaners or workers outside the family. Key boxes are available from locksmiths.

■ GARAGE DOORS

My garage door squeaks and groans

OIL THE MOVING PARTS With all those metal parts scraping together—no wonder. You won't eliminate all the noise of a moving garage door, but you can reduce the harshest sounds by lubricating the metal parts. First, try a few drops of an all-purpose lubricant, such as 3-in-One oil, on rollers, hinges, torsion spring (the big spring that helps lift the door), and bearings alongside the door. Keep the tracks clean and dry, so the rollers won't drag. Don't use grease, and don't use WD-40, which will dry out more quickly than a regular lubricating oil. If the lubrication does not stop the problem, disconnect the door from the door opener (if it's automatic) and operate it by hand to see whether the noises are coming from the door or the moving parts inside the opener motor. Once you've pinpointed the source, lubricate.

REMOVE ANY GREASE Never use grease on a garage door. Grease on the runners and rollers acts like a brake, especially in winter when cold temperatures harden grease into a sticky obstacle course. By making the door work harder to open and close, grease on your runners could be causing the noise. Use a spray-on degreaser, such as WD-40, to break down any old grease you see. Wipe away the residue with paper towels and then lubricate the parts with oil. Now open the door. And close it. Open it again. It should run smoothly and quietly.

My automatic garage door won't close

CHECK THE PHOTOELECTRIC SENSORS The door slides down, but before it can touch the ground, it heads back up again. No, it's not just a door with a bad attitude. On the contrary, this door means well. Something is triggering the door's safety feature, the one that keeps the door from closing on your car hood or the neighbor's kindergartner. In newer garage doors, this safety feature typically has an infrared beam source and a matching photoelectric sensor on either side of the garage door opening. They are located about 10 inches (25 centimeters) or so above the ground. If the beam is obscured or is not properly lined up, it can malfunction. To fix the problem, try cleaning the beam lens, following the manufacturer's instructions. Make sure the indicator light (if it has one) signals that the feature is working and that the beam is aligned properly. Use a tape measure to check that the sensors are at the same height. Rough-moving or out-of-whack doors could also be the cause. If so, try lubricating the door (see previous problem) or having it realigned.

PROBLEM STOPPER

Reducing Noise When Getting a New Garage Door
A cheap garage door is like a banjo: Thin and tinny, it amplifies all the noises its parts make. If your garage door makes too much noise, maybe it's time for an upgrade. Buy an insulated door. While the working parts will still need to be lubricated to keep them moving smoothly and quietly, the layers of insulation will muffle any sounds the door makes.

Electrical Problems

PROBLEM STOPPER

Replace Flickering Fluorescents

If your fluorescent tube is flickering, replace it. Flickering tubes can burn out the fixture's ballast, which regulates the electric current traveling into the tube. If the ballast fails, you're in for a more expensive repair.

■ LIGHTING

A bulb broke off in my light socket

REMOVE THE BULB BASE WITH PLIERS OR FRUIT Before you start, sweep up any glass on the floor. Then turn off the circuit breaker controlling the light socket. For a ceiling or high wall socket, you'll need a step stool or stepladder. Wear protective goggles and gloves.

The best tool for removing the base of the bulb is a pair of needle-nose pliers. Don't grab the remaining glass portion of the blub with the pliers; it might break. Instead, use the tip of the pliers to grab the edge of the bulb's metal base and turn it counterclockwise. If you don't have needle-nose pliers, insert a piece of fruit in the broken base of the bulb (oranges and apples work great) and turn. A potato or a wad of newspaper will also do the job.

I can't reach a hall light to change the bulb

USE A POLE LIGHT CHANGER Many modern front entryways have towering ceilings with a light fixture high overhead. They look great—until the bulb blows out. You can reach some of these lights with a stepladder, but a safer and easier solution for out-of-reach fixtures is a bulb changer. These suction-cup or clamping devices, available at hardware and home improvement stores, screw onto a telescoping handle to give you 10 to 12 feet (3 to 3.6 meters) of extra reach. They're great for exterior floodlights as well. Some are designed for floodlights, others for round bulbs—make sure to buy the right kind for your needs. Some bulb-changing kits come with a variety of heads for different bulbs.

I can't unscrew the bulb in my recessed ceiling fixture

STICK A TAB ON THE BULB Those flat floodlight bulbs are so wide that sometimes people can't get their fingers around the bulbs to twist them out when it's time to change them. The solution: Make a tab out of a 6-inch (15-centimeter) length of duct tape by folding the middle section over on itself, sticky side to sticky side. Stick the free ends across the bulb face so that the tab is in the middle of the bulb. Twist the tab. It will give you enough grip to loosen the bulb.

My lightbulbs burn out too quickly

MAKE SURE THE BULBS ARE DYING TOO SOON Before you do anything, make sure the bulbs are, indeed, giving out prematurely. Check the package for the bulb's estimated life expectancy and then try to calculate how long yours are actually lasting. A bulb with a 1,000-hour life, for example, should burn for a little over four months (120 days) if it's used an average of eight hours per day.

KEEP THE BULB FROM OVERHEATING Check for heat, which will shorten the life span of a bulb. If it's a high-wattage bulb in a small shade, such as a tight glass globe, then the bulb might be overheating. If so, replace it with a lower wattage bulb. Bulbs in recessed fixtures surrounded by attic insulation can overheat as well. Go up into the attic and remove the insulation around the fixture. Unless the fixture is UL listed as safe for use with insulation, it shouldn't have insulation around it anyway.

KEEP THE BULB FROM SHAKING Check for vibration. Ceiling fixtures beneath springy floors can jiggle so much that a bulb's filament snaps prematurely. The same goes for lights on or

WORLD-CLASS FIX

Mir Heroism

Thanks to a quick-thinking fix by Commander Valeri Korzun, the crew of six on the Russian space station *Mir* escaped a fiery death in 1997.

Late one Sunday evening, *Mir*'s master alarm sounded. Two-foot flames were shooting from one of the space station's oxygen-generating canisters. Sparks and molten metal were flying, and smoke choked the central passageway. Donning oxygen masks, crew members fought the fire, but the water-based fire extinguishers were useless against the burning lithium perchlorate. So the crew had to wait for the canister to burn itself out and hope that the flames would not burn through *Mir*'s aluminum hull, causing the capsule to decompress 250 miles from Earth.

Thinking fast, Commander Korzun sprayed the wall with the fire extinguisher to keep it from melting. It took 14 minutes for the pressurized canister to burn out. When the smoke cleared, ash was everywhere, but miraculously, the damage was minimal and no one was hurt.

near a wobbly ceiling fan or near a door that often slams shut. If you can't stop the vibration, use either a screw-in fluorescent bulb, which is not affected by vibration, or a shock-resistant regular incandescent bulb made especially for this purpose.

CALL THE POWER COMPANY Sometimes the voltage on a 120-volt line can exceed 120 volts. An extra half-dozen volts on the line can cut a bulb's life span in half. Special 125- or 130-volt bulbs can handle the extra voltage. But if you suspect this may be the cause, ask your power company to test for overvoltage, because it might be able to fix the problem.

■ ANNOYANCES

The exhaust fan in my bathroom rattles

SCREW IT TIGHTLY TO THE JOIST Exhaust fans usually rattle because they're not secured firmly. These fans are often attached to a wooden cross-support—a joist in the ceiling or a stud in the outside wall. Get a step stool or ladder, climb up, and remove the cover of the fan. Identify which side of the fan casing is against a joist. Using a power drill, drill two or three holes for 1-inch (2.5-centimeter) screws going through the side of the fan casing into the wood. Then drill smaller diameter pilot holes in the wood for the screws and drive the screws through the casing to secure it to the joist.

My bathroom outlet goes dead every time I run my hair dryer

HIT THE GFI RESET BUTTON To keep you from getting electrocuted, electrical outlets known as GFIs (ground fault circuit interrupters) are now commonly required in places where you might encounter moisture—kitchens, garages, unfinished basements, and bathrooms. They trip whenever they detect a harmful leakage of current. Unfortunately, GFIs grow more sensitive with age. They trip more easily, especially when used with heat-producing appliances such as hair dryers. The instant solution, which you probably already know, is to press the outlet's reset button, which reconnects the circuit.

REPLACE THE GFI To really solve this problem, you'll need to open the receptacle, take out the old GFI outlet, and replace it with a new one. Once you've cut off the power to the GFI at the main service

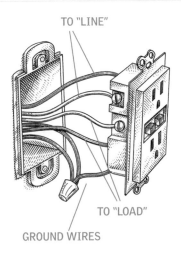

TO "LINE"

TO "LOAD"

GROUND WIRES

panel, it takes only a couple of minutes to detach the wires from the old GFI and attach them to the corresponding screws on the new one. In a typical installation, you attach the black wires in the box to the brass screws, and the white wires to the silver screws, and twist the green tail wire on the GFI to the bare wire in the box using a caplike wire connector. If you are afraid to deal with electricity, call a handy friend or an electrician.

My doorbell sounds muffled

VACUUM THE BELL'S INTERIOR You never think about your door chime—much less consider cleaning it. But a blanket of dust can build up inside, giving your bell a fuzzy sound. So just remove the cover and vacuum inside with the brush attachment. Your chimes will return to their former glory.

■ LARGE APPLIANCES

My dryer is hot but the clothes don't dry

CHECK FOR A BLOCKED VENT If your clothes dryer feels really hot, but your clothes take forever to dry, the vent may be clogged. A clogged vent traps the excess hot air inside the dryer's drum. But the low circulation of air keeps clothes from getting dry. This is a big problem—the extra heat can damage fabrics and can start a fire—but it's nothing you can't fix yourself.

1. Start by checking the vent flap or hood on the outside of the house. Make sure that you feel a strong flow of air coming out when the dryer is running. If not, try cleaning out the vent with a straightened clothes hanger.
2. If the vent flap is not the problem, check for a kink or sag in the duct and straighten the hose if necessary.
3. If a kinked or sagging duct is not the problem, disconnect the duct from the dryer and look for blockage inside with a flashlight. To remove the blockage, shake it out or run a wadded cloth through the duct. If the duct is damaged, replace it.

PROBLEM STOPPER

Phone Won't Ring?
If your phone has a dial tone but doesn't ring, or if you find that messages were left on your answering machine while you were at home, check the phone's volume control, often a slider or wheel on the side of the phone's base. It may have been turned down or off by accident.

My refrigerator wobbles

ADJUST THE LEG HEIGHT There is an easy solution to this problem. The legs of most large appliances—refrigerators, as well as washing machines and dryers—can be adjusted to level the unit. Some legs are threaded so that you can screw them in or out. You simply screw a leg in to lower a corner and screw it out to raise it. Put a level on top of the fridge to figure out which corner is low or high and adjust accordingly. If your refrigerator has rollers instead of screw-legs, use a screwdriver to turn the adjusting screw just above the roller.

Here are some tips to keep in mind when leveling a fridge:

- If you have trouble screwing a leg in or out, tilt the fridge back slightly and prop it up with a block of wood.
- If the threads on a screw-leg are locked tight, slide a wedge under the low corner. Hardware stores carry plastic shims for this purpose. They're shorter than wooden shims and less likely to split under the heavy weight.

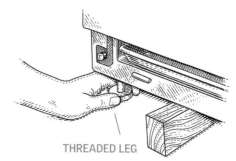

THREADED LEG

- If your refrigerator door doesn't close automatically from an open position, tilt the fridge backward ever so slightly. However, if your fridge has an ice maker, the unit should be perfectly level.

My refrigerator rattles

CHECK IF IT'S OFF-BALANCE OR TOUCHING SOMETHING Make sure the refrigerator is balanced and that it's not rubbing against anything, such as a cabinet or countertop appliance.

CLEAN THE COMPRESSOR COILS The problem could be a compressor that is overworked. Clean the dust from the compressor coils, which are usually located on the bottom of the refrigerator, behind the plastic or aluminum grille just below the door. The grille probably pops on or off. (On models that are *not* frost-free, the coils are usually on the back of fridge, and you have to roll the refrigerator out to access them.) First, unplug or turn off the refrigerator and remove the grille. Then use a vacuum cleaner with a brush or crevice attachment to clean the coils thoroughly.

TRICKS OF THE TRADE

Quick Fix for a Broken Dryer Switch

If the dryer doesn't start after you close the door, there's a good chance the button switch that activates the motor has worn down. Cut a thick piece of cardboard, just a couple square inches, from a cardboard box. Tape the cardboard to the inside of the door, where it will make contact with the button switch when the door is closed. The cardboard will fill the gap and activate the button until you can get the switch replaced.

Plumbing Problems

■ KITCHEN PLUMBING

The water pressure in my kitchen faucet is too low

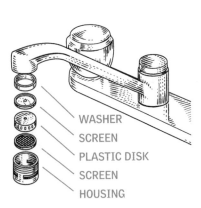

WASHER
SCREEN
PLASTIC DISK
SCREEN
HOUSING

CLEAN THE AERATOR SCREEN If your kitchen faucet has been underperforming lately, the likely source of the problem is its aerator—the round, screenlike device right where the water pours out that causes the water to bubble slightly. Unscrew the aerator by hand. If it's too tight, use groove-joint pliers. Put masking tape on the pliers' jaws to avoid scratching the chrome. Disassemble the aerator carefully, laying out the parts in proper sequence and orientation. Typically, there are two or three screens, a perforated nylon disk, and a washer. (Some newer aerators aren't meant to be taken apart, so you'll have to replace the entire aerator.) Use an old toothbrush to remove any sediment from the parts. Soak the screens in vinegar to remove minor corrosion. If a screen is too corroded, replace it or the entire aerator. Reverse the procedure to reinstall.

If you can't remove the faucet's aerator, there's still a way to clean it. Pour white vinegar into a sandwich bag and then use a rubber band or duct tape to secure the bag around the spout. Make sure the aerator is fully immersed in the vinegar and keep the bag there overnight. You can use this trick for a clogged showerhead as well.

My kitchen sprayer just dribbles

STRAIGHTEN OR REPLACE THE HOSE A sluggish sink sprayer is a sign that the hose feeding it is kinked. Check under the sink to make sure the hose is straight. If it is twisted or pinched, you may have to disconnect the hose to straighten it. The hose is connected to the

TRICKS OF THE TRADE

Finding a Reliable Contractor
Next time you need a plumber—or an electrician or a tile installer—don't ask a friend for a recommendation or look in the Yellow Pages. Instead, ask a wholesaler, the place where the pros shop. Ask a plumbing supply dealer (not the plumbing desk at a big box home center) for the names of two or three plumbers. Ask the electrical supplier for electricians. It's in the interest of the wholesaler to give you the names of skilled, reliable contractors, who spend money at their stores and are reliable and pay their bills.

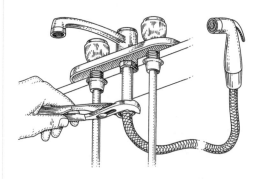

faucet by a simple hex (six-sided) nut that you can loosen with loose-joint or locking pliers. But because it is behind the sink, it's difficult to reach. You may find it easier to unscrew and remove the sprayer's head so that you can untangle it from the hose. If the hose is old and permanently kinked, replace it with a new nylon-reinforced vinyl hose of the same diameter. Take the old hose with you to the hardware store to buy a replacement.

There's water coming from under my dishwasher

PACKING NUT

TIGHTEN THE HOT-WATER VALVE If the flood seems to be originating under the sink, it may be due to a loose packing nut at the hot-water shutoff valve. Remove the screw holding the handle and take off any slip-on covering. Then tighten the packing nut with a wrench, if there are signs that it is leaking.

CHECK THE INLET VALVE CONNECTIONS A flood originating under the dishwasher may be due to a loose connection at the inlet line. To check, shut off the power to the dishwasher's circuit at your home's main electrical service panel and cut off the water at the hot-water shutoff valve under the sink. Then remove the dishwasher's lower front panel to access the valve. The valve is usually close to the front, and you can identify it by the pipe entering it and the hose leaving it.

- Check first for a loose nut on the inlet pipe, and if necessary, use a wrench to tighten it.
- Next, check for a loose or damaged hose. Secure a loose hose connection with a hose clamp or by twisting a wire around it. You can temporarily fix a cracked hose with duct or electrical tape, but don't wait long to replace it.
- If the leak seems to be coming from the pump underneath the middle of the machine, check the hose connection at that end.

Or call for service. The pump seals probably need to be replaced.

- While you're under the dishwasher, you should check two other possible sources of a leak: Make sure the nuts that hold the heating element in place are tight. And look for holes rusted though the tub; you can fix them with an epoxy patch kit sold by appliance repair stores.

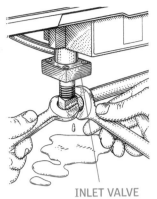

INLET VALVE

My sink has a chip in it

FIX IT USING AN EPOXY REPAIR KIT Chips in sinks, bathtubs, appliances, and even glazed tiles don't have to be permanent. The repair is quick, inexpensive, and easy. There are several types of repair materials available, ranging from simple paints to tough epoxies. Epoxies are best and are usually available in a variety of colors, so you should be able to find one that matches the damaged area.

1. Scrub the chipped area with soapy water. Then rough it up with a small piece of medium-grit sandpaper to remove rust or debris. Roughening also gives the damaged area some "tooth" for the repair material to cling to.
2. Mix together equal parts of hardener and color, using the plastic bubble package as a mixing tray. Then wait about ten minutes for the mixture to thicken.
3. Brush the epoxy onto the damaged area. Confine your repair to the damaged spot rather than trying to feather it out or blend the old with the new. If the chip is deep, don't try to fill it with one coat. Instead, wait eight hours and then apply a second coat. Repeat the procedure if necessary.

Wait 24 hours before getting the area wet and seven days before scrubbing it.

■ TOILET TROUBLES

My toilet doesn't flush

RECONNECT THE CHAIN GOING TO THE FLUSH VALVE If your toilet isn't flushing, it's probably a problem with the chain that connects the handle to the flapper that opens the flush valve at the bottom of the

TRICKS OF THE TRADE

An Impromptu Toilet Plunger

While vacationing in a rental cabin in Canada, Jake Jacob found himself with a clogged toilet but no plunger. All the toilet needed, he says, was a compressive shot in the arm. His nifty solution: He cut an empty 1.5-liter plastic soft drink bottle in half, jammed a broom handle into the spout, and secured it with duct tape. Then he used his one-shot plumber's helper as you would any plunger: He placed it in the toilet bowl, removed as much air from the bell end as possible, inserted the end in the drain, and plunged it in and out to loosen the clog. Jake's friends thought he was a hero.

TRICKS OF THE TRADE

Testing for a Leaky Toilet

Here is a quick test to see whether you have a leaky toilet:

1. Remove any color-producing in-tank bowl cleaner so that you can start with clear water in the toilet.

2. Color the tank water with enough food coloring or powdered drink mix to give it a rich color.

3. Wait half an hour. If some of the coloring has entered the toilet bowl, your toilet is leaking.

If your toilet is leaking, here is an easy way to determine the cause:

1. Inside the tank, make a pencil mark at the water-line.

2. Turn off the water to the toilet at the shutoff valve just under the tank.

3. Wait half an hour. If the water in the tank remains at the level of the pencil mark, the refill valve is the source of the leak. If the water drops below the mark, a worn flapper valve is the culprit.

toilet. Lift the cover off the toilet tank. Inside, you'll find a long trip lever that moves up and down when you operate the flush handle. Chances are, you'll find that the lift chain has fallen off the trip lever. Just reconnect the chain and flush away.

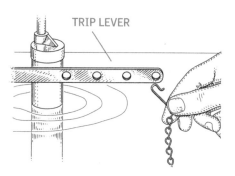

TRIP LEVER

My toilet keeps running, even when I jiggle the handle

"Running" is usually a sign of a problem with either the flapper or with the refill valve. (To isolate the problem, see "Testing for a Leaky Toilet," left.)

- To check these parts inside the tank, first turn off the water at the shutoff valve under the tank and then flush the toilet to empty the tank.
- To get the right replacement part for either the flapper or the refill valve, look under the toilet tank cover for the toilet's manufacturer and model number. Take this information along with the old part to a home center or plumbing supply store.

TROUBLESHOOTING THE FLAPPER The flapper is basically a hinged plastic or rubber plug in the bottom of the toilet tank. It is connected to the handle, so that when you flush a toilet, the flapper lifts, releasing water into the bowl. When the tank is empty, the flapper reseats itself, allowing the tank to refill. If the flapper fails to seat properly, water will flow constantly into the tank and down the drain.

Here's how to troubleshoot a flapper:

1. Check the valve seat that the flapper fits into for mineral deposits and sediment that may be keeping the flapper from seating properly. Clear that stuff out with a plastic scouring pad.
2. Try reviving an old flapper by rubbing it with petroleum jelly or spraying it with silicone spray, which will make it more supple and better able to seal.
3. For a more lasting fix, replace the flapper: Move the bowl refill tube out of the way, slip the old flapper off the overflow tube, and slip on the new one.

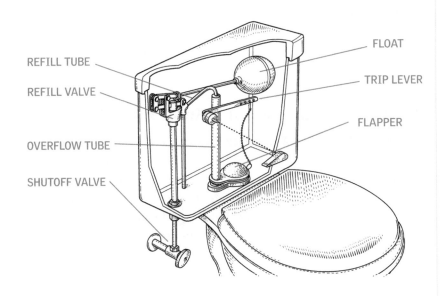

REFILL TUBE

REFILL VALVE

OVERFLOW TUBE

SHUTOFF VALVE

FLOAT

TRIP LEVER

FLAPPER

An older toilet may have a tank ball instead of a flapper. It's usu-ally best to replace the tank ball, its lift wire, and the clamp that holds the lift wire with a flapper and a lift chain.

REPLACE THE REFILL VALVE The refill valve—also known as the ball cock—is the tank's faucet, filling the tank up and stopping it at the optimal point, about half an inch below the top of the overflow tube. A large float ball on an arm usually controls the valve. When the valve begins to wear out, causing the water to flow continuously, the only solution is to replace it. You may prefer to have a plumber or a handy friend replace the refill valve, but the task is not terribly complicated:

1. Unscrew any float arm and ball that's attached to the valve and lift the refill tube (also called a filler tube) out of the larger overflow tube.
2. Under the tank, unscrew the coupling nut that attaches the water supply line to the valve.
3. Also under the tank, unscrew the locknut that holds the refill valve to the bottom of the tank. Use a second pair of pliers inside the tank to keep the refill valve from turning as you unscrew the locknut.
4. Lift out the valve and reverse the steps to replace it.

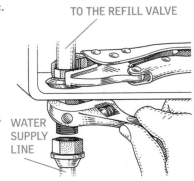

TO THE REFILL VALVE

WATER SUPPLY LINE

Besides the traditional valve that uses a float ball on an arm, you can get a floating cup refill valve, which has a float cup on the valve. Or you can get a floatless model, which has a screw that you turn to control the water level in the tank.

I smell sewage when I flush my toilet

CHECK THE TOILET BOWL'S WATER LEVEL No matter how clean your toilet is, it will still reek if sewage gas seeps out. Escaping gas could be caused by several things. First, check the level of the water in the bowl. If it is low, that may be allowing the gas to escape. It could be that your pet is drinking from the bowl, a problem easily solved by keeping the lid closed. Evaporation of water from a rarely used toilet (in the basement, for instance) could be the problem. If so, flush it periodically to keep it full.

CLEAN THE RIM HOLES Bacteria can develop under the rim of the toilet bowl, giving off a funky odor every time you flush. This is more apt to happen under hot, humid conditions. Kill any bacteria by pouring several cups of household bleach into the toilet tank's overflow tube (the one sticking up about half an inch above the water). This will flow through the rim holes and into the toilet bowl, killing any bacteria hiding there. Flush the toilet to get rid of the bleach.

CHECK YOUR PLUMBING'S ROOF VENT Leaves or a bird's nest might be clogging the roof vent on your plumbing system's main vent pipe, known as the soil stack, and this may be blocking the path of escaping sewage gases. Other symptoms of a blocked vent are sluggish drains and sink or tub drains that gurgle when you flush the toilet.

My toilet tank sweats, making puddles on the floor

VENTILATE THE ROOM When humid air hits a cold porcelain toilet tank, condensation forms. This is a common problem in humid weather, after showers, and for homes that use well water (since well water stays cool, even during hot months). First, see if just keeping your bathroom well ventilated will solve the problem. After showering, leave a window open or the exhaust fan running for a half hour or so. Also make sure you don't have a toilet leak, which brings a constant flow of cold water into the tank, chilling it and causing it to sweat. (See "Testing for a Leaky Toilet," on page 114.)

TRICKS OF THE TRADE

A Better Plunger
Your plunger can become a more effective tool with the aid of a little petroleum jelly. Just smear some jelly around the edge of the suction cup. This will create a better seal between the suction cup and the drain. If the handle on your plunger is loose and easy to pull out of the cup, use a hose clamp to secure the cup to the handle.

INSULATE THE TANK If the problem is chronic, the solution is to line the inside of the tank with ½-inch polystyrene or foam rubber insulation, available in kits at home centers and plumbing supply stores.

1. Empty the tank and dry it thoroughly.
2. Cut the liners to fit your tank's walls and floor.
3. Glue the liners in place with silicone cement and let the adhesive dry for at least 24 hours before refilling the tank.

■ NOISY PLUMBING

My pipes are banging

Usually, the problem is something called water hammer, a pressure shock wave sent through a plumbing system by a sudden change in the flow of water when you shut it off. Apart from being annoying, water hammer can exert tremendous pressure that can damage pipes and valves and weaken joints.

REESTABLISH YOUR SYSTEM'S AIR CUSHION Many plumbing systems cushion the shock waves by having pipe risers filled with air rather than water (or specially designed pressure arresters to do the same thing). When these pipes fill with water—due to very cold water, high chlorine content, or recent plumbing work—they lose their effectiveness. To make them effective again and solve the banging problem, you need to reestablish the system's air cushion.

WORLD-CLASS GOOF

The Flush That Stopped the Rush

A few years ago, a clogged commode shut down the busy McPherson Square Metro station in Washington, D.C., early one morning. The toilet in a nearby building flooded a pair of power company feeder boxes that service the station, knocking out elevators, escalators, fare machines, turnstiles, and even the electric rail itself. Metro authorities restored train service at 5:50 A.M., after an hour and a half. But all other power remained off until nearly lunchtime, forcing passengers to board and exit trains by dim, generator-powered lights. The bright side? Everyone rode free.

To do this, you have to drain your home's plumbing system, which is easier than you might think:

1. Turn off your home's main water supply.
2. Shut off the water to the dishwasher, the washing machine, and each toilet in the house. Each of these should have its own shutoff valve.
3. Find your home's lowest sink or spigot (usually the one nearest the water main) and open the cold-water tap.
4. Open the cold tap of the highest sink (or the one farthest from the water main).
5. When all the water has drained out of the system, close the two water taps. Open the main water valve. Turn on the water to the dishwasher, washing machine, and toilets. Flush the toilets and turn on all hot- and cold-water faucets—tubs and showers included.

You'll likely hear banging pipes and sputtering faucets. That's normal. Leave each faucet open until the sputtering stops and the water flows uniformly. Now that you have reestablished your system's air cushion, the ghostly pipe banging should vanish.

My steam radiator makes a knocking sound

TURN THE VALVE ON FULLY The cause of a knocking sound is usually water that condenses from the steam and collects in the bottom of the radiator. The water normally flows back out through the inlet valve; if it can't, it causes a knocking sound. First, make sure that the inlet valve is turned all the way on so that the water can flow out. A steam radiator's valve should be either completely on or completely off; if you've set it in between, it blocks the flow of returning water.

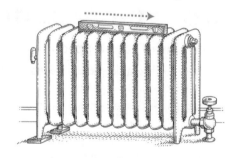

TILT THE RADIATOR If that doesn't end the racket, try tilting the radiator toward the inlet valve to encourage the water to flow out. To do that, turn off the heat, let the radiator cool, and disconnect the inlet pipe from the radiator. Then place shims—thin wooden wedges—under the far legs and reconnect the inlet pipe. Open the inlet valve fully.

Emergencies and Home Safety

■ PLUMBING DISASTERS

My tub is overflowing

SOP UP THE WATER WITH TOWELS Finally, a
use for those old towels in the back of the
linen closet. But first, turn off the running
water and open the drain. Now toss the
old towels on any floor puddles. When
the towels are saturated, wring them out
over the sink, the toilet, or a bucket and toss
them back down. If the pools are big, contain the water
by soaking it up from the outside to the center. Finish by mopping
and then air out the room. Use a fan or a dehumidifier to dry the
room faster. If you work fast, a little spilled water won't hurt much.

*Tub flooding over?
The quick solution
is right in your
linen closet.*

My toilet bowl is about to overflow

TURN OFF THE TOILET'S SHUTOFF VALVE If your toilet looks like it's
about to flow over the rim, keep calm. Most toilet bowls are designed
to hold all the water in the tank without overflowing. If you do flush
again before the water level has had a chance to settle back to its
normal level, however, you can cause an overflow. If this happens,
you need to stop the water immediately. Turn off the shutoff valve
under the tank (see illustration on page 115). If there is no shutoff
under the tank, stop the water by removing the tank lid and lifting up
on the float ball or pushing down the flapper at the bottom of the
tank. Then send someone to the basement to find the main shutoff
for the house. Don't try flushing again until the water level has
dropped back to normal, which even clogged toilets will do.

PLUNGE AWAY THE CLOG If the toilet remains clogged, try using a
plunger to remove the clog. Place the plumber's helper in the toilet
bowl, remove as much air from the bell end as possible, insert the
end in the drain, and plunge in and out. The pressure should loosen

the clog. If that does not work, call a plumber. There might be a foreign object—a hairbrush or a toy—lodged in the toilet trap. If you can see an object blocking the drain, slip a plastic bag over your hand and pull the offending item out.

My pipes are frozen

USE A MOIST RAG TO FIND THE BLOCKAGE The first order of business is locating the frozen spot in your plumbing, which is all too easy if the pipe has already burst or is bulging to the point of bursting. But if you're lucky, the frozen section of pipe is simply plugging the water so it can't run. To find the frozen plug, check the piping in the unheated areas of your house or in exterior walls. On exposed pipes, you can pinpoint the frozen area by swabbing along the pipe with a moist rag. Frost will form as you hit the frozen spot.

THAW IT WITH A HAIR DRYER When it comes to thawing out pipes, the slower the better. Use a hair dryer set on high to elevate the temperature. Never use propane torches—the heat they produce can turn water into steam, which could build up and burst the pipes.

Start thawing the ice in your frozen pipe from the side closer to a faucet, so the melting ice will have somewhere to drain. (You *have* opened the faucet, right?) Gradually work with the hair dryer from the faucet side back toward the frozen area.

Sewage backed up, and my floor is a mess

Sewage is really dirty stuff, so don't touch it. And don't worsen the situation by flushing the toilet or running water in the sink or tub. Find alternatives, such as using your neighbor's facilities, until the backup is fixed. If you live in a city or town and your house is part of a municipal sewage system, call the right city department. The office will send someone to diagnose and fix the problem—if it was the city's fault.

SNAKE OUT THE CLOG AND CLEAN UP If the fault lies in your home's plumbing lines, call a plumber—or unclog the waste line using a plumber's snake. If you do the cleanup, don a good pair of rubber gloves and some old work clothes. Use a wet vac or a mop to remove the mess. Mop floors and wipe walls with a heavy-duty disinfectant-style cleaner. Clean plumbing fixtures. Carpets and rugs may need professional cleaning.

■ FURNACE AND CHIMNEYS

My furnace just belched soot everywhere

STOP OR CONTAIN THE SOOT Soot is even more troublesome than it looks. Oily and acidic, it is made up of extremely fine particles that can corrode metal and be permanently ground into fabrics and finishes. But don't panic and make the situation worse. Before you reach for a dust cloth, turn the furnace off or cut the power feeding it. If it's so cold that you have to keep it running, install an additional, temporary filter system to contain any more soot. Here's how: Remove register and return covers throughout the house, fold two layers of cheesecloth over the duct openings (spray these lightly with a penetrating lubricant such as WD-40 to help them hold the soot particles), and loosely screw the covers back on.

TURN OFF ELECTRONIC GEAR Next, turn off all electronics, such as computers and stereos. If soot gets inside a component (or is sucked into a computer by a motor fan), it can damage the circuitry.

NOW CLEAN UP You'll be itching to vacuum, but resist the itch unless your machine has a HEPA filter with a minimum of 2 micron entrapment. If you have such a vacuum, use the brush attachment to avoid grinding soot into things. Likewise, don't touch anything covered with soot. The body's natural oils will set soot stains on surfaces. Wipe doorknobs, hinges, and other exposed metal with an alkaline degreaser, such as Simple Green.

CALL IN A PRO TO FINISH That's about all you, the homeowner, should do in the wake of a furnace accident. If the problem is severe, hire a professional cleaning company. Make sure the company is familiar with furnace soot cleanup.

Smoke is pouring out of my fireplace

MAKE SURE IT'S NOT A CHIMNEY FIRE First and foremost, make certain that you don't have a chimney fire. If the built-up creosote in your chimney is on fire, sparks will probably accompany the smoke, and you might hear a loud roaring sound coming from the chimney. If it is a chimney fire, call the fire department. (See "My chimney is on fire," on page 123.)

PROBLEM STOPPER

What to Do If You Smell Gas

If you smell gas, leave the vicinity immediately, taking everyone and all family pets with you. Go to a neighbor's house and call your gas provider. Typically, they will send someone right away, free of charge, to locate the source of the smell. To avoid igniting the gas, remember these major don'ts if you smell gas:

• Don't light a match or lighter.

• Don't use computers, appliances, or garage door openers.

• Don't turn any lights on or off.

• Don't operate combustion engines.

CHECK THE DAMPERS AND INCREASE THE AIRFLOW If you're convinced you do not have a chimney fire, then most likely the chimney is not drawing well, say experts. First, make sure all dampers are open. If so, your house might be too "tight," meaning there is not enough airflow to keep the smoke headed up the chimney. To improve the draft, open a door or window on the windy side of the house. If the smoke has pooled in the house, open more windows and doors on the windy side. Use fans to circulate air.

CLEAN FABRIC AND METAL SURFACES Get rid of the lingering smoke smell by washing drapes and cleaning upholstery. Generally, cleaning upholstery is like cleaning carpet: You never want to overwet the fabric and the cushion beneath it. Instead, apply a commercial foam-

Home, Safe Home

What constitutes a safe house these days? Glenn Haege, host of *The Handyman Show*, a widely syndicated radio call-in program, has compiled a list of devices for warning and protection against fire, flooding, and more. Here's what he recommends:

- **Fire extinguishers** Have at least three: one in the kitchen, one in the basement, and one in the master bedroom.
- **Carbon monoxide detectors** Have at least one on each floor, including one in the basement and one in the bedroom hallway.
- **Smoke detectors** Have at least one per floor. Install them in every bedroom, in the main hallway, and by the furnace.
- **Antiscald devices** Install them on sinks, tubs, and showers, especially those used by very young or very old people. Some faucets come with them. Or you can retrofit your faucets using antiscald products available at plumbing supply stores. You need to hire a plumber to install them.
- **Excess flow valve for your gas line** These inexpensive valves fit on the gas line into your house. In the event of a leak, these valves shut off the gas flow and reduce the chances of a major catastrophe. Ask your gas supplier about them.
- **Automatic water shutoff valve** Like the gas valve, these valves are designed to automatically shut off the main water flow if a leak develops or a pipe bursts.
- **Lighting motion detectors** Install on exterior floodlights. They are available from electrical supply stores and home centers.
- **Sump pump** A water-powered backup sump pump (if you're on city water) or a battery-powered backup sump pump (if you use a well) are great in storms, when your basement is flooding and your power is out.
- **Whole-house surge protectors** These are available for electric, cable, and phone lines. Have them installed by an electrician.

type upholstery cleaner. Let it stand and then vacuum it off, following the label instructions. Before cleaning upholstery, always check the tag for cleaning instructions (usually found on new upholstery fabric sold after 1970). Since smoke is drawn to cool surfaces, such as metal, wipe down all exposed doorknobs, hinges, drawer pulls, and other metal surfaces with a degreaser, such as Simple Green. This also prevents the acidic soot from etching the metal.

My chimney is on fire

CALL FOR HELP AND EVACUATE If a buildup of combustible material in your chimney catches fire, you'll probably see smoke and sparks shooting out of the chimney, and you might hear a loud roaring sound. Chimney fires burn fast and furiously, melting flue liners, damaging chimneys, and even igniting roof shingles. If you have a chimney fire, call the fire department and get everyone out of the house. Have everyone meet at the mailbox or front gate, so that all can be accounted for. Here are some other steps you might be able to take:

- If possible, put a chimney fire extinguisher in the fireplace or wood stove. (A chimney fire extinguisher looks like a large road flare. When you strike it and toss it in the firebox, it emits a lot of smoke to put out the fire. It's sold by stove shops and chimney cleaning professionals.)
- Close any doors or dampers feeding air to the fire to cut the airflow as much as possible. Don't bother dousing water on the fire. It won't do any good and may crack your hearth or wood stove.
- Go outside and hose down the roof around the chimney to prevent sparks from starting new fires.
- After the fire is out, call a chimney sweep to come and inspect the chimney. And call your insurance company. Most home insurance policies cover chimney fire damage.

■ POWER OUTAGES

The power just went out, and I can't see

FIND A LIGHT SOURCE Don't panic. Find a flashlight, preferably the one with fresh batteries you keep around for just such an occasion. If you must use a candle or hurricane light, never leave it unattended. Take it with you as you move from room to room. Make sure a candle is well seated in a candlestick or other solid holder.

PROBLEM STOPPER

Preventing Chimney Fires

Creosote, a tarlike substance that collects on the chimney flue when you burn wood, is what causes chimney fires. The more your fire smokes, the more creosote is deposited. The higher the moisture content and sap level in the wood you burn, the more your fire smokes. To prevent chimney fires:

• Burn only well-seasoned hardwoods. Never burn freshly cut wood or softwoods, such as pine or fir.

• Build small hot fires that burn out completely rather than big smoldering fires.

• Clean chimneys don't catch on fire. At least once a year, have your chimney cleaned and inspected by a reputable chimney sweep.

TURN OFF YOUR APPLIANCES Once you have an alternate light source, turn off all nonessential appliances that were on—TVs, computers, stereos, and air conditioners. When the power comes back on, it could damage them. Leave the furnace and fridge on. Keep the refrigerator and freezer closed.

DETERMINE THE EXTENT OF THE OUTAGE Take a look across the street and next door to see whether your neighbors' homes are also out. If the power is off in just your house, call the power company.

CHECK YOUR WATER SUPPLY If you use city water, then you might still have flow. If you have a well, the pump won't work when the power is out. But there may be pressure in the system, so conserve water to conserve the pressure. You might just have enough pressure to keep the toilet flushing for a day or two.

MAKE USE OF YOUR CAR If you don't have a battery-operated radio, you can always get the latest news on the extent and expected duration of a blackout from your car's radio. You can also use your car to plug in a cell phone that has an exhausted battery. But don't overdo using the car, especially if you are low on gas. And, of course, don't run the car in a closed garage.

Be Prepared for a Blackout

- Fill extra space in your freezer with plastic jugs of water (leaving enough room for the ice to expand). If the power goes out, this ice will extend the life of the food in the freezer. Put one or more jugs of ice in the fridge for the same effect.
- Know where the manual door release is on your garage door.
- Have an old-fashioned cord-connected telephone in the house, even if you store it in a drawer or closet. Cordless phones and answering-machine phones won't work when the power goes out. For your cell phone, get a cable that lets you use and charge the phone in your car.
- During periods of increased likelihood of a power outage, always try to keep your car's fuel tank as full as possible. When power goes out, service stations can't pump gas.
- Consider getting a generator and having a supply of fuel for it on hand. But never operate one inside your house or in a basement. The fumes can be dangerous. Put it on a porch or in a carport.
- Keep a blackout kit handy. Make sure everyone knows where it is. Include
  - a flashlight with extra batteries
  - a portable radio with extra batteries
  - potable water (at least 1 gallon [3.7 liters])
  - a small supply of food that doesn't need preparation

Pests

■ FLYING INSECTS

I can't keep flying insects out of my house

CHANGE YOUR OUTDOOR LIGHTING You use window screens, weather-strip doors, and seal cracks, but moths, mosquitoes, and gnats still get in and flit around your ceilings. The cause could be your outdoor lighting. Porch and door lights that are on for hours at night attract lots of insects. Open the door, and you sweep them into the house.

Here are some ways to fix this problem:

- Turn on outdoor lights only when they are needed. Even better, install motion sensors, which turn lights on automatically when needed and switch them off after a few minutes—before the bugs have had a chance to congregate. Outdoor light fixtures with built-in motion sensors are available at home centers and electrical supply stores.
- Use yellow bulbs, which are not as appealing to insects as white bulbs.
- Consider modifying the outdoor lighting by your doors. Replace lights above doors with floodlights a few feet away, aiming them at the places you want to illuminate, such as stairs and walkways. Another benefit of more strategic lighting: fewer spiderwebs, since you will be attracting fewer insects.

Moths have munched my sweaters

FREEZE YOUR SWEATERS Clothes moths—or more precisely, the larvae of clothes moths—eat wool sweaters. Usually we figure this out when we pull a sweater out of the closet during winter's first cold blast. Even if we see no moths, how do we know the minuscule larvae are gone? Here's a clever way to kill these unseen sweater-destroyers: Freeze them. If it's below freezing outside, leave your sweaters on a porch or in an unheated garage. The cold will kill the larvae. Put the sweaters in plastic bags to keep them clean.

If it's not cold enough outdoors, put the sweaters in your extra freezer (or your refrigerator's freezer compartment if there is room). Leave them overnight and let them thaw before wearing. It's also a good idea to vacuum and wipe down your closets and drawers to make sure you get the stragglers.

Clothes-moth caterpillars, which chew holes in clothes, hatch from eggs laid by clothes moths. Because the larvae are fragile, they don't usually survive in clothing that is worn regularly. Instead, they prefer stored clothes. Since they also seek out stains, such as perspiration, urine, fruit juice, and other foods, be sure you wash or dry-clean your wool, silk, and other clothes before you store them.

Fruit flies are driving me bananas

MAKE A FUNNEL TRAP During warm months, these harmless but pesky critters enter your home as invisible eggs riding piggyback on fresh fruit. Before you know it, a bunch of grown-up fruit flies are taking over your fruit bowl. You can solve the problem by putting the fruit you buy in the refrigerator and keeping a lid on your kitchen garbage. If you don't like the idea of chilling fruits that ripen better at room temperature— bananas and peaches, for instance—create a fruit-fly trap. Here's how: Put some banana peel or

WORLD-CLASS FIX

A Plague of No-See-Ums

The problem usually begins like this: An office worker starts to itch. He swats at what he thinks are tiny bugs pricking his arms and neck with bites. Soon his office mates are itching and swatting, too. The office manager calls in a pest control company. But after monitoring for insects, the exterminators report that there are none.

The real culprit? Static electricity. It frequently happens in large offices with a lot of people working on computers, which hold a tremendous static charge. The static electricity causes a prickling sensation. And the dry winter air that produces excess static electricity also causes itching. Experts suggest misting the air in the area with plain water to solve the problem. The water raises the humidity level and reduces the static charge. But take care not to spray water directly on computers and other sensitive electronic gear.

melon rind in the bottom of a quart (liter) jar. Make a paper funnel (standard copier paper works fine): The small opening should be about ½ inch (12 millimeters) across, and the large opening should fit snugly into the top of the jar. Insert the small end of the cone in the jar and tape the wide opening to the jar's rim. Taking the bait, fruit flies will fly into the jar and lay their eggs, but they will have trouble finding their way back out again. Every couple of days, fill the jar with hot tap water and cap it to kill the larvae and flies. Discard them and start over with fresh bait and a new paper funnel.

USE FLY CATCHER RIBBONS Adhesive fly catcher ribbons—the kind you uncurl and hang from a hook—are also effective in capturing fruit flies. You can buy them or make your own with a length of sticky tape weighted at the bottom with a coin or a binder clip.

■ ANTS

I've got ants all over my kitchen counters

SEAL CRACKS AND ELIMINATE THEIR FOOD To get rid of ants, follow these steps:

1. Wipe up any ants you see with soapy water. This erases the odor trails they leave for other ants to follow.
2. Look for their entry point—often a crack around a window or plumbing pipe—and seal it with caulk.
3. Eliminate all food sources, including crumbs, spilled sugar and fruit juice, pet food, and garbage. Sweep and vacuum often, especially around pet dishes and under children's places at the table. Set pet dishes in slightly larger pans of water with a drop or two of dish detergent, creating a moat. The detergent breaks the surface tension so the ants can't float across.

Ants are nesting in my houseplants

WRAP STICKY TAPE AROUND THE PLANTER Ants like dirt. And they love the honeydew that drips from aphid-infested plants. The instant solution is to wrap two-sided tape around the plant containers. The ants won't cross the sticky barrier.

SET THE PLANTER IN WATER If the planter is small enough, you can place it in a tray or plate filled with water. This will create a barrier.

Ants: Over 1 Billion Sold

Some people are desperate to get rid of ants. Others pay to have them shipped to their homes. Since Milton Levine created the Ant Farm, a see-through ant habitat, in 1956, his company, Uncle Milton Industries, has sold more than 20 million and shipped *1 billion* ants through the mail.

The ants—called red harvesters—are gathered in the deserts of the western United States. About the only problem related to mailing live ants is the weather. "The big culprit is the outdoor mailbox," a company spokesman explains. "We won't ship them to Fargo, North Dakota, in the middle of the winter, or you'd end up with antsicles."

The ants come with simple instructions, including a useful tip for transferring them from vial to farm: Put the ants in the fridge first for 15 minutes. The cold makes them groggy and less apt to escape.

Early on, Levine appeared on many radio and television talk shows. Once, according to the company spokesman, he literally got ants in his pants when—on national TV—the vial he was carrying in his pocket broke and dozens of red harvesters escaped. In the hot studio lights, the ants were anything but groggy. They scurried over his legs, biting furiously, while Levine tried to maintain his composure.

Levine has received countless letters from customers. One favorite reads: "Dear Uncle Milton, Please send me more ants. My little brother peed on them."

■ FLEAS

I think my house is infested with fleas

TRY THE WHITE SOCKS TEST Not sure whether your home has fleas? Stroll through the rooms wearing white kneesocks. If you have fleas, you'll notice the little varmints leaping onto the socks. Or create a trap by putting a gooseneck lamp on the floor 6 inches above a shallow pan of water containing a squirt of dishwashing liquid. The fleas will jump for the light and drown in the water.

VACUUM THOROUGHLY To control fleas, you've got to hit them on all fronts, say the experts. Most likely, your pet has introduced them to your home. If so, treat the pet (see "My dog is scratching, and I think he has fleas" below). And then treat your home, since the flea spends most of its life cycle off the host pet and in carpeting or upholstery in some preadult stage—egg, larva, or pupa. For a couple of weeks, vacuum rugs and upholstery regularly, making sure to get under furniture and beneath chair and couch cushions. Even if the vacuum bag is not full, remove it immediately, seal it in a plastic bag, and throw it away. It may seem wasteful, but you don't want to risk fleas hatching in your vacuum and spreading. Wash throw rugs. Try to find easy-to-clean sleeping quarters for your pet—a carpetless mudroom, for instance—and clean that area more often than the rest of the house.

My dog is scratching, and I'm afraid he has fleas

USE A FLEA-KILLING SHAMPOO To make sure it's fleas, roll your dog over and inspect its bare stomach. Or gently blow back its fur and look at the skin. If you spot fleas, wash your dog in a pyrethrin flea shampoo, which will kill adult fleas and their eggs and is not as toxic as other chemical-based shampoos. (For a cat, ask your vet for a recommendation; pyrethrin-based products can be toxic to cats.)

CLEAN YOUR PET'S BED Wash your pet's bedding to kill flea eggs. Do it often, until all signs of fleas are gone. To make life easier, cover your pet's bedding with a blanket. That way, you won't have to wash the cushion every time, only the blanket. Remove the blanket carefully, lifting it by all four corners so the flea eggs won't roll off.

APPLY A FLEA REPELLENT For a quick and easy (though relatively expensive) long-term flea deterrent, try one of the topical liquids, such as Frontline or Advantage, once available only from vets but now sold at pet stores. Typically, they work this way: You squeeze a prescribed amount of the oily liquid on the animal's back; this guards the entire animal against fleas for a month or more. Insect-growth regulators are another long-term solution—Precor, for example, whose active ingredient is methoprene. Such growth regulators don't kill adult fleas, but they prevent them from reproducing. And they do not harm the pet.

■ CREEPY BUGS

I've got roaches

DUST BORIC ACID INTO YOUR HOME'S OUTLETS As many people know, boric acid is a relatively safe way to kill roaches. And it is widely available at supermarkets and other stores. But if you're not painstaking in applying it, the roaches will find a wall space you can't get to. Here's a way to treat your whole house once and for all. Remove the plates from your electric outlets and dust inside the walls around the outlets with boric acid. Use a squeeze bottle and

TRICKS OF THE TRADE

How to Use Boric Acid
More is not best when it comes to getting rid of roaches with boric acid. Many of us put down a heavy layer of the powder, thinking that the more we use, the better. But the best way to apply boric acid is to lightly dust it on. Boric acid works in two ways: First, it is abrasive, so that when a roach cleans itself, it rubs holes in its exoskeleton, which causes it to slowly dry up. Second, the roach ingests the boric acid and is poisoned. If you apply boric acid sparingly, like salt, roaches walk through it and pick it up on their legs, but if they encounter a lot of it, they avoid it. It takes boric acid about a week to kill a roach.

PROBLEM STOPPER

Make Roaches Die of Thirst

Like all organisms, cockroaches need water to survive. Here are ways for controlling common moisture sources:

• Repair leaky faucets.

• Insulate pipes that collect condensation.

• Ventilate bathrooms by using an exhaust fan or cracking a window after showering.

• Dehumidify moist basements by using a dehumidifier or by having good cross ventilation.

• Empty refrigerator and dehumidifier drainage pans regularly.

• Cap abandoned drain lines; cover active drains, like ones in basements, with tight wire mesh.

• Clean dirty dishes immediately. If you must let them stand in the sink, fill the sink with water and mix in dishwashing detergent.

puff the boric acid in. (Boric acid often comes in squeeze bottles, but an old mustard or ketchup one will do.) Do this to every outlet in every room, and you will have covered the perimeter of each room, blocking the roaches' ability to travel. Since boric acid stays active as long as it remains dry, this solution should work for years.

It's still a good idea to put boric acid into as many other roach hangouts in a room as possible, especially in an old house that has few electric outlets per room and walls that are not tightly sealed. Puff a little boric acid along baseboards; in corners of cabinets and closets; under and behind the fridge, stove, sink, dishwasher, washer and dryer; and in openings around drain pipes. If you are building a new house, dust inside the walls as they are going up to nip the problem in the bud.

Silverfish have invaded my basement

MAKE A TRAP WITH A JAR Silverfish are small, scaly-looking insects that love warm, moist environments—basements, kitchens, and bathrooms. Here's a way to trap them: Wrap the entire exterior of a small, clean glass jar with masking tape. Set it upright in an infested area, such as in a damp basement corner or around bathroom and kitchen plumbing. The silverfish can climb the taped sides, but once they fall into the jar, they cannot climb the smooth glass surface inside. Drown the silverfish in hot water and dispose of them. Reset the trap.

Eek! A spider

TRAP AND RELEASE IT OR KILL IT If you want to get rid of a spider in your house, you can either transport it outdoors or kill it. To remove it, cover it quickly with a jar and then slide a stiff piece of paper under the jar to cover the opening. Pressing the paper firmly against the opening so the spider can't escape, carry the jar outside and let the spider go. Or, if you decide to kill it, swat it with a flyswatter or a rolled-up newspaper.

Although their webs may seem to reflect on your housekeeping, spiders are mostly beneficial, because they trap other bugs, including pesky ones like mosquitoes. Many spiders do have venom glands, but they rarely bite humans. The spiders you need to worry about—most commonly the black widow and brown recluse—don't typically show up in living areas, although you do have to be on the lookout in crawl spaces and sheds.

■ MICE

I have mice in my home

SEAL ENTRY POINTS AND MAKE INVITING TRAPS Act the minute you see signs of a mice infestation. A female mouse gives birth to an average of six mice—and can do it every three weeks. All those babies will be ready to mate in about two months. Under ideal conditions, a single female can produce 2,500 heirs in six months!

At the first sign that you have mice, follow these tips for eliminating them:

- Seal cracks and crevices. Use steel wool, which the mice can't chew through. Fill gaps between the outside of the house and the inside, and between unfinished areas, such as basements and crawl spaces, and finished living quarters.
- Set traps around a room's perimeter. Place the trap perpendicular to the wall, with the baited side facing and touching the wall. Mice travel along walls, whiskers touching the walls, for security. Set enough traps in the right spots, exterminators say, and you won't even have to bait them.
- Wear gloves when setting traps. Otherwise, mice may smell your human scent and steer clear. Rubber gloves work well.

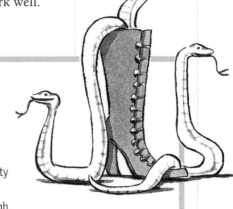

WORLD-CLASS GOOF

Soft on Snakes

A woman in Pennsylvania called the JC Ehrlich pest control company because she had a snake in the house. When the exterminators arrived, they learned that the homeowner had let snakes live in her basement, since they were a nonpoisonous species that kept the rodent population in check. But during a party one Saturday night, a snake slithered across the living room floor, frightening the guests, and the woman decided she had had enough.

"It was an old house with a stone foundation," recalled Dave Fisher, one of the exterminators. "There were snakes in the basement rafters and around the sill plate. Black rat snakes."

The company's snake expert sealed himself in the crawl space and spread wet burlap sacks on the ground. As the moisture-seeking serpents crawled under the burlap, he grabbed them, put them in a sack, and handed them to Fisher. He did this for two hours at a time on and off for three weeks. By the end they had removed, and later disposed of, 33 snakes.

"The homeowner thought she had one or two snakes living in the basement," Fisher says. "She wasn't very comfortable with the idea of 33 snakes down there."

- Bait with peanut butter. It's fragrant and hard to snatch without triggering the trap. Smear the peanut butter on the top and bottom of the bait pedal.
- Bait with a cotton ball. Cotton makes a great nest liner, so this will appeal to a mouse's nesting instincts. It's also great for long-term traps—those you might set in the garage or basement to catch new intruders—because cotton doesn't get stale and moldy.

I'm not sure if I have mice

MAKE SOME TESTS If you suspect you have mice, test for their presence before you go spreading poison and setting traps. Mice are basically shy. They prefer places, such as basements, where humans are rarely present. They are active at night and rarely travel into the center of rooms, sticking to the walls instead. To test for them, sprinkle some unscented talcum powder on the floor next to the walls. Check the talcum powder in a day or two for footprints. Be sure to use unscented powder because any scent could put them off. And use only a sprinkling of powder because they might avoid a heavy layer of it. Also be on the lookout for tiny black pellets, which also indicate the presence of mice.

The mouse in my trap is still kicking

SCOOP UP THE TRAP AND DROWN IT IN A BUCKET It's hard enough for some people to dispose of the dead mice they trap. But when one is still alive, they panic and don't want to go near the injured captive. But the most humane thing to do is to kill the animal as soon as possible. Here's a solution: Scoop up the mouse, trap and all, with a shovel and drop it into a bucket of soapy water. In no time, the creature will be out of its misery. Drain the bucket, holding the shovel over the top. Then collect the dead mouse in a plastic bag and dispose of it in the trash.

I can't stand the sight of a dead mouse

PUT THE TRAP IN A PAPER BAG You are not alone. Lots of people blanch at the sight of dead rodents. Here's a solution that lets you trap mice without the unsightly aftermath: Set the snap trap in an open paper bag. Once the trap is sprung, throw the bag and its contents into the garbage.

■ LARGER INTRUDERS

A bird got into the house

CLOSE INSIDE DOORS AND OPEN WINDOWS
A bird that mistakenly gets into a house
through a window, door, or chimney usually
panics and can't find its way out. To help a
bird along, close all interior doors into the
room so the bird won't be able to escape into
another part of the house. Open the windows in the room
and take out the screens. Turn off the inside lights and, if it is dark
out, turn on a light outside (your porch light or a security light, for
instance). Your winged guest will be able to see an exit more easily.
Luckily, this rarely happens in the winter, when opening the windows means also opening or taking down storm windows.

*To quickly get rid
of an unwanted
winged visitor,
open the window
and turn off the
lights.*

Help! A bat flew into my living room

CLOSE INSIDE DOORS AND OPEN WINDOWS Occasionally, a lone bat
will fly into your home through an open window or door. Don't
panic: Bats are typically not aggressive, although they can bite if
handled. Caution: Never handle a bat with bare hands. If you are
bitten, call your local health department immediately. Bats can carry
diseases, such as rabies.

If the bat is active, do just as you would for a bird: Close all interior doors into the room, so the bat cannot escape into another part
of the house. Open the windows and remove the screens. The bat
should fly out.

CAPTURE IT IN A BOX If the bat has landed or is inactive, cover it
with a shoe box or some other small box. Carefully slide a piece of
cardboard (at least as large as the box opening) between the box and
the surface the bat is on, nudging the bat into the box. Holding the
cardboard firmly against the box, carry the bat outside and release it.
Remember: Wear sturdy gloves when dealing with a bat.

Five Knots for Solving Your Knotty Problems

There are many useful ways to knot a rope, but only the most dedicated sailors—and the occasional Boy Scout—know how to tie anything other than a basic square knot. Here are five bare-minimum best-knots-to-know. Learn them, and you're prepared any time you need to tie-down, haul, hoist, or keep your shoe from coming untied.

■ PILINGSPIKE HITCH

Gives better grip on a thin rope

Thanks to forward leaps in rope-making technology, today's ropes are thinner and stronger than ever. That's great in terms of price and reduced bulk but not so good when it comes to actually handling the rope. Tugging on twine can cut you, and there's not much surface area to keep your hands from slipping. Here's a knot, called the pilingspike hitch, that is especially useful while tugging on rope when hauling or hoisting.

To tie this knot, you'll need some sort of "spike," such as a screwdriver, a large nail, or a dowel.

1. Bend the rope over an index finger. Grasp the two parts of the rope between your thumb and middle finger of the same hand, leaving some slack in the rope. Insert the spike, its tip pointing away from you, between the rope and your index finger, above the other fingers.

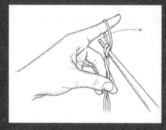

2. Rotate the tip of the spike away from you one-half turn and bring the spike tip up and through the loop that is around your index finger.

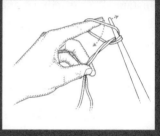

3. Push the spike up through the loop and take your index finger out to finish the knot.

4. Pull on both ends of the rope to draw the knot tight. Now you can use the spike as a handle for pulling.

Tip: If you're using slick rope, such as waxed twine, make two turns of the spike before inserting the tip through the loop.

DOUBLE CONSTRICTOR

Binding knot for clamping things

Maybe a rubber hose has come loose from your car's engine or your washing machine. You need a way to secure it until you can buy a hose clamp. Here's an ingenious knot that can do the trick. It's called the double constrictor, and it is a binding knot, used for clamping things. In addition to clamping hoses, it will bind the ends of canvas sacks, keep rope ends from unraveling, secure a bundle of tubes or rods, and splint a piece of cracked wood, such as a chair leg. But this knot is nearly impossible to untie. Don't use it unless you're prepared to cut the knot loose.

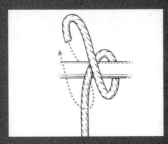

1. Lay the working end of your rope, pointing away from you, over the hose or other object to be constricted. Pass the working end around the hose and up, so that the rope crosses itself, forming an X on top of the hose.

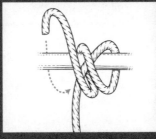

2. Pass the rope around the hose again, forming a second X.

3. Pass the working end of the rope around the hose a third time, but this time bring it up on the outer side of the standing (or nonworking) part of the rope. Bring the working end across the standing rope and thread it under the first two loops (that is, between the loops and the hose). Pull the working end out between those loops and the third loop.

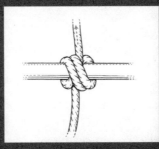

4. To finish, pull hard on each rope end in opposite directions, drawing the knot tight.

BUNTLINE HITCH

Strong enough to tow a car

A strong rope will tow a car—but you need a strong knot to match. Compact, easy to tie, with a breaking strength of about 80 percent of a rope's overall strength, the buntline hitch is one of the best when you need strength. Like all hitches, it's good anytime you need to tie a rope end onto something else, like a climber's carabiner or the eye hook of a clothesline pole. It's also good for tying down cargo.

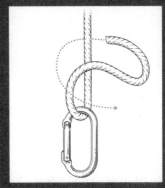

1. Bring the working end of your rope toward you through the hitching ring. Cross the working end over the long end of the rope and then behind it. This will form a figure 8.

continued

continued from 135

2. Pass the working end in front of the bottom part of the 8. This will divide the bottom part of the 8 into two sections, upper and lower. Then pass the working end behind the long part of the rope again and bring it out through the upper section of the 8's bottom part. Note that the working end comes out on top of itself.

3. Work all the slack out of the knot and snug it down against its attachment point. Front and back views of the finished knot are shown here.

■ BUTTERFLY KNOT

Versatile, stable, and easy to tie

A hand winch, a block and tackle—anything with a hook on one end—can be tricky to attach to a rope when you're hoisting something heavy, such as a piece of machinery. The butterfly knot is the answer. While not as strong as the buntline hitch (60 percent as opposed to 80 percent of the rope's strength), the butterfly is more versatile, allowing you to create stable loops as small or big as you want anywhere in a length of rope, not just at the ends. It doesn't slip, is easy to tie, and is handy when using extra-long rope. You can also use it for making handholds in a rope, so that several people can haul at once, and for clipping carabiners to when climbing, hoisting gear, or conducting a rescue operation.

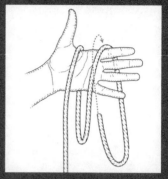

1. Make two loose turns around one hand. Start the turns on the palm side of the hand. Bring the end up to make a third turn, which should hang between the other two turns across the top of your hand.

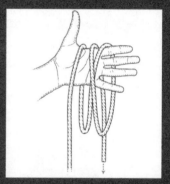

2. The three turns should now look like this.

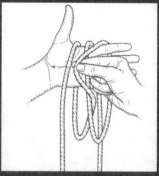

3. Pick up the turn farthest from your wrist. Pull it toward your wrist, over the other two turns.

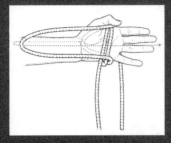

4. Pull the same turn back the way it came, but under the other two turns.

5. Draw up by pulling on all four parts that exit the knot. Pull on each, in turn, until the knot is firm.

■ SHOELACE SQUARE KNOT

Better way to keep shoes laced

The most common solution to loose laces—the double knot—is flawed. It often slips, especially with slick shoelaces. And it often jams, making it hard to untie. A better solution is a variation on the good old square knot that surgeons use for tying sutures. The next time you tie your shoes, try it.

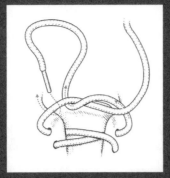

1. Begin as you always do, with an overhand knot. But before drawing it up, take one end around once more, forming a multiple overhand.

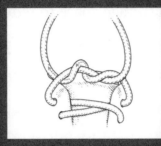

2. Now pull it tight. See how it stays put? The extra turn means more friction and more security.

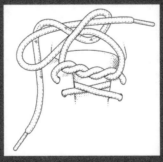

3. Now, as you always do, form a loop to make the first half of the bow. Again as usual, wrap the other end of the shoestring around the loop. However, instead of wrapping it around just once,

wrap it around twice before pushing the string through the little hole to make the second half of the bow.

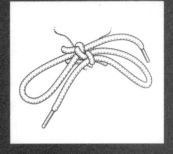

4. Pull tight, and you are done. This knot will stay put, will never jam, and can be untied simply by pulling on either end. It's especially handy for runners, kids—and anyone with a bad back.

PART TWO

Decorating and Organizing

Wish you could perk up a blah living room? Need some extra storage space to reduce clutter? Want to give a room more light—or less? Tired of people tracking in mud? Want to give your house a new look in a hurry? Got a window shade that won't roll up? Boy, is this part of the book for you! It's full of ingenious solutions for everyday problems all around the house.

Keeping Up Appearances

■ ROOM SPACE

The walls are closing in on me

USE MANY SMALL MIRRORS You may know the time-honored decorator's trick of using a huge mirror to make a room look larger. But large mirrors are costly. Small mirrors can create the same effect—or even a more interesting one—for pocket change. Buy several inexpensive small mirrors at garage sales or thrift stores. Pick different shapes and sizes. If you like, spray-paint all the frames the same color or using colors that will look good together. Decide which wall of your small room you want to mount the mirrors on and use masking tape to design a pattern for the mirrors on that wall. Mount the mirrors according to your design and then remove the masking tape.

An interesting collection of small mirrors is a quick way to open up a room.

How can I create an illusion of height?

DRAW THE EYE UPWARD A combination of lighting, picture-placement, and curtain-hanging strategies will create the illusion of height, making your room look more spacious than it is.

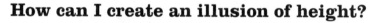

- Hang the pictures in your room 2 or 3 inches (5 to 7.5 centimeters) higher than eye level to draw the eye upward.
- Use indirect lighting to illuminate the ceiling. (A light-colored ceiling reflects light better.) Torchères and lamps with heads that can be aimed upward will allow light to hit the ceiling and bounce off, bathing the rest of the room in soft light. This creates an illusion of height, making your room seem bigger.
- Raise the curtains. You can help create the illusion of a higher ceiling in a small room by hanging the curtains higher. Instead of placing curtain rods at the level of the window frame, install them up against the ceiling (or at the crown molding edging the ceiling, if you have it). Then hang long curtains that reach the floor. This super vertical treatment will add a sense of

height to the room. Drape the curtains to hide the wall above the window or put a scrim under the curtain to hide the wall.

My living room seems cramped

UNCLUTTER AND USE LIGHT COLORS You can make your living room seem airier through the artful choice of furniture and accessories. Decorators recommend these techniques:

- Choose just a few pieces of furniture—declutter!
- Choose light colors for the furniture and your wall paint, and match some of the furniture to the walls. Avoid busy prints in upholstery.
- Choose low-slung, unobtrusive furniture and don't block windows or doors.
- Choose tables with glass or mirror tops.
- Choose sheer fabrics for window treatments and tablecloths.

My room feels like a corridor

USE STRIPES ACROSS THE SPACE Got a long, narrow room? Choose carpeting or rugs with stripes that run the width of the room rather than length. This will give the illusion that the room is wider.

Dark wood paneling makes my living room seem dank

PAINT IT WHITE OR OFF-WHITE Nothing opens up a room with dark wood paneling better than a couple of coats of semigloss white or off-white paint. First, lightly sand the paneling to a smooth finish. Dab sealant on any wood knots and then apply a washable flat paint. You may need two coats. You'll discover that the grooves between wood panels will provide a pleasing visual texture to your walls.

If you include the brickwork around the fireplace in the paint job, the room will seem even cheerier and bigger. Add color with rugs, slipcovers, decorative pillows, plants, and bouquets of flowers.

The sofa is dominating my family room

MAKE IT LESS CONSPICUOUS One way to solve the problem is to make the sofa stand out less. Place it against a wall—if possible against the wall with the main entry door for the room. That way, the sofa is

TRICKS OF THE TRADE

Using High Ceilings to Make Up for Meager Floor Space
Room is at a premium in the home of veterinarian Arnold Plotnick in New York City. Fortunately, his 400-square-foot (37-square-meter) loft has 14-foot (4.3-meter) ceilings. So instead of devoting a lot of his precious floor space to furniture, he tapped into his unused vertical space.

He painted his walls light beige to make the loft appear larger. His sleeping space is elevated, and he converted the closet under the stairs leading up to it into a mini-office with a desk, a computer, and lots of shelves. He keeps his collection of CDs and books in tall, narrow bookcases. He also positioned his furniture to define separate kitchen, dining, and living areas. A tall armoire against one wall holds his television and stereo. The armoire is closed when not in use to give a clean, spacious look to his small apartment.

not the first thing that hits your eyes when you come in. Also consider giving it a new slipcover that makes it less noticeable, preferably a light-toned solid color that blends with the wall. Keep other furnishings in the room to a minimum. Especially avoid large upholstered chairs or recliners.

BUY A SMALLER SOFA In small rooms where you want to keep a cozy feeling but still have space to move around, you may want to consider using two comfortable upholstered chairs instead of a big sofa. Or consider a love seat or a condominium-sized couch, which is smaller than a standard sofa but bigger than a love seat.

An oriental rug is overpowering my family room

ADD MORE COLOR You may have been proud—and a little nervous—when you spent a lot of money on a beautiful Oriental rug for your family room. But now, stepping back, you realize that its colors and complex pattern totally dominate the room. Fight back with color: Add some multicolored throw pillows and bright artwork to the room. Cover a chair in a vivid pattern. These strong new elements will force the rug to settle into the overall scheme of the room.

■ WARMTH AND COLOR

I have trouble picking colors for my walls

PICK FROM YOUR FAVORITE THINGS Look for inspiration in your favorite furniture, fabrics, or china patterns. Let's say your favorite living room furnishing is a chair upholstered in a multicolored fabric that features sage green. Paint your walls to match this green. Use other colors in the upholstery fabric to help you pick accessories for the room.

I painted the room too dark a color

TEMPER DARK COLORS WITH LIGHT COUNTERPOINTS Navy blue, hunter green, and chocolate brown walls can make a dramatic statement in a room. But they need tempering with light-colored, or even white, trim and upholstery fabrics, as well as window treatments. For example, a light-colored painting or tapestry against a dark wall can create a beautiful focal point in a room. Make sure a room with dark walls also has plenty of light fixtures and lamps.

I want to reflect the changing seasons in my house

USE COLOR ACCENT PIECES Without completely redecorating for every season, a few well-placed pillows and throws can give a seasonal touch to your decor. In the winter, place some red and green accents around. During the spring and summer, use blues and yellows. When autumn rolls around, mix reds and yellows in with a little brown. When you find seasonal accents on sale, buy the ones you like. At the start of the appropriate season, place a few of these accents around the house. Out of season, store them on a shelf in the guest room.

I want to give my house interior a new look in a hurry

PAINT THE TRIM Concentrate on the trim. If your walls are white, for example, paint the trim a contrasting color, such as a gray-blue or misty green that picks up a color in your curtains or upholstery. Or, if your walls are colored, paint the trim white. The fresh trim will give the room renewed energy.

Redecorating is so expensive that I worry about making a mistake

GO CONSERVATIVE ON BIG ITEMS Interior designers suggest that you stick with conservative colors, patterns, and styles for big-ticket items, such as sofas, dressers, carpeting or rugs, and custom curtains. Go wild with accessories, such as lamps, side tables, and artwork. The smaller, less-expensive items are easy to relocate in your house, and the cost of your mistakes won't leave you with lasting regret.

I want to add sparkle to my rooms, but I haven't much of a budget

SHOP RESALE STORES You probably already know about the Salvation Army and Goodwill stores, as well as local resale shops that support a hospital or other community charity. You can often buy

PROBLEM STOPPER

How to Make Wall Painting Easier

• Wear clothes that you expect to get splashed with paint.

• Remove all switch and outlet plates, doorknobs, and other hardware and place each in a plastic bag with its screws.

• Cover or remove all furniture, rugs, and light fixtures. Cover the floor with drop cloths.

• Prepare a paint station where you keep a paint tray, masking tape, brushes, rollers, stir sticks, a can opener, cleaning rags, a screwdriver, a hammer, a ladder, and, if necessary, paint thinner or turpentine.

• Paint in this order: ceiling, walls, doors, and woodwork.

• Don't rush. Give yourself plenty of time.

• When you've finished, keep a supply of paint for touch-ups in small plastic containers or glass jars with airtight lids. Label each with the color and brand name.

excellent second-hand goods at one-third of the retail price at such places. For the best bargains, make sure you shop in a second-hand store in a well-to-do neighborhood, where you're likely to find items donated by people who can afford to give away perfectly good furnishings when they redecorate. And do your shopping on Friday and Saturday mornings, when the stores first open. That's when you are most likely to find treasures.

I don't know which types of wood furniture will go together

USE WOODS OF THE SAME HUE If you inherit furniture from relatives or buy bargain furniture at garage sales, you may end up with a lot of furniture made from a variety of woods. Which ones harmonize and which clash? The answer is simple: When decorating a room, stick with woods of the same hue to avoid a look of confusion. For instance, don't mix a hard, dark wood such as cherry with a soft, light wood such as pine. But you can mix furniture made of cherry and maple quite effectively. And pine paired with walnut works well.

My bedroom needs spark

USE A DECORATIVE SHEET AS A WALLCOVERING Cut the hems off a flat bedsheet that has a decorative pattern you like. Soak the sheet in full-strength liquid starch. The starch will act as a natural adhesive. Smooth the sheet over the wall behind the bed, starting at the ceiling line and working down. Use a squeegee to smooth out wrinkles. When you want to redecorate, you can easily pull down the sheet; the original wall finish will only need wiping down to be restored.

Five Minute Decorating Ideas Using a Bedsheet

A bedsheet is more than just a mattress covering. It can perk up a room for very little money, as the following:

- a tablecloth over a real or improvised dining room table
- a curtain, by threading a curtain rod through the broad hem across the top of a flat sheet and mounting it over a window, an open doorway, or an exposed closet on a tension rod
- a canopy to hang over your four-poster bed, with ribbons added to tie the ends to the four posts
- a pillow appliqué, by cutting out a pretty design from the sheet and stitching it on a plain pillow
- seat cushion covers, by cutting decorative sheets to fit over padded seat cushions that have become faded or worn

■ ROOM LIGHTING

I can't get the right lighting effects in my living room

INSTALL DIMMER SWITCHES You will have many more options for good lighting if you install dimmer switches on your overhead lights and floor lamps. Dimmer switches allow you to control the intensity of light from each fixture. With a series of dimmer switches, you can regulate the light in each part of the room. (Dimmers come with instructions for installing them; it is not very different from installing an ordinary light switch.) To light a room properly, the first goal is to provide a uniform lighting that lets the eye scan from one end of the room to the other without interruption. Then you can concentrate on highlighting pieces of art or plant arrangements.

The lights in my living room seem to be getting dimmer

CLEAN YOUR LAMPSHADES Take a close look at your lampshades. Dust and household dirt can collect on them, cutting down on the lamp's illumination. You can remove that dust with a stiff paintbrush (designated for lampshade cleaning duties only). Remove the lampshade from the lamp and head outdoors. Holding the lampshade steady in one hand, use the other hand to briskly brush the dust away. Start at the top and work down, slowly turning the shade as you go. Back inside, wipe off the lightbulb with a dry cloth before putting the shade back on the lamp.

No one ever uses that chair in the corner

ADD A LAMP Maybe the problem isn't the chair, but the lack of light around it. A standing lamp can open up underused corners of a room for reading, and adding a small table would give you a place to put a book or a cup of tea.

My chandelier looks lopsided

ADD WEIGHT TO ONE SIDE If your chandelier has arms supporting several glass light globes, you may be able to rebalance the fixture yourself. Identify which light globe is higher than the others. Lift that globe off its holder. (You may have to remove the lightbulb first.)

TRICKS OF THE TRADE

What Color Choices Will Do in a Room

Before decorating a room, keep in mind these basics on color:

• **Primary colors:** Bright blues, reds, and yellows bring out bold, strong statements in active rooms. These are good choices for a child's room or a family room where there are lots of get-togethers. Primary colors spark conversations.

• **Autumn colors:** Muted oranges, greens, blues, and purples give a room a sense of calmness and relaxation. They make ideal wall colors for bedrooms, reading libraries, and other retreats from the hectic stress of your on-the-go life.

• **Neutral colors:** Shades of white, beiges, and grays are best used to connect one room to the next. They purposely take a backseat to items you want to showcase in a room—such as a red brick fireplace or that large, framed oil painting of your grandfather.

Take a yard or so of soldering wire off its spool and lay it in a circle around the bottom of the holder to add a little weight. Make sure the wire is not on the lip that holds the globe so that won't interfere with the way the globe sits in the holder. Then put the globe back into place and check the balance of the chandelier. Add or remove soldering wire as needed. You may have to put soldering wire in more than one holder to get the right balance.

■ ARTWORK AND FOUND ART

I don't have wall space for all the pictures I want to hang

ROTATE YOUR DISPLAY Install two or three long, narrow display shelves on a wall where you usually hang pictures. Arrange some of your favorite pictures, putting several frames on each shelf and leaning them against the wall. After a few months, take these pictures down and put up some of the others. Store the pictures not on display in document boxes, where they will be protected from light and dust. You will catch your family's and friends' attention when you regularly change your gallery.

A display shelf is the easy way to rotate your picture collection.

There is a lot of bare wall above my bedroom window

HANG A HAT If your bedroom has a low window or a high ceiling, you may wonder how to decorate the unexpected space above the window. Try gluing some dry or silk flowers on a straw hat. Add colorful ribbons. Then hang the hat on a hook centered over the top of the window.

How should I light artwork on a wall?

BE WARY OF THE LIGHT FROM LAMPS If you want to bring out the best in your photos or mounted artwork, do not place them near a lamp with a shade. The shade tends to give the lightbulb a soft, yellow glow rather than the ample light you need to showcase your artwork. Go with a white or clear glass lightbulb, which will cast eye-pleasing illumination on your prized piece of art. You can get small lights that attach to the top of the frame and shine on the artwork or you can direct light at the piece from a track light.

I can't get my pictures to hang straight

TRY A LASER If you have trouble getting pictures lined up and level, consider getting a little device called the LaserVision iLine (available at major building supply stores). This tool does the work of a 4-foot (1.2-meter) level and more. It emits a level laser line in four directions, which makes hanging pictures (and installing bookshelves) a snap. It sells for less than $50.

I hate to throw away this beautiful calendar

FRAME THE PICTURES Appoint yourself curator of your own "art collection." Say you have a calendar featuring paintings by Vermeer. Or you brought back a calendar from China that has exquisite silkscreen prints of birds, flowers, and mountain scenes. Cut out or detach your favorite pictures from the calendar, place them in inexpensive frames, and group them on a wall. (Buy several frames at a time on sale at your local discount store, or snap them up at neighborhood yard sales.)

I need a new slant on decorating

FEATURE NATURAL DECORATIONS Bring a little bit of the outdoors inside. There are lots of free items to be found in nature that will give your rooms a creative and distinctive look. Instead of hanging a landscape portrait behind your sofa, for instance, hang an interesting branch or a piece of driftwood from your favorite beach. Arrange seashells as wall art. Pile pinecones in a basket.

TRICKS OF THE TRADE

What You Need to Know Before You Hang Pictures

• Never hang artwork in direct sunlight. Exposure will fade images.

• Keep a series of related pictures no farther apart than the width of a hand.

• Use incandescent or halogen lights to illuminate artwork. Both types are less harmful to artwork than fluorescent light.

• Never hang artwork above heat vents; changes in temperature can cause condensation and harm the artwork.

• Larger pictures slide out of kilter easily. Use two picture hooks instead of one and press mounting putty (available at craft stores) behind each bottom corner to hold the frame against the wall.

Getting Your Rooms in Order

ENTRYWAYS

My front hall is claustrophobic

HANG A MIRROR You may not be able to do anything to enlarge the space, but hanging a mirror in the hallway will make it seem bigger and brighter. A hall mirror is also great for last-minute checks of your appearance before you head out the door.

I want my front entry to be welcoming

ADD LIGHT COLORS AND FRESH FLOWERS For an inviting look in your hallway, choose light colors for paint or subtle patterns for wallpaper instead of dark colors or busy patterns. Install an attractive light fixture with a dimmer to control the light. Hang a small gallery of pictures or put a piece of treasured pottery on a table. And finally, nothing welcomes guests at the front entrance better than a vase of fresh flowers.

Vanquish the mess of muddy footware in your entryway with a cabinet.

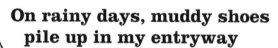

On rainy days, muddy shoes pile up in my entryway

BUY A CABINET FOR WET SHOES Look for a knee-high cabinet with a row of cubbies for shoes and boots. (Many home furnishings stores sell just such cubby cabinets.) Each family member gets his or her own cubbyhole for wet shoes and boots, and the top of the cabinet makes a place to sit while taking them off.

People track a lot of mud into the house

USE MATS If you protect your doorways inside and out with large mats, you will cut down on all the things that shoes can track into a house. A waterproof rough mat outside allows family and guests to scrape their feet before coming in. Indoor mats long enough for several steps protect rugs and floors from wetness and debris.

I have new carpets and want my guests to remove their shoes at the front door

PROVIDE SLIPPERS A no-shoes-indoors rule is a good way to keep the house clean, but some visitors just aren't used to this custom. Adopt a Japanese practice and place "guest slippers" in many sizes by the front door. This will give guests a hint of your wishes and make it easy for them to shuck their shoes. Make sure there's a chair or bench where guests can sit comfortably to don and doff their shoes.

My front hall is always a mess

ASSIGN FAMILY BINS To straighten out your entryway, assign everyone in the family his or her own in and out "basket." This could be a bin in a set of stacking bins, a drawer in a dresser, or one shelf in a standing cupboard. Incoming residents can dump their school supplies, hats, briefcases, and other such items in their own bins. And everyone can use the bins as a staging area for the next morning's departure. One organizer calls this area the "launching pad" for the house. Every few days, each person must be responsible for completely emptying his or her bin.

I am forever losing my keys

DESIGNATE A BOWL OR BASKET It would be nice to think that everyone would carefully hang keys on a hook where they'd be easy to find when needed again. But the reality is that most people toss their keys on the first available table when they come in the door. Don't fight it: Put a sturdy but attractive bowl or basket on the table by your front door and designate it for car keys, sunglasses, cell phones, and the other portable necessities of modern life.

■ FAMILY AND LIVING ROOMS

Cushions won't stay on my wooden chairs

USE HIGH-FRICTION DRAWER LINER Cut a piece of high-friction drawer liner (designed to keep utensils or tools from sliding around)

to fit your chair seat. Place it on the seat frame directly under the seat cushion. The liner, which comes in many colors, will grab the seat cushion and keep it in place.

My family room has turned into toy land

GET A TOY CHEST Buy a decorative toy chest (a lid is a must) in a color that harmonizes with your family room furniture. Each day, allow your child to pick three or four toys or games to play with in the family room. Just before dinnertime, ring a bell to signal that it's time to pick up the toys and put them in the toy chest.

I can't figure out how to showcase my fireplace

PAINT THE FIREPLACE WALL A DIFFERENT COLOR When your guests walk into your living room, you want them to admire that majestic fireplace with the mantel you inherited from your grandfather. Paint the wall that includes the fireplace a different color from that of the rest of the room. This helps focus all eyes on the fireplace.

My fireplace is no longer safe to use

MAKE IT A DECORATIVE CENTERPIECE Even if the log-burning days of your fireplace are over, you can still use it as the focal point of your room. Buy a decorative fireplace screen and place candles in front of it to finish a cozy look. Or clean out the old burned logs and ashes, vacuum the area, and place decorative candles of various sizes and colors on a plant stand inside the fireplace.

■ WINDOWS

My window trim is not very attractive

HIDE IT WITH CURTAINS If you don't like the trim around your windows, the easy solution is to hang nice curtains so that they cover the trim completely. Mount a curtain rod 2 or 3 inches (5 to 7.5 centimeters) above the window opening and extend it at least 3 inches to either side. Conversely, if you have attractive window casings or trim, showcase these features by using shades or blinds that fit only the interior of the window.

The pleats in my window shades are beginning to sag

USE THE SHADES REGULARLY Over time, the pleats in fabric window coverings tend to settle a bit, leaving billowy pleats at the bottom of the window and fresh-creased pleats at the top. The solution: Regularly open and close the shades to help keep all the pleats crisp and new looking.

I'm afraid to wash my sheer curtains

USE THE GENTLE CYCLE Most sheer curtains are made of synthetic fabrics that are machine washable in warm, not hot, water on the gentle cycle. Rinse with cold water and diluted fabric softener. Place the curtains in the dryer with several hand towels and dry on the cool or permanent press setting for two or three minutes. Hang them back up so that they can shake out as they air-dry.

The curtain rod snags my sheers when I hang them

COVER THE ROUGH EDGES To prevent snags, cover the end of the curtain rod with cellophane or duct tape before pushing it through the pocket.

My drapery cords tangle easily

ADD A SMALL WEIGHT Keep cords straight by tying a small weight (such as a fishing-line sinker) to each cord. Position the weight on the cord so that it hangs above the floor whether the drapes are fully opened or closed.

The easy way to keep drapery cords from tangling is to add a lead fishing weight.

My curtains don't hang evenly

ADD WEIGHTS TO THE HEM Unruly curtains can be brought into line by adding weights to the bottom hem. Fabric stores sell lengths of weighted beads that can be threaded through the hem of sheer curtains to keep them from billowing in slight breezes or the forced air from furnaces. To keep heavier curtains straight, sew small lead weights with two holes in them, like buttons, to the curtain hem. The neatest way to do this is to sew these weights inside a tiny pillow of matching fabric to hide the weights and prevent the metal from discoloring the curtain fabric. Many such weights now come already covered in vinyl or cloth.

I want a new look for some single windows in my house

USE NYLON CORD Hang "found objects" in the window instead of a shade or drapes. Thread nearly invisible monofilament fishing line through beads, crystals, Christmas ornaments, children's toys, or small pieces of driftwood, and attach the lines at the top and bottom of the window frame with wire brads. (You may want to hide the brads by touching them up with the same trim paint that's on the windows.) Or use fishing line to lash together a latticework of beautiful dried branches from a small tree or shrub, with fall berries or dried flowers attached.

■ FURNITURE

I want my wood furniture to look better

USE NEW HARDWARE The easiest way to enliven chests, desks, and dressers without the hassle or expense of refinishing is to replace the hardware on the front. Attaching a bright new set of knobs or replacing one style of pull with another can transform a piece.

My sofa is too soft

ADD A STIFF BOARD You can firm up a sagging sofa by placing a stiff insert under the cushions. Sofa Saver and Sav-A-Sofa are two brands of folding, fabric-covered particleboard inserts for couches, love seats, and chairs and are available at home improvement stores. Or you can ask your local lumber dealer to cut a piece of ⅜-inch (9.5-millimeter), grade AA plywood to fit under your seat cushions. Cover the plywood with a matching fabric if you're worried that the board might show.

My sofa is sagging

REATTACH THE SPRINGS A sagging couch may be easy to fix. First, turn it over. If the bottom is covered with plastic or gauze, peel back the covering to expose the springs. The springs often are attached to a bracket at either end with a simple hook, and sometimes one or

more springs come unhooked. Simply reattaching the springs can fix the problem. (If the springs or pieces of the wooden frame are broken, that's a job for a professional repairperson.)

I have a living room cabinet with doors that won't open

RAISE THE CORNER Try lifting each corner of the cabinet a half-inch (1.25 centimeters) and then testing the door. If a boost to one corner frees up the door, put a sliver of wood under that leg to shim it up. Sometimes a cabinet warps slightly, and a little lift is all it needs to regain its equilibrium.

My furniture doesn't match

USE ACCESSORIES FOR CONTINUITY An eclectic look can be interesting and even very stylish. Instead of worrying about your furniture not matching, concentrate on using accessories to tie the room together. Choose pillows, planters, rugs, and artwork that incorporate the same dominant color. Coordinate fabrics for upholstery and curtains. The eye will be drawn to these elements and not to your mismatched furniture.

Where do you start in arranging living room furniture?

START WITH A CONVERSATION CIRCLE Designers say that the key to successfully arranging a living room is to first

PROBLEM STOPPER

Bookshelves
Taking a Bow?
Kevin Moore of Washington, D.C. is a retired U.S. Navy Seabee whose building talents came in handy when his bookshelves began to sag under the weight of his books. To reinforce each shelf, he screwed a strip of wood along the front edge. Then, for additional support, he screwed a L- bracket into the wall under the heart of the sag. In no time, his shelves were ship-shape.

WORLD-CLASS GOOF

Ahhh, I Think I'll Just Sit Right Here...

A tired visitor to the Minneapolis Institute of Arts, trying to take a load of his feet, suffered acute embarrassment when he sat in a chair in one of the exhibit halls and broke it into three pieces, sending him crashing to the floor. Unfortunately, the chair belonged to the museum's collection. It was a 16th-century Ming dynasty piece from China, valued at around $500,000. The man apparently missed or ignored the "Do Not Touch" sign posted beside the chair. Fortunately, the chair was insured and was fully restored.

place the couches and chairs in a rough circle for conversation. None of these pieces should be more than 10 feet (3 meters) from one another. After this furniture arrangement is set, you can use other parts of the room for other purposes. You might want a listening area around the stereo system. You could also create a reading nook.

How can I antique new brass hinges for an old cabinet?

AGE THE BRASS WITH AMMONIA FUMES To give new brass an old look, pour an inch or two of nonsudsy ammonia into a bucket. Then suspend the hardware above the ammonia in the following way: Run a string or wire across the bucket, securing each end where the handle meets the bucket's rim. Hang the brass hinges over the string and put plastic wrap over the bucket and suspended hinges. The hinges will turn black within a day or two. Scrub off the black with a soft cloth until the hinges look the way you want them to.

■ BEDROOMS

I am forever knocking things off my crowded nightstand

MOUNT A WALL LAMP To free up space on your nightstand, remove the lamp. Use a swing-arm floor lamp instead, or mount a swing-arm wall lamp above the headboard. Such fixtures allow you to adjust the lamp exactly the way you want it for reading. Install the lamp about 18 to 20 inches (45 to 50 centimeters) from the top of the headboard for best results. If you don't have a headboard, position the lamp 3 feet (1 meter) or more above the mattress, so that it will be within easy reach but won't hit your head when you sit up in bed. With the lamp out of the way, you'll have ample room on your nightstand for your alarm clock, book, and telephone.

My bedroom doubles as my home office

USE A DECORATIVE SCREEN You need to separate the two areas so that work worries won't keep you awake. Find a folding decorative screen to define the two spaces and block your view of your files while you are in bed. A screen, which you can find at home improvement stores, won't be cheap, but it will cost far less than building a

TRICKS OF THE TRADE

"Aging" Furniture

To give wood furniture a weathered, antique look, buy some sodium sulfate fertilizer at a garden center. Fill a spray bottle one-quarter of the way with sodium sulfate and the rest with water; then shake. Working outside, spray the solution on the furniture. Let it dry in the sun (about an hour). The wood will darken and look as if it had aged 5 years. Repeat to "age" it more.

wall. Some screens have fabric panels that can be custom-made to match your curtains or bedspread.

I can't part with my memento T-shirts

MAKE A MEMORY QUILT For some people, a vacation is not complete without a souvenir T-shirt. Those wonderful mementos, however, can quickly fill up your dresser drawers. Still, how can you part with a T-shirt that proudly proclaims that you survived that scary ride at the amusement park, visited a Hollywood movie set, or hiked in the Rocky Mountains? One solution is to save the memory and make rags of the rest of the shirt. Cut out the logos from these cherished T-shirts and make them into squares for a memory quilt that you can mount on your wall.

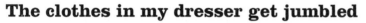

To get rid of a drawerful of beloved T-shirts, clip the logos and turn them into a quilt.

The clothes in my dresser get jumbled

ADD DRAWER DIVIDERS If athletic socks, casual socks, and dress socks make up that mess, you can solve your problem with a couple of drawer dividers. Buy them in closet shops or home improvement stores or make your own by cutting wooden yardsticks so that the ends fit snugly at the front and back of the drawer.

■ CHILDREN'S BEDROOMS

My kids need more storage space

INSTALL OLD SCHOOL LOCKERS Head for your child's school the next time a remodeling project is announced. Schools often host sales to get rid of old lockers, desks, and other gear to make room for the new. An old locker—or a set of them—would certainly add more storage space. Paint the lockers bright colors to match each child's décor. Then stow away their collections, toys, and sports equipment.

My child throws everything on the floor

INSTALL A ROW OF HOOKS OR PEGS If you line a bedroom wall with a row of pegs or hooks, your child will have a place to hang up jackets and coats as well as small bags filled with such treasures as Legos, dolls and doll clothes, and plastic space figures. Sacks work better than a toy chest because they free up floor space and keep toys divided, so there is less chance of losing pieces.

I want to redecorate my child's room to celebrate the crib-to-big-bed move

PICK TODDLER-FRIENDLY COLORS AND TEXTURES Pick bold colors for walls and furniture; pastels seem too tame to toddlers. Select objects in the room with tactile appeal, because young children love to touch different textures. Choose a faux fur bedspread or throw, for example, that your child can snuggle into. Or pick a rug with another kind of snuggly feel. Create an environment that will make your child feel secure and sheltered. Provide storage spaces.

I don't want to be too strict, but my child's room is a jungle

PUT UP A TENT Let your child exercise some creativity in his or her personal space. Raise a colorful small tent or build a little castle of cardboard and fabric in the room. Inside the tent or castle, your child can play with favorite toys, which will now be out of sight. The result will be a room that both you and your child will like and that will give the child some privacy.

■ BATHROOMS

I need to make my bathroom look bigger

USE A LIGHT COLOR SCHEME As with any small room in your home, you can create the illusion of more space with a subdued color scheme. Use neutral or light colors for your walls, countertops, and sink basin. Pick a clear or light-colored shower curtain and light-colored towels to match.

My bathroom drawer is a jumble of tubes and bottles

TOSS OLD STUFF AND ORGANIZE THE REST Bathroom drawers are one of the final frontiers of household organizing. Attack each drawer with

PROBLEM STOPPER

Corral Those Crayons
Do your children litter the floor with coloring books, and other art supplies? Here's a solution from Claudia Kadia, a set and costume designer in Toronto: Create armchair pockets to hang on an upholstered chair.

To make the pockets, buy machine-washable material. Starting about a foot (30 centimeters) below the armrest on one side of your chair, measure up over the armrest, down across the cushion-less seat, over the other armrest, and down about a foot on the other side. That will be the length of your main piece. Depending on your chair, its width should be 15 to 18 inches (37 to 45 centimeters). Cut two separate squares of fabric to serve as pockets. Fold over the top of each piece and sew a hem. Sew a pocket on each end of the main piece, right sides together. Invert the pockets and hem the main piece.

a grocery bag in hand for disposing of unwanted items. Toss out anything that's more than two years old, that's past its expiration date, or that you can't envision needing. If there are items that don't belong in the bathroom, set them in the hallway and put them in their proper places when you're finished with the bathroom drawers. Organize the things remaining in the drawers into groups of like items and cluster them in zipper-sealed bags, small boxes, or plastic bins.

Bottles keep tumbling into the tub

PUT THEM IN A RACK There are only so many corners where you can store shampoo and conditioner bottles around a bathtub before you start an avalanche. The simple solution: Move all the bottles to a waterproof rack that mounts easily on the wall or hangs from the showerhead pipe. These racks are available at bath, discount, and home improvement stores.

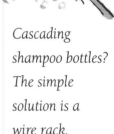

My spouse and I fight over cabinet space

PUT SHELVES OVER THE TOILET If you don't have enough counter or cabinet space in your bathroom, consider a cabinet above the toilet. You can buy units with several shelves, with and without doors, to store toilet articles, extra toilet paper, tissue boxes, and extra hand towels. Look in bath shops and home improvement centers.

Cascading shampoo bottles? The simple solution is a wire rack.

I don't have enough towel rack space

USE A COATRACK You can maximize the space in a small bathroom by standing a coatrack in the corner. A coatrack is perfect for hanging towels and bathrobes. These items dry quickly without taking up much horizontal space.

Hey, you're using my towel

COLOR-CODE TOWELS Sharing a bathroom is difficult enough, but everybody in the family should at least have his or her own towel and washcloth. Institute a color-coding system in your household. Designate one color for each person—say, blue for your spouse, red for you, green for your son, and yellow for your daughter. Then make sure each person has at least two towels and washcloths, one to use

TRICKS OF THE TRADE

Hampered by Little Space? Make a Bag for Dirty Clothes

Give an old bedsheet a second life by converting it into a laundry bag for storing dirty clothes until washday. A laundry bag hanging from a hook on the back of the bathroom door takes up less space than a hamper. Follow these five easy steps:

1. Use a double, queen, or king-size flat bedsheet.

2. Buy about 80 inches (2 meters) of sturdy nylon cord from a home center or camping store.

3. Make a 1-inch (2.5-centimeter) hem in each short end of the sheet, keeping the ends open so that the cord can be threaded through. Then fold the sheet in half widthwise and sew the two sides together.

4. Thread the cord through the hem. Tie the two ends of the cord together to form a drawstring.

5. Pull the cord to close the top, and hang your homemade laundry bag.

now and one in the wash, in his or her color. Of course, this won't work if you want a coordinated look in your bathroom.

I keep collecting hotel shampoos and conditioners

MAKE A GUEST BASKET There may be something in human nature that requires us to snap up all of those complimentary shampoos, conditioners, hand lotions, shower caps, and sewing kits provided during hotel stays. To make use of your collection, stock a small wicker basket with two hotel-size shampoos, two conditioners, two lotions, and one shower cap. Put the basket out on your bathroom counter when you have guests. Donate the rest of your minis to a shelter. Don't bring any more home until the basket needs replenishing.

I need better light at the bathroom mirror

CHANGE THE LIGHTBULBS The harsh lightbulbs often used in bathrooms tend to throw shadows and make delicate work, such as applying makeup, difficult. Nowadays, the choices in lightbulb shapes and colors are almost limitless. For better bathroom lighting, replace exposed lightbulbs with incandescent vanity globes.

My bathroom towels never seem to dry completely

INSTALL A VENTILATING FAN You don't have to resign yourself to towels that never seem to get dry. Do this today: Fold your towels once and place them on towel racks. Position a small oscillating fan on your bathroom counter aimed at the towels. Tomorrow, consider installing a ventilating fan in your bathroom.

■ LAUNDRY ROOM

I keep missing stains in my wash

INSTALL A BETTER LIGHT Maybe you're not noticing stains because it's too dark in your laundry room. Try installing a wall-mounted spotlight by the washing machine. Look over each item of clothing under the bright light, and you'll catch more stains for treatment before they go through the wash.

I have no place to hang wet clothes

BUY A RETRACTABLE CLOTHESLINE If your laundry area is too small for a drying rack, install a retractable clothesline across a shower stall or hallway. These inexpensive devices can accommodate a load of clothes on hangers. Put a towel under the clothes to protect the floor, if necessary. Or, if you have a full bath, install an extra shower curtain rod above the middle of the tub—a perfect place to hang and dry clothes.

I can't keep up with lost buttons

PUT UP A BULLETIN BOARD A laundry room bulletin board goes a long way toward keeping the laundry organized. Tack up small, zip-sealed plastic bags to hold pins, threaded needles, spare buttons, and other items for quick repairs. The bulletin board is also a good place to hang specific washing and drying instructions for favorite clothes that take special handling.

My bulk detergent is a pain in the back

USE A SHELF OVER THE MACHINE Buying laundry detergent in bulk saves money, but it can be heavy to manage. To save your back, repackage the powder or liquid in smaller containers. An alternative, if you have a shelf above your washer: Buy a big jug of liquid detergent with a dispenser button and lift it just once, to put it on the shelf. When it's laundry time, let gravity do the work. Push the dispenser

TRICKS OF THE TRADE

To Speed Bathroom Clean-ups

Install a paper towel rack in your bathroom. When you need to clean the counters and the toilet lids, just reach for the spray cleaner and a paper towel. Then toss the used towel in the trash. Paper towels eliminate the need to keep a sponge under your bathroom sink, where its dampness can create mildew.

WORLD-CLASS FIX

Low-Gravity Laundry

There's never been a washer or dryer aboard a U. S. space shuttle, but astronauts have managed to change their underwear and even do laundry. John Grunsfeld, a veteran of four shuttle missions, recalls that he and his colleagues washed their dirty clothes by hand inside a plastic bag and then towel-dried them. With zero gravity, there was no need to string a laundry line. Instead, Grunsfeld said, the astronauts used "towel grommets"—rubber disks, about 2 inches (5 centimeters) in diameter, with an X cut into the center—attached to the shuttle walls to hang their damp laundry. The astronauts stuffed a corner of a wet towel or T-shirt into the X, and the item floated in the air. "The humidity is low on the shuttle," Grunsfeld explained, so the towels dried fast.

PROBLEM STOPPER

End Orphaned Socks
It's the age-old laundry mystery: Where did that second sock go? Several companies sell small plastic rings that neatly hold together pairs of socks. (Sock-Locks and Sockpro are brands available on the Internet.) For generations, people have used safety pins for this purpose, but the modern version is as quick to use and won't corrode in the wash. As soon as you take off a dirty pair of socks, slip them through one of these rings and toss them into the laundry hamper. Wash and dry the socks while they're linked together and return them to your sock drawer ready to wear.

button and let the liquid flow directly into the washer, or fill a measuring cup and pour a cupful into the wash.

I need laundry cabinets

USE OLD KITCHEN CABINETS At any given moment, somebody within a few blocks of your home is probably remodeling a kitchen. Watch the curbs on trash day to see whether there's a set of cabinets you can pick up at no cost. Check out yard sales or used-furniture shops for kitchen or bathroom cabinets that are being sold off after a remodeling job. These happy finds can sit on the floor or be installed on the walls of your laundry room by a carpenter. Slap on a coat of paint to match the room, and you'll have custom laundry cabinets.

I have no place to put my ironing board

BUY A WALL-MOUNTED IRONING BOARD You can install such an ironing board on a door or on the wall of your laundry room. These fold-down ironing boards are not only easier to set up than the freestanding models, but they are also sturdier. When you're not ironing, they disappear.

My kids don't pitch in with laundry

USE PERSONAL BASKETS Designate and label a basket in your laundry room for each family member. When you sort the clean laundry, put each person's clothing in his or her basket. Make each person responsible for folding his or her own items and returning them to the proper closet or dresser.

I spend forever folding laundry!

MAKE FEWER FOLDS Reorganize your closets and drawers to accommodate clothes and linens with fewer folds. Fold a towel in half instead of thirds, for example. It may not sound like much, but an extra fold or two in each shirt, towel, sheet, and pair of jeans adds up to many hours over hundreds of loads.

Closets and Clutter

■ ORGANIZING AND STORING

I want to store my magazines where I can find them

USE RACKS OR HOLDERS Space-saving magazine racks are available at home improvement stores. You might attach a six-tiered magazine rack to the back of a door with wood screws, for example. Or keep magazines in upright magazine holders (available in office supply stores) on a bookshelf so they will be within easy reach but out of the way. After you have collected two year's worth of magazines in the holders, it's your signal to start discarding the older issues.

My den is inundated with catalogs

USE A LARGE FILE FOLDER Keeping catalogs "just in case" can use up a lot of den or family room space. Buy an accordion-style file folder to hold catalogs you are not ready to throw out. Give each catalog a two-month life span. After that, throw them out. (You will undoubtedly get a replacement soon.) You can also save space by jotting down the Web sites of each company and going online the next time you want to place an order.

The coffee table is littered with magazines

USE A BASKET OR BUCKET Keep the current issues of your favorite magazines within easy reach by rolling them up and inserting them in deep wicker baskets or decorative metal buckets. If you can lay your hands on some old metal nail bins (find them at hardware stores, yard sales, and house and farm auctions), spray-paint them in bright colors, allow them to dry thoroughly, and add the magazines. The baskets and buckets keep your magazines from littering.

Our CD collection needs storage space

USE SQUARE WICKER BASKETS You can dress up your family room and organize your CD collection with wicker baskets. Pick square or

PROBLEM STOPPER

Finding Room for Extra China
A construction worker from Laurel, Maryland, found a novel way to free up precious kitchen cabinet space while adding a distinctive look to his living room. He bought 12 wire plate holders (available at craft, framing, and kitchen-and-bath stores). On a blank wall in his living room, he measured out three rows of the holders, four per row, and mounted them on the wall with screws. He then placed his 12 dinner plates in the holders. When he wants to entertain guests, he grabs the plates he needs from his "wall art." After dinner, he washes the plates and returns them to their holders.

rectangular baskets in colors and designs that match the room's décor. Designate different colors for different types of music. Line up the CDs in the baskets so that you can read the titles. Baskets are often prettier and handier than the metal CD holders you can buy at music stores.

I can never find the CD I want

USE SIMPLE CATEGORIES You don't have to arrange all your CDs alphabetically by artist to keep track of them. An easier system is based on types of music—classical, big band, jazz, and rock, for example. Designate separate sections in your CD holder for these categories. It will be easy to find what you want and even easier to put your CDs away later.

I need more storage space

You'll be able to find your coat in a jiff—if you keep only outerware in your hall closet.

USE THE BOTTOM STEP IN THE BASEMENT If you have wooden steps leading down to your basement, you can convert the bottom step to a storage bin. Pry up the bottom step with a crowbar or claw hammer and screw a pair of hinges at the back of the step. The step becomes the lid for your new storage space. This is a great spot to tuck away tools, batteries, or spare lightbulbs.

■ HALL CLOSETS

My hall closet is so jammed that it is hard to find my coat

TRANSFER ITEMS TO OTHER STORAGE SPACE To reduce the clutter in your front closet, stop using it for anything except coats, hats, gloves, and scarves. Vacuum cleaners, kitchen supplies, spare lightbulbs, and other pantry or cleaning items should go somewhere else. Then begin periodically purging old or outgrown coats and donating them to Goodwill, the Salvation Army, or another charity. If the closet is still overcrowded, move out-of-season coats and boots to the attic or to a lower-traffic closet in another part of the house. This way, everyone in the family will be able to find what they need quickly and make nimble exits for school and work. You will also have room for guests' coats.

I'm embarrassed to let guests open my hall closet

DECORATE THE CLOSET "Who says you can't decorate a hall closet?" asks one interior designer we consulted. Obviously, the first step to an attractive front-hall closet is to remove the junk. (See previous item.) But after that, why not decorate the closet with wallpaper, a coat of bright paint, an unusual light, or an intriguing piece of artwork on the inside of the closet door?

I don't have a hall closet

BUY A COATRACK Many apartments and small homes don't have coat closets near the front door. Depending on your space, you can improvise a satisfactory way to handle family and guest coats, gloves, scarves, and hats. Buy a sturdy coat stand to keep by the front door, or install a row of hooks or pegs. A small table with a drawer or a compact chest of drawers can provide a place for gloves and such. Some hallways are large enough for an armoire to hold outerwear. Include an umbrella stand in the mix for rainy days.

My kids never hang their coats up

PUT HOOKS WITHIN REACH Your little ones may be staging a coat-hanging strike because the hooks are out of reach. On the inside of the hall closet or below your hallway row of pegs, install a second row of hooks at child height.

■ CLOTHES CLOSETS

Shoes have overrun my closet

Here are strategies for optimum shoe storage:

- Save up-front space for the three or four pairs of shoes you wear the most.
- Store and stack your shoes in clear plastic containers so you can quickly select the pair you want to wear. If you can't bring yourself to throw the cardboard shoe boxes out, label each box so you can easily identify what's in it without lifting the lid.
- Each time you buy a new pair of shoes, throw out or give away two or three pairs of old or rarely used shoes.

TRICKS OF THE TRADE

Creating More Storage in the Front-Hall Closet

- If you don't already have some, install high shelving near the ceiling, above the coat rack.
- Install a second coat rack below the main one—this will be the perfect height for hanging the kids' jackets.
- Make sure to use the back of the closet door for pegs, coat hooks, small shelves, or other storage options.

**PROBLEM
STOPPER**

They're on a Roll
Nobody understands bedroom space constraints better than Hal and Judy Abrams. They travel throughout the United States, hosting a radio show that touts the benefits of adopting dogs and cats. Their home—and their workspace—is a 36-foot (11-meter) recreational vehicle.

With the radio studio inside their RV, space was at a premium. Two of the first items sacrificed were their iron and ironing board. Here's how they save on closet space and still keep wrinkles to a minimum: As soon as their shirts and pants come out of the dryer, the Abramses roll them up, to compress their volume, and store them in see-through plastic containers. If any clothes get badly wrinkled, they hang the garments in their shower and let the steam smooth the material.

- When shoes and boots are out of season, store them in boxes under your bed.

My closet is bursting with clothes

MAKE UNDERBED STORAGE BINS Try this simple way to store more clothes and shoes in your bedroom. Buy some inexpensive small casters at the hardware store. Screw them to the bottoms of shallow wooden boxes or drawers from an old dresser. (Make sure the drawers, with casters attached, will fit under the bed.) You can fill the drawers with seasonal clothes because they can easily be rolled out when you need an article of clothing.

I need even more clothes storage

USE BIG BASKETS Creative use of baskets can make up for a lack of closet space. Large wicker baskets with flat lids that look like trunks can easily hold more folded sweaters or T-shirts than a drawer. Plus you can use these baskets as bedside tables or coffee tables.

I don't have much room to store out-of-season clothes

USE VACUUM SEAL BAGS You can store seldom-used clothes (such as evening gowns and tuxedos) in very little space if you use special vacuum-seal bags, which are available at hardware stores. Put the clothing in the special plastic bag and use a vacuum cleaner to suck all the air out before sealing the bag. The clothes compress and are totally safe from insects and dust.

I can't find my favorite sweater

REORGANIZE YOUR CLOSET Instead of grouping all your clothing by type (that is, sweaters together, pants together, and shirts together), group clothes by frequency of use. Put your most-used items on the most accessible shelves, which are those at waist height. Seldom-worn clothes should go on top shelves. Clothes you wear fairly frequently should be stacked on shelves below your waist. You will discover that this system can save you time in finding things.

■ PANTRIES

My pantry isn't big enough

ADD SHELVES TO YOUR DOOR If your walls and floor are jammed with cans and boxes, look behind you: Is the back of your pantry door being used effectively? Install narrow shelves or hanging racks on the door to hold frequently needed items such as spices, condiments, and snacks. (Don't hang anything too heavy on the door, or the weight may cause it to drag on the floor.)

I'm wasting space under the stairs

USE THE BACK OF THE CLOSET Closets under stairwells often serve as convenient pantries. However, the space in back, where the ceiling slopes down to toddler height, sometimes goes to waste. Here are ways to use that space:

- Store out-of-season items you don't need very often, such as jumbo lobster pots or holiday lights, in the back.
- Buy boxes or bins on wheels, so that the items in back can be rolled out.
- Install a second light in the back to make it easier to see what's lurking there. A battery-powered camping light will do.

I need a wine cellar

USE THE BASEMENT Unless you're a certified oenophile, you probably don't keep the quantity or quality of vintage wines to justify a full wine cellar, which is a small refrigerator calibrated to keep wine at a consistent temperature and humidity. To store wines properly, you just need a dark, cool space. (The optimal conditions are constant temperatures of between 54° and 63°F (12° to 17°C) and between 60 and 80 percent humidity.) Wine should not be jostled, so keep it in a part of the basement where the traffic is low. Since wine bottles should be stored on their side, look for adjustable racks that will fit on shelves or stand on the floor. One more suggestion: Strong odors can infiltrate an aging bottle of wine, so keep your wine far from the garlic cloves and ammonia.

PROBLEM STOPPER

How to Save Plastic Bags Neatly for Reuse
Whether you save them for recycling, for lunch bags, or for pooper-scoopers, plastic bags quickly pile up. Here's a great solution from professional organizer Maxine Harris of Winona, Texas. She taped shut a medium-sized cardboard box and covered the top with attractive contact paper. Then she cut a hole 4 inches (10-centimeters) in diameter in the top. She says she can stuff an "endless amount" of plastic bags in this box, yet it's easy to reach in and grab a bag when she needs one.

Another way to make a holder is to sew a long cloth tube, elasticized at each end, that can be hung on a hook. You stuff bags in at the top and pull them out the bottom.

PART THREE

Kitchen and Cooking

Key ingredients go missing. Pot roasts dive for the floor. Unexpected guests show up for dinner. Considering the hurricane of logistics that sweep through the kitchen every day, it's no wonder this room is the center of crises in the home. Sure, you can always order out in a pinch, but hold the phone—we have a host of ingenious solutions for the most common culinary catastrophes.

Food Troubles

■ SAUCES

My sauce is too thin

THICKEN IT WITH FLOUR The simplest and quickest way to thicken a too-thin sauce (or a stew) without altering its taste is to add some flour. Knead together equal parts soft butter and flour. About a quarter of a cup each should be enough for most dishes. Now make marble-sized balls out of the paste and drop them into the simmering sauce one at a time. They'll dissolve instantly without lumps. Keep adding flour pellets until you get the consistency you want.

If you have the more expensive, instant-blending type of flour, whisk a few tablespoons of it into three times as much liquid removed from the pot and pour a small amount of the mixture into the sauce while it's at a low boil. Stir it in, turn the heat down, let it simmer a few minutes, and then test the consistency. If it's still too thin, turn up the flame, pour some more dissolved flour in, and repeat the routine.

BOIL IT DOWN Often when you have a thin sauce, it's because you added too much water. If that's the case, thicken it up by boiling it down. Turn the flame up high and leave the lid off. Keep stirring, so that the sauce doesn't stick and clump up on the bottom. Let the excess water evaporate until the liquid level is where you want it. Since only water was lost, you'll have a thicker sauce.

If you have a watery stew that needs to be boiled down, separate the liquid from the meat and vegetables. Either take the solids out with a slotted spoon or pour the whole dish into another pot through a colander. Boil the liquid down to the thickness you want and then put the meat and vegetables back in. This way, you won't overcook the meat and vegetables.

If your spaghetti sauce resembles red soup, the fast fix is to add tomato paste—half a can at a time.

My spaghetti sauce is watery

ADD TOMATO PASTE If you want thick spaghetti sauce rather than red soup, the simple solution is to stir in more tomato paste. But don't overdo it—add half a small can or less at a time until you get the thickness you want. If you don't have time to let the sauce simmer more, add a teaspoon or so of sugar. The sugar will add a hint of caramelizing flavor, making the sauce taste as if it's been cooking longer. Also put in a pinch of baking soda; it will neutralize the acid and bring out the tomato flavor. But if you do have time, let the additional tomato paste simmer in the sauce for a while, then taste to see whether it needs any last-minute seasoning.

ADD FLOUR Tomato paste has the advantage of being compatible with the spaghetti sauce taste. But an alternative is to add flour, as you would to thicken a sauce or gravy. Don't just dump the flour into the sauce, though. Either make flour-butter pellets, as described in the previous problem, or spoon a quarter cup of the sauce into a measuring cup, add a tablespoon or so of flour, and blend well; then mix that into the sauce.

My gravy is lumpy

STRAIN OUT THE LUMPS AND RETHICKEN Gravy develops lumps because the thickening agent—flour, cornstarch, or arrowroot—didn't get incorporated into the liquid. And once that stuff balls up and declares its independence, nothing will change its mind. You can't whisk away or press out or otherwise urge those lumps to dissolve. There is a simple solution to gravy lumps: Get rid of them! All you need is a good-sized colander with holes big enough for the liquid but not the lumps to seep through. Set it over a container, fill it halfway with gravy, and gently press the liquid through with the underside of a ladle or big spoon. Throw away the lumpy material that's left behind. Repeat until you have strained all the gravy.

To get the thickness back (without lumps this time), put about as much flour as you think you lost into a small bowl. Add enough water, wine, or stock to dissolve the flour with whisking. Now slowly stir this slurry into the simmering, but not boiling, gravy. Add a little at a time and let the gravy cool slightly each time before checking the thickness.

■ SOUPS AND STEWS

My soup has zero taste

ADD A BOUILLON CUBE Surprisingly, the culprit often isn't inadequate seasoning or the wrong mix of ingredients. A soup usually

TRICKS OF THE TRADE

Keeping Sugar from Clumping in the Bag
When your sugar forms clumps, the problem is humidity. Whether you are dealing with white or brown sugar, you can prevent clumping the way the chefs at the Four Seasons Hotel in Toronto do: Put a slice of bread in your sugar bag. The bread sucks up any moisture, leaving the sweet stuff ready to spoon. Change the bread every two or three days to prevent mold.

Similarly, you can add a few grains of rice to your saltshaker to prevent the salt from clumping. They recommend $1/2$ teaspoon of rice to $1/4$ cup of salt for best results.

**How Not to Overcook
Veggies Ever**
Give fresh vegetables like
green beans and broccoli
your full attention and
you'll never overcook
them again.

1. Before you do any-
thing else to prepare
your meal, drop your
chosen vegetables into
boiling water. Pull them
out before they're done.
(You've just "blanched"
your vegetables.)

2. Immediately plunge
them into a bowl of ice
water. (You've just pre-
vented your vegetables
from continuing to cook
while locking in the color
and taste.)

3. After the vegetables
have cooled down—a
minute or two—take
them out of the ice water
and drain them in a
colander over a bowl.
Forget about them while
you cook dinner.

4. When everything else is
finished, dunk the vegetables in boiling water again
for less than a minute.
Drain, season, and serve.

tastes bland because the original broth or stock is weak. You can take care of that by whisking a beef, chicken, or vegetable bouillon cube (or two, if it's a big pot) in a little hot water to dissolve it and then stirring it into the soup. Just like that, you've cranked up the taste without changing the soup's volume or altering the ingredients. This flavor booster works in a stew or sauce, too.

ADD MORE SPICES To bump up the taste a little more, there's no law against adding more generous amounts of whatever spices were called for. Recipes tend to be conservative in their spice recommen-dations, and what's right for a cookbook aimed at a mass market may not be right for your taste buds. Add and taste till you're satisfied.

ADD A LITTLE SALT "Salty" doesn't equal "tasty," but salt does bring out flavors lurking in your sauce, stew, or soup. So give the pot a few shakes of salt, stir it in, let the liquid simmer a bit longer, and give it a taste.

My soup is choking with fat

USE AN ICE-COLD LADLE With almost any cooking liquid—whether it's a soup, sauce, or stew—fat con-geals at the top as it cools. So here's a shortcut that the pros use to cool it: Fill your biggest metal ladle with ice. Run the ice-filled ladle bowl along the surface of the liquid. Push the ladle down far enough to submerge most of the outside but not so far that liquid spills into the ice in the ladle. Fat will stick to the cold underside of the ladle. Wipe it away with a paper towel and keep skimming, adding more ice as needed to keep the ladle really cold. You won't get every drop of fat out this way, but you'll definitely end up with a more artery-friendly soup or sauce.

PUT IT IN THE REFRIGERATOR If you have enough time, cool the dish in the fridge for a few hours. Then simply skim the coagulated fat off the top with a spoon. Sometimes fat forms so firmly that you can actually lift it off.

■ OVERCOOKED FOOD

My vegetables have turned to mush

CONVERT THEM INTO A CREAMY SOUP Nobody likes mushy broccoli or asparagus, or any other overboiled or oversteamed vegetable. But everyone likes cream of vegetable soup. The solution, then, is to turn your overcooked veggies into a creamy soup. And it's easy to do.

1. Drain those limp vegetables and throw them into a blender. Just a few pulses will yield a vegetable puree that nobody will ever suspect was once a soggy disappointment.
2. Bring a similar volume of chicken or vegetable stock to a boil in a pot on the stove; then turn the heat down.
3. Stir in the vegetable puree, add salt and any seasonings you want, and let it simmer for five minutes. There's no need to add cream or milk. But if it's not smooth enough, run the whole thing through the blender again.

Serve the soup in a wide, flat soup bowl to further the illusion that you'd planned this treat from the beginning.

Help! I burned the meat

The only problem with overcooked meat (once the burned parts are removed) is dryness. So your mission is simple: Make it moist again.

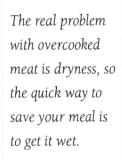

MAKE A CASSEROLE Here's the quick solution to meat you left on the grill or in the oven too long:

1. Trim off the burned outer layer and discard it.
2. Cut the dry interior meat into thin slices.
3. Put the pieces in a casserole dish with some beef broth and your favorite salsa. There's your moisture.
4. Stir in some pinto or black beans from a can and, if you like, some canned or frozen corn kernels and some chopped onion. Let it sit for a few minutes. Warm the mixture on the stovetop.
5. Grate a thick layer of hard cheese on top. Put the whole thing, uncovered, in the oven long enough to melt the cheese. Serve with warm tortillas or tortilla chips.

The real problem with overcooked meat is dryness, so the quick way to save your meal is to get it wet.

SHRED THE MEAT AND PUT IT IN GRAVY Here's another solution for burned meat: After you've trim off the charred outer layer, shred the dry interior meat with a fork or your fingers. (It should shred easily in the state it's in.) Stir the meat into a cup or two of barbecue sauce, canned gravy, or real gravy made by mixing flour with the roast's drippings. Then warm the dish on the stove for five minutes. Pour it over potatoes or biscuits.

■ TOUGH MEAT

I know this roast won't be tender

BRAISE A LARGE CUT If you have a large piece of meat that you know is tough, remember these three basics for tenderizing it:

- Use liquid.
- Keep the heat extremely low.
- Cook it slowly.

Say you have a 5-pound (2-kilogram) chunk of boneless chuck—tough stuff from one of the hardest-working parts of a cow, the shoulder. If you roast it, it's going to get even tougher. Instead:

1. Rub the meat with flour, salt and pepper it, and brown it briefly on all sides in hot shortening in a flameproof casserole dish on the stovetop.
2. Turn off the heat and pour in a cup of seasoned broth, stock, tomato juice, or wine along with some extra flavorings, such as chopped onion, crushed garlic cloves, thyme, or other herbs.
3. Cover the casserole dish, set the burner on low simmer, and let the meat cook that way for at least three hours. Turn the meat once or twice, but never let the liquid boil.

What you've done is braise the meat—that is, you've cooked it very slowly in liquid. The result will be a tender, moist delight (essentially a pot roast) that you'd never have dreamed could result from the monster you started with.

MARINATE IT AND MAKE A CASSEROLE You can also get tender results by cutting tough meat into large cubes and making a stew—the very essence of low, slow cooking in liquid. But there are still other options. For example, steep that tough chunk of chuck or rump in a marinade containing some kind of acid, such as wine or vinegar. Try 2 cups of water, 1 cup of dry red wine, some salt, a sliced onion, and 1 or 2 teaspoons of some combination of the following: coriander, mustard, dill seed, allspice, bay leaves, cinnamon, ginger, and cloves. Bring the mixture to a boil on the stove and then turn off the heat and let it stand. When it has cooled down, pour the marinade over the meat in a glass bowl, seal the top with aluminum foil, and put it in the fridge overnight or, preferably, for two days.

When you're ready to cook the meat, reserve the marinade. Brown the meat in hot shortening on the stovetop. Then strain the marinade, pour the liquid over the meat, and let it cook for two hours in a 350° F (175° C) oven. You'll be amazed by the tenderness as well as the taste, which will be much like sauerbraten.

I'm afraid this steak will be tough as nails

POUND IT INTO A THIN MINUTE STEAK If you have sliced fresh meat (round steak, for example) that you fear is too tough, your best—and fastest—bet is to pound it into submission. Pounding itself will break up the tough fibers and sinew. Just lay the meat out flat on a wooden carving board and flail away with a meat mallet (or the bottom of a strong coffee mug) until the cuts are as thin as can be. Coat each slice generously with flour, cornmeal, or ground cornflakes (don't use an egg wash); then sear the meat for a minute of two on each side in hot oil over a burner turned to high. You'll end up with meat so tender you won't even need a knife.

■ TOO MUCH SALT

I overdid the salt in the soup

ADD MORE WATER There's a possibility that you didn't oversalt the soup. A lot of water may have evaporated during cooking, leaving an off-kilter salt-to-liquid ratio. If that seems to be the case and the liquid volume has shrunk noticeably, simply put water back in. Add it a little at a time, taste-testing as you go.

ADD POTATOES If the problem really is too much salt rather than not enough water, add potatoes to the soup, along with a bit more water or broth. If you're lucky enough to have discovered the excess saltiness while the soup is still at an early stage of cooking, you can add the cut-up raw potatoes directly to the pot. But if the soup is already cooked (or very nearly so), you'll want to turn it off and cook the potatoes in a separate pot before adding them. If you don't have potatoes, add another starch, such as noodles, (cooked) rice, or pasta, to absorb the excess salt.

TRICKS OF THE TRADE

Avoid Contamination from Meat
Bacteria from meat are easily transferred to other foods, and merely cleaning kitchen surfaces and utensils with soap and water will not prevent contamination.

The solution: Mix $\frac{1}{8}$ teaspoon of unscented household chlorine bleach with 1 cup of cold water in a spray bottle and label it as sanitizing solution. When you've finished preparing meat, clean all surfaces—cutting board, counter, utensils, and such—with dishwashing liquid and hot water. Then spray them with the sanitizing solution and wipe with a paper towel.

ADD MORE OF ALL INGREDIENTS You can also increase the volume of the entire recipe, adding more of all the ingredients (except salt, of course) in their original proportions. Like the potatoes, the ingredients can be raw or cooked separately, depending on the stage at which you catch the problem.

I oversalted the meat

ADD SOME SUGAR To pull a cut of meat back from the salty abyss, just sprinkle a pinch of sugar over it. It may seem a little strange to put sugar on meat, but the idea is to keep the amount small enough that you don't really taste it. At the same time, the sugar will subtly offset the excess salt.

I used too much salt in the vegetables

ADD SUGAR TO VEGGIES, TOO A touch of sugar is actually recommended to bring out the natural taste of vegetables, so adding a little bit to counteract saltiness is not such a radical idea. Or try a splash of vinegar or lemon juice. It probably won't neutralize the salt as completely as sugar will, but it'll give a slight edge to the taste so that your taste buds won't focus on the salt.

■ HOT SPICY FOODS

My dish is too hot for anyone

INCREASE THE NONSPICY INGREDIENTS The most common reason for an overly spicy dish is that you added too much liquid hot sauce or hot chili powder to your dish. The fast fix is to add more of whatever's not hot. If it's a chili dish, add more beans, beef broth, or meat. For any sauce or other stirrable dish that's too hot, increase the proportion of everything in the recipe except the hot stuff.

SERVE WITH A STARCH For further fire-extinguishing, serve your spicy dish over rice or with tortillas and sour cream. There's a reason such things are often on the same plate as spicy Indian, Chinese, Thai, or Mexican dishes—they blunt the burn.

PICK OUT THE HOT CHILI PIECES Another reason for an overspiced dish is that you've put diced or sliced jalapeño, serrano, or habañero chilies right into the dish (for instance, a tamale pie, Thai vegetables, or any other chili-loaded recipe). There's a quick remedy for this problem. Get in there with a spoon or fork and remove all the chili pieces. Put the extracted chili pieces in a small glass bowl and let the fire-eaters serve themselves.

Call the fire department— I just bit into a chili

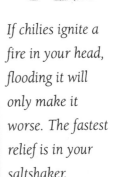

DON'T GRAB THE WATER Most people instinctively react to this emergency by taking the worst possible course of action—namely, flooding their mouths with water, beer, or a soft drink. The sting in chilies comes from a chemical called capsaicin, which does not dissolve easily in water. So sloshing liquids around in your mouth will only spread the pain.

If chilies ignite a fire in your head, flooding it will only make it worse. The fastest relief is in your saltshaker.

REACH FOR SALT, MILK, OR BREAD In Mexico, where they *know* what hot chilies can do to unsuspecting mouths, three instant chili-extinguishing remedies have proved themselves over the centuries:

- Salt is the quickest and most reliable pain reliever for anybody who is, as they say, *enchilado.*
- Milk, cream, yogurt, or cheese will also help, thanks to the proteins known as caseins in dairy products. Caseins disrupt the bond between that burning chemical capsaicin and your taste receptors, giving your tongue a break.
- A piece of white bread, a cracker, or a tortilla popped into your mouth will provide some relief, too, by absorbing the pain-producing capsaicin.

■ MISSING INGREDIENTS

I need buttermilk for pancakes

ADD LEMON JUICE TO MILK Most homes don't keep buttermilk handy in the fridge anymore. But it still shows up in recipes. You can substitute sour milk for buttermilk. To make it, just add 1 tablespoon of lemon juice or white vinegar to 1 cup of regular whole milk and let it stand for 15 minutes. Use the amount the recipe calls for.

USE YOGURT OR SOUR CREAM Depending on the recipe and your preference, you can also use an equal amount of plain yogurt or use

Getting a Sneak Preview
Once you've baked a meat loaf or similar meat dish, there's nothing you can do to adjust the seasoning. So before you put a meat loaf in the oven, steal a little piece and make a patty the size of a quarter. Cook it in a pan with a touch of oil. (You don't want to be eating raw meat, which isn't safe and may not reveal the true taste of the final product anyway.)

Now give it a taste. If it's not flavored the way you want it, adjust the seasoning of the dish. Retest with another fried patty if you're still not sure. Then go ahead and bake, confident that there will be no surprises when it's done.

sour cream, thinned with milk to a pourable consistency, as a substitute for buttermilk.

I'm out of baking powder

MAKE YOUR OWN BAKING POWDER If you have cream of tartar and baking soda, make your own baking powder by mixing ¼ teaspoon of baking soda with ½ teaspoon of cream of tartar, which will yield the equivalent of 1 teaspoon of baking powder. Unlike commercial baking powder, your homemade baking powder will start using up its leavening power as soon as it mixes with liquid. So get that batter into the oven right away.

USE BAKING SODA AND AN ACIDIC LIQUID If you don't have cream of tartar, use baking soda and an acidic liquid. Your choices: sour cream, buttermilk, yogurt, or a citrus juice, such as lime or lemon. Add the baking soda to the dry ingredients, using about one-quarter the amount of the baking powder called for. When it's time to blend in the liquid ingredients, add 4 fluid ounces (120 milliliters) of your acidic liquid for every quarter teaspoon of baking soda you used.

I'm out of cinnamon, ginger, or other spices

SUBSTITUTE ONE SPICE FOR ANOTHER If you don't have a spice that's called for in a recipe, substitute a similar one:

If you're out of...	try using...
Allspice	Equal amounts of cinnamon, cloves, and nutmeg
Caraway seeds	Anise seeds
Basil	Oregano, marjoram, thyme, rosemary, or savory
Cardamom	Ginger
Cayenne pepper	Ground chili peppers
Chervil	Parsley or tarragon
Chili powder	Cumin plus a dash of hot sauce
Cinnamon	¼ as much nutmeg or allspice
Cloves	Cinnamon, nutmeg, allspice, ginger, or mace
Fennel seeds	Anise seeds
Ginger	Mace, nutmeg, allspice, cloves, or cinnamon
Italian seasoning	Any mixture of oregano, thyme, basil, rosemary, savory, or marjoram, plus a little ground red pepper
Nutmeg	Allspice, mace, ginger, cloves, or cinnamon
Poultry seasoning	Sage mixed with rosemary, thyme, or marjoram
Rosemary	Savory, oregano, thyme, basil, rosemary, or marjoram
Sage	Thyme
Tarragon	Chervil or fennel seed

The important thing to remember is that most sweet spices (cinnamon, nutmeg, allspice, cloves, ginger, and mace) can be substituted for one another. And the same goes for herbs associated with Italian and other Mediterranean cooking (basil, oregano, thyme, rosemary, and marjoram). When making spice switches, start by using half the amount the recipe calls for and then add more (or another spice) until you're happy with the taste.

I just ran out of barbecue sauce

MAKE YOUR OWN You probably have everything you need in your kitchen cabinets. Start with a classic basic recipe:

1½ cup ketchup
1 cup cider vinegar
⅓ cup vegetable oil
⅓ cup Worcestershire sauce
½ cup firmly packed brown sugar
3 tablespoons prepared yellow mustard
3 cloves of garlic, minced
Juice of 1 lemon

Combine the ingredients in a nonreactive (that is, stainless steel, glass, enamel-coated, or nonstick) saucepan and heat slowly—for about 15 minutes—to blend flavors. Makes about 3 cups.

To personalize the sauce, substitute tomato sauce or paste, honey, molasses, brown mustard, or lime or orange juice for their obvious counterparts. Or add smoke flavoring, chili powder, paprika, hot sauce, chopped and sautéed onion or celery, celery seed, cumin, French or Western salad dressing, or even ground coffee.

The recipe calls for white wine and I'm out of it

USE WHITE WINE VINEGAR Try this quick substitute: Dilute white wine vinegar with water in a 50-50 ratio. Add a little sugar and use this concoction instead of the white wine called for. Nobody will be able to tell the difference.

USE DRY VERMOUTH Another solution: Keep a bottle of dry vermouth in the kitchen and substitute it whenever white wine is needed, using only half the amount called for. Add a little water or broth to make up for the smaller volume.

■ FLAVOR FAILURES

My perfectly cooked meat has no taste

LIVEN UP THE SAUCE If your bland-tasting meat happens to be in a stew or other liquid, there's a quick solution. Heighten the taste of that sauce or gravy, and nobody will notice that the meat is bland. You can do this by adding a bouillon cube, more spices, or salt, as described in "My soup has zero taste" on page 169.

MAKE A TASTY CONDIMENT TO GO ON IT What about meats that aren't swimming in a sauce that can be jazzed up? What if you've prepared a roast, steak, or other stand-alone meat cut to lean and tender perfection, yet it's weak in the taste department?

If your problem is an underseasoned meat loaf, a good solution is to yank out the steak sauce, salt, and ketchup. But your perfectly cooked roast, steak, or veal deserves better. Give it its own exotic little brush-on sauce that will garnish it subtly but with an unmistakable zing. Here are three quick, simple, surefire meat rescuers:

- Mix salsa, as spicy as you wish, with an equal amount of apricot preserves. Heat in the microwave just long enough to marry the flavors (about a minute), and spread lightly on your meat slices.
- Put together a sweet-and-sour sauce by blending apricot preserves with apple cider vinegar to taste, again heating for just a minute in the microwave.
- Mix a bit of honey, horseradish, mustard, and fresh chopped mint (or dried mint mixed with fresh parsley—or even mint jelly) to taste. This is sure to add pizzazz to the blandest meat.

Any of these three taste enhancers can be helped along with a little lemon juice, vinegar, ground red pepper, curry powder, or cumin. Add small amounts at a time and taste.

My potato salad tastes too mayonnaisey

ADD BREAD CRUMBS Once you've stirred too much mayonnaise into your potato salad, carrot salad, or fruit salad, you can't really take it out. But you *can* stir in a liberal amount of plain bread crumbs as a quick fix. They'll absorb the extra mayonnaise as they disappear into the dressing. Don't worry; your cold dish won't taste like bread crumbs—and it won't taste like pure mayonnaise either.

■ NO TIME TO COOK

I don't have four hours to cook a turkey

BOIL THE TURKEY FIRST Assuming you have a fresh turkey or one that you've defrosted, you can cut the cooking time in half—with the bonus of serving a bird that is tastier and juicier than usual—by boiling the bird before baking it. Here's how to proceed with a typical 12-pound (5.4 kilogram) turkey:

1. Place the turkey in a large pot and add enough cold water to cover it. Toss in salt, pepper, cut-up onion, and a total of 2 tablespoons of combined parsley, thyme, or other herbs.
2. Bring the pot to a boil on the stovetop and then lower the heat to a simmer (with tiny bubbles rising along the side of the pot). Simmer uncovered for one hour; then drain the turkey.
3. Prepare the turkey to roast as you normally would. Roast at 400° F (200° C) and check for doneness after an hour. (Pull a leg away from the body enough that you can puncture the inner thigh near the hip joint. If there's no blood, the turkey is done.)

The result will be a succulent, moist turkey, in half the normal cooking time! Try it if you're tired of turkey the consistency of polystyrene foam plastic.

■ MARGINAL FOODS

My fruit is getting too ripe

TURN THEM INTO A RAW PUREE As long as those peaches, plums, strawberries, or other fruits aren't rotten or moldy, why waste them? Cut away any parts that look particularly bad, but don't toss anything out just because it's a little soft or mushy. Throw the fruit in the blender, add some sugar, and turn it into a delicious puree that you can blend into salad dressings, use instead of syrup on pancakes, or pour over ice cream, pie, or other desserts.

Believe it or not, you'll get a better-tasting bird and it will cook faster if it gets a hot bath before roasting.

MAKE A COOKED PUREE For flavor variation, cook down the fruit puree by simmering it in a pan for a few minutes and then letting it cool. Perhaps add food coloring or some brightly colored juice. Freeze whatever you can't use right away in sealable, portion-size plastic bags.

My salad greens are a little withered

SOAK THEM IN WARM WATER Slightly wilted lettuce, spinach, and other leafy salad greens are still good; they've just lost water. They will perk up if left in a pan of warm water for an hour. Then drain them, splash them with cold water, and let them drain again in a colander. When no more water drips out, shake them dry as best you can or use a salad spinner. Your greens will be resuscitated.

My cheese is moldy

JUST CUT OFF THE MOLD That moldy surface may look like a major problem, but it's usually not. Cut away the moldy areas and enjoy the clean cheese that's left.

Be careful not to reinfect the cheese.

- Don't slice the cheese with the same knife or cheese slicer that you used to remove the mold. Wash the utensil first if you want to reuse it.
- Don't set the cheese back on the cutting board where the moldy cheese sat. Wash the board first.
- Don't put the cheese back in the same packaging, which may harbor mold. Toss out the old wrapper and use fresh plastic wrap.

WORLD-CLASS FIX

You're Alone in the Kitchen

The late Julia Child, the noted TV chef, took the snobbery out of French cuisine and made it fun and easy for amateur cooks across the globe. She also once imparted a wonderful all-purpose solution to many a kitchen woe.

One time, Child was demonstrating how to flip a patato pancake on her popular television show when she accidently spilled the contents of the pan on the stovetop. As viewers watched in amazement, she promptly scooped up the spill and put it back in her pan and continued cooking, advising her audience, "You can always pick it up if you're alone in the kitchen. Who's going to see it?"

The message was clear: What people don't know won't hurt them. As long as you are being sanitary, a so-called kitchen disaster is no disaster at all.

Serving Glitches

■ TOO MANY GUESTS

My china is for eight; dinner's for ten

MAKE THE MISMATCH LOOK PLANNED If the dinner's informal, chances are nobody will care that two of the plates come from a different set. If dinner is more formal, consider this quick solution: Instead of using your full eight-piece formal china and two everyday settings, use five and five. Alternate the settings: formal, everyday, formal, everyday. The esthetic effect will be pleasing and look as if you planned it that way.

I cooked for six but ten showed up

MAKE EXTRA PASTA AND EAT FAMILY STYLE The nanosecond you find out that there will be more mouths than you cooked for, get some water boiling for pasta. Once the pasta is cooked and drained, stir in a can of undiluted, condensed mushroom soup (or something similar), add minced garlic, season liberally, and put in plenty of grated parmesan cheese or other grated cheese, the harder the better. Without delaying the meal much, you now have a delicious and filling dish that will guarantee that nobody will leave the table feeling the least bit hungry.

The second you find out there will be more mouths to feed than you expected, get some water on the stove and boil pasta.

Pasta is not the only solution. If you broiled six steaks, for example, what do you serve the extra four people? A simple and quick solution is to convert your meal to family style. Put the entire meal on the table in serving dishes and encourage your guests to help themselves. Cut the steaks or other main meat dish into appetizing slices or portions and arrange them on a serving platter. Display the vegetables in a casserole dish or vegetable bowl with a serving spoon. By some tacit rule of manners, people will help themselves to less meat than they would have eaten if served individually. And with the extra pasta and a generous basket of bread, what seemed to be not enough will turn out to be a generous and enjoyable feast.

■ SPECIAL DEMANDS GUEST

Now he tells me he's a vegetarian

ASK YOUR GUEST WHAT HE WANTS TO EAT Just as you're putting the final touches on your veal cutlets, you get word that the guest of honor follows a strict meatless diet. What do you do? Actually, there's only one person who can answer that question—your vegetarian guest. Ask the guest what you can prepare for him. It probably won't be the first time this has happened, so your guest may be ready with a suggestion or two. Take him into your kitchen, apologize for not knowing, throw open your fridge and cupboards, and say, "Here's what I have. Let's see what we can do." Not only will your guest eat happily, but the two of you will have established an intimacy that may have been the point of the dinner in the first place.

Only one person can say what your vegetarian guest would prefer instead of the steak you cooked. Feel free to ask him.

■ LAST-MINUTE FOOD DIFFICULTIES

The butter's too hard to spread

MICROWAVE IT VERY BRIEFLY Your microwave oven will take care of that in 15 seconds—but no more than that. Put the cold butter on a dish and set the microwave on the defrost setting. Remember that the inside of the bar will get soft sooner than the outside, so be careful not to overdo it.

I squirt everybody when I squeeze my lemon

TWIST A FORK IN THE LEMON Squeezing a lemon into your drink or onto fish without embarrassing consequences is all a matter of control. To squeeze lemon juice into your glass or on food:

1. Take the lemon slice in one hand and your fork in the other.
2. Hold the lemon over your glass or food and stick the fork into the pulp. Then move the fork from side to side and twist it.
3. Remove the fork, pierce another spot, and twist again.

Repeat this process until the lemon slice is used up. There will be not one unfortunate squirt.

■ WINE AND BEVERAGES

The party punch is sickeningly sweet

ADD LEMON JUICE OR DRY WINE Don't add water. By the time you dilute the punch enough to tone down the sugar, you're stuck with a tepid, watery swill. Instead, add a tart juice—lemon or grapefruit—a little at a time until the punch's sugar ratio is just right. A dry wine will produce equally good results.

The same strategy works for cocktails that are too sweet. You can even use lemon juice or dry wine to reduce the sugary taste of desserts such as pudding and pie filling.

I don't have a corkscrew for the wine

DIG IT OUT WITH A SCREWDRIVER If you have a Swiss Army Knife, it most likely has a corkscrew. If you don't, use a screwdriver tip to dig out the cork bit by bit. Once you've removed about half of it, you should be able to push the rest into the bottle and decant the wine— just as you would if the cork broke off during a normal opening process, as described in the problem below.

USE A LONG SCREW Round up utility pliers, a nail, a screwdriver, and a long (2-inch [5-centimeter] or more) wood screw. Place the tip of the nail against the center of the cork and use the pliers to work it in about a half-inch to create a starter hole for your screw. You can also do this with an ice pick. Drive the screw into the hole, leaving enough protruding to grip with the pliers. Pull on the screw with the pliers, dragging the cork steadily straight out of the bottle. If the screw pulls free, make a new starter hole to the side of the old one and try again. Or, if the cork is far enough out, grab the sides of the cork with pliers and pull, twisting the cork slightly to loosen it.

The cork broke off in the wine bottle

TRY AGAIN WITH THE CORKSCREW First try to twist your corkscrew into the remaining half of the cork. It's a little tricky, because the now-jagged surface of the cork is below the level of the bottle opening. But often you can penetrate the cork enough to pull it out.

PUSH THE CORK IN If you accidentally push the remaining cork into the bottle, don't worry. That was Plan B anyway. By pushing the

PROBLEM STOPPER

Always Have a Corkscrew Handy
To avoid the situation of not having a corkscrew when you need it, buy at least four wine openers. Keep one in the kitchen, one with your wine supply, one with your picnic gear, and one somewhere for just such an emergency. So supplied, you'll never have to dig out a wine cork again.

Add Life to a Dull Salad
Ho-hum salad? Here's a simple but zingy salad dressing that will make taste buds snap to attention, courtesy of Chief Warrant Officer 3 David J. Longstaff, team manager of U.S. Army Culinary Arts in Fort Lee, Virginia. It takes less than five minutes to make:

SUN-DRIED TOMATO BASIL VINAIGRETTE

1 tbsp sun-dried toma-
    toes (dry or
    oil-packed), chopped
1 tbsp fresh garlic,
    peeled
2 tbsp white wine
    vinegar (or white
    vinegar)
4 tbsp lemon juice,
    freshly squeezed
1 tbsp grated lemon
    peel
1 tbsp fresh basil,
    chopped
1 cup extra virgin olive
    oil
¼ tsp salt
    Black pepper, to taste

Blend the sun-dried tomatoes and garlic in a blender until smooth (about one minute). Add the remaining ingredients and blend until smooth (45 seconds to one minute). Cover and refrigerate until ready to use. Makes four servings.

remaining cork into the bottle, you've successfully opened the bottle and can pour the wine. Because cork bits may be swimming around in the wine, pour the wine through a cone coffee filter into a decanter or a clean glass pitcher. If the floating cork makes it difficult to pour the wine, use a shish kebab skewer or chopstick to hold it at the bottom of the bottle.

Dinner's ready, and I forgot to chill the white wine

USE AN ICE BUCKET Don't put the wine in the freezer; wine bottles tend to get forgotten and end up freezing or exploding. Instead, fill a bucket half and half with ice and cold water and put the bottle in it up to its neck. You don't need a fancy wine bucket. Any clean bucket that's almost as tall as the bottle will do. Some swear that stirring salt into the ice and water helps the wine chill faster. In about ten minutes the ice-and-water treatment will chill your wine sufficiently. You want your white wine just cold enough to be light and fresh. Overchilling dulls the taste.

The red wine's too cold to serve

POUR IT INTO GLASSES Is it really too cold? True, most red wines are best served at or near room temperature. But that tradition began centuries ago, when houses lacked central heating, and the room temperature was considerably cooler than what we're used to today. It's usually just fine, and often preferable, to drink a red wine that's a little bit cool. If the bottle is really too cold (because it was stored it in the refrigerator or left out in the car in winter), open it and pour the wine into wineglasses, just as you normally would. The liquid will warm to room temperature much faster once transferred from the thick bottle into thinner, airy glasses.

WARM THE GLASS WITH YOUR HANDS To warm wine even faster, bring out your secret temperature-control tools—your hands. Wrapping them around the bowl of the wineglass will warm the glass and get your wine to the temperature you want surprisingly quickly. In fact, while wineglasses for white wine are made to be held by the stem (to keep the chill), the more bulbous wineglasses for red wine invite bowl-fondling, which raises the temperature and releases the aroma, enhancing the taste. If you have guests, show them how they can warm the glass with their cupped hands.

I think the wine has gone bad

DO A COMPARISON TEST Sometimes it's hard to tell whether that peculiar taste is indicative of wine gone bad or something you're just not used to. If you have another bottle of the same wine, open it and compare. If the second bottle undeniably tastes better, the first bottle has been found guilty.

GET ANOTHER OPINION If both bottles taste the same, or you don't have a second bottle, get a second opinion. If you get a definite thumbs-up or thumbs-down from your accomplice, consider the decision made. But if your helper is just as uncertain as you, err on the side of caution. Open something else and use the unproven bottle to cook with the next day.

■ DESSERT DISASTERS

My cake fell, my mousse is lumpy, my flan is tough

MAKE AN ICE CREAM TOPPING Desserts can turn into semidisasters: Cakes fall, bread puddings take on strange consistencies, mousses get lumpy, flans firm up to an eggy butte of toughness. Such emergencies are the reason you keep vanilla (preferably French) ice cream in the freezer. Stir the ice cream with a spoon to help it melt to a creamy sauce consistency (not a liquid). Add a little liqueur if you wish. Put individual servings of your dessert in

WORLD-CLASS GOOF

Champagne Surprise

A correspondent to wordbanquet.com tells of a family calamity of epic proportions. For a large Sunday luncheon, Mom had laid out a wonderful buffet for guests to enjoy. But before they could, Dad accidentally aimed the Champagne bottle at the fluorescent light above the table, launching a cork-missile that sent a shower of broken glass on the food below.

The fix? A second-best meal of barbecued chops found in the freezer, followed by a dessert that had survived in the refrigerator. Of course, this will never happen to you, because you know to drape a towel over the cork, point the Champagne bottle at empty ceiling space, and hold the cork steady as you twist the bottle, not the cork.

bowls, chop the portions up if that will help, and then cover each serving with a generous pour of the ice cream sauce. Maybe top it with a cherry. Your guests may not be sure what they're eating, but they'll know it's cool, sweet, and delicious.

My cake is just too rich and sweet

SERVE SMALL PORTIONS If you're worried that the density, butterfat, and sweetness of your chocolate cake are over the top, serve half as much as you normally would. Announce to the table, "This is extremely rich, so proceed with caution." Then add that there's plenty more for those who want it. But stall a bit before obliging guests who ask for seconds. Give their stomach signals enough time to reach their brains. After five minutes or so, offer second helpings. Your guests may have realized how full they are and changed their minds by then.

Smaller servings are also the best way to deal with too-rich main course offerings, such as quiches or casseroles. But you can correct rich sauces or cream soups by diluting them with vegetable or chicken soup stock. In these cases, the perceived richness is usually the work of butter, cream, or cheese. The thin stock will tone down the richness without diluting the taste.

My pie turned out so runny that the slices fall apart

MAKE A FAUX COBBLER There is a fast solution: Just spoon the entire pie into a bowl, break up the crust into medium-sized pieces, and call it a cobbler—that's essentially what it has become. Put a shot of whipped cream on top, and you'll hear your family and guests express their appreciation for the nice change of pace from the usual pie.

Cleanup Hassles

■ HARD-TO-CLEAN ITEMS

My coffee carafe has an ugly brown residue

USE ICE, SALT, AND LEMON The glass carafe that comes with your coffeemaker can quickly develop a brown, splotchy haze—especially when you leave it on for long periods of time. For the quickest cure, gather up ice, salt, and a lemon.

1. Fill the empty pot one-quarter of the way with ice.
2. Cut the lemon into quarters and squeeze two of the quarters into the pot.
3. Add 2 tablespoons of salt. Swirl the mixture in the pot for two minutes, and the inside surface will come blessedly clean. Rinse under the faucet.

The quickest cure for a brown, splotchy coffee carafe is ice, salt, and a lemon.

Tomato sauce stained my plastic container

LET THE SUN BLEACH IT OFF Simply take your stained plastic container—the one that sat in the fridge for a week with spaghetti sauce in it—out to the part of your patio or garden that gets the most sun. An apartment balcony or even a sunny window will do. Leave it there all day. When you retrieve it at sundown, the stain will be gone, and your plastic container will look like new.

The only difficult thing about this method of cleaning plastic containers is believing that anything so easy really works. But the sun is a great bleacher of tomato-based stains, which are precisely the stains that often won't scrub off. In fact, spaghetti-stained T-shirts and tablecloths will also come cleaner if you sun-dry them after washing.

USE A LITTLE BLEACH Of course, in some regions months can pass between sunny days. In that case, bleach is your best bet. Fill the container with water and a capful of household chlorine bleach and

PROBLEM STOPPER

Keeping Tomato Stains at Bay

Avoid tomato stains in the future by spraying the plastic container with a spray cooking oil, such as Pam, before spooning in the leftover spaghetti sauce or tomato soup. Or line the container bowl with plastic wrap (but never with aluminum foil, which the sauce will eat away). The surest stain-prevention strategy? Store your tomato-based sauces in glass jars with tight-fitting lids.

let it sit for at least an hour. With most heavy-duty plastic containers, the stain will be gone when you rinse it.

A sun or bleach bath will also work for white plastic spatulas. Remember, though, that they're usually made of rubber, so don't let them sit out in intense heat for long.

Burned-on food won't come off my pot

BOIL AND SOAK IT OFF The easy way to dislodge burned food from a pot or pan is to fill it with water and a little dishwashing soap. Bring the water to a boil, turn off the heat, and let it sit for at least 15 minutes. The burned food should now be soft enough to scrape off with a plastic scraper. Then scrub the bottom clean.

If this treatment doesn't work the first time, try it again. Stubborn burned-on food may need three boilings. For extra power, stir 2 or 3 teaspoons of salt into the water. Or add a spoonful of vinegar.

I can't get the cheese off the grater

USE AN OLD TOOTHBRUSH This is a pesky challenge whether the problem is cheese or lemon zest, especially with a grater's smallest holes. There's no way to scrub them without shredding whatever you're scrubbing with. Instead, use an old hard-bristled toothbrush. Get it wet and brush away the stuck bits, inside and outside, top to bottom. Then wash the grater and rinse.

■ GREASE AND FOOD SPLATTERS

My kitchen walls are stained and greasy

WASH PAINTED WALLS WITH A BLEACH SOLUTION Most kitchen walls are painted. To clean them, add ½ cup of household chlorine bleach to 1 gallon of water and use it to wipe down the walls with a sponge.

If that doesn't work, use a commercial wall cleaner, the concentrated kind that mixes in water and includes a degreaser and disinfectant. Spray it over the entire wall surface, let it sit for about ten minutes, and wipe it off with a soft towel.

WASH WALLPAPER WITH SOAPY WATER Wallpapered kitchen walls require a different strategy. First vacuum them, bottom to top, using the brush attachment. Then check whether your wallpaper is washable. Find a spot that nobody can see and use a sponge to wipe it gently with a mixture of water and dishwashing liquid. If the wall-paper is not damaged, you can clean the entire wall with the soapy water. Rinse it off right away with a clean sponge and fresh water.

For wallpaper that can't be washed, hardware stores sell special cleaners that spread on like paste and then wipe off. Test it first in an out-of-the-way spot.

The inside of my microwave is dirty

STEAM OFF THE SPLATTERS Water is all you need to get rid of those dried-on food splatters. And you don't need to scrub. Just put a glass of water in your microwave and heat it for about a minute, until the inside of the microwave is steamy. Then let the glass of water sit in the microwave for about 20 minutes with the door closed. The mois-ture condensing on the walls will soften the food residue. Finally, wipe off the residue with a sponge or paper towel.

You just spared yourself elbow grease—and saved yourself money. Most microwave oven cleaners are nothing more than bags that release steam when they're heated. Your glass of water accom-plished the same thing without added chemicals, extra trash, and unnecessary spending.

■ CUTTING BOARDS

My cutting board is too grimy to use

SAND AND OIL A WOODEN BOARD If scrubbing with soap and water won't clean a wooden cutting board, sanding will. Use a very fine-grit piece of sandpaper and press lightly. It won't take long to sand the entire surface. Finish with a coat of mineral oil or olive oil. That will keep the wood from drying out and give the board a pleasing sheen and color.

BLEACH A PLASTIC BOARD If you have a plastic cutting board, your best option is to spray on a 50-50 water-and-bleach solution (wear rubber gloves) and wipe it off with a paper towel. Bleach is not the best option for wooden cutting boards.

My wooden cutting board has deep cuts

SAND THEM DOWN If your cutting board looks like a map of the Grand Canyon, it's time to sand it. But unlike sanding for surface

TRICKS OF THE TRADE

Take the Stick Out of Your Cast-Iron Pan
Most cooks know that you should never use dish detergent on your cast-iron pan and never scrub it with anything abrasive if you want to maintain its well-oiled nonstick sur-face. Then how do you clean it? Use salt. If the pan won't rinse clean with water and a soft dish-cloth, rub it with a few tablespoons of salt and a paper towel and rinse. Then replenish the oil film by coating the inside sur-face with a dab of cooking oil.

cleaning, you need to start out with a larger-grit sandpaper for this task. The deeper the groove, the more roughness you want. Sand the whole surface evenly, not just the grooved areas. The trick is to use progressively smoother grits of sandpaper as the board starts smoothing out. (The higher the number, the smoother the sandpaper.) That way you won't dig into the board any more than you have to.

When you've finished sanding, rub on a coat of mineral oil or olive oil to keep the wood from drying out.

■ KITCHEN ODORS

My hands reek of fish

RUB YOUR HANDS WITH LEMON Whether you've handled fish in the kitchen or out on the water, here's a sure-handed way to get rid of that fishy odor: Cut a lemon in half and squeeze each half over your hands. Rub your hands together and rinse.

WASH WITH SOAP AND SUGAR If there's no lemon handy, pour a teaspoon of hand soap onto your palm. Add a tablespoon of sugar to the soap and rub the mixture thoroughly over your hands. Then rinse. The combination of soap and abrasion from the sugar will remove the odor.

That fishy smell lingering on your hands can be quickly killed by rubbing them on stainless steel.

RUB YOUR HANDS ON STAINLESS STEEL Some chefs swear by stainless steel as a fish-smell remover. Rub your hands on your stainless steel sink or fixtures and then wash your hands as usual.

The kitchen still smells like last night's dinner

BURN TOAST AND SET OUT AMMONIA There's nothing wrong with a kitchen smelling like food. But if a food odor becomes unpleasant, food chemists say the fast solution is to burn some toast. That's right: Burn a slice of bread in the toaster. That will absorb the lingering odor. Just make sure the bread doesn't catch fire. Of course, now you have a kitchen that smells like burned toast, but this odor at least won't linger long. Help it along by leaving a small, shallow bowl of ammonia out in the kitchen for a day.

SIMMER SOME ORANGE PEELS For a food odor that appears to be fading, you can take less drastic action by creating a pleasant smell to overwhelm the unpleasant one. To do that, simmer some orange peels and cinnamon in water for a few minutes. Then turn off the flame and leave the open pot of warm, sweet-smelling water on the stove all day.

My kitchen is filled with smoke

GET THE AIR CIRCULATING If you plan to eat in the kitchen and don't have time to wait—or if the smoke is working its way into the dining room where all your guests will soon assemble—it's time to spring into action.

Open all the kitchen doors and windows to get the air moving. Place a portable fan by a door or window that opens to the outdoors or that leads away from where the guests are or where you'll be eating. Face the fan so that it will blow out through a door or window. The room will be clear in a few minutes, or ten minutes max if you've really got a lot of smoke.

SET OUT A BOWL OF VINEGAR If you have time, there's a very easy way to rid a room of smoke odor. Set out a shallow bowl of vinegar, which will absorb the smell as the smoke dissipates.

▪ REFRIGERATORS

My refrigerator has smelled bad for days

ABSORB ODORS WITH BAKING SODA, COFFEE, OR CHARCOAL The first course of action is the obvious one: Quickly sniff out the mal-odorous culprit lurking in your fridge and get rid of it. To absorb lingering odors, baking soda really works. You may already keep an open box in your refrigerator to prevent bad smells. But to get rid of a smell that's already there, pour a cup of fresh baking soda onto a plate and leave it inside the fridge for a day. For stronger odors, fill a plate with dry unused coffee grounds and leave it in the fridge for several days. Freshly ground coffee beans work best. For sour odors, charcoal often works amazingly well. Just put several briquettes on a dish and let them soak up the odor for a few days.

PROBLEM STOPPER

Smaller Bottles Mean Smaller Spills
Make sure that future spills of oil or other kitchen liquids will be a matter of drops rather than rivers. Take some small glass bottles to a cookware shop (or get some nice new ones there) and buy pour tops that fit them. These are plastic attachments that control the flow and won't let any liquid gush out if the bottle tips over. (You've probably seen bartenders use them with liquor bottles.)

Funnel oils, vinegar, and other cooking liquids into these little bottles and keep them handy. The larger jugs and cans the liquid came in will stay safely in the cupboards while you're cooking.

STEAM WITH HOT LEMON WATER AND CLEAN If none of the above gets the job done, you've probably got some combination of food, mold, mildew, and bacteria hiding in the refrigerator. You need to clean them away. First take all the food out and put it in a closed cooler with a bag of ice so you won't have to worry about it. Unplug the refrigerator. Squeeze a lemon into a cup of water, throw the peels in too, and heat the liquid on the stove. Pour this hot lemon water into a bowl, put the bowl in the fridge, close the door, and wait a few minutes. This will start cutting the odor but, more important, it will also loosen the food accumulations on the walls and shelves, making them easier to clean away. To give your fridge a quick cleaning, follow the instructions in the Problem Stopper box at left.

My freezer has iced up

HEAT IT WITH A HAIR DRYER If your freezer frosts up or accumulates ice, count your blessings. It must have lasted many years, since most refrigerators have been frost-free models for quite a while. To melt the ice, unplug the unit. The ice or frost will melt eventually, but you don't want your fridge turned off that long. To help the defrosting process along, get your hair blow-dryer and aim the hot air at the ice. Brush the resulting water into a bucket with a rag, and soon your problem will melt away. Never stab at the ice with a knife. You could easily poke through a wall and burst a tube, letting coolant escape. That's dangerous and expensive to repair.

■ ACCIDENTS

I spilled oil all over the counter

USE PAPER TOWELS, THEN SUGAR Quickly stop the flow with a dishcloth, paper towels, or whatever is nearest at hand. Then get as much of the oil as you can up with paper towels or sponges. Sprinkle sugar over the remaining oil to absorb it, then wipe with paper towels. You still may have an oily film left, so spray a strong degreasing all-purpose cleaner on the surface and wipe it off.

My plastic bowl melted onto the stovetop

PULL IT OFF WHILE IT'S WARM This sticky situation can happen with plastic mixing bowls, plastic serving spoons, plastic cutting boards, and such. As soon as you see it happening, turn off the burner and get as much of the melting plastic away from the heat source as you can by pulling from the end farthest from the stove. Heat won't conduct through the plastic, but you still should use a pot holder or oven mitt for safety's sake. If you're lucky, the melting end will still be hot enough to peel off the stove.

SCRAPE IT OFF SMOOTH SURFACES Once it cools, plastic sticks on pretty hard. If you have an electric range with a ceramic glass cooktop, carefully scrape off the plastic with a single-edge razor. Scraping can also work on the smooth surface areas of any stove.

TORCH IT OFF ROUGH SURFACES If the plastic has stuck to an uneven surface, such as one of the burner grates on a gas stove or the drip pan underneath, remelting will get the plastic off better than anything. Remove the grate or drip pan and take it out to the driveway or patio. Then melt the plastic with a blowtorch—which is not as drastic as it sounds. Hardware stores sell little canisters of propane gas with screw-on attachments that will send out a modest jet of flame when you flick the little wheel like a cigarette lighter. Hold the grate or drip pan away from you with a long-handled clamp or tongs. Or remove the grill from your barbecue and set it across two stools. Spread some newspapers on the ground below so you won't get melting plastic on your driveway or patio. Then aim the blowtorch at the stove part. As the plastic heats up, it will melt and fall to the newspapers below. When the plastic stops smoking, your problem has also melted away.

I burned my finger while cooking

COAT IT WITH MUSTARD Reach for the mustard, if you have a meal to finish and haven't time to search your medicine cabinet for remedies. For quick first aid, some professional chefs cover the burned area of their fingers with mustard. Good old yellow hot dog mustard will do. Don't stick your finger into the mustard jar (unsanitary!). Just spoon some out, spread it on your finger, and keep it there. You'll feel a coolness and enough pain relief that you can keep on cooking with one hand and four-fifths of the other.

THE BETTER TREATMENT If you have time, the proper first aid for a superficial burn on your finger is to soak it in cool water for several minutes and then treat it with aloe vera cream or an antibiotic ointment before covering the area with a dry gauze bandage.

Kitchen Clutter

■ TABLES AND COUNTERTOPS

My kitchen is littered with mail, newspapers, and homework

GET A ROLL-AROUND FILE CABINET The kitchen is a great place for opening mail, reading newspapers, and doing homework. The problem is the newspapers, magazines, letters, notebooks, books, and other stuff that pile up on the table and countertops. Those things need a place to be stashed right in your kitchen but out of the way. There's an easy answer—a small portable file cabinet on wheels, found at any office supply store. Place a one-level in-basket on top for mail. The student of the house gets the file drawer for his or her homework materials. (Two students, of course, mean two drawers or two cabinets.) Simply roll the file cabinet under the counter or the table or into an out-of-the way corner.

For that collection of clutter on your kitchen table, a filing cabinet with wheels provides a fast fix.

GET A POCKET OR A STAND FOR PERIODICALS Your portable filing cabinet may come with a side pocket for newspapers or magazines. If it's not big enough, see if there's room in your kitchen for one of those wooden magazine racks that many people keep in their living rooms or bathrooms.

TRY MAKING A WORK NOOK As an alternative to the portable filing cabinet, consider a small permanent cabinet or a small two-shelf bookcase that you can position discreetly as a kind of homework nook. It may not be a typical kitchen design, but it will keep the rest of your kitchen clear for culinary pursuits.

■ REFRIGERATOR CLUTTER

My fridge is chock-full of leftovers

THROW OUT USELESS LEFTOVERS Accept a radical idea: It's sometimes OK to throw away food! The four squishy asparagus spears and the rubbery leftover hamburger patty wrapped in aluminum foil are no more "wasted" in the garbage than they are taking up space in the refrigerator for an entire summer. With this philosophy, you can rid your refrigerator of many of its accumulated leftovers in a single day.

MAKE A LEFTOVER SUPPER Plan on having leftovers for dinner. Take out and open every leftover you've saved—refrigerator and freezer. (The one exception: food you've frozen for a specific future use, such as spaghetti sauce.) If it looks or smells funny, if you can't tell what it is, or if you doubt that anybody will eat it, chuck it. You may throw out a lot of old food and feel a bit guilty, but it's a one-time fix that's worth it.

Now, reheat (if appropriate) and serve for dinner all the leftovers that didn't get tossed. You may end up with a dozen different small servings, a sort of minibuffet. Or you may need to cook more food to round out the meal. Either way, nothing will be left over tonight. It either gets eaten or thrown away. Period. Your fridge is leftover free.

Condiments are taking over my refrigerator

MAKE A FIRST-PASS CLEANUP Condiments have a way of hiding when you need them and getting in the way when you don't. Here's how to take control: Start by checking whether each condiment has to be refrigerated in the first place. Ketchup, for example, is usually exempt from the "refrigerate after opening" requirement. Check the expiration dates on your entire condiment inventory; then open them up and take a whiff. Throw out any that have expired or that don't pass the smell test.

KEEP EVERYDAY CONDIMENTS HANDY Put the three or four condiments you use virtually every day—mayonnaise, mustard, ketchup, or whatever—in a prominent, easily accessible part of your refrigerator, perhaps in a door shelf.

PUT THE OTHERS TOGETHER IN ONE AREA Keep the rest of your condiments together in their own home—in a contained space so they can't scatter. Ideally, designate a refrigerator door shelf as a condiment-only zone. If space is tight, use a boxy lidless plastic container as a condiment corral. You'll always know exactly where your condiments are, and access to them will be as easy as pulling out the plastic container.

PROBLEM STOPPER

Controlling Leftovers in the Fridge

• Before you put any leftover in the refrigerator, decide if that food's really going to get eaten. Be honest. Most of the time you know that nobody's going to eat it.

• Never store a leftover in your refrigerator without a specific plan for when it's going to be eaten. The extra pot roast, for example, is an easy call because it's perfect for sandwiches. A container of leftover rice, on the other hand, is likely to be sitting there two months from now.

• When you do save food, label and date the container. Keep masking tape and a marker handy.

• Follow the pros' FIFO (first in, first out) system. Don't push old leftover containers to the back. Each time you put in a new leftover, bring whatever leftover has been in there the longest to the front.

GIVE AWAY ONES YOU'LL NEVER REUSE To control your condiment inventory, get rid of "one-shot" condiments. Tartar sauce and mint jelly are not one-shot condiments—you'll want them for your next fish or lamb dinner. But the banana chutney you bought for a special duck dish is probably a one-shot condiment. Give the unused portion and the recipe to a food-loving friend or neighbor.

■ FOOD AND SUPPLIES

I hate having to toss out expired food

STORE FOOD SO YOU USE THE OLDEST FIRST If you frequently have to throw away packaged food because it's passed its expiration date, start using the LIFO (Last In, First Out) method of pantry stocking. Always put your newest purchases on the back of the shelf or on the bottom of a stack. That way, you and your family members will always use up the oldest (and easiest to grab) food first.

My food cupboard has a jumble of bags and boxes

PUT LIKE ITEMS TOGETHER IN BASKETS To control the mess of boxes and bags in your cupboard, you need some flat-bottomed baskets or low-sided wooden boxes not quite as deep as your shelves and maybe a foot or so wide. Kitchen supply stores give you lots of attractive options, but in a pinch you can simply cut down the sides of some cardboard boxes and use those. Line up the boxes on your shelves and let each one hold a category of food. One box could hold sweet stuff—white sugar, brown sugar, syrup, vanilla, molasses, sugar cubes, and so on. Another could be for baking-related items, such as flour, bread crumbs, and cornstarch. Even breakfast cereals could have a box. However you organize your containers, future fumbling and searching will be limited to an area the size of your box or basket, which you can pull out and set on the table or counter for hassle-free searching.

I can never find the can I'm looking for

INSTALL STEPPED MINISHELVES To corral the chaos of cans in your food cupboard, try a stair-style minishelf unit. You can find these two- or three-tiered shelves at kitchen supply stores. Buy one that's about one can-height short of touching the shelf above it and one can-width less wide than the main shelf you'll be setting it on. Fill the mini-shelves with your canned goods. Now not only can you see the can you want, but you can also pull it out without toppling others.

I've got soup packets and dried-food bags falling from every shelf

PUT THEM IN TRANSPARENT CONTAINERS Use see-through, stackable plastic containers to hold loose packets of soup mix, hot cocoa, tea, and condiments. They'll be much easier to find than tucked away in piles of plastic bags. Also repackage cereal, pasta, rice, and beans—those half-empty boxes and bags are space wasters and are almost impossible to keep neat. Most dried foods can be emptied into large jars with tight-fitting tops or into airtight stackable plastic containers. Kitchen supply stores carry nice-looking sturdy glass or plastic containers, or you can convert jars you already have. If you have counter space or areas available on top of your wall cabinets, keep the jars of dried foods outside the cupboard, where you won't forget they're available.

The same principle applies to dried dog and cat food. A large, rigid container on the floor, such as a 5-gallon (19-liter) bucket, will keep your pet's food easily accessible without spills.

WORLD-CLASS FIX

The Cost of Kitchen Clutter

Organizing consultants get paid to suggest ways to declutter your home, including your kitchen. Identifying clutter sources is easy. Persuading their perpetrators to get rid of them is often harder. Christy Best, a professional organizer from Aromas, California, found an ingenious way to persuade a wealthy client to part with the hundreds of mayonnaise jars he had stockpiled. The thrifty gentleman planned to start a pickling business when he retired and thought he'd save money by having the jars ready when the time came. Sure, he was only in his 40s, but he couldn't resist the thought of saving a few dollars 20 years down the road.

Best fought fire with fire. She calculated the total value of his home mortgage plus household expenses. She divided that number by the square footage of his pricey home. The resulting figure told Jar Man how much it was costing him to store those containers. Surely there were better uses for such expensive space. Once he saw the figure, the mayonnaise jars were history.

I don't have enough shelves for food

INSTALL WIRE SHELVES Use freestanding, plastic-coated wire units to create more horizontal space in your pantry. These "helper shelves" let you store twice as many cans, boxes, or other items on a given shelf without perilously piling them on top of each other. Helper shelves are widely available at home and kitchen supply stores.

I *still* don't have enough shelves for food

PUT SCREW-ON JARS UNDER SHELVES If there's a lot of space wasted between shelves, try this trick from the workshop: Attach mason-type jars to the underside of the shelves. Using a small nail and a hammer, punch a hole or two in each metal jar lid. Then screw the lid to the shelf using half-inch (1.25 centimeter) wood screws. Install a lid about every 5 inches (12.5 centimeters). Now, fill the jars with rice, beans, and other staples and screw them into their lids.

I don't even have a pantry!

CONVERT A SMALL CLOSET OR CUPBOARD Even the smallest apartment or home usually has a closet or cupboard near the kitchen that can be treated as a pantry. The key is to adopt the same principles used in larger spaces. Organize the space by putting the most frequently used items in front. Group like items together. And use sliding shelves, lazy Susans, and door-mounted racks or shelves to make the most of the space. Install a small light on the "ceiling" of the cupboard to complete the pocket pantry. (A battery-powered car or camping light works great.)

I have six half-empty boxes of snack bars

PUT THEM IN A BASKET Put an open-topped basket on a shelf and dump energy bars, granola bars, and the like into it. Your choice: Make the basket easily accessible to your kids or stash it on a higher shelf out of reach of temptation.

Exotic foods pile up in my pantry

MAKE SPECIAL MEALS TO USE THEM UP Instead of letting seldom-used foods languish in your pantry or throwing them away, use them as an excuse for creative cooking. Every month or so, explore your pantry and pick out one or two things that you haven't used in ages. Now go through your cookbooks and create a meal plan that uses those ingredients. You'll have more room in your pantry, and you'll please your family or guests with your "pantry surprise"!

My spices are in permanent disarray

GET A SPICE RACK Store spices together in a way that you can see and grab what you're looking for without moving the rest. Nothing can beat a spice rack if your spices are in, or can be put in, bottles that fit the rack and if you have a good place to put the rack—a handy exposed wall or the inside of a cabinet door. A spice rack stuffed into your food cabinet with everything else will end up creating more disarray, not less.

GET A LAZY SUSAN If you have a potpourri of containers that don't always fit right in a spice rack, put them on a revolving lazy Susan. A lazy Susan can accommodate spice containers of any shape—tall skinny bottles, short fat ones, little bags, bigger bags, and plastic containers as well as the classic little bottles. And as long as you keep it on a shelf at or near eye level, you can easily spot the spice you're looking for as you turn the tray.

I have more spices than will fit on a rack

FILE THEM IN A DRAWER If you're a true spice aficionado, do what many chefs do: Buy a supply of sturdy medium-sized zip-sealing plastic bags. Except for the three or four spices you use most often, transfer each of your spices from its store container to its own plastic bag. Use masking tape and a permanent marker to label each spice bag. Date the bag as well, because spices do lose their potency and should be replaced after a year or even sooner. Give your spice bags their own drawer, and simply line them up in alphabetical order. Finding a spice is just a matter of opening the drawer and thumbing through the rows—provided you remember to put the spice bag back in its proper place.

I can't find my garbage bags

KEEP THE BAGS IN THE TRASH CAN Bulky items like that 30-count box of garbage bags often end up down the hall in a closet, forcing you to march around the house looking for a fresh bag every time you take out the garbage. To end this little annoyance, take some or all of the garbage bags out of their cardboard box. Put the bags loose in the bottom of the trash bin. That way, every time you take out the trash, there's a fresh bag lying there ready for service.

■ POTS, PANS, AND UTENSILS

My plastic food containers are a real mess

REPLACE THEM WITH NEW MATCHING CONTAINERS Your plastic food containers won't stack, don't have matching lids, take up too much space, and fall out when you open the cabinet door. The fix may seem a little drastic but it works: Start over! If you have a typical collection of plastic food containers—an assortment of yogurt containers, margarine tubs, and ice cream cartons, as well as better quality items—get rid of them. Then go out and buy brand-new matching plastic containers. Buy fewer than you think you need. Most important, get just one shape and style and just three sizes (big, medium, and small). Now matching lids to containers will be a snap, and they'll all stack or nest.

Keep your new storage container collection in its own drawer or a plastic bin or box to keep the lids and containers from drifting apart. And don't be tempted to augment your container supply. If now and then you need extra food storage, use disposable food-storage containers sold at supermarkets.

My undercounter cabinets are a nightmare

HANG YOUR MOST USED POTS AND PANS Here are some steps you can take to clean out that space. Start by putting your most-used pots and pans on racks. These are simple wooden or metal bars with hooks that attach to your kitchen ceiling or wall. The holes on your pot or pan handles fit the hooks. Just like that, you've cleared out a good chunk of clutter from your cabinet and positioned your pots and pans for easy access.

GET MIXING BOWLS THAT NEST If you don't have a set of mixing bowls that nest, buy one and get rid of your old ones. Three or four bowls now take up the same space of one old one. You can even keep them on the countertop or on an overhead shelf to free up more undercounter space.

GIVE AWAY OR EXILE NEVER- OR SELDOM-USED ITEMS What about bowls that don't nest? Pots and pans that don't hang? Or that paté pan and circa-1974 popcorn maker? If you won't ever use an item, give it away. If you use it less than once a month, store it in a distant cabinet or in a box in the garage. When you do need it, you can get it.

You'll still have plenty of stuff to keep in those cabinets, such as pitchers, casserole dishes, and gelatin molds.

It's hard to reach items in the back of undercounter cabinets

PUT THE ITEMS ON SLIDING RACKS To make undercounter items readily accessible, place them on "totes," sliding racks that pull out like file cabinet drawers. You can find a tote that fits your cabinet at a kitchen supply or hardware store. All you need is a screwdriver to install one.

One glass is stuck in the other

USE HOT AND COLD WATER Don't use brute force to pull them apart. That could lead to broken glasses and cut hands. Instead, take advantage of how materials expand or contract with temperature change. Put cold water in the top glass and wait a minute while the glass contracts. Then see if it lifts right out. If not, set the bottom glass down in an inch or two of warm water in a pot or sink. Then fill the top glass with cold water. That should do it. One caution: If you use the hot-and-cold combination, don't use water that's extremely cold or extremely hot. The glasses could crack.

Also learn this lesson: It's not a good idea to stack glasses.

PART FOUR

Outdoors

The world outside seems so fraught with peril:
Creatures large and small skulking about, unruly plant
life, weather disasters. And that's just in your backyard!
Venturing into the wilderness, we find campfires
that won't light, bears that won't go away, and
that eau de skunk on your clothes that just
won't quit. Never fear! Here are solutions
to your outdoor problems.

Outdoor Maintenance

■ HOUSE EXTERIOR

My porch light keeps blowing out

USE A FLUORESCENT BULB Front-porch lights often get left on all night. With an average lifetime of just 750 hours, a typical 75-watt incandescent bulb will last only a couple of months. The solution is simple: Fit your porch lights with compact fluorescent bulbs. They cost five to ten times more than incandescent bulbs, but they last around ten times longer and use only about one-third as much electricity for the same light output, saving significant money—and the nuisance of bulb-changing—over the long haul.

My vinyl siding is dingy

IS IT MILDEW OR DIRT ON YOUR SIDING? If you have vinyl siding that is off-color, you should first determine whether the discoloration is dirt or mildew. Put on rubber gloves and goggles, mix one part chlorine bleach to four parts water in a bucket, and rub a discolored spot with a sponge. If the spot comes off, the problem is mildew. If not, the problem is dirt.

CLEAN OFF MILDEW WITH BLEACH SOLUTION To remove the mildew, first protect yourself with gloves, goggles, and some old clothing and then scrub the siding with a stiff brush and the same 1:4 bleach-water solution you used for testing.

CLEAN OFF DIRT WITH DETERGENT To remove dirt, wear your protective gear and scrub the siding with a stiff brush and diluted detergent. One detergent that works for this purpose is trisodium phosphate (TSP), but you can find more environmentally friendly outdoor cleaning products that don't contain phosphate at home improvement stores. Follow the manufacturer's directions on the label for diluting the cleaner in water.

If you're always changing the porch light, the quick solution is a long-life compact fluorescent.

RENT A PRESSURE WASHER If your siding has dirty areas that are too extensive to clean by hand, rent a pressure washer from your area tool-rental store. In general, you'll want to use 1 pound (450 grams) of detergent for every 4 or 5 gallons (15 to 19 liters) of water in the pressure washer. This is just for dirt; don't use a pressure washer to clean mildewed spots, because you don't want to be spraying chlorine bleach all around you.

Put on goggles and start spraying at the top of the wall and work your way down. Afterward, rinse any remaining detergent out of the washer's tank, refill it with clear water, and rinse off the siding from the top down.

My new wooden roof shingles don't match the old ones

USE BAKING SODA TO "AGE" THEM Fixing roof leaks by replacing wooden shakes or shingles on your roof does your house a world of good. However, sticking a new piece among the old ones is akin to having a gold tooth in the middle of your smile—it's valuable, but it stands out more than necessary.

Before installing new shingles or shakes on your roof, lay the shingles out on the ground. Mix ½ pound (225 grams) of baking soda in 1 gallon (3.7 liters) of water, pour the mixture onto the shingles, and let them sit for a few hours. The solution will gray the wood so it will fit in better with the rest of your roof.

My awning has a tear

USE COLORED DUCT TAPE The trick with a tear in an awning or tarp is to stop it from tearing further. Try this quick solution: Lay equal-length strips of duct tape on both the top and underside of the tear. Strong and waterproof, duct tape will withstand the elements until you can properly patch the rip. For inexpensive tarps, the duct tape patch should be enough. Auto parts stores sell duct tape in a variety of colors, so you should be able to find tape that doesn't look bad.

USE A PATCH REPAIR KIT For a proper repair to a vinyl and acrylic awning, get a patch kit specially designed for awnings. Most patch glues require temperatures of 50° F (10° C) or more for three days straight to cure. If you live in the northern climes and your awning tears in October, you'll have to wait until springtime to repair it.

PROBLEM STOPPER

A Weeping Shame

Maybe you've noticed missing mortar in the joints along the base of your brick house. Don't fill them, as one Florida homeowner did after his wife saw a small snake slither out of one of the gaps. Those are weep holes (usually in vertical joints one brick up from the foundation). They're left open intentionally in brick veneer houses so that moisture that naturally seeps into the brick and mortar can exit. If you plug them up—with mortar or, as this fellow did, with Styrofoam insulation—you'll welcome all sorts of moisture-related problems, including the growth of unhealthful mold and termite infestation. Make sure your landscaping does not block the weep holes either. Keep mulch 3 to 6 inches (7 to 15 centimeters) away from the sides of the house.

PROBLEM STOPPER

Preventing Roof Leaks

Once a year or so, inspect your roof for deterioration and missing pieces. Check the seals around vent stacks and chimneys. Make sure the flashing is secure and tightly sealed. You don't have to climb up there to inspect it. A pair of binoculars is a great aid in getting a close-up view.

Even with maintenance, not all roofs will last as long as their warranties promise. Roof life depends on what it is exposed to and for how long. The sun ruins a shingle roof. It warps shingles; it dries out rubber flashing and caulk. And once a roof has leaked for a while, you'll have a large repair job inside the house as well as on the roof.

■ WATER LEAKS

My roof has sprung a leak

STAPLE PLASTIC OVER A DAMAGED ROOF A storm-damaged roof can be temporarily repaired by covering the hole with plastic sheeting, available at home centers. Fold over the edges of the plastic and staple them to sound roofing shingles surrounding the opening. Note: A tarp, particularly a plastic one, is very slippery when wet, so be careful when working with one on a roof.

LOCATE THE LEAK AND DIVERT IT
First, find the leak's source. Trace it back from the inside by looking for water marks on the underside of the roof and for cone-shaped impressions on the surface of fiberglass insulation. Follow the trail upward and mark the uppermost location with a waterproof marker. Check the suspicious spot for dampness or dripping water the next time it rains.

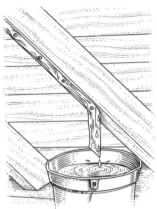

Try to contain an active leak before it does serious damage to the attic joists and the walls below. If the water is dripping down a rafter, for example, divert it temporarily with a rag "wick" until you can stop the leak. Tack a long strip of cloth to the rafter in the water's path and let the lower end of the cloth strip dangle down a few inches. Set a bucket under the lower end. The strip will redirect the minor river into the bucket.

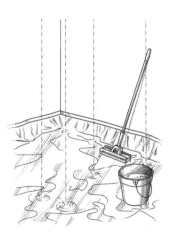

CREATE A PLASTIC CATCH BASIN
If there are several active leaks in one room that you can't get to the roof to fix, capture the dripping water in a catch basin made of plastic sheeting (the kind painters use for drop cloths, for instance). Turn up the sides of the plastic and tape or staple them to the walls to create a large, shallow bowl that can contain the water. Mop up the water frequently so that it won't overflow.

A crack in my basement wall is leaking

FILL THE CRACK WITH HYDRAULIC CEMENT Try this quick fix for water that is seeping through visible cracks. Use a cold chisel and hammer to chisel out the crack slightly—about ¼ inch (6 millimeters). Then mix up some hydraulic cement and smear it into the crack, smoothing it out flat over the surface of the masonry wall. Unlike regular cement, which shrinks as it hardens, hydraulic cement expands and will fill gaps and block seeping water. It's available at hardware stores and home improvement centers.

My downspout is blocked

BLOW DEBRIS OUT WITH A LEAF BLOWER The rain runs off your roof and into the gutter—but it doesn't come out the downspout. Some stray debris must be blocking the spout. Try blasting out the offending blockage. Stick the business end of a leaf blower into the bottom of the downspout and give it a blast of air. The pressure should blow the blockage out the top of the gutter, relieving you of the chore of climbing up to clean it out.

My window well floods and leaks inside

CLEAR THE DRAIN Basement window wells that don't drain properly can collect rainwater and snow and cause leaks. If your window well is a permanent masonry or metal structure, the problem may be leaves and debris blocking the drain. Clean out any clogs in the drain line with a plumber's snake or a long wire; a thin-wire coat hanger, cut and straightened, will even do the job.

IMPROVE THE DRAINAGE If you have the more common window well, which has a corrugated steel semicircular liner, its earth bottom may have become hard with debris or clay-rich soil, so that water collected in the well can't seep deeper into the ground. In that case, your best bet is to remove the liner, dig out the compacted soil, and then put gravel underneath to improve drainage. Dig out the liner and, if necessary, unbolt it from the foundation. Then dig deeper and remove 2 feet (60 centimeters) of earth. Replace that with 8 inches (20 centimeters) of coarse gravel, then 8 inches of fine gravel, and 8 inches of topsoil. Put the well liner back into position. The layers of gravel and topsoil will let water that collects in the well seep down deeper into the ground.

PROBLEM STOPPER

Rain, Rain, Go Away
Rainwater coming off the roof is one of the biggest causes of moist basements. If not properly drained, the water sinks into the soil and seeps into foundation walls. Waterproofing foundation walls is an expensive job involving heavy machinery used to dig out around the foundation. But you can often greatly reduce the amount of seepage with one simple step: extending your downspouts. Buy a length of 4-inch (10 centimeter) black corrugated plastic drainpipe at a home improvement center or hardware store. Slip it over the end of the downspout so that it carries the water a few feet away from the house.

Don't add to the problem by soaking the sides of your house with the lawn sprinkler. Keep the sprinkler stream well away from the house. Water foundation plantings with a hose on low pressure.

There are white stains inside my fireplace

FIND AND STOP THE LEAK A white stain on masonry is usually a sign of efflorescence, salt deposits leeching out of the brick, stone, or mortar. Although the white stuff is easy to clean (scrub gently with a 50-50 solution of vinegar and warm water, drying with a towel afterward), efflorescence is a symptom of a moisture problem. Water seeps into the masonry, dissolves the salts, and then evaporates, leaving white powder stains on the surface. Efflorescence is common in fireplaces because fireplaces often leak.

Whether you do it yourself or hire a pro, here's how to stop a fireplace leak—and put a halt to efflorescence:

1. Make sure you have a chimney cap and that it is functioning properly. A chimney cap is like a small roof covering the top of the chimney. It lets smoke out but keeps rainwater from entering.

2. If the cap is in good shape, water may be seeping into loose mortar joints in the chimney, either at the top, just below the chimney cap, or along the sides. If so, you'll be best off hiring a pro to replace the loose mortar in the joints between the chimney's bricks.

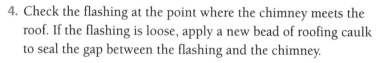

FLASHING

3. Check the space between your tile flue liner and the chimney. If there's a gap, fill it with mortar or roofing caulk.

4. Check the flashing at the point where the chimney meets the roof. If the flashing is loose, apply a new bead of roofing caulk to seal the gap between the flashing and the chimney.

■ COLD WEATHER

It's too cold outside to clean windows

USE WINDSHIELD WASHING FLUID Don't despair. There is a way to wash your home's windows even when the temperature is below freezing. Use automobile windshield washing fluid, which won't freeze. Fill a bucket with the fluid. Wearing rubber gloves, wash the windows with a sponge or rag. Use a small squeegee to wipe away the solution. Keep a clean, dry rag in your back pocket for wiping spills and sills. Use this same no-freeze solution to clean metal, plastic, and other outdoor surfaces in cold weather.

Snow sticks to my shovel

SPRAY THE SHOVEL WITH OIL To keep wet snow from gluing itself to a shovel, spray the shovel with cooking spray (Pam, for instance), silicone spray, or a household lubricant (such as WD-40) before you use it. Snow slides easily off a lubricated shovel, sparing your back from the excess weight. And store your shovel outside or in a cold shed or garage—never inside the house. Snow won't stick as much to a cold shovel.

My snow shovel is wrecking my porch

USE A PUSH BROOM To save wooden porches or decks—not to mention your back—from the ravages of a snow shovel, use a janitor's push broom to clear light snowfalls. A broom is lighter and easier to maneuver than a shovel, and it won't chip paint on a deck or porch the way a shovel will.

On bitterly cold days, you don't want to spend a lot of time outside washing windows. The answer is windshield washing fluid.

My downspouts are frozen solid

CREATE MELTERS WITH ROAD SALT AND PANTY HOSE If you live in an area with cold, snowy winters, it's hard to avoid ice dams. Warm air in the attic causes the snow on the rooftop to melt, but the runoff freezes again when it reaches the gutter line, where the air is colder. The ice is usually thickest at the tops of the downspouts, which is bad, because when the gutter ice does melt, the thick plugs block the runoff. Here's a quick solution: Cut the legs off a pair of old panty hose. Fill each hose leg with calcium chloride pellets or flakes, the "salt" used to melt sidewalk ice and sold at home improvement centers. Tie the leg ends and lay these homemade ice-melting devices over the frozen downspouts—or any other section of gutter that is especially thick with ice. Remove once the ice has melted.

My gutters are frozen over, and water is trickling into my house

BLOW COLD AIR INTO THE ATTIC If you see water trickling down your interior walls, you need to stop it—now! Here's how: Take a box fan or two into the attic and set them up near a window or louvered gable vent. Turn them on high to suck cold air into the attic. The water on the roof will quickly freeze, stopping it from trickling into the house. The reason that cooling the attic solves the problem is that you have what is known as an ice dam. Warm air in your attic melts rooftop snow, and the runoff freezes again near the roof's edge, where the air is cooler. The ice that forms acts like a dam, pooling water behind it and causing it to creep under the roof shingles, run down the rafters, and eventually trickle down your interior walls.

COOL THE ATTIC WITH VENTS The long-term solution to ice dams is to keep the air in the attic consistently cool so that the snow on the roof will melt evenly and run off without refreezing. A well-insulated attic floor helps. If your insulation already reaches the top of the joists in the attic, try installing new bats of insulation over the joists, going at a right angle to the joists. It also helps to install vents under the eaves and, perhaps, along the ridgeline. The easiest vents to install are vent plugs that fit into holes that you drill into the soffit under the eaves.

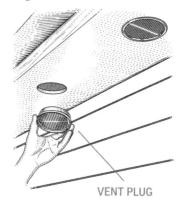

VENT PLUG

■ DECKS AND PATIOS

My deck's a discolored wreck

CLEAN IT WITH AN OXYGEN BLEACH Is your once beautiful deck now a greenish-black eyesore? The fast and best solution, according to the experts, is to clean your deck with an oxygen bleach, a bleach that doesn't contain chlorine. (See the Problem Stopper on page 212.) Many brands of the bleach are available from online sellers and home improvement centers, and any oxygen bleach should do the trick.

Mix the product in water according to label directions and apply it liberally to all the deck surfaces. Leave it on for ten minutes. You may need to reapply it to vertical surfaces a time or two, since it will run off. Lightly scrub the surfaces with a push broom; then rinse them with a garden hose.

My patio has a sunken brick

PRY THE BRICK OUT AND FILL UNDER IT It's easy to fix a sunken piece, but first you must remove it. Here's how:

1. Slide a thin chisel or a stiff putty knife into the crack between the sunken brick and a neighbor. Wiggle the tool back and forth to create a bigger gap. Repeat on all four sides of the sunken brick.
2. When you have created a gap on all sides, use the tip or edge of your chisel or putty knife to pry the brick upward. You may need to pry it up from all four sides. Eventually you'll raise the brick far enough that you can grab it with your fingertips and pull it out.
3. Add sand in the hole where the brick was removed. Tamp it down with a mallet or other heavy object. Keep adding sand and compacting it until the surface is level with the sand under the surrounding bricks.
4. Set the extracted brick in the hole. Drive it into place by laying a short board over it and tapping it with a rubber mallet until it's level with the surrounding bricks.

■ HOT TUBS AND POOLS

The water in my hot tub looks dirty

SCRUB THE FILTER WITH DETERGENT Monthly maintenance is not always enough to keep a hot tub *really* clean. Filters trap natural oils from your skin that you leave in the water, and these oils can combine with other material to form a claylike sludge. Clean this sludge away by scrubbing the filter with a soft brush and a dishwasher detergent containing grease-busting ingredients. Then thoroughly rinse with a garden hose until the detergent is gone. One detergent that works well is Cascade, say hot-tub maintenance specialists.

Don't overlook monthly maintenance as the main way to keep the filter in your hot tub working properly. All you have to do is remove the filter and spray it with a garden hose.

PROBLEM STOPPER

Keep Replacement Pavers Outdoors to Age Them
If you install a sidewalk, patio, or other structure made of bricks or pavers, store some extras outside in an out-of-the-way location. When a brick or paver becomes cracked or damaged someday, you'll be able to replace it, as well as any others that may get damaged during the repair process. If you store the replacements indoors, they won't have weathered at the same rate as the ones outside. Their bold colors will stand out among the faded bricks around them. By keeping the replacements outdoors, they'll weather at the same rate.

PROBLEM STOPPER

How Not to Clean a Deck
Don't use a pressure washer or a chlorine bleach solution to clean your deck.

A pressure washer will erode the wood grain, making the boards rough. And chlorine bleach takes the color out of the wood and weakens the fibers. It also corrodes the nails or screws.

I'm afraid my pool will become pitted like my brother's

MAINTAIN YOUR POOL YEAR ROUND Many people don't do a good job of maintaining their swimming pool chemistry during the winter off-season. If the water has too little "calcium hardness" over the winter, it can cause the floor surface of the pool to become pitted and abraded. This will be uncomfortable on your feet, and you'll have to sand the bottom or resurface the pool. Take a sample of your water to a swimming pool store two times over the winter to get it tested.

■ DRIVEWAYS

My concrete driveway is cracked

FILL IT WITH AN EPOXY COMPOUND If a concrete driveway or sidewalk is cracked, attend to it as soon as you can, before water freezing inside the crack or a car passing over it can increase the damage. If you catch it early enough—while the crack is a quarter-inch wide or less—fixing it is a cinch and only takes a few minutes. Pick up a tube of concrete-patching compound at your home improvement store. This is an epoxy-type material that's

WORLD-CLASS GOOF

The In-Ground Pool That Isn't

Frank Goldstein, a Maryland swimming pool maintenance consultant, has seen the following sad sight four times in his life: an in-ground swimming pool that has popped out of the earth.

When you totally drain the water from your pool for the winter, the pool becomes much lighter. Water in the ground surrounding the swimming pool freezes and expands, pushing against the empty shell, which can pop the shell several feet out of the ground.

Goldstein recommends that you remove 6 inches to a foot (15 to 30 centimeters) only of water from your pool during the winter. This will get the water below the tile band around the edge of your pool. Water freezing around this tile could damage it.

However, the amount you should remove will vary depending on the severity of your winters and the type of pool cover you have. Both affect how much the water in the pool will freeze. Talk to a local pool supply company about how much water to remove.

slightly flexible so that it expands and contracts with the concrete. It comes in a tube that fits into a standard caulking gun, which you will also need.

Blow any dust and debris out of the crack or clean it out with a wire brush. Be sure to wear goggles. Following label directions, squeeze the material into the crack and smooth it with a putty knife until it is level with the surrounding concrete.

My car leaked oil on the carport

ABSORB IT WITH CAT LITTER You can buy absorbent products especially marketed for soaking up oil spills on your garage floor. But there's nothing that works better, is handier, and is less expensive than cat litter. Just pour cheap, basic cat litter over the oil and let it soak up the liquid for one hour. Then sweep the litter into a dustpan and discard it.

■ OUTDOOR FURNITURE

My patio chair's webbing is unraveling

STOP THE FRAYING WITH A MATCH FLAME One little nick on the edge of a folding patio chair's plastic webbing and before you know it the fabric is fraying and unraveling. There's a simple solution: Strike a match and run the flame quickly across the frayed edges. Apply just enough heat so that the material melts slightly and forms globs along the edge. Be careful not to burn yourself with the flame or the material's hot edge.

My metal lawn furniture is rusted

POWER-BRUSH OFF THE RUST AND PAINT If a little patch of rust has discolored your outdoor furniture, use a metal scouring pad (an SOS pad, for instance) to scrub off the rust. If the furniture is rustier than the Tin Man after a hurricane, the quick way to remove the rust is to pick up an inexpensive circular wire brush drill attachment for your electric drill at a home improvement store. Then, wearing safety goggles, use the drill and wire brush to knock off the rust.

After you remove the rust, protect the furniture from future rust by applying a coat of primer—you can find it in a spray can for about $3—followed by a coat of rust-inhibiting spray paint.

PROBLEM STOPPER

What's Good for the Deck...
Protect your outdoor wooden furniture with a quick coat of penetrating finish, such as Thompson's Water Seal, each year. Apply a coat of this liquid sealant with a paint pad or rag. Steer clear of film finishes, such as lacquer or varnish, however. They look great at first but blister in the sun and require frequent touch-ups.

My plastic resin lawn furniture has mildew

WASH IT WITH A BLEACH SOLUTION If you don't want to sit in your molded plastic lawn chair because it's already occupied by a lower life form (we're talking about mildew, not a pesky neighbor), there is a quick answer: Mix a solution of one part chlorine bleach to four parts water. Wearing latex gloves, scrub the furniture with a sponge or brush dipped in the solution. Then rinse with a hose.

My aluminum patio furniture is dingy

WASH WITH VINEGAR SOLUTION; THEN APPLY AUTO WAX To brighten aluminum furniture, wash it with a solution of 1 gallon (4 liters) of water and 4 tablespoons of vinegar. If the surface is dotted with tiny pits, use a soapy steel-wool pot cleaner on it. Rinse the furniture carefully to remove any traces of the steel wool, as rusting steel could discolor the furniture. Then, to prevent pitting, coat the aluminum with a thin layer of automobile wax.

■ YARD TOOLS

I overfilled my mower's gas tank

ABSORB THE EXCESS WITH A TAMPON Whether it's a lawn mower, leaf blower, weed eater, or some other small internal combustion engine, if you overfill the tank, you risk spilling gasoline in your garage or on your driveway when you move the engine or try to replace the cap. And then you've got a smelly, dangerous situation on your hands. Quick! Run and grab an unused tampon—yes, a tampon—and carefully insert it in the overfilled tank. In a matter of seconds it will absorb the excess fluid. Just make sure the saturated tampon does not expand so much that it sticks in the tank opening. And be careful in disposing of it. It's best to let it dry out first before putting it in a garbage can or other enclosed space.

My garden hoses never seem to last long

BUY THE RIGHT HOSE If your garden hose is prone to springing leaks, there's an easy way to cut down on this outdoor hassle. Buy a hose that's made of rubber or a rubber-nylon blend; avoid the ones made totally of nylon. Nylon hoses dry out in the sun and crack, and they're easily damaged as you pull them around the yard. If you can't

PROBLEM STOPPER

Get a Good Handle on Your Tools

Sometimes the handle on your shovel, sledgehammer, or other outdoor tool isn't up to the challenge of a heavy job, and it snaps.

To save yourself this aggravation, condition the wooden handles on your tools with mineral oil once a year. Just soak a rag in the oil and rub it down the length of the handle. Dry handles become more likely to break; the moisture from the mineral oil helps preserve their flexibility. But wait until the oil is well absorbed into the handle before you use the tool, to avoid having it slip out of your hands and cause an accident.

Store your tools indoors or in a storage shed, too. Don't leave them exposed to the elements.

tell from the packaging what kind of hoses you're looking at in the store, lift a few different kinds. The hoses containing rubber are heavier than ones made of just nylon.

■ BARBECUE GRILLS

My grill is caked with crud

DON'T CLEAN THE GRILL'S INSIDE If your barbecue grill is getting greasy, sooty buildup, the cleanup might be quicker and easier than you think. To start with, grilling experts say, it's not necessary to scrub the interior of your grill, whether you have a charcoal grill or a gas grill. In fact, allowing residue from cooking smoke to accumulate inside the grill seasons it, imparting a better flavor to the food you cook. This is similar to seasoning a new cast-iron skillet with oil before you cook with it. You may even want to season a new grill before using it the first time. (See sidebar, right.)

If flaky stuff falling off the inside of the grill bothers you, just remove it once a season using a wet, soapy sponge, followed by a wipe with a wet, nonsoapy sponge. That's all you need to do.

CLEAN THE GRATE WHILE IT'S HOT Although you'll save time by not cleaning the inside of the grill, experts advise that you regularly clean the grate that holds the food. Greasy clumps of burnt food that accumulate on this grate can give a bad flavor to the next round of food you grill.

To clean the grate easily, first preheat your grill with the lid down for a few minutes until the grate is hot. Then scrub it with a long-handled brass-bristled brush. Be careful not to touch the hot grate with your hand.

Do this after you've finished cooking. If you clean the grate like this each time you use it, it shouldn't ever get so messy that you have to remove it for a more heavy-duty cleaning.

The electric igniter on my gas grill is on the blink

SAND A DIRTY ELECTRODE This is a common problem. The igniter sends a spark that ignites a small amount of gas that pools in a collector box. The electrode or electric connections can become corroded. Getting the igniter working again can simply be a matter

TRICKS OF THE TRADE

Seasoning Your New Grill

When you buy a new grill, whether gas or charcoal, season the inside so that it imparts a better taste to the food. Here's how to do it, says Elizabeth Karmel, the guru behind girlsatthegrill.com, who learned the tricks of the trade from years of doing public-relations work for a grill manufacturer. You have to sacrifice a little meat in the process, but it will pay off in your future cooking.

Buy enough sausages to cover the entire cooking grate with just a little space between them. Fire up the grill, lower the lid, and cook the sausages over low heat "until they're practically turned to charcoal," Karmel says. The fat and juices pour out of the sausages and vaporize into smoke that coats and seasons the inside of the lid.

of cleaning the electrode, the tip that sparks when you push the igniter button. Make sure the gas is turned off or disconnected. Use your instruction manual to help you locate the electrode. You may need a mirror to see inside the collector box. Sand the tip gently with fine sandpaper and then swab it with alcohol. Lightly sand the roof of the collector box. If that doesn't solve the problem, check all electrical connections between the button and the electrode. Make sure they are intact and corrosion-free.

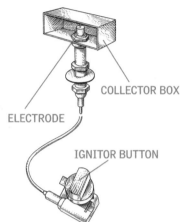

COLLECTOR BOX

ELECTRODE

IGNITOR BUTTON

REPLACE A CORRODED ELECTRODE
If the electrode is too corroded to clean, you can replace it. Remove the electrode by loosening a set screw or (in newer models) releasing a clip. Take it, along with the make and model number, to your local gas grill dealer. Or locate a mail-order replacement parts business on the Internet.

My gas grill's window keeps breaking

CLEAN THE BURNER Most likely, your glass is fine. What you've got is a burner problem. Fix the problem by cleaning or replacing the burner.

1. Turn the gas off and disconnect the gas line from the grill.
2. Place the cooking grid on a piece of newspaper. Pile the lava rocks on the grate and lift grate and rocks out all at once.
3. Remove the burner, following the manufacturer's instructions.
4. Clean the burner by scraping the outside with a wire brush to remove spiderwebs, rust, and cooking buildup. Then clean each gas outlet hole with a piece of wire or a paper clip. Use a bottle brush to clean inside the burner tube. You can also flush the burner with a garden hose.

REPLACE THE BURNER If you find split seams or corroded gas outlet holes on the burner, you'll need to replace it. If you don't know the make and model of your grill, look for a label near the controls or on the cart. The American Gas Association requires a label that contains manufacturer name and model numbers.

Gardening Problems

■ PLANNING AND TENDING

I need help planning my garden

CHECK OUT NEIGHBORS' GARDENS Gardening experts often say that planning a garden is just a matter of putting the right plant in the right place. But in practice, it can be hard to find the right plant and the right place. If you're new to gardening, where can you turn for help?

Start with your neighbors, gardeners advise. Walk around the neighborhood and check out the gardens that catch your eye. Ask your neighbors what kinds of plants they enjoy and how much maintenance they require. Gardeners tend to love talking about their work. You'll get ideas for plants you'd like to have in your own yard, as well as tips on where to buy them and how to care for them. Neighboring gardeners may even offer you plants or cuttings to get started with.

If you don't have helpful gardeners in your neighborhood, attend local garden club meetings or visit a plant nursery or two. Nurseries often offer gardening courses in the spring and should be good sources of information about weather and soil conditions for gardening in your area.

Not sure of what to do with your garden? The instant answer is to steal an idea.

I'd like to save money on seeds

COLLECT SEEDS FROM THE GARDEN Vegetable gardens are the gift that keeps on giving. If you collect the seeds properly, you won't have to go to the store next year to buy more to start the new crop. Keep these tips in mind, though:

- Find out whether your vegetables are hybrids. The packet they came in has this information on it. If they are hybrids, don't bother keeping the seeds, because you'll just get a wide variation in the quality of the vegetables in the next round.

Heirloom vegetables are typically not hybrid, so seeds from plants grown from heirloom seeds should be OK.

- Make sure you're giving the plant time to produce good seeds. Some vegetable plants, such as melons, tomatoes, peppers, and eggplants, need to be ripe or slightly overripe. Beans and peas must stay in their pods until the pods are dry before the seeds are mature, and sweet corn should be left until the ears and kernels are dried on the cob. It's probably not worth trying to get seeds from carrots, beets, lettuce, cabbage, broccoli, or radishes, since they don't produce seeds in the same year the crop grows.
- Take your seeds from fully ripe, good-quality large vegetables, and spread them on paper towels in a warm, dry, shaded location for two to three weeks, until they are completely dry. Remove any bits of dried pulp or debris from the seeds—using your mouth to blow the material away sometimes does the trick. Then place the seeds in containers for storage.
- Store your seeds in a cool, dry place. They can keep for up to three years if they're stored well. A good spot for them is in a sealed jar or plastic container in a refrigerator.
- Take the seeds out of the refrigerator a week before you plan to use them, and let them warm up to room temperature and adjust to the humidity. This is particularly important for beans and peas, which develop a hard coating during storage that can make sprouting difficult if you don't let them warm up before planting them.

I want to start seeds indoors

USE PLASTIC FOOD CONTAINERS The simple solution is to start saving plastic containers whenever you visit a salad bar or deli. These clear-topped containers are perfect for starting seeds indoors, either at a window that gets a lot of natural indirect light or under an artificial plant light. Wash each container and fill the bottom halfway with a lightly moistened seed-starting mix. Place the seeds and close the lid, securing it with a rubber band. The clear lid allows light to pass through, holds moisture in, and lets you keep track of your sprouting seeds. If the containers are next to a window, be sure to turn them regularly so that the seedlings don't tend to lean one way. Or place an aluminum foil reflector behind the containers to even out the light. Putting reflectors on three sides of—and under—the containers is a good idea if your window doesn't have sufficient light.

Herbs are hijacking my garden

PREVENT HERB ROOTS FROM SPREADING Whether the herbs are in the garden or on your plate, the same holds true: A few are nice, but you don't want them on everything. Gardeners soon discover that herbs like to take over their surroundings.

Oregano, thyme, and mints are particularly bad about busting out all over and spreading by underground runners. To keep them in their place, cut the bottoms out of 5-gallon (19-liter) buckets or use chimney tiles. (A chimney tile looks like a square clay box with no top or bottom.) Sink your buckets or tiles 18 inches (45 centimeters) into the ground and plant your herbs in them. That's deep enough to curb their underground spread.

That clump of perennials looks a little peaked

DIVIDE PERENNIALS TO KEEP THEM HEALTHY Some perennials (plants that live over from one growing season to another) multiply by putting out adjacent roots and stems, so you can wind up with a cluster of plants growing out from the center, which might not suit your garden design. Moreover, the leaves and flowers at the center of clumps of perennials may become sickly and weak looking, a signal that too many plants are competing for food and moisture.

The solution is to uproot the clustered perennials and divide them into pieces occasionally. The separate pieces, which will grow into replicas of the parent plant, can be planted elsewhere on your property, or you can give them to a friend.

Here are some tips to keep in mind when dividing perennials:

- Do the dividing when the plant flowers are dormant. For instance, if the perennial flowers in the spring, divide it in late summer or in the fall. If it flowers in late summer, divide it in the spring.

- Dig about 6 inches (15 centimeters) around the plant with a spade or shovel. When the plant has been loosened, pull it out of the ground. Once it's out, experienced gardeners say, you can sometimes reach into the clump and pull the roots apart easily with your fingers. But if the clump is tightly bound, you will need to cut it in half or into several sections.

If you're not sure where one plant ends and another begins, put the cluster in a bucket of water and wash off as much soil as you can. This will help you see how to divide the cluster.

I'm melancholy about my small melons

PROTECT THE LEAVES, PRUNE, AND COVER THE GROUND It's an unpleasant surprise when the melons you've been hoping will turn out huge and sweet turn out small and bland. (Another melon sur-prise is that they're technically *vegetables*, not fruit. Bet you didn't know that.)

Horticulturists who particularly enjoy growing melons know how to turn out good ones. Here's what they suggest:

- Make sure the plants keep the leaves on their vines as long as possible. Don't let beetles or other bugs chew up the leaves, and make sure you deal with any leaf diseases promptly. (Talk to your local Cooperative Extension office about particular bugs and diseases you can expect to see.) The leaves produce sugars that get transferred to the melons, giving them their sweet taste. No leaves, no sweetness.
- If you want big melons, once you get a nice-looking melon growing, prune off any others that start on the same vine. The remaining melon will grow larger without competition for nutrients.
- Melons respond well to growing on raised beds with a layer of plastic on top of the soil for mulch, which keeps the soil warmer and keeps the fruit—er, vegetables—from directly con-tacting the ground.

I want straighter garden rows

USE A CORD AND JUGS OF WATER To establish straight rows in a garden, fill two plastic jugs with water and set one at each end of the row. Then stretch a cord between them. When you've finished planting the row, move the jugs into position to mark the next row. This technique is easier than driving in stakes to hold your string.

■ NURTURING PLANTS

I keep feeding my vegetables, but they don't perk up

USE FERTILIZER WITH CARE One mistake gardeners commonly make is that they overfertilize their plants, which can damage their roots and lead to poor fruiting, poor flavor, and excessive vine growth. In fact, some horticulturists say many more problems are related to overfertilization than to underfertilization.

Fertilizers, which provide nitrogen (N), phosphorus (P), and potassium (K), are a good way to give your plants the nutrients they need. (The three numbers prominently featured on fertilizer labels represent the percentages of these nutrients in this order.) However, you should have a sample of your soil tested by your local Cooperative Extension office (see box, below) if you know nothing about its fertility, so that you can better judge what type of fertilizer the soil needs.

Keep in mind that more fertilizer isn't better. In general, you should apply less than the bag indicates; certainly don't apply more than indicated. Most packages recommend using a strong dose so you'll purchase more product. Don't go above the package's recommendation unless you know your specific soil needs it.

My plants need an extra boost

ADD SOME BENEFICIAL FUNGI Whenever you plant seeds or seedlings or transplant a plant, consider adding some mycorrhizal

---

Cooperative Help for Your Garden

If you want to have the alkalinity and acidity of your soil tested, or if you want to get free reliable information on your area's gardening conditions, one of the best places to turn to is your local Cooperative Extension Service. The service has a university-affiliated headquarters in every state and a local office in most counties. You can find your local office listed in the telephone directory under U.S. Government, Department of Agriculture. You can also find it on the Internet by searching for Cooperative Extension Service and your state's name. There is no similar service in Canada.

fungi to the soil or sprinkling it on the plants' roots before you put them into the ground. These fungi are becoming a popular tool for gardeners. They form a beneficial relationship with the plant, improving its root system's ability to pull nutrients from the ground. This allows the plant to grow stronger and larger.

Name brands that you might find in nurseries or garden-supply catalogs include Myke and MycoGrow.

I want compost—not a lifetime project

ENCIRCLE A COMPOST PILE WITH STRAW Some gardeners take their compost piles *very* seriously. You can find entire books on the topic, and you can spend a lot of time measuring ingredients and tending the stuff. It's true that compost, which is a mixture of leaves and grass clippings, table scraps, and other natural wastes, decomposes and enriches your existing soil with nutrients. But you don't *have* to lavish a lot of attention on your compost pile, say experienced gardeners.

Here's a simple way to generate compost: Get a couple of bales of straw at a garden center, pop the strings off them, and break them into chunks. Use these chunks to make a 4-foot (1.2-meter) circle. Fill it with your leaves, grass clippings, table scraps, fruit and vegetable peelings, and even weeds and old plants. Avoid putting in meat, fat, and bones or pet droppings, which can spread disease and attract pests. Sprinkle a little dirt and some more straw on top. As your layers of compost grow taller, keep stacking chunks of straw on the circle; it should eventually look like a little igloo.

Let the stuff decompose over several months, and you will wind up with great compost to spread on your garden.

Composting takes forever

PUREE SCRAPS FOR FASTER DECOMPOSITION An easy way to speed up the composting process is to take your collection of fruit and vegetable peelings, eggshells, and other easily biodegradable scraps (no meat or dairy) and put them in a blender along with a cup of water. Puree the scraps and pour the mixture on the compost pile. The mush will decompose quickly—usually in a few weeks. To minimize the mess, collect the scraps in a small plastic bag and puree them every few days.

■ URBAN GARDENING

My yard's too tiny for a garden

GROW PLANTS IN CONTAINERS Even if you have some yard space, you might not have enough for a garden. Growing plants in containers might be a solution. Just keep the following hints from gardening experts in mind:

- Use big enough containers that your plants will have plenty of room to grow. Ask your local nursery how much soil each plant will need. Although scientists have developed vegetables that don't require as much growing space, some still need a lot of soil. For example, you would need at least a 5-gallon (19-liter) container for a single tomato plant.
- Use potting soil in your containers rather than soil from the ground. Potting soil is lighter, drains better, and is sterilized to kill weed seeds and diseases that could hurt your plants.
- Use a slow-release fertilizer in pellet form. Since you need to water container plants frequently, a regular fertilizer would tend to wash right out of the soil. But in pellet form, one application will release the plant food slowly and last for several months.
- Don't overwater your plants. Make sure that you thoroughly soak the entire container each time you water, but pour away any extra water that fills the saucer underneath the container. Making the plant sit in water encourages root rot. Since the signs of rot include wilting, many people think that the plant needs *more* water, which does even more damage. If you're not sure whether the wilting is from too much or too little water, gently pull the plant up out of the container. If the roots are brown and slimy, it's root rot. Water it less.

I'd love to garden, but I live in an apartment building

USE BASKETS AND PLASTIC POTS Even if you're in a high-rise apartment and live far above the nearest soil, let alone gardening space, you can still grow plants in containers and hanging baskets. Just keep these tips in mind:

- In high-rise buildings, balconies can get extremely hot and dry from sunlight reflected off the building, so you may need to

TRICKS OF THE TRADE

Don't Make Your Bulbs Skip Lunch

If you have spring flowers that grow from bulbs, such as tulips and daffodils, don't chop down the plant after it's finished flowering, urges aptly named Rose Lerner, a consumer home horticulture extension specialist for Purdue University. And if you cut off flowers for a display, leave as many leaves on the uncut part as possible. The foliage on the plant is making sugars to store in the bulb for *next* year, she explains. If you cut the plant down as soon as the flowers are gone, the bulb will do poorly the following year. Once the leaves fade and wilt, you can cut the plants down. If you're bothered by the flowerless foliage, plant other perennials around them that will bloom at different times and hide the withered ones.

water your plants every day. Since you'll probably be carrying water from your sink or tub faucet, keep this chore in mind when you're planning how many plants to grow.

- Use plastic pots rather than clay pots. Plants in plastic dry out less quickly because the pots aren't porous like clay ones. Put 2 inches (5 centimeters) of an organic mulch on top of the soil in the container to reduce water evaporation from the soil.

- When you're planning for hanging baskets, consider how you're going to water them. Can you safely stand on a step stool and water with a watering can? Will you get tired of taking the basket down to water it frequently?

My house plants will die if I go away

ADD WATER-RELEASING CRYSTALS A fast, affordable, and practical solution is to stock up on little crystals that soak up and then gradually release water. Specific brands include Water Crystals and WaterSmart Crystals, which are sold by garden centers. When you add water to these polymer granules, they absorb many times their weight in water. By mixing them in with the soil in your plants' containers and then watering, the crystals soak up and then slowly release the water to keep your plants watered while you're gone.

Be sure to follow directions on the label, because putting more crystals in a container is not necessarily better. Since they expand when wet, too many crystals can swell up and damage your plant or push it out of the pot.

I need to get the lead out of my veggies

TEST THE SOIL AND CHANGE PLANTINGS ACCORDINGLY
Researchers studying soil have found that people who grow vegetables in urban areas may be getting an added ingredient in their fresh veggies: lead.

This metal is particularly dangerous for fetuses and children. It can cause developmental problems in the brain and nervous system, including mental impairment. Lead accumulates in soil in urban areas from chips of paint from older homes that were long ago painted with lead-based paint or from the exhaust of vehicles that burned leaded gasoline decades ago.

Here's what gardening experts suggest you do if you're gardening in an older urban neighborhood or you live near a major highway. First, take a sample of your soil to your local cooperative extension service and have it tested for lead. If it's high in the metal, you have these alternatives:

- Grow flowers instead of vegetables.
- Stick with "fruiting" vegetables like tomatoes, peppers, and squash. They accumulate less lead. Steer clear of leafy vegetables, such as lettuce and spinach, and root vegetables, such as carrots, potatoes, and beets. They absorb more lead than other vegetables.
- Grow your vegetables in containers or raised beds. Fill the containers with potting soil. Fill the raised beds with new topsoil and compost that you've brought in from elsewhere. Of course, you should have soil for your raised beds tested before you plant things in it to make sure it's safe, too. If you use raised beds, first put down a plastic barrier between your old soil and the new soil and build the beds up 12 to 18 inches (30 to 45 centimeters). That should give your vegetables enough new soil for growth, and the plastic will keep them from tapping into the lead-tainted soil.

■ TOOLS AND TECHNIQUES

My gardening sessions leave me aching

PICK COMFORTABLE TOOLS AND WORK HABITS Thinking about your garden should give you a glow in your heart. But if it gives you more of a dull ache in your back, you probably need to adjust your gardening routines.

The easy solution to gardening aches and pains is to change the way you work.

- Make sure you're using tools that fit your body. (See "Tool School," next page.)
- Examine the repetitive movements you're doing that you may not have realized. Are you on your knees a lot? Are you constantly using your arms above your head? Are you continually bending and twisting? All of these can cause or aggravate aches and pains. You may need to sit down on a bench rather than kneel, enlist some help in the garden, or find new ways to do your tasks that don't involve repetitive movements.
- Break up your tasks so that you're not repeating the same motion for an hour straight.

If you must pull weeds, do so for only 15 or 20 minutes at a time, then rest or tackle another chore for a while.

My fingers are sore from pinching mums

USE GARDEN SHEARS INSTEAD By removing buds from your chrysanthemums, you can make the plant flower later in the year. However, pinching off all those little buds can be a time-consuming chore. Forget all that pinching and break out a big pair of garden shears or a stringed weed trimmer, such as a Weed Eater, experienced nursery workers advise. They recommend that you whack the plant off about halfway up. This will also encourage the plant to become bushy and compact rather than tall and spindly.

■ SICK PLANTS AND PESTS

My vegetable plants keep getting diseases

CHANGE YOUR WATERING SYSTEM If your vegetable plot stays sicker than an emergency room during flu season, the problem could be the way you water the plants.

First, refrain from watering at night, experienced vegetable growers say. When plants stay wet all night, it sets them up for disease. Second, keep the spray from the garden hose off the leaves and other aboveground parts of the plants. These don't take up water; the roots underground do. Keeping water off the plants will help cut down on diseases.

Vegetable plants also commonly get diseases by touching the ground. If your plants are prone to disease, follow these guidelines:

- **Mulch properly.** Mulching is great for plants in general, since it holds moisture in the soil, and organic mulches can supply some nutrients as they decompose. Mulch also keeps the plants, vines, and vegetables from coming into direct contact with the soil. So make sure you have a 1- to 3-inch (2.5- to 7.5-centimeter) layer of organic mulch, such as wood chips, shredded bark, or grass clippings, in your vegetable garden beneath your plants.
- **Get your plants up off the ground.** If any crop can be trellised, staked, or caged to force it to grow vertically, that's good, say experts. Tomatoes are grown this way, of course, but you can do the same with peppers, eggplants, cucumbers, and peas. You generally get less disease and better-quality vegetables. And picking them is easier, since they're higher off the ground.

My tomatoes have black bottoms

PLANT CRUSHED EGGSHELLS WITH TOMATO PLANTS Seasons that are very wet or very dry often spell trouble for tomato plants and the people who love them. The tomatoes get a vile condition called blossom end rot, and the gardeners get sad.

Blossom end rot causes a very nasty blackening at the bottom of the tomato fruit that makes it unusable. The problem is caused by excessive water or hot, dry temperatures. Ideally, your plants will get a long soak each week or so, but nature—or your watering schedule with the garden hose—can sometimes provide them with too much or too little.

The solution is to share your eggs with your plants. In February, start saving eggshells from your cooking. Set them in a cool, dry place for 24 hours, so they can dry out, and then crush them into a powder. If you don't eat eggs, get eggshells from a restaurant.

When tomato-planting season comes around, put the crushed shells from a dozen eggs into each hole before you put in a tomato

Of Hoses and Roses
Diana Kilmer, in Temecula, California, sees all sorts of sick roses caused by improper watering. She advises keeping these tips in mind:

• Water roses before noon. If they sit in wet soil overnight, particularly if the soil is heavy in clay and doesn't drain well, roses will get root rot. If your roses develop this problem, you may detect a distinctive smell like rotten eggs. Further, any water droplets that stay on the leaves during the bright afternoon sunlight will act like magnifying glasses, burning brown spots on the foliage.

• When you prune roses, cut the stems at a 45-degree angle. If you cut them straight across, water droplets can sit on them and soak in, causing "dieback," or a brown color that spreads down the stem until it kills the plant.

plant. The plant will take in the calcium from the shells, which will greatly increase its ability to regulate its own reserves of moisture, experts say. No other type of calcium seems to work as well.

My water garden turned into a slime garden

ADD WATER-CLARIFYING PLANTS Has the water in your decorative water pond turned green, murky, and just plain gross? The solution is simple and involves adding two types of plants.

- First, make sure that two-thirds of the surface of your pond is covered with floating plant material, such as water lilies. The large leaves of these surface floaters create shade, which helps thwart sun-loving algae.
- Second, add some oxygenating plants. Some of these seaweed-like plants are floaters and others need to be planted on the bottom, but they stay hard at work underwater keeping the water clear. In most ponds, you plant them in a pot and then sink the pot. Adding these plants, which are available at your local nursery or water-garden center, will clear the water in a few weeks.

Slugs love my flowers—for lunch

SET UP A COPPER BARRIER Slugs have an aversion to copper, say those who have successfully coped with slugs. This gives you an opportunity to protect your outdoor plants and decorate your flower boxes and raised beds at the same time. Go to your local hardware store or a store that sells roofing supplies and ask for a roofing material called copper flashing. Many stores will cut this into strips for you. (Yours should be at least 1 inch wide.) Use weatherproof nails to fasten a strip of copper around your flower box or planter midway between the top and bottom. It makes a handsome adornment and posts a warning sign: "No slugs served here."

■ TREES

I fear a windstorm will damage my trees

PRUNE WEAK BRANCHES Big and strong as most trees are, they can take a beating when a powerful wind whips through their branches. Here's how to help yours suffer fewer broken limbs the next time they tangle with the wind:

- A general rule of thumb is to avoid what experts call double leaders—two equal-sized branches that come out of the trunk at the same spot. This causes both of them to be weaker. Which one should you lop off? Cut off the branch that's emerging from the tree at a narrower angle. Limbs that come out at a 90-degree angle (right angle) are stronger than those that emerge with a narrower angle. The more limbs that grow out at 90 degrees, the stronger your tree will be.
- Pick up the phone and have an arborist (a tree-maintenance professional) check out your trees and trim hard-to-reach, weak, and dead branches so they won't break off and fall on your house, your car, or your head during the next windstorm.

A snapped branch left a wound on my tree trunk

MAYBE TRIM IT, BUT OTHERWISE DO NOTHING For the most part, the tree will take care of itself. Trees naturally close off wounds to prevent rot and damage from spreading. Trying to help the process along might cause additional damage. For example, packing a cavity with insulation or painting a wound will only trap moisture and promote rot. What you can do to help your tree is to prune off any remaining portions of the branch in stages, as close to the branch collar as possible without cutting into the trunk. As a preventive measure, cut off any other dead limbs before they break off.

■ LAWNS

I'm afraid road salt will hurt my lawn

SPREAD GYPSUM ON YOUR LAWN If you get a little road salt on your lawn, it will delay grass growth in the spring. But if you get a lot of salt, it can kill the lawn. The solution: gypsum. This mineral can absorb and neutralize excessive amounts of salt. To save salt-contaminated grass, use a spreader to apply gypsum after the snow has melted and the top inch of soil has thawed. Lawn and garden gypsum is available in garden centers. You'll need about 40 pounds of gypsum per 250 square feet (18 kilograms per 23 square meters).

It's important that you apply the gypsum before the new roots start feeding and growing. Once the salt is drawn into the grass, it's too late.

Weeds are overtaking my lawn

The soil in your lawn is *full* of weed seeds, and they're just waiting to pop up in a bare spot in your lawn. That's kind of a downer to think about, but it's true. Three simple techniques—proper mowing, fertilizing, and watering—will dramatically cut down on weeds invading your lawn while minimizing the need for chemical herbicides, say turf specialists. Here's how these three steps can keep weeds from taking over:

MOW HIGH AND OFTEN Most homeowners typically mow their grass too low and wait too long between mowings. You should usually keep

WORLD-CLASS GOOF

The Plant that Ate the South

In 1876, Americans got their first look at an exotic Asian plant called kudzu at the Centennial Exposition in Philadelphia. During the Great Depression, farmers and government conservation workers were paid to plant it liberally to reduce soil erosion. It also made good food for farm animals.

But planting it turned out to be a *really* bad idea. The lush, vinelike kudzu grew to engulf about 7 million acres in the southeastern United States, where it still thrives. The plant can grow 60 feet (18 meters) annually and smother telephone poles, homes, junked cars, and fields in a dense green blanket. It's been found as far north as Connecticut and as far west as Oregon.

Its deep root systems make it hard to kill once it gains a foothold. To eradicate a new growth of kudzu, cut the vines close to the ground with a mower every month or two, and bag up and burn all the cut vines or send them to the landfill.

your grass between 2 and 3 inches (5 and 7.5 centimeters) tall. Never mow off more than a third of the height of your grass at any one time, experts say. This may require measuring the grass with a ruler and inspecting your lawn mower's manual to learn how to set the blade the appropriate distance from the ground.

By mowing the grass at the proper height, the leaves form a dense canopy over your lawn. It also helps grass form new leaf-bearing shoots. These factors crowd out the weeds.

FERTILIZE YOUR LAWN REGULARLY Depending on where you live, you'll need to fertilize at different intervals. In northern climates, lawns need to be fertilized in May, early July, early September, and again in late October. In the south, that schedule should be concentrated in the summer, with applications in May, June, July, and August. In the West, the schedule depends on elevation. Call your local Cooperative Extension office for more information.

Be sure to buy fertilizer that has package directions telling you what setting to use on your kind of spreader. The setting determines how heavily your spreader dispenses the fertilizer.

Don't worry that you'll be fertilizing your weeds, too. They're so handy at utilizing existing nutrients in the soil that the extra fertilizer will make little difference to them.

WATER YOUR LAWN WHEN NEEDED Most lawn grasses need about an inch of water each week during the growing season. Signs that it needs water are that the grass turns bluish green or that your footprints remain in the grass after you walk across it.

The best time to water is early in the morning before the wind and sun cause water to evaporate. Avoid watering in the evening, since the leaves will stay wet overnight, raising the risk of lawn disease. To tell how much water is coming out of your sprinkler, and to ensure that it's hitting your lawn evenly, place coffee cans 5 and 20 feet (1.5 and 6 meters) away from it. Check the depth of the water that the cans have accumulated after 30 minutes and multiply by 2 to estimate the hourly amount. Move the sprinkler accordingly to spread the water around.

If water is puddling on the ground, turn off the sprinkler and let the water soak in. Finish watering in another two or three days.

PROBLEM STOPPER

Scorched Earth Policy
An urban garden specialist in Wisconsin tells of a woman he met at a neighborhood gardening function. He noticed that *everything* around her house was dying: shrubs, perennials, trees.

The stuff looked like it had weed killer on it, he recalls. The woman reported that she had indeed doused everything with herbicide in an effort to kill her weeds—mistakenly thinking that the chemicals somehow knew to kill only the weeds, not the good plants.

Yard and Garden Invaders

■ BIRD PESTS

Pigeons are nesting on my house

PUT UP A WIRE MESH BARRIER When pigeons, swallows, and other birds build nests under your eaves and overhangs, they usually set up housekeeping on ledges. To send these squatters packing, change the ledge so that they won't have a level surface to work with. Take a length of hardware cloth—a woven wire mesh available at hardware stores—that's long enough to cover the ledge that the birds are roosting on. Use rustproof staples or nails to fasten one edge of the mesh to the wall a few inches above the ledge. Then pull the cloth taut across the corner and fasten the free edge of the hardware cloth to the ledge. On each end, nail down a flap of hardware cloth to cover up the hole so no little pests can get under the cloth. The invading birds will sound a retweet and find some other place to call home.

Blackbirds are heckling me

SHINE RED LIGHT IN THEIR EYES Blackbirds and other pesky birds, such as starlings and grackles, can be party animals of the worst kind. They sometimes roost in large numbers in people's trees and on their homes, make a lot of noise, and occasionally leave huge messes. One way to solve the problem is with light. Blackbirds don't like having strong lights shined into their eyes any more than you do. And for some reason they *especially* hate red lights, say wildlife-damage-management specialists, who do such things as chase critters away from airports so that they won't collide with planes.

Arm yourself with a red laser pointer, found in gift stores and novelty shops for less than $20. (An alternative is to use a flashlight. Cover the lens with a piece of red cellophane, held in place with a rubber band.) Go outside early in the morning or in the evening when it's somewhat dark so the birds will see the light better. Shine the light in the birds' eyes while making a noisy commotion. They'll learn to stay away.

HANG UP SHINY METALLIC STRIPS Experts say you'll get the best results if you combine the red-light strategy with multiple harassment techniques. An example: Buy shiny strips of Mylar—a thin, durable metallic material—and hang them around problem areas. The strips flutter and flash in the light, making the birds uncomfortable.

The strips should be at least 1½ feet (45 centimeters) long to be effective; 2 feet (60 centimeters) is better. You can hang them from tree limbs, fences, or other structures that let them flutter in the wind. How many you'll need to hang depends on the size of the flock you're trying to deter, but three dozen strands is a good average number in a yard. You can buy Mylar strips at garden supply stores and from online animal control businesses for about $4 per 300-foot (91-meter) roll.

Geese are leaving drops on my yard

SPRAY THEM WITH A MOTION-ACTIVATED SPRINKLER Geese droppings create an unsightly obstacle course of waste on sidewalks and lawns. The simple solution is to buy a motion-activated yard sprinkler that will give them an alarming blast whenever they decide to visit. Set up the sprinkler near the goose hangout and attach a garden hose. When the birds waddle too close to the device, an unwelcome spray of water will frighten them away. Motion-activated sprinklers sell for about $70 and are available at garden and hardware stores or through mail order.

WORLD-CLASS GOOF

Honk Next Time

In 1999, publicists for a Virginia amusement park learned the recipe for a public relations nightmare: Take an internationally known model and give him a goose.

According to news accounts, Busch Gardens brought in Fabio—whose flowing mane and muscular torso have graced the covers of countless romance novels—to promote its new roller coaster, Apollo's Chariot.

Unfortunately, during a ride on the roller coaster, Fabio's nose collided with an airborne goose. As the roller coaster descended back into the station, news photographers snapped photos of Fabio's blood-spattered face. He wound up with only minor injuries, but the bird was reportedly later found dead.

■ INSECT AND OTHER SMALL PESTS

Cutworms are slicing up my plants

SPRINKLE CORNMEAL AROUND THE PLANTS Cutworms, which are actually moth larvae, live just below the surface of your soil and, true to their name, can tear right through your flowerbeds. They come in many colors and range from 1 to 2 inches (2.5 to 5 centimeters) in length. One way to recognize them is to remember that "*C* is for *cutworm*"—they usually curl up into a *C* shape when you touch them. You can quickly get rid of them with yellow cornmeal, say entomologists who specialize in nontoxic pest control. The cutworms like to eat the cornmeal, but unfortunately for them they can't digest it, so they die. Sprinkle it on the ground around your plants and let them enjoy their last meal.

Snails are feasting on my veggies

ATTRACT THEM TO A SHADY RETREAT When snails proliferate in your yard or garden, you can get rid of them in no time by putting a roof over their heads. Make a little tablelike structure by nailing 1-inch (2.5-centimeter) risers, such as short pieces of thick dowel rod, under the corners of a 12-inch (30-centimeter) square of plywood or other board. Place this shelter wherever the snails are appearing and toss a few slices of raw turnip or potato under it as bait.

Snails like to hide in dark, cool places during the day, and they'll gather under the board after their night's activities. Each morning, collect the snails from under the board and relocate them as you see fit. This technique will also work on the squash bugs that like to infest zucchini.

Aphids are killing my garden

HOSE THEM OFF Research shows that just blasting aphids with a hard stream of water from the garden hose is a super way to kill most of the bugs and chase away the rest. Cradle your plant with one hand and hit the aphids with a narrow stream of water. Most of the time you'll take care of the pests with the first session of water therapy, but you may need to return the next day to get the stragglers. Though you may knock some petals from flowers with this approach, you're unlikely to damage the plant with a hard stream of water.

APPLY INSECTICIDAL SOAP Sold at garden supply stores, insecticidal soap is also an effective tool against aphids. When the soap lands on the aphid, the stuff washes away the protective coating on the bug's body and causes damage to its cells, killing it. Insecticidal soaps also won't harm birds, other animals, or people. These soaps must be thoroughly applied by spraying them onto plants that you want to protect. Follow the label instructions carefully for proper use of the product you buy; insecticidal soaps can damage certain plants.

ADD LADYBUGS TO YOUR GARDEN Another way to annihilate aphids: Fight bugs with bugs. Increase the population of ladybugs around your yard. Also known as lady beetles or ladybirds, these familiar red-and-black-spotted bugs rely on aphids as a primary food source. You can order ladybugs from a number of beneficial-insect supply companies. A half-pint of the bugs—about 4,500—costs about $30. Scatter the ladybugs around your property, making sure to follow directions from the company about what time of day to scatter **them and how to make your property attractive to them so**

The Movie Bug Wrangler

You think you've got insect problems? They pale in comparison to Steven Kutcher's. He's had to make a fly clean itself on cue. He's made a cockroach run out on the floor, then flip over on its back. He's had to coax a live wasp to fly into actor Roddy McDowall's mouth.

Kutcher, a California entomologist, regularly wrangles bugs for films. His 75-plus credits include *Spider-Man* and *Arachnophobia* as well as many commercials and music videos. For *Spider-Man* he came up with the special red-and-blue spider that gives Peter Parker his superpowers. He used a secret technique to paint the spider without harming it.

Kutcher needs all his skills on movie sets, given the unusual circumstances he and the bugs often find themselves in. A director wants a shot of a butterfly, but at *night*. Or of ants, but during a *rainstorm*. Or of a moth circling a porch light—when the studio is full of more attractive floodlights.

He has four toolkits filled with food and bug-handling accessories as well as four vacuum cleaners to pick up his bugs when they've finished their close-ups.

His recommendation for keeping bugs away from your home is to think of all the things you would do to lure all the bugs in the world to your house, then do the opposite.

Bugs want water, food, and shelter. Therefore, don't have standing water or food sitting around for the bugs to eat, including bowls of pet food and rotting fruit underneath trees. Keep window screens repaired and free of holes, and use weather stripping to make doors and windows bug-tight.

Baiting Pill Bugs with a Potato

Pill bugs—also known as roly-polies—aren't actually bugs. They're crustaceans, kin to crabs and lobsters. They're flat and oval-shaped, and when you bother them, they roll up into a little ball. But they do eat your plants. The fast solution to this problem is to cut a large raw potato in half and hollow each half out with a spoon. Take the halves outside and place them hollow side down on the ground where the pill bugs gather. Next morning collect the pill bugs, which will gather under the potatoes. Drown them in a bucket of water with a squirt of dishwashing liquid.

they'll stay. To find out the best time of year to do this in your area, talk to your local Cooperative Extension Service (listed in the yellow pages under federal government offices).

Grubs are gobbling up my lawn

KILL THEM WITH NEMATODES Grubs are actually immature beetles. They live in the soil and eat grass roots, which can cause large patches of your grass to die. They're also bothersome because they are a food source that attracts other pests, such as raccoons. Here's a simple, natural way to control grubs: Attack them with nematodes. Nematodes are crudely built, microscopic worms that will attack and kill grubs underground. They're available from commercial nursery and pest control suppliers, and you typically apply them to your lawn by attaching a container of them to a garden hose or by putting them in a watering can and sprinkling them on.

Check with your local university cooperative extension office about the best time to apply nematodes to your lawn. You'll want to do it when grubs are closest to the surface of the ground, so the nematodes will work most effectively. The best time of year will vary from region to region.

Keep in mind that nematodes are fairly fragile, so follow the instructions for using them carefully. You generally want to apply them in the evening, since ultraviolet light kills them. Then keep the soil well moistened so they will stay alive, but not so wet that they can't attack their prey.

Yellow jackets are menacing my yard

FLOOD THEIR NESTS WITH SOAPY WATER These little wasps, with bold black and yellow stripes, look like trouble with a capital T. They tend to build nests underground, and if they feel threatened—when you run a lawn mower nearby, for instance—they sometimes attack aggressively, quickly leaving you with many painful stings. You may also find them swarming around garbage cans and fruit trees that have dropped their fruit, both of which provide food.

To get rid of a nest, take a large watering can—the kind you use to water your garden—and add 2 gallons (7.5 liters) of water and ½ cup of liquid dishwashing detergent. The detergent makes the wasps drown more easily. Go out about half an hour before sunrise and pour the mixture from your watering can into the ground where you've seen the yellow jackets emerge. It's important to do this early in the morning while the yellow jackets are all in their nest and the cool temperature limits their ability to fly out.

Mosquitoes are after my blood

DRAIN ALL STANDING WATER Mosquitoes were bad enough when they just made you itch. Now that some of them carry the West Nile virus, their bite can even be deadly in rare cases. The little bloodsuckers like to lay their eggs in standing water. To keep the mosquito population around your house to a minimum, make sure you have no still water anywhere. That means *all* standing water, even what you would find in flowerpots and gutters. Change the water in your birdbath daily to clear away mosquitoes' eggs and larvae.

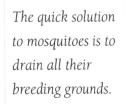

PUT MOSQUITO-EATING FISH IN PONDS If you have spots where you *want* water for landscaping purposes—in ornamental ponds and water gardens, for instance—stock them with mosquito fish (*Gambusia affinis*), which are available at pet stores. These little fish are skeeter-eating machines: An adult can put away 500 larvae a day.

The quick solution to mosquitoes is to drain all their breeding grounds.

Fire ants have set up camp

DUMP BOILING WATER ON THEM Fire ants can damage electrical equipment by chewing on insulation around wires, and they can kill small birds and mammals. When they bite *you*, they leave painful spots that often become infected. On occasion their bites have killed people who were sensitive to them. The red imported fire ant, the most troublesome type, is predominantly found in the southeastern United States, from North Carolina to Texas. Here's a simple, non-toxic way to douse fire ants: Pour boiling water onto the mound. Boil about ½ gallon (2 liters) of water in a pot that you can carry safely and add a squirt of dishwashing liquid. The detergent sticks to their bodies and makes the hot water more likely to kill them. Carefully pour the water on the mound, making sure you don't burn yourself or get bitten by ants. This technique can kill up to 90 percent of a mound's residents.

Don't do this if the mound is near flowers or other vegetation you wish to keep, because the solution can kill vegetation.

PROBLEM STOPPER

Checking for Mosquito Breeding Grounds

Here's how to make sure there are no water sources near your home where mosquitoes can breed:

• Cover garbage, recycling, and compost containers. Drill holes in the bottoms of containers that must be left uncovered.

• Remove water from easily overlooked spots, such as flowerpots, tire swings, and swimming pool covers.

• Store wheelbarrows and boats upside down.

• Replace birdbath water at least once a week to stay ahead of the seven- to ten-day breeding cycle.

• Keep gutters clean. Empty rain barrels at least once a week.

• Fill any low areas in your yard where puddles form with earth. Check under shrubbery for hidden containers.

• Repair leaks in hoses and sprinkler systems. Fix dripping outdoor taps.

Everyday black ants are making me antsy

KILL THEM WITH A BORIC ACID PRODUCT If run-of-the-mill ants have invaded your yard, here's a low-toxic and effective way to kill them: Use a commercial ant poison containing boric acid and sugar. Ants, like people, like sweet tastes, so the sugar attracts them. These ants won't have to worry about cavities from the sugar, because the boric acid kills them. A boric acid–sugar mixture can decimate an ant colony. It may take a while, but this is one occasion when slow and steady works the best. This is because ants feed by a process called tropholaxis, in which one ant eats food, then brings it back up for other ants to share. If ants eat a poison that's too strong, they'll die before they can share it with other ants in the colony.

You can find this type of commercial ant killer in many supermarkets and hardware stores in a liquid form or in bait stations, which you leave around areas of ant traffic. It should be effective in killing most kinds of ant species, say pest control experts. Follow the label directions for outdoor use and keep in mind that it will take time for the poison to reach the queen ant, who sustains the colony.

Ants are nesting too close to the house

FLOOD THE NEST Encourage ant colonies to move away from your house without using poisons, which might harm your family or pets. Here are some measures you can take:

• Periodically flood the nest with the garden hose. For stubborn ants, pour boiling water on the nest.
• Put tomato or walnut leaves on the nest. These will repel ants.
• If the ants are climbing the trees near your house, block their paths by wrapping the tree trunks with two-sided tape.

■ ANIMAL PESTS

Skunks are a real problem in my yard

PUT OUT BUNCHES OF BALLOONS These black-and-white members of the weasel family can dig up your lawn, get your trash, or spray you or your pets with their terrible scent. One way to run them off is to blow up regular latex balloons and tie them in bunches around your house, patio, and property where the skunks hang out. This works for raccoons, too, say pest management specialists. The balloons rustling around may be enough to frighten the little stinkers. But if a skunk happens to *pop* a balloon, the noise will really get them running. (However, if a young skunk pops a balloon, it may be scared so badly that it will emit a little scent.)

SPRINKLE FOX URINE IN YOUR YARD You can also scare skunks away by sprinkling fox urine around your yard. The smell will make them fear that a predator has been nearby and will encourage them to move along. Try a product such as Shake-Away Fox Urine Powder, available from online pest control dealers.

GET RID OF GRUBS Controlling the grubs in your lawn will cut down on your skunk problem, since skunks feed on them.

Got skunks? Balloons will get rid of them in a hurry.

The dogs are in my trash again

SPRAY WITH A VILE-TASTING PRODUCT If neighborhood dogs seem to enjoy strewing your trash bags down the street, chewing your fence, or indulging in other forms of canine tomfoolery at your expense, this trick will leave a bad taste in their mouths. Spray a product called Ro-Pel Animal, Rodent, and Bird Spray Repellent on any surface that you want to keep a dog from slobbering on. According to experts, it's the most vile-tasting product on the market, so don't let a gust of wind blow it into your mouth. You can order the product from online suppliers for about $15 for a quart (liter).

Cats are tap-dancing on my car

SCARE THEM OFF WITH PREDATOR URINE If you find muddy cat footprints all over your freshly washed car or little droppings left as "presents" on your lawn, be careful in how you discourage the offenders. You don't want to harm someone's pet cat.

Try marking areas that you want to keep off limits to cats—around your driveway, for instance—with predator urine, suggest experts who focus on low-toxic ways to control pests. If a cat thinks that a wolf or coyote has been in the area, it may decide that its safety is a higher priority than decorating your car. You can find a number of products containing predator urine in lawn and garden shops. Brands include PredatorPee and Shake-Away Coyote Urine Powder.

TRICKS OF THE TRADE

Don't Leave Takeout for Raccoons

There are two common takeout foods that especially tempt raccoons into tearing open your trash bags and strewing them across the driveway: pizza and chicken bones. So says Michael Bohdan, a Plano, Texas, pest-control specialist, author, and television personality.

So if you want to avoid inviting raccoons to invade your trash, you might try keeping your leftover pizza and chicken bones indoors in a sealed container until trash day. Then set them out with the garbage.

I don't like the idea of killing pests

TRAP THEM LIVE IF IT'S LEGAL One fast way to rid your yard and garden of animal pests is to trap them live and have them escorted from your property. In some cases you can do this by yourself, but you should check with your local animal control authorities first. Laws in many areas regulate trapping, since animals may be protected, other people may not want to deal with your relocated pests, or the relocated animals may spread disease to a new area. In addition, some animals can harm you: A skunk could douse you with its stinky spray, for instance, or a rabid raccoon could give you rabies. If trapping is legal, your local animal control office may provide you with a trap to use.

Moles think my lawn is Grand Central Station

APPLY A CASTOR-OIL PRODUCT These underground pests can make a mess of your yard with their tunnels and mounds. But here's a little secret: Moles don't like castor oil any better than you do, say entomologists who specialize in pest management. So applying a product containing castor oil to your lawn will have the little tunnelers buying one-way tickets out of town.

One such product is called Mole-Med, available at garden centers, hardware stores, and plant nurseries. It comes in a granular form that you can scatter or a liquid form that you can spray on your yard with a garden hose. You can buy 3¾ pounds (1.7 kilograms) of the dry version for about $15, or a quart (liter) bottle of liquid for about $30.

Raccoons are a real problem in my area

BAIT YOUR TRAP WITH FISH For raccoons, possums, and skunks, it's best to bait your trap with any food that has a fishy smell. That includes sardines, tuna, and canned cat food.

I need to get rid of armadillos

CATCH ARMADILLOS WITH A PANTY HOSE TRAP Here's the perfect trap bait for these armor-bearing pests of southern states: Cut the toe off an old pair of panty hose, drop in several earthworms, and tie it closed with string or a rubber band. Then put it in your trap. Keep in mind, though, that there's a trade-off involved in relocating armadillos. They may be a pain because they dig up your yard, but they also eat many bothersome insects.

Squirrels are pests in my yard

BAIT SQUIRRELS WITH AN APPLE TREAT Here's the best bait: Take half an apple and cover it with loganberry paste. A company called Trapper's Choice makes this fruity rodent lure, which is available from online pest control vendors. Embed six pecan halves in the paste. The combination makes an aroma and taste that a squirrel can't resist. If you relocate the squirrel, make sure to take it at least 9 miles (14.5 kilometers) away from your home, since it may return to your home from any lesser distance.

My traps aren't catching mice

BAIT TRAPS WITH PEANUT BUTTER If you're tired of mice scurrying around your yard and invading your house, rethink how you bait your traps. Cheese is overrated as bait, as mice aren't instinctively attracted to it. Instead, bait your traps with a dab of peanut butter. And to make it *extra* appealing, put a shelled pecan or sunflower seed in front of the trap. A mouse will eat that as an appetizer and then attempt to snap up the peanut butter main course.

Deer are eating my plants

SPRINKLE THE PLANTS WITH HOT PEPPER If deer have turned your garden into a salad bar, turn up the heat on them by giving your plants a zing of cayenne pepper. Sprinkle the cayenne on your plants and reapply after it rains. Eventually the deer will figure out that the plants are hot—and they'll make someone *else's* garden their favorite mealtime destination. Several bulk-spice outlets sell cayenne pepper in large quantities online. To find their Web sites, do an Internet search for "bulk spices."

WRAP TREES WITH WIRE MESH If the deer are stripping the bark off the trees in your yard, wrap the tree trunks in hardware cloth. This wire mesh will keep the deer from sinking their teeth into the bark. Check your local hardware store, home improvement center, or plant nursery for this material.

TRICKS OF THE TRADE

Protecting Your Pets from Coyotes
If you have coyotes in your area, one of the most painful consequences could be the loss of your pet. Coyotes are extremely cunning and hard to scare away, and they can climb an 8-foot (2.4-meter) fence to attack their prey, says Robert Stalbaum, a Texas wildlife damage management biologist. Their favorite foods include cats and small dogs.

The best way to protect your pets from coyotes is to keep them inside your house or garage or in enclosed pens, especially at night. Keep their food dishes inside, too.

You can tell that coyotes are in your area by their droppings, which often contain hair and bones from their prey. Their tracks look similar to those of dogs, but coyote tracks are more pointed at the front; a dog's tracks are rounder.

Dealing with Neighbors' Pets

Pets are a common cause of friction between neighbors—whether it's a yowling tomcat at 2 A.M. or a Pekinese that poops on your manicured lawn. Pet experts offer this advice:

- **Assume goodwill at first.** Calling the cops or threatening to sue will usually make matters worse.

- **Talk to the neighbors.** They may have no idea their pet is bothering you.

- **Say it nicely.** Pick an opportune moment—a sunny afternoon when your neighbor is enjoying the yard, not some workday at 5 P.M. when she's trying to get the kids and the groceries into the house.

- **Look for allies.** The dog-owning neighbor might write off one complaint as hypersensitivity, but if he hears the same complaint from two or three others, the message gets reinforced.

- **Seek mediation.** Many local governments refer people to low- or no-fee mediation services. Ask your local small claims court about mediation services in your area.

- **If all else fails, call animal control.** For extreme offenders, especially violent dogs, the law is on your side. Do your homework by finding out what the local statutes say about pets. Then call animal control to report your problem.

Rabbits think my garden is a salad bar

PUT UP A CHICKEN-WIRE FENCE An easy-to-build fence will keep those bunnies from enjoying your vegetables before you do. Get a roll of 3-foot (1-meter) chicken wire and several lengths of rebar. Chicken wire is the wire fencing with honeycomb-shaped holes, and rebar is the metal bar used to reinforce masonry walls. Check for both at your local hardware store or home improvement warehouse. Pound the rebar stakes into the ground, several feet apart, around the perimeter of your garden.

Unroll the chicken wire flat on the ground and, down one long edge, bend 6 inches (15 centimeters) of the fencing out at a 90-degree angle. Stand the chicken wire up next to the rebar stakes so that the bent portion is on the ground, facing outward. Attach the fencing to the bars using short twists of wire. When you've run the fencing around the enclosure and you're back to the starting point, attach the loose end of the fence to the post with a twist or two of wire. This way, you can remove the fastening easily so that you can open and enter the enclosure when you want to work with the plants.

The fencing will keep rabbits out, and the portion at the bottom that sticks out along the ground will discourage rabbits from digging under the fence.

You versus Nature

■ HOT AND COLD WEATHER

I can't light my campfire, and it's cold

CARRY A COTTON-BALL FIRE STARTER You light a match and set it into a little pile of pine needles, twigs, and branches. The match goes out. You dig for another, dreaming of a cozy fire. Unfortunately, you have no more matches. It's going to be a cold night. Here's the experts' ultimate hint for avoiding a situation like this:

Before you go out into the wilderness, take a cotton ball and rub petroleum jelly all over it. Make sure you saturate the cotton. Do this to several cotton balls, stick them in a film canister or a little baggie, and put the container in your backpack or jacket pocket along with waterproof matches or a lighter.

The cotton is flammable, and the petroleum jelly will keep the cotton balls waterproof. When you need to light a fire, just assemble your pile of tinder and wood, tease some strands of fiber loose from a cotton ball, insert the ball into the pile, and touch your match or lighter to it.

Even a spark or a quick flame will light the cotton, which will then burn for several minutes, greatly improving your chances of lighting your campfire.

Cotton balls soaked in petroleum jelly are instant fire starters.

Everything's wet, and I need tinder for a campfire

LOOK FOR AN EVERGREEN TREE You'll find fire-starting salvation in a cone-bearing tree (a pine, for instance), say knowledgeable campers. The tree you select may be wet from rain or snow, but the base of the trunk is usually well protected from the elements. Two or 3 feet (60 to 90 centimeters) up the trunk, you will find dead, dry twigs that will make great tinder for your campfire. The dead twigs snap off easily. If a twig bends without breaking, leave it alone. It's alive and won't burn well anyway.

I'm going to a sporting event, and it's bitter cold

OPEN AN UMBRELLA Odd as it may seem, one of your best defenses against a cold, windy day is a large golf umbrella, say knowledgeable sporting enthusiasts. Open your umbrella, point it toward the wind, and seat yourself close up inside the umbrella so that it protects you from the bluster. You'll be surprised to discover how much warmer you'll feel in this makeshift shelter.

My car is stalling in the heat

STAY WITH YOUR CAR If you're motoring through a desert and your car decides it's not up to the challenge, feel free to be angry with the vehicle, but don't abandon it, recommend desert-survival experts. Pull off to the side of the road and stay near the car. Find some shade nearby—the car might even cast some shade for you. Don't go hiking for help. Odds are good that another motorist will come along and help you out, experts say.

I'm getting overcome by the heat

You were having such a good time out in the summer sunshine, soaking up the warmth and trying to store away some good memories to warm you next winter. But now you're a little *too* hot. That warmth suddenly feels more like a burning sensation. Choose your next steps carefully to avoid a medical emergency, desert-survival experts advise.

REST AND COOL OFF Common signs of *heat exhaustion* include a pale face, clammy skin, and dizziness. These are indications that you've pushed yourself too hard. You need to rest, cool off, and get some water and salty snacks in you, say the experts.

HEAD TO THE HOSPITAL You may need to do more if you have *heatstroke*, a medical emergency that requires prompt treatment at a hospital. Signs of heatstroke are skin that is red, hot, and dry. You may also be confused and hallucinating, so listen to your companions if they tell you that you need help.

■ DANGEROUS SITUATIONS

I'm lost in the woods

Getting lost in the woods can be scary. Here's how to keep yourself alive until someone finds you or you find your way back:

DON'T PANIC Most people who die as a result of being stranded in the boonies do so within 36 hours, but the average person can survive without eating for 40 days, survival experts say. Keep your wits about you, and you can last longer than you think. By panicking and running around frantically, you will burn up energy and get yourself sweaty, setting yourself up for hypothermia when the sun goes down.

KEEP WARM Staying warm and getting sleep so you can make rational decisions are crucial to wilderness survival. Since your surroundings have changed, your habits may need to change, too. That could mean moving around at *night* to stay warm, preferably walking in a circle so you won't injure yourself in the dark, and sleeping during the *day* when the sun's out. Avoid lying down directly on the ground. The cold earth will draw the heat out of your body. Gather up a nice pile of leaves and get into it. This will get you off the ground and trap your body heat.

DRINK WATER WHEN YOU FIND IT The water may have nasty microbes like giardia in it, but you can

WORLD-CLASS FIX

Surviving a Hot Spot

Australian volcano explorer John Seach was in the South Pacific a few years ago climbing a volcano that had erupted just four days earlier.

"I was just commenting how the ground was hot enough to cook dinner, when one of my boots melted," he says. "I reached for my backpack and took out some electrical tape, which I wrapped around my boot to keep the soles on." He hotfooted it a few hundred yards down the mountain to safety.

"I used electrical tape because it was all I had available," he adds. "It was in my backpack because it was small, light, and waterproof."

always visit the doctor when you get back to civilization. If you don't stay hydrated, you might die, say survival experts. If you're in a forest, you can often find a creek flowing down between two big hills. Even a dry streambed typically has water in it if you dig down a few feet. Or wipe your shirt on dewy grass and plants in the morning and wring it into your mouth.

The current is pulling me out to sea

THE PROBLEM IS A RIP CURRENT A rip current is a panic-inducing threat that can get you into real trouble at the beach. More than 80 percent of lifeguard rescues at ocean beaches are due to rip currents, say experts who train lifeguards.

When waves travel from deep to shallow water, they break near the shore. When they break strongly in some places and weakly in others, rip currents—narrow, fast-moving strips of water moving seaward—can form. Rip currents (also called riptides) often form in low spots or breaks in sandbars or near piers and other structures.

Most rip currents head straight back out to sea, perpendicular to the beach, but some go out diagonally. When people are caught in them, they often struggle in a futile attempt to swim directly toward the shore. But a strong rip current can make swimming seem like walking on a treadmill or up a down escalator, the experts say. Swimmers may grow exhausted and panic.

SWIM PARALLEL TO THE SHORE If you're caught in a rip current, instead of struggling to swim against the current toward the shore, swim *parallel* to the shore, experts advise. Most rip currents are fairly narrow, and you don't have to swim far to get out of their path. Once you're out of the current, *then* swim to shore.

REVERSE DIRECTION IF NECESSARY If you happen to be in a rip current that's headed diagonally away from shore, swimming parallel with the shore may put you into the swifter part of the current. If you feel as if you aren't getting out of the rip current quickly, turn around and swim parallel to the shore the *other* way.

I've cut myself badly, and I'm in the wild

CLOSE THE WOUND WITH DUCT TAPE You've cut your knee badly and need stitches, but you're on a hike and are miles from a hospital. Fortunately, you have that backpacker's staple, duct tape. Apply pressure to the wound to control the bleeding and then apply a stretch of duct tape across it to hold the two sides of the gash together. This should allow you to walk to a place where you can get help and a ride to a doctor or hospital.

■ INSECT BITES

Ouch! I just got stung

USE MEAT TENDERIZER You are just minding your own business when a bee or wasp gives you a painful sting. If you act quickly, you can minimize the pain and swelling. Here's what experts who have studied insect bites suggest:

Apply meat tenderizer immediately, if available. Protein enzymes in a venomous sting cause much of the inflammation. Meat tenderizers work by breaking down proteins. If you mix tenderizer with water to form a paste and then smear the paste on your sting, you will reduce pain and swelling by breaking down the enzymes in the venom. You have to do this within a few seconds after being stung, however, the experts say. So if you're going out where you might be exposed to yellow jackets or other stinging insects, take a little container of meat-tenderizer paste with you. Make sure the label on the meat tenderizer says it contains a protein-busting component, such as papain or bromelain.

PULL OUT THE STINGER Some insects, such as honeybees, will leave behind their stingers when they sting. A widespread belief is that you should scrape away the stinger with a credit card or knife edge to avoid squeezing more venom from the stinger into your skin by pinching. But experts say most of the venom is injected within 20 seconds of the sting. You can easily take that long looking through your wallet or purse to find something to scrape with. Instead, pull the stinger out of your skin and forget about scraping it.

TAKE AN ANTIHISTAMINE PILL Take an antihistamine, such as Benadryl, after getting stung. This, too, will help reduce swelling.

CARRY EPINEPHRINE IF YOU ARE ALLERGIC Keep in mind that insect stings can trigger a life-threatening condition called anaphylactic shock in highly allergic people. This requires a more sophisticated level of treatment. If you know you have these reac-

tions, consult with your doctor on how to treat insect stings. You may need to carry the drug epinephrine with you and, if you're stung, inject yourself with it before seeking emergency medical care.

The bee-sting itch is driving me nuts

RUB WITH ICE The best way to minimize the itching of a sting is to rub ice on it, say medical specialists. Rub an ice cube or hold an ice pack on it for a few minutes and repeat as needed.

■ ANIMAL ATTACKS

I've been sprayed by a skunk

MAKE A PEROXIDE-BAKING SODA SOLUTION You've probably heard that bathing in tomato juice will eradicate the notorious odor. But, scientists say, tomato juice only temporarily masks the stench. Here's a surefire remedy from camp nurses who have tended to many skunk victims: Mix 1 quart (1 liter) of 3 percent hydrogen peroxide, ¼ cup of baking soda, and 2 squirts of dishwashing detergent in a large container. Soak a hand towel or washcloth in the solution and wring it out so that it's no longer dripping wet. Rub the cloth over the spots that have been skunked, on both skin and clothing, as if you were scrubbing a really dirty spot. Go over the spot several times. If you're wearing bulky clothes, such as long pants and a sweater, remove the clothes and soak them in the solution for ten minutes before washing them as usual in the washing machine.

Be sure to handle skunk-sprayed clothing carefully so that the spray does not drip onto or rub against anything else in your house.

Running or screaming is not the answer when faced with a threatening dog.

A mean dog is growling at me

DON'T INTRUDE OR STARTLE Dogs are very territorial and may act aggressively to defend their turf. And dogs may attack if they're startled. So pay attention if you're walking or jogging and see a dog that hasn't noticed you; it may be startled when it sees you.

WATCH FOR PEAKED EARS AND BARE TEETH Dogs often exhibit warning signs that they're about to attack. They may hold their tails stiffly aloft, their ears may stick up, the hair on their backs may stand up, and—not surprisingly—they may bare their teeth.

DON'T RUN OR SCREAM If you're confronted with a threatening dog, resist the impulse to scream or run. The dog's natural instinct is to chase and catch prey, experts say. And avoid making direct eye contact with the dog, because the animal will see it as a challenge. Instead, try to remain motionless until the dog has lost interest and leaves. Then slowly back away until the dog is out of sight.

PUT SOMETHING IN THE WAY If a dog does attack, try to put something between it and you, such as a purse or package. If a dog bites you and holds on, avoid pulling away from it, because that can cause you further injury.

I've stumbled upon a bear

Black bears and grizzlies that have been fed by humans often make a connection between people and food, and they sometimes become aggressive. A bear may also attack if it is startled or feels that you're threatening its cubs. If you come across a bear while hiking, it will usually run away. But if it doesn't flee, follow these steps:

TRY TO CALM THE ANIMAL If you see a bear, never turn and run. That will arouse its predatory instincts. Instead, stand your ground and make yourself look larger by raising your hands over your head. Say something like, "Whoa, bear, calm down, bear," in a calm, authoritative voice, experts advise.

EXPECT A FEIGNED ATTACK The bear may wander away. But another possibility is that it will try a "bluff charge" at you. If it does, stand still. Keep your eyes on the bear and slowly back up after it stops charging. Don't turn your back on the animal until it loses interest in you and leaves.

A bear is attacking me

HAVE PEPPER SPRAY HANDY AND PLAY DEAD Unfortunately, bears sometimes *do* attack. If one does, here's what to do:

Keep a canister of bear-repellent spray containing capsaicin (the stuff that makes hot sauce hot) easily accessible on your person when you're out in bear country. Attach it to your belt or the shoulder harness of your backpack so you can get to it immediately.

If the bear keeps charging you and gets up close, spray the burning repellent in its face. Unfortunately, these sprays have a limited range,

PROBLEM STOPPER

Don't Attract Bears with Food
Bears have a keen sense of smell and will quickly home in on your food. If your clothes and your tent smell like food, bears will be more likely to attack.

• Do your cooking 100 yards (90 meters) away from your tent. Save a change of clothes to do your cooking in and leave them in the cooking area.

• Store all your food, garbage, and cooking and eating utensils in a weatherproof bag (available at camping stores, or use a backpack or plastic sack). Tie a rope to the sack. Find a tree with a sturdy branch at least 15 feet (2.5 meters) off the ground. Throw the rope over the branch at a spot 8 to 10 feet (2.5 to 3 meters) out from the trunk. Hoist the bag up until it is at least 10 feet (3 meters) high and a couple of feet below the branch it's hanging from. Then tie the rope around the trunk of the tree.

so you'll have to have steady nerves to let the bear get close enough, park experts warn. It's a good idea to test your canister when you purchase it by spraying it downwind in an isolated spot so you can see how far the spray reaches.

If the bear continues to attack, drop and play dead. Roll up in the fetal position or lie on your stomach, lace your hands together over the back of your neck, and stop moving. This will help protect your head, neck, and belly. A daypack will help protect your back, too.

I'm facing down one mean kitty

MAKE YOURSELF LOOK LARGER If you're an adult, it's unlikely that a mountain lion will attack you. Mountain lions, which typically weigh 100 to 140 pounds (45 to 64 kilograms), rarely attack humans. They're interested in smaller prey, although this does sometimes include children and pets. Mountain lions tend to stalk and sneak up on prey, and if you're bending down to tie your shoe or pick something up, you may look smaller and more vulnerable.

If you do encounter a mountain lion, slowly raise your arms or spread open your jacket to look larger. Don't turn your back to the animal. If it attacks, don't play dead. Fight with all you've got, experts say. Strike the animal with your hands or any objects handy.

Why does "playing possum" protect you from bears but not from mountain lions? Bears typically attack because they see you as an intruder or a threat, according to one school of thought, whereas mountain lions attack because they see you as a potential meal.

Owww—a venomous snake just bit me

DRIVE TO A HOSPITAL OR CALL FOR HELP Don't panic. People rarely die from snakebites within the first 24 hours, say snake experts. This gives you time to seek help calmly. The best first-aid tool for a snakebite is a set of car keys, the snake researchers advise. Another good tool is a cell phone. Call for help or drive to a hospital.

DON'T CUT AND SUCK THE BITE OR USE A TOURNIQUET Forget about doing any field surgery on the bite. Many people are under the impression that cutting into a snakebite and sucking out the poison is a useful treatment. Unfortunately, say the experts, cutting into the skin can damage blood vessels, nerves, and other delicate tissue, particularly if the bite is on a hand or foot, which it often is. Besides, up to 30 percent of bites from venomous snakes are "dry" bites, which

PROBLEM STOPPER

Be Prepared for Snakes
If you're concerned about encountering venomous snakes when you're out hiking, here are some hints from snake specialists:

• *Wear tall boots.* They're not guaranteed to protect you from all bites when you're out hiking in snake country, but wearing calf-high boots can protect you from many strikes.

• *Keep your eyes open.* If snakes are out and about, you'll often find them basking in the sun. Scan the ground in and around the trail as you hike. Logs, boulders, and piles of rocks are favorite basking areas for snakes.

• *Carry a field guide.* Most bookstores carry books with pictures of poisonous snakes found in your area. If you spend time outdoors, familiarize yourself with these snakes. The local ranger's headquarters can also provide useful information.

means they inject little or no venom. So people often inflict injuries on themselves trying to tend bites that weren't serious in the first place. Furthermore, if you have little cuts on your lips or gums and you *do* suck out venom, it could be absorbed through the open wounds just as if the snake had injected it.

If you're bitten on the arm or leg, don't tie a tourniquet on it. As soon as the tourniquet is removed, any venom and digested tissue that's built up in your limb will flood into the rest of your body, possibly causing serious damage.

I'm afraid of a shark attack

FOLLOW COMMON-SENSE RULES Sharks attack several dozen people in the world each year in unprovoked incidents, but the total per year since 2000 has been below 100, according to shark experts and naturalists. Over the past 100 years, the number of such attacks has been growing slowly but steadily, perhaps partly because the number of people vacationing at the ocean has risen, partly because there has been better reporting of incidents involving sharks, and partly because of faster and more widespread media coverage of attacks. Given the number of people who take a dip each year, your odds of being one of the shark-bitees is pretty slim. Follow these precautions, recommended by shark experts, and you'll improve your chances even further:

- Swim in groups. Sharks prefer solitary targets.
- Swim during the day. Sharks are most active during the night and twilight hours.
- Skip the water if you have an open wound or are menstruating.
- Don't wear jewelry that's shiny into the briny. The flickering light from jewelry looks like fish scales to a hungry shark.
- Steer clear of waters where people are fishing or feeding fish. If you see seabirds diving for food, shun those areas, too.
- Be wary when you're between sandbars or near steep drop-offs.
- Don't get into the water if you know sharks are around.

TRICKS OF THE TRADE

Was There Venom in That Bite?
Here's an easy way to tell whether the snake that bit you is cause for concern, according to snake experts. A venomous snake, such as a rattlesnake, copperhead, cottonmouth, or coral snake, will leave only one or two punctures in your skin. A nonvenomous snake will leave multiple puncture wounds on your skin; 8 to 12 or more wouldn't be unusual. That's because venomous snakes use a fang or two to inject their venom, not their teeth. (Yes, snakes have teeth.) The nonvenomous snakes bite you with their teeth.

PART FIVE

Clothing and Appearance

The clasp fell off your earring? Reach for your kid's school bag. Want a brown tint for your hair? Visit your pantry. Got a rough fingernail? Snap up a pack of matches. Keeping yourself looking sharp is no small task, but the good news is that there are surprising solutions everywhere you turn.

Everyday Attire Problems

■ CLOTHING MISHAPS

My button popped off at the worst possible moment

WIRE IT BACK ON You're on your way to an important meeting, and a button lets go. Fear not. Find a thin piece of wire, even a small paper clip or a trash-bag tie. (If you use the tie, strip off the paper or plastic covering, exposing the wire beneath it.) Thread whatever wire you use from the inside of the garment up through the hole where the original thread had been, through one hole in the button, down through another buttonhole, and then through the second hole in the fabric. Twist the metal ends together until the button is secure. Bend the metal ends so that they will lie flat against the garment.

If you lose a button at a bad time, a trash-bag twist tie (or even a paper clip) can save the day in seconds.

My zipper's glider is off the track on one side

MAKE A CUT TO GET IT BACK ON TRACK You're rushing to go out. You start to pull up your zipper but discover that the glider is attached to only one side. Grab a pair of sharp scissors and, at the bottom of the zipper, cut between the last two zipper teeth on the open side. Reinsert the glider here over the zipper teeth. Zip up. Then fasten a safety pin across the bottom of the zipper on the inside above the cut, to keep the glider from coming off the track when you unzip.

It's a struggle to move my zipper

LUBRICATE THE ZIPPER Your zipper has all its teeth, but it no longer moves easily up and down. Lubrication is the answer. Rub the teeth on either side with a lead pencil, a dry bar of soap, or a ball of beeswax.

Either my slacks shrank or my waist grew

PUT ELASTIC IN THE WAISTBAND You pull on a pair of slacks you haven't worn since last season. Could they have shrunk while in storage? Well, maybe. Take a tip from maternity-wear designers. Stop by a fabric store and pick up a short length of elastic with buttonholes already in it. Sew or pin one end of the elastic inside the waistband of your slacks. Use the button already on your slacks at the other end. Presto! You've put some slack in your slacks.

I'm forever fighting static cling

USE A FABRIC SOFTENER SHEET The easy solution: Stash a fabric softening dryer sheet in your purse or pocket. Rub the sheet lightly over your panty hose and on the underside of your skirt whenever you're having a static-cling problem. Residue from the sheet will prevent static buildup.

Here are two more ways to cope with the problem:

- Swoosh the underside of your skirt with hair spray, which will also prevent static electricity.
- Wet a paper towel or even your hand with water and lightly run it down the exterior of your panty hose and the interior of your skirt. This trick is used in the theater by wardrobe supervisors, who often stand at the ready with a spray bottle of water to get the static out of costumes before performers go onstage.

My hem has become unstitched

STAPLE IT IN PLACE Both trousers and skirts are prone to having hems come undone, usually at the most awkward times. Staple your hem into place. If you're careful, you can do this from the inside so that the staple will be barely noticeable. Staples make tiny punctures in fabric and are easy to remove once you get your hands on a sewing kit.

My dress's neckline keeps gaping open

KEEP IT IN PLACE WITH TOUPEE TAPE You look great, except for a problem with the neckline on your dress or blouse. It keeps gaping open in a way the designer never imagined. It's a problem that can be caused by wear and tear or improper fit. Double-sided toupee tape will come to your rescue. Products such as Vapon Topstick will

TRICKS OF THE TRADE

Getting Rid of Pet Hair Pronto
Frustrated by dog or cat hair all over your clothing? An expert's advice: Lightly mist your hair-covered garment with water from a spray bottle. Then put the garment in the dryer with a damp towel, along with a fabric softener sheet. Tumble-dry on the air cycle for up to 15 minutes. The softener sheet will reduce the static electricity that helps the hair stick to the clothing, while the tumbling and airflow pull the hair off the clothing and suck it out of the dryer. (Be sure to clean the filter afterward.)

TRICKS OF THE TRADE

Pull the Plug on Static Electricity

In the dry winter air, you can walk around feeling like one big electrical charge, expecting to be shocked at every door-knob and lamp. A moisturizer—hand cream or body lotion—will prevent this problem if you use plenty of it on your body in the morning and apply more on your hands during the day.

adhere to your skin and the garment at the same time, and it won't hurt when you pull it off. The tape comes in segments about 2 inches (5 centimeters) long and can be cut and shaped easily. Toupee tape is also great for stopping straps from falling off your shoulders. Look for it in beauty aid supply shops.

I slipped up and forgot to pack a slip

SUBSTITUTE A T-SHIRT You're traveling, and as you put on your favorite dress or skirt, you realize you need a slip and don't have one. A T-shirt will rescue you. Snip the neck opening near the shoulder seam with scissors, an inch (a couple of centimeters) on either side for starters. Then pull the skirt up over your hips to your waist. If the first cut doesn't do it, snip a little more. If that still isn't enough, try sliding the T-shirt over your head rather than pulling it up to your hips. Once the T-shirt is on, cut off the arms at the seams, pull on your dress, and you're presentable again.

My clothes are wrinkled, and I don't have an iron handy

LET THE SHOWER STEAM THEM Hang your clothes in the bathroom, shut the door, and run the shower on hot for five minutes. The steam from the shower will smooth out the wrinkles. You can even unwrinkle the clothes you're wearing with this technique. And it's great for gowns that are difficult to iron.

For ultra efficiency, try spraying your outfit lightly with water and hanging it in the bathroom while you shower. Then shake the clothing, and if you still have wrinkles, press them out by laying the clothing on a flat surface and running your hand over it. For washable silks, spray the fabric, press it with your hand, and leave it on a hanger for 15 minutes before wearing it.

PUT THEM IN A DRYER WITH A DAMP TOWEL If you have access to a dryer, put a damp towel in the dryer with the outfit and turn it on to air-dry. Your outfit should be wrinkle free in about 10 or 15 minutes.

My clothes smell musty, and I have no time to wash them

SPRAY THEM WITH VODKA If your clothes are giving off a musty odor—or even a whiff of perspiration—and you don't have time to wash or dry-clean them, here's a trick that Russian theater managers have used for centuries: Put some unflavored vodka into a spray bottle and mist the garment. The vodka kills odor-causing bacteria (it's alcohol, after all), and because it is relatively odorless, it won't make you smell like you just came from a bar.

I just spilled greasy food on my shirt

ABSORB IT WITH TALCUM POWDER If you act quickly, you can rescue fabric from oily stains (such as butter, peanut butter, or greasy fast food). First, scrape away any food. Then sprinkle on a generous amount of talcum powder, enough to cover the spot completely, and leave it for five minutes. The powder will soak up the oil. Flick off the powder and launder as usual. If the oily stain is older, follow the instruction in "I've struck oil, but it's on my clothing," page 265.

The seam in my pants split open

PIN OR STAPLE IT SHUT Your pants split, and suddenly you're air-conditioned in a way you never intended to be. The classic solution is safety pins, if you have some on hand. Retire to a restroom, remove the pants, and work on the interior of the garment. Gather a half-inch of material on each side of the seam and fasten the sides together with a small safety pin or two. No safety pins? Staple the seam closed.

USE DOUBLE-STICK TAPE A better remedy is double-sided tape, because it's less likely to show. Duck into a drug, hardware, discount, or home improvement store and buy the kind of tape used to hold carpeting in place. Find a private place where you can remove the garment and lay it out on a table or counter. Cut a strip of the double-sided tape just wide and long enough to fit invisibly between the two pieces of fabric that have separated, and press it into place.

I have a run in my hose—and no nail polish

USE SOAP TO FIX IT Yes, the traditional quick remedy for a run in your hose is a light coating of nail polish that will harden and hold the fibers in place, preventing further damage. But if you don't have nail polish, take a slightly wet bar of soap, or even a small amount of liquid soap, and gently rub it over the edge of the run. When the soap dries, it will harden and prevent further running.

PROBLEM STOPPER

Stop Those Runs in Your Hose Cold
You can reduce the likelihood that your hose will run with this cool tip: Put your nylons in a plastic bag and stick them in the freezer. The temperature hardens the material, making it less likely to snag as you get dressed.

■ WEATHER-RELATED PROBLEMS

I forgot my umbrella, and it's pouring rain

WEAR A PLASTIC GARBAGE BAG Get your hands on the largest plastic garbage bag you can find. Cut holes for your eyes, nose, and mouth. Then slip the bag over your head. You may look like the Creature from the Landfill, but your upper body will be well protected.

My coat got soaked in a downpour

DRY IT WITH A HAIR DRYER A rainstorm surprised you, and there you are dripping water in the foyer. That sopping coat of yours—not designed for a downpour—needs some special attention. You can't just stuff it in the closet, where it will dampen all the other coats. Hang it up on a good wooden hanger where there's plenty of air circulation to help dry it out without its turning musty. (The laundry room, maybe?) If you're in a hurry to go back out, hang the coat up and use a hair dryer, moving it up and down the coat about 6 inches (15 centimeters) from the fabric. Don't drape the coat on a radiator or stove: Some fabrics are flammable and others might shrink. Hanging your coat near a fan is fine, however.

Hang your drenched coat on a wooden hanger and use a hair dryer to get the moisture out of it in a hurry.

My shirt is dripping with sweat

USE A HAND DRYER A hot, humid day is taking a toll on you. You feel wilted, and your shirt or blouse is showing signs of sweat. If you are not able to change your top, find a restroom with a blower-type hand dryer and angle the spout so that the air can blow you and your shirt dry. Paper towels don't do the job quickly enough.

The snow's a foot deep, and I don't have boots

WEAR PLASTIC BAGS INSIDE YOUR SHOES If you're going to be out in the cold for any length of time, keeping your feet dry is essential. Here's what to do: Take off your shoes. If your socks are dry, slide your sock-covered feet into a pair of plastic bags (plastic grocery bags will do). If your socks are wet, peel them off, dry your bare feet thoroughly, wrap them in rags, and slip them into the bags. Then put your shoes back on. For extra weatherproofing, tape (with duct or packing tape) the tops of the plastic bags to the cuffs of your trousers, the tops of your socks, or your legs.

■ GARMENT WEAR AND TEAR

I have small pinholes in my garment

DAMPEN, RUB, AND IRON THE HOLES You may have pin or staple holes in your clothing from tags that the store put on or from the pins that marked a hemline. In either event, they are probably not literally holes. More likely, the pin or staple has pushed the weave apart. To close such holes, wet your fingertip and use your fingernail to gently move the weave closer together. Or dampen the fabric around the holes with a small wet paintbrush. Then ironing with a press cloth should close the weave.

Clothes hangers are puckering my dresses' shoulders

STEAM OUT THE PUCKERS If you notice that your hangers leave little pucker marks at the shoulders of garments you take out of the closet, the solution is to use a blast of steam from a steam iron to relax the puckered fibers. Or drape the garment over a towel rack in the bathroom when you shower.

I have a snag in my sweater

PULL THE SNAG THROUGH TO THE INSIDE Your watchband catches a thread in your sweater and yanks it out into an ugly loop. When knit garments suffer this kind of damage, pull that irritating loop to the inside of the sweater where it can't be seen. A needle and thread will do the trick. Put the eye-end of a threaded needle through the fabric from the inside. Wrap the thread on the end of the needle around the snag and pull the needle and thread and the attached snag to the inside of the garment. Don't clip the little loop—that would cause a hole.

My sweater cuffs are stretched

DIP IN HOT WATER AND DRY WITH A HAIR DRYER You're in the habit of shoving your sweater sleeves up your forearms, and the cuffs have

A Quick Stabilizer for a Buttonhole

You have a small buttonhole project, but making a special trip to the sewing store for the stabilizer material used to back fabric so it won't stretch seems like a hassle. The easy solution: Use an old dryer sheet retrieved from the laundry room waste basket instead. (Don't use a fresh sheet, because the chemicals in it could stain the fabric.) Like commercial stabilizer material, a dryer sheet adds body to the area being sewn.

Place the fabric over the dryer sheet where you want the buttonhole to be while you create the buttonhole. Clip away the excess dryer sheet from the back of the fabric when you're done.

become stretched. If the sweater is cotton or wool, a little hot water will do the trick. Dip the cuffs in the water and then dry them with a hair dryer. You might be out of luck, however, if the cuffs contain elastic, spandex, or some other fiber that stretches. Once they lose their elasticity, they can't be fixed.

My sweaters are looking fuzzy

RUB LIGHTLY WITH FINE SANDPAPER Sweaters look worn when little bits of material pill up on them. There's an easy fix for this. Before laundering, brush the fabric gently with a piece of extra-fine sandpaper. If you go gently, your sweater will look like new. Or try one of these higher-tech methods:

- Sweater Stone, a product sold at sewing shops, has a pumice-like surface that removes fuzz.
- An electric fabric shaver, which costs around $10, will also keep your sweaters looking sharp.

The buttons keep getting pulled off my sweater

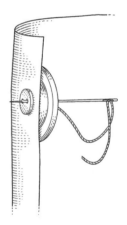

ADD A SECOND BUTTON INSIDE When you are resewing the main button, sew a small clear button on the back of the fabric. Because it's clear and small, it won't be conspicuous when the garment is open. Line up the holes on both buttons and stitch right through from bottom to top and back again. The inside button will prevent the thread from pulling through the back of the fabric, a particular hazard in loosely woven or knit cloth.

Everything I wear is missing a button

KEEP A BUTTON-FIXING KIT NEXT TO YOUR DRYER Buttons work loose or come off completely quite regularly. In your busy day, it's difficult to regularly check for and fix recalcitrant buttons. Answer: Keep a miniature sewing kit right next to your dryer. It should consist of three or four needles, each threaded in a different color; a pair of scissors; and a selection of buttons. When you pull a buttonless garment out of the dryer, you can fix it on the spot.

For buttons that pop off more than you think they should, stop the problem before it starts. Put a dab of clear nail polish on the center of each button to seal the thread and prevent wear and tear on it.

I have a pull in my shirt

STROKE THE MATERIAL WITH YOUR FINGERNAIL A woven fabric such as linen, twill, or denim can get a pull when a thread catches on something sharp, causing the threads to bunch up in an ugly line. To fix the problem, stroke at the damaged material with your fingernail. This will pull the thread back into position.

The collar on my favorite blouse is frayed

BOND THE FIBERS WITH LIQUID SEALANT Everything on your garment looks fine except for the frayed edge of the collar. If you can tuck the edge out of sight inside your collar, you can just put cellophane tape over the fray. But a better solution would be to use a liquid seam sealant that holds fibers together. It is available at sewing stores with brand names such as Fray Check, Fray Away, Sullivans Glue Pins, Sullivans Fray Stop, and Liquid Stitch.

The crease in my pants is gone

PRESS IN FUSIBLE THREAD Your crease is not as sharp as it used to be? Fusible thread can help you, especially in polyester and cotton pants—but not silk or wool. You can buy fusible thread in fabric stores or quilt shops. Place a long length of the thread in the crease, on the inside of the fabric. Then press over the crease with an iron. The thread melts onto the fabric, creating a permanent crease. Getting a straight crease is tricky, so practice on scrap material first.

The gathers on my little girl's dress have come undone

USE DENTAL FLOSS TO MAKE GATHERS If you don't know how to sew gathers neatly, dental floss can save the day. Instead of using basting stitches, which are the longest stitches on your machine, use a zigzag stitch over a length of dental floss along the fabric to be gathered. Sew over the floss, but not through it, so that you can pull on the floss until the gathers look just right. Then sew across the top of the gathers to hold them in place, and pull out the strip of dental floss.

PROBLEM STOPPER

When Scissors Can't Fly

You know how modern air travel is: tight security, and anything that even approximates a weapon is not allowed. That can make it tough on passengers who stay busy with sewing and needlework, because scissors are not allowed on today's aircraft. But you can solve the problem with a disc-shaped metal thread cutter, which is safe and permitted on planes, according to Cheryl Wray, founder of a Canadian-based sewing club network called Sewers Forum. Made by a company named Clover, this thread cutter can be worn as a pendant or can be placed on top of a spool of thread and has grooves for cutting yarn and thread. The disc is available at many sewing stores and several Web sites.

■ SEWING GEAR

My sewing machine vibrates

PUT A RUBBER TREAD RUNNER UNDER IT You're trying to put the finishing touches on a delicate sewing job, but your machine is vibrating and dancing all over the place. An easy solution: Buy a rubber tread runner, such as those used on basement or outdoor steps, at a hardware store. Put the runner under the machine to absorb the vibration and help hold the machine in place. Or buy cushiony, no-slip rubber shelf lining by the yard to use in the same way.

My sewing machine needs a good cleaning

USE A SQUEEZE BOTTLE TO BLOW AWAY LINT To clean out the little bits of fluff and lint that collect in tiny spaces in your sewing machine, an empty dish detergent squeeze bottle can come to the rescue. Clean top and bottom thoroughly so that there's no detergent left and let both parts dry. Screw the top back on. Then simply squeeze the empty bottle so that it makes puffs of air. Aim it at the lint, and poof! the problem is solved. You can use this tool for cleaning computer keyboards, too.

My scissors don't cut well anymore

CUT THROUGH SANDPAPER You grab your scissors for a bit of work around the house, but they just won't do the job—too dull. Sandpaper can help you. Use the scissors to cut through a sheet of sandpaper several times. That will remove grime and also sharpen the metal edges a little.

My hem is uneven, and I don't have a skirt marker

USE A BATHROOM PLUNGER AS A GUIDE To adjust the hem of a skirt when the original hem isn't even, the humble bathroom plunger can help you. It has a handle and a firm base when you stand it up. Determine how high you want the hem to be from the floor and mark the distance on the handle of the plunger. Put on the skirt and have a friend use the plunger to mark the new hemline as you turn slowly.

Laundry Problems

■ STAINS

My pen stained my pocket

REMOVE THE STAIN WITH ALCOHOL AND PAPER TOWELS How many shirts have been ruined by leaking pens? You can't hear it, and you can't smell it. But you sure can see it—that horrifying blue or black ink stain at the base of your shirt pocket. Can you rescue the shirt? Yes, with the help of rubbing alcohol. Put three paper towels, one on top of the other and folded in half, on a flat surface, such as a kitchen counter. Put the shirt pocket over the paper towels and pour rubbing alcohol onto the ink—just enough to cover the area. The paper towels will absorb the alcohol and draw the ink away from the fabric. Replace the paper towels when they become saturated. Repeat the process after about two minutes. The alcohol will loosen up the ink. Rinse by pouring water on the stained area, again changing the paper towels. If there is still a slight ink stain, apply nail polish remover (acetone) to a cloth and rub it on the stained shirt. Rinse with water; then presoak with a stain remover such as Shout and let it soak for 15 to 20 minutes before laundering.

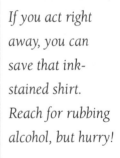

If you act right away, you can save that ink-stained shirt. Reach for rubbing alcohol, but hurry!

I spilled coffee on my shirt

USE COLD WATER; THEN PRETREAT If you drink your coffee black, the stain will be easier to remove than if you put milk in it, because the protein in milk works against you. Either way you take your coffee, however, the solution is the same: Hold the garment under a faucet, stain side down, and run cold water through it for a couple of minutes. Next, rub laundry detergent or a prewash product into the stain and let it stand for five minutes. Then launder as usual.

My favorite garment has a mildew stain

REMOVE THE STAIN WITH BLEACH You tossed your soaked sweatshirt into the trunk of your car and promptly forgot it. When you finally pulled it out again, the sweatshirt had developed a mildew stain. If the shirt is white and all cotton, and the stain is relatively new, you're in luck. Mix 1 ounce (2 tablespoons) of chlorine bleach with ⅓ cup of water and pour it on the stain. Then launder. The bleach should kill the spores that caused the mildew. For colored clothing and items made of synthetic fabrics, washing with an all-fabric bleach should do the trick. Remember, however, that the older a mildew stain is, the more difficult it will be to remove. Be sure to treat mildew stains as soon as possible.

The underarms of my blouse are stained

LAUNDER WITH BLEACH Your favorite clothes are being ruined by what appear to be sweat stains, which can show up as a yellow blotch. You can tell whether it's actually caused by perspiration by feeling the fabric. Sweat may stain, but it will leave the cloth feeling normal. Stains from antiperspirant will feel either oily or stiff. For cotton and linen, launder the garment with chlorine bleach, according to the package directions. Use oxygen (all-fabric) bleach on synthetic fabric. These methods should work whether the stain is caused by antiperspirant or sweat. Take a silk or wool garment to a dry cleaner.

My lipstick has left its mark

PRETREAT WITH LAUNDRY DETERGENT OR ACETONE Lipstick can easily stain clothing. Removing it is tricky because not all lipsticks are made of the same ingredients. First, try rubbing a lipstick stain with liquid detergent before laundering. If that doesn't work and the clothing is white, you can use acetone-based nail polish remover to remove the spot. Acetone can harm colored clothing, so be careful. And even with white items, test it on an inconspicuous spot before you go after the lipstick stain.

I've got grass stains on my pants

PRETREAT AND WASH WITH AN ENZYME BOOSTER Grass stains can mar a perfectly good pair of pants in an instant. The sooner you treat such stains, the better. Rub laundry detergent on the fabric; then rinse with hot water. If that doesn't remove the stain, rub more detergent on the stain and wash the garment, adding an enzyme laundry product, such as Amaze or Spray 'n Wash In-Wash Laundry Stain Remover, that will help remove the protein in the stain.

Here are two other ways to remove a fresh grass stain:

- Mix 2 tablespoons of rubbing alcohol with ¼ cup of water and spray it on the stain. Rub the area with an old toothbrush. Rinse the stain before the alcohol completely evaporates.
- Mix a few drops of household ammonia with a teaspoon of hydrogen peroxide. Rub it on the stain and then rinse with water as soon as the stain disappears.

Grass stains that are not fresh are tougher to remove, especially if you've washed the garment and then dried it at a high temperature.

A child used my clothing as a napkin

CLEAN UP WITH BABY WIPES Tots tend to be untidy eaters, to say the least. Some of the resulting grime gets smeared from ear to ear and then on whatever piece of cloth is nearby. If that's the shirt or jacket you're wearing, there are a couple of solutions. First, get as much off your clothing as you can by blotting it with a paper towel. Then see whether the parents have any baby wipes; these are perfect for taking food smudges off clothing.

My favorite blouse has rust stains

TREAT THE STAIN WITH LEMON, SALT, AND SUN Got a persistent rust spot on a prized garment? If the garment is washable, sprinkle salt on the stain; no need to wet it first. Then wet the area with lemon juice, either fresh or bottled. Lay the garment out in the sun, which helps to bleach the fabric, for a few hours. Then rinse to remove the lemon juice and salt. You may have to repeat the process a few times. On colored fabrics, test the method in an inconspicuous place first. Take dry-clean-only garments to the dry cleaner.

I've struck oil, but it's on my clothing

ABSORB WITH POWDER AND DEGREASE WITH DETERGENT The fabrics in your life—clothing, tablecloths, bedspreads, and the like—face all sorts of oily perils. Cooking oil at the stove, baby oil in the nursery, and cosmetics in the bathroom can mean trouble. To remove such stains, follow these steps:

1. Blot up as much of the oil as you can with paper towels.
2. Cover the remaining spot with an absorbent powder, such as talcum powder, cornstarch, or baking soda.

PROBLEM STOPPER

Get Your Ducts in a Row
You have a hunch that it's taking longer than it should for your dryer to get the job done. The air duct leading from the dryer to the outside could be the problem.

Experts say you should try to use ductwork of at least 4-inch (10-centimeter) diameter, preferably made of rigid aluminum or galvanized steel. A flexible plastic duct can kink, sag, or be punctured, reducing airflow and extending drying time. If you absolutely must use a flexible duct, get the kind that has a wall of sheet metal inside, as opposed to the type with a thin foil wall. You should try to keep ductwork as straight and short as possible. It should end with an exhaust hood with a swing-out damper.

Never put a screen over the exhaust outlet; it could collect lint and stop the airflow. And dampers that close with a magnet will lose their magnetism over time.

3. After about 30 minutes, brush the spot with a toothbrush or soft nailbrush. (Soft bristles won't damage or wear away the fabric.) Repeat until the powder has absorbed as much as it can.
4. Coat the spot with a clear degreasing dish detergent. Brush it in with a second toothbrush or a rag. Let it stand for two minutes.
5. Soak the spot in hot tap water for 30 minutes to help dissolve the grease.

The garment is now ready to be laundered in a hot water wash.

My shirt collar has an ugly ring of dirt

PRETREAT AREA WITH SHAMPOO The insides of shirt collars pick up oil and dirt from our skin, which leave a dirty ring on the cloth. Shampoo is the solution. Put a little bit of shampoo on the collar and gently rub it in with an old toothbrush. Then wash as usual.

My kid left Silly Putty in his pocket

SCRAPE IT OFF; THEN APPLY WD-40 You can work it like clay, you can bounce it like a ball . . . and you can seriously gunk up fabric with this oozing plaything. Start by picking off as much of the substance as you can. Then scrape with a butter knife or some other dull, hard-edged object. Spray the stained area with WD-40, let it sit for ten minutes, and scrape again. Spray the spot one more time with WD-40, let it sit another ten minutes, and blot the stain with a clean cloth. If a stain still remains, douse an unused area of your cloth in rubbing alcohol and blot the spot repeatedly. Then launder the clothing as usual.

Sticky pockets from gooey play clay? WD-40 will remove the stain in minutes.

I have water spots on my dress

DAMPEN THE AREA AND PRESS A little spill here, a little splash there, and you can end up with watermarks on your garment. The first thing to know is that the water didn't cause the mark. Rather, it's something in the fabric, such as dust, dirt, body oils, or even fabric softener, that causes the stain. When water mixes with one of these substances, it creates a spot. The solution lies in more water:

1. Put an absorbent rag, such as an old gauze diaper or an artificial chamois, over the mark.
2. Spray this covering material with a fine mist of water from a spray bottle until the material is damp to the touch.

3. Press the covering material with an iron set at a temperature for the garment fabric. The extra moisture will often disburse the ring, while the heat from the iron dries the sprayed water.

Alternative: Dampen a small artist's paintbrush, lightly brush over the water spot, and use a pressing cloth to iron over the spot.

■ WASHING PROBLEMS

My white cotton top came out of the wash with a pink blush

REMOVE IT WITH A BLEACH SOLUTION White or light clothing washed with darker colors can come out with a new hue. The fix can take a while, but there's hope. Soak the clothing overnight in a solution of 1 part household chlorine bleach to 10 parts water. Then thoroughly rinse the garment in cold water and wash as usual. Hang the item in the sun to dry. (The UVA rays will help to further lighten the fabric.) If the dye isn't quite gone, repeat the procedure. The bleach and water solution works on colors too—for instance, if a top was yellow and it turned a little pink. The dye in clothing is set chemically and professionally to prevent it from running, so the diluted bleach solution can remove the dye that has come from another item because it hasn't been set in the garment.

For delicate fabrics that can't be treated with chlorine bleach, use peroxide, which isn't as aggressive. To remove a color stain, mix ¼ cup of peroxide in a gallon of water. Soak for half an hour, rinse, and wash as usual. Dry in the sun to help the peroxide lighten the clothing.

I accidentally spilled bleach on my new navy skirt

RINSE WELL AND APPLY AMMONIA Bleach spilled on colored clothing can easily ruin the garment. Laundry experts caution that time is of the essence. As soon as you see the problem, take these steps:

1. Rinse the garment with cold water. It takes a few minutes to flush bleach out of a fabric.
2. Put the garment on a counter with an old towel beneath it. Pour ammonia, which deactivates bleach, over the area.
3. Wet a rag with more ammonia and rub from the outside toward the center of the spill. This should take about five minutes.

TRICKS OF THE TRADE

Ironing Needlework without Flattening It
If you have cross-stitch or other embroidery on a tablecloth or clothing, directly ironing it normally against a hard surface like an ironing board would ruin the look of the stitches. Instead, lay a folded bath towel on your ironing board and gently iron the reverse side of the embroidery. This will provide enough pressure to get the ironing done without mashing the stitches.

The result may not be perfect; you may end up with a spot a little lighter than the rest of the garment.

Caution: Apply the ammonia in a well-ventilated area, and only after the bleach has been thoroughly rinsed out of the fabric. The combination of bleach and ammonia can create a dangerous gas.

My white socks are dingy

BOIL THEM WITH LEMON White socks that have become a strange shade of gray or yellow, even though you've washed them with bleach, are one of the tougher laundry problems to solve. Your once washed socks may never be as bright as the day you bought them, but here's your best bet: Boil some water on the stove, drop in a slice of lemon, and add the socks. Let them bubble away for 15 to 30 minutes.

I left my laundry in the washer too long, and it smells

REWASH WITH BAKING SODA You were busy and forgot that load of laundry. Days later, you opened the machine and were greeted by an unpleasant smell. There's an easy solution: Run the clothes through the wash cycle again with warm or hot water, depending on the fabrics in the load, and 1 cup of baking soda. Then put the laundry in the dryer with fabric softener sheets. If a piece of clothing in the batch is something you need right away and it is dry, spray it with a fabric freshening product, such as Febreze. That should neutralize the odor.

■ IRONING PROBLEMS

I lengthened my dress, but the old hem's crease still shows

DAMPEN WITH VINEGAR SOLUTION AND IRON You have carefully removed the stitches from a hem and have lowered it and rehemmed it. But the crease from the original hem still stands out like a beacon. Sponge the crease with equal parts of white vinegar and water and then iron. Or sandwich the crease between two pieces of aluminum foil and press with a hot iron.

If there's a mark, as opposed to a crease, where the original hem was, use a spot remover to erase it. Or hide the mark by adding a decorative row of trim.

I scorched my favorite dress with the iron

USE PEROXIDE ON THIN FABRIC With a flatter, thinner fabric, such as linen, cotton, or wool, place the garment on a folded white towel. Then mix a 50-50 solution of hydrogen peroxide and water and pour it on the mark. Leave the solution on for several minutes; then blot with a clean towel.

Here are two other ways to handle a burn mark:

- Make a paste with powdered dishwasher detergent and water and put it on the mark. Then lay the fabric in the sun to bleach.
- Use chlorine bleach for white cotton or linen fabrics, and all-fabric bleach for synthetic fabrics. Leave either product on the scorch mark for 10 to 15 minutes. Then blot the area with water and launder.

Caution: Test any remedy on an inconspicuous area first. If you scorch a delicate fabric like silk, take the garment to the dry cleaner.

USE SANDPAPER ON THICK WOOL Sometimes you can smell the fabric overheating before you actually see the scorch mark. You end up with an ugly light-brown mark on your garment. What remedy you use depends on the fabric you're dealing with. On a thick, fuzzy wool fabric (or on heavy upholstery linen), you can actually use extra-fine sandpaper. Very lightly abrade the surface of the scorched fiber until you see undamaged fabric beneath the surface.

My iron left unwanted lines on my clothing

PRESS THEM OUT You went a little heavy on the ironing, and one of your favorite garments now has ridge lines and smashed-looking fibers or unwanted creases. You have four options, starting with the simplest:

- Place a press cloth over the area and see whether the heat of the iron will fix the problem. The press cloth can be a white tea towel, anything made of muslin, or an old diaper.
- If that doesn't do the job, try steam. Don't put the iron right on the cloth, though. Hold the iron just above the fabric and let the steam spray. Then use your fingers or a brush to fluff the area.
- Still have a problem? Try misting the press cloth with water, then pressing.
- The last resort: Mist the press cloth with a half-and-half solution of water and white vinegar; then press without steam.

Scorched wool? Run to the workshop and grab some extra-fine sandpaper.

Appearance and Accessories

■ HAIR PROBLEMS

Static electricity is making my hair stand on end

USE ANTISTATIC FABRIC SPRAY Static electricity will send your locks flying every which way, but never the way you like it. To fix the problem, squirt some antistatic fabric spray on your comb and then run it through your hair. (It won't damage your hair.)

 If you don't have antistatic fabric spray, dousing your comb with regular hair spray will also help. Misting your hair with water from a spray bottle is the last resort.

Got hair-raising static? Get it out in a jiff with anti-static fabric spray.

My hair is so matted I can't comb it

LOOSEN IT WITH OLIVE OIL The solution is as close as your pantry. Olive oil can help loosen matted hair. First rub some oil into the matted area. Wait a few minutes and then slowly work out the matting with a large-tooth comb. After you've combed out the mats, shampoo your hair to remove the oil.

 Bonus: If you rub the oil into your entire scalp, it will act as a deep-cleansing conditioner. After rubbing in the oil, wrap your head in a towel for half an hour before washing your hair.

I'm frustrated with my frizzy hair

RUB IN SKIN LOTION Is your hair all frizzy and uncontrollable, and you have no hair-care products handy? An easy remedy is to rub a generous amount of skin moisturizer onto your hands and work it into your skin. If you've used enough, you'll still have some residue left on your hands after a few minutes. Now rub your hands lightly over your hair. That should provide enough moisturizer to get the frizzies out.

My thick hair takes forever to dry

USE SUPERABSORBENT PAPER TOWELS People with thick hair face special challenges when it comes to drying hair quickly. A professional hair stylist says superabsorbent paper towels are the answer. After drying your hair with a bath towel, scrunch sections of hair up in a paper towel, which can absorb more moisture than a regular towel. When the paper towel is saturated, toss it out and repeat with another. This technique will reduce the amount of time you need to use a blow dryer.

How dry I am—or at least my hair is

SPRAY IT WITH DILUTED CONDITIONER Some people have naturally dry hair. Others develop dry hair from exposure to heat and hair-styling chemicals. Dry hair owes its rough texture and dullness to raised cuticles on the hair shaft, which allow moisture to escape.

To treat dry hair, fill a spray bottle halfway with any hair conditioner and fill it the rest of the way with water. This makes a spray-on conditioner that you can leave in. If you've just washed your hair, spray the conditioner on your wet hair to help you comb and condition it further. You can dampen dry hair a little with a spray bottle of water and then spray the conditioner on.

I'm a brunette, and I need an inexpensive color rinse

MAKE A COFFEE RINSE Want a way to make your brown or red hair richer and shinier? Brew some dark, rich coffee and let it cool. Mix 3 tablespoons of the coffee with 1 tablespoon of shampoo. Rub the shampoo into your hair and leave it in for 15 to 30 minutes. (Put on a shower cap if you want to walk around the house without creating a mess.) Then rinse the mixture out of your hair and condition as usual.

Overtreatment has made my hair look like a bad wig

GIVE IT A BEER RINSE Even after loading your hair up with leave-in conditioner, antifrizz products, hair-volume enhancers, mousse, and hair spray, you can get it back to normal. Shampoo your hair and then pour a can of regular beer on it. Leave the beer on for a few minutes and then rinse.

PROBLEM STOPPER

Food for Your Hair

If you have dyed, thick, or dry hair, you can keep it healthy with a weekly deep conditioning. A professional hair stylist says you can use common ingredients from the supermarket: mayonnaise or avocado blended with a couple of teaspoons of olive oil. First shampoo your hair, towel it dry, and comb either the mayonnaise or avocado oil mixture through your hair until it's saturated. Leave the treatment on your hair for 20 minutes or so before rinsing.

■ FACE AND SKIN

My eyebrows are out of control

GROOM THEM WITH A TOOTHBRUSH Having a hair-raising experience with your eyebrows? Get a new soft toothbrush, spray it lightly with hair spray, and groom your unruly brows. (Just keep it in a place where you won't mistake it for the one you use on your teeth.)

Rain has made my makeup messy

BLOT WITH TISSUE AND CLEAN UP WITH LOTION Getting caught in the rain can undo the makeup you so carefully applied in the morning, particularly your mascara and rouge. To save face: First blot your face with tissues to absorb the moisture without removing or distorting your rouge and foundation. Then use hand lotion on a tissue to clean up smudges under the eyes. (Most mascara is not waterproof.) You can even use olive oil in an emergency, if you happen to be in a restaurant. Dab a napkin or tissue in the olive oil and then head for the restroom to remove the dark spots under your eyes.

I need to zap a zit

COVER IT WITH TOOTHPASTE Like many of life's little crises, pimples arrive when they are least wanted. Regular white nongel toothpaste has a drying agent that can speed a zit's healing process. Wipe enough toothpaste over the pimple to cover it, and leave the toothpaste on overnight. The pimple won't disappear immediately, but the toothpaste should reduce the redness.

My skin is oily, and I'm prone to acne

GIVE YOURSELF A HOMEMADE FACIAL Try a homemade facial mask to help with the problem. In a small bowl, mix one egg white and the juice of half a lemon. Apply the mixture to your face with clean fingers. As the egg white dries, it closes and tightens pores; the lemon juice helps dry up oil on your skin. You can also make a facial mask by mixing baking soda and warm water in a small bowl until you get a creamlike consistency.

As the face mask dries, you will feel your skin tighten. Once the mask is completely dry, rinse it off with warm water. Then rinse your face again in cool water to help close the pores. Apply moisturizer to rehydrate your face. These masks can be used once a week.

My lipstick doesn't go on neatly anymore

PUT ON FOUNDATION MAKEUP FIRST Lipstick, as we grow older, tends to "feather" into the fine lines around the lips, giving the lips an uneven appearance. You can fix that problem by applying foundation makeup to your lips and face. Foundation fills in the fine lines around the mouth, preventing the lipstick from spreading into them. Foundation also helps keep the lipstick looking fresh longer. After applying lipstick, you can create an added border with lip liner to further prevent the lipstick from feathering.

I had a late night, and my eyes are puffy

PUT CUCUMBER SLICES OVER YOUR EYES If you've stayed up too late and maybe had a drink or two too many, the area around your eyes may acquire a puffed-up look by morning. You've seen the solution in fashion pictures a hundred times: cucumber slices. And they work. Take a cucumber straight from the fridge. Cut two slices, about ¼ inch (6 millimeters) thick. Lie down and place the cucumber slices on your eyes for about 20 minutes. The cold cucumber, which is more than 90 percent water, feels soothing. The moisture, plus the natural sodium in the vegetable and the cool temperature, will help reduce the swelling.

It's true! Cold cucumber slices really do help reduce the swelling of puffy eyes.

I have a rough nail and no emery board

SUBSTITUTE A MATCHBOX If a ragged fingernail is catching on everything and there's not an emery board to be found, use a box or book of matches. Rub your nail against the little strip designed for striking matches. It's not as abrasive as an emery board, but it will help.

■ JEWELRY PROBLEMS

The clasp on my earring has fallen off

SUBSTITUTE A BIT OF PENCIL ERASER You've lost the clasp that goes behind your earlobe on an earring for pierced ears. No matter: Find a pencil and something sharp, such as a steak knife, a pocketknife, a razor blade, or scissors. Clip off a bit of the pencil's eraser, run the point of the earring shaft through your ear hole, and press the bit of eraser onto the point to serve as an improvised clasp.

My brass jewelry is turning green

MAKE A VINEGAR-BASED TARNISH REMOVER The condition suggests that the plating beneath the surface is damaged. But there's a way to take care of the green: Mix together a tablespoon of vinegar or lemon juice, a tablespoon of salt, and a cup of hot water. Dip an old toothbrush or a nylon scrubbing pad into the solution and use it to wipe away the green. Dry completely with towels and a hair dryer set on cool.

Ketchup can help, too. The acid in the tomatoes will eliminate the tarnish. Use a cotton swab or a toothpick to put it on the jewelry. Leave it on for five to ten minutes and then clean the jewelry with a soft, damp cloth and dry it with a hair dryer. Repeat if necessary.

My sterling silver jewelry is tarnished

SOAK IN A FABRIC SOFTENER SOLUTION There are three solutions to tarnish that has made your sterling silver jewelry look dull, as long as the jewelry doesn't have stones set in it. The first is to soak the jewelry in a mixture of fabric softener, salt, and water. Heat 4 cups of water, add 4 teaspoons of salt, and stir to dissolve the salt. Then stir in enough fabric softener to make the mixture cloudy. Soak the pieces in the pot for an hour, remove, rinse under warm water, and rub lightly with a clean, dry cloth. Repeat the process if you need a higher sheen.

RUB WITH A BAKING SODA PASTE Put 2 tablespoons of baking soda in a bowl and add enough lemon juice to make a paste. Brush it on the jewelry with a soft toothbrush. Let the solution dry a bit and then run it under water, using a clean toothbrush to remove the mixture. Dry thoroughly with a clean cloth.

USE ALUMINUM FOIL AND BAKING SODA Line a pan with aluminum foil (or use a disposable aluminum baking pan). Put the jewelry on the aluminum. Dissolve a tablespoon or two of baking soda in 2 cups or so of hot water and then pour the solution over the jewelry. You'll see the foil getting darker and the jewelry getting lighter. Note: This method works so well that it will even remove tarnish from crevices in the jewelry. So if you value the antique look, use one of the first two methods. For silver jewelry with stones, use a paste silver polish and soft cloths; soaking stones can loosen or discolor them.

My ring just fell down the sink drain

OPEN THE SINK DRAIN TRAP Some people swear that you can retrieve jewelry lost down the sink drain by putting a small kitchen magnet on string and dangling it

down the drain. But that works only if your drainpipe is plastic and if your jewelry contains iron, which is not common. The real solution is to open the drain trap—that large U-shaped pipe under the sink. Many traps have a clean-out plug at the bottom. Put a bucket under it and use a wrench to unscrew the plug, as

shown in the illustration. Your jewelry should come out along with hair and soap scum. If the trap does not have a plug, remove the trap: Use a wrench or channel-type pliers to loosen the slip nuts at either end of the trap. Tape the jaws of the wrench or pliers to avoid scratching chrome-finished slip nuts.

My jewelry stones have lost their sparkle

USE WINDOW CLEANER Glass cleaner will get those precious stones to shine once more. Spray some commercial window cleaner, such as Windex, on a clean, lint-free cloth, making it barely damp. Then wipe the jewelry. This will also clean the metal around the stones.

■ EYEGLASS EMERGENCIES

I broke a stem of my eyeglasses

FIX IT WITH DUCT TAPE Make a temporary repair with duct tape. Grab a toothpick or even a small twig to serve as a splint, position it at the broken spot on the glasses frame, and wrap both together with tape. In a pinch, duct tape can also be used to secure the hinge.

I lost my eyeglasses hinge screw

FIX IT WITH FISHING LINE That minuscule screw fell out of the hinge on your glasses, and the stem is separated from the frame. Nylon fishing line makes an excellent temporary repair. Move the loose stem to the open position, as if you were about to put the eyeglasses on, to get the proper alignment. Thread a piece of the nylon line through the screw hole. Then trim the excess line with scissors, leaving ¹⁄₁₆ inch on each end. Heat the tip of a knife and touch it to each end of the line. The melting line will form just enough of a bead to prevent it from slipping through the holes. When it's time to make a permanent repair, snip an end off the line and slide it out.

My plastic sunglass frames no longer fit

USE HEAT TO RESHAPE THEM Plastic frames have a way of getting stretched into slightly different shapes. To get them back to the way you like them, immerse them in hot water or heat them with a hair dryer. The plastic will become flexible, allowing you to bend the frame back into shape.

■ SHOE PROBLEMS

My shoes are too tight

USE RUBBING ALCOHOL You need to stretch your shoes in the spots where they're too tight. Put them on and apply rubbing alcohol with a rag or tissue to those snug areas. This will soften the leather and, with the aid of the heat of your feet, allow it to stretch to fit your foot better. The stretching will take a day. If they are too painful to wear all day, take them off and stuff them with socks or panty hose to push them into shape. Some experts suggest that you dampen thick socks with rubbing alcohol and wear them in the shoes until the socks are dry.

My sneakers smell

SPRINKLE THEM WITH BAKING SODA Running and sweating will make your shoes stink. Baking soda, famous for its odor-absorbing ability, is an easy antidote. Sprinkle some of the powder inside your shoes, leave it overnight, and vacuum it out. For a longer-term solution, toss your sneakers in the wash and let them air-dry thoroughly.

A puddle got my shoes all wet

STUFF THEM WITH NEWSPAPER You have two challenges when your shoes get soaked: One is to dry them, and the other is to retain the

original shape of the shoe. Crumpled newspaper can do both jobs better than paper towels because it holds its shape while absorbing water. Ball the newsprint up into tight wads and press them firmly into the shoe until it's packed. Replace the newspaper stuffing every 20 minutes until the shoes are dry.

My shoes are caked with mud

LET THEM DRY BEFORE BRUSHING On leather shoes, wait until the mud has dried and then brush it away with a stiff brush. Rub a damp rag over the shoe to remove any remaining mud. Dry the shoes with a clean rag and then dab with a good wax shoe polish, which will penetrate the leather and protect the shoe from future stains.

I have white salt marks on my shoes

REMOVE WITH A VINEGAR SOLUTION A trudge home over a well-salted sidewalk on a winter day can leave your favorite shoes with stubborn salt stains. The quick solution: Mix 2 tablespoons of white vinegar with ½ cup of water and dab the mixture on the salt stain with a sponge or rag. The acidity in the vinegar will dissolve the salt. For suede shoes, first brush the stain with a suede brush and then apply a milder solution—1 tablespoon of white vinegar in ½ cup of water. Machine-wash canvas shoes.

The heel of my shoe came loose

NAIL IT BACK ON FROM INSIDE You're rushing out the door, and the heel comes loose on one of your shoes. What's more, they're the only shoes that go with the suit you're wearing. Find a short nail or thumbtack and a hammer, peel back the lining on the inside of the shoe, and hammer the nail through the sole and into the heel. This trick might make your shoe repair folks wince, but it will get you through the day.

I can't lace my frayed shoestring

DIP IT IN CLEAR NAIL POLISH When the end of your shoestring is frayed, it's hard to thread the lace through the eyes of your shoe. The solution: Snip the frayed end off the lace. Then dip the tip in clear nail polish to harden the material, wait for the polish to dry, and you're in business.

TRICKS OF THE TRADE

Is One Foot Larger than the Other?
Many people would tell you to buy the size of shoe that's comfortable for your larger foot and then pay extra for an insole to fill the extra space in the roomier shoe. Melissa Waden, director of a homeless shelter in Greensboro, North Carolina, has an easier and less expensive approach: Buy a pair of shoes to fit the smaller foot. Then reach into the shoe that needs to accommodate the larger foot and peel out the lining and padding that covers the bottom. You'll find another layer of fabric underneath, which is perfectly comfortable. This works on virtually any kind of shoe, she says, from walking boots to dress shoes.

PART SIX

Social Life

The tipsy guest with an obnoxious mouth.
The acquaintance whose name you forgot. The partygoers
who don't know when to call it a night. The thunderstorm
at an outdoor wedding. The friends arguing loudly
at your party. In this part of the book, you'll find
safe passage through these social minefields.

Parties and Weddings

■ PARTY PLANNING

I'm hosting a bash at a fancy hotel, and I'd like to save on the liquor bill

SUPPLY YOUR OWN ALCOHOL Buying the liquor yourself will be cheaper than having the caterer or venue provide it. You'll also know your exact liquor bill up front and how much your guests actually consume. (The caterer could exaggerate both of these amounts, and you'd have no way of knowing.) In addition, if you have any unopened bottles left over, you can usually return them to the store where you purchased them. (Be sure to ask about the store's return policy before you buy.) When deciding how much alcohol to buy, consider the age of most of the guests (younger adults drink more), the time of day (people drink more at night), and how many guests even imbibe in the first place.

Alternative: Instead of buying your own, try to negotiate a flat fee for the alcohol from the caterer or venue.

I don't know how much food to get

FOLLOW THE CATERING RULES OF THUMB Want to see party guests start gathering their coats in unison? Just run out of food or drinks and see how long the festivities continue. Fortunately, there are time-tested guidelines. Here are the basics:

- Overall amount of food: 1½ pounds (70 grams) per person for a meal; about 1 pound (45 grams) per person for a cocktail party
- Hors d'oeuvres: six pieces per person for a dinner party; twelve pieces per person for a cocktail party (or four to six pieces per person per hour)
- Alcohol: Plan on two drinks per person per hour for the first two hours; half that amount afterward. A 750-milliliter bottle of spirits (vodka, rum, scotch, etc.) contains about sixteen 1½-ounce (45-milliliter) shots; a 750-milliliter bottle of wine yields about five glasses

- Soft drinks: Plan on three bottles of mix for every bottle of spirits. Stock plenty of bottled water, soft drinks, and juices for nondrinkers and to give drinkers of alcohol a break. For a cocktail party, also buy 1 pound (.45 kilograms) of ice per person.

If you're serving an expensive, "special treat" food item, such as caviar, plan on serving a lot of it, because that's where your guests will go first. And remember, when planning food amounts, it's always safer to round *up*.

The weather forecast for my party is looking bad

HAVE A BACKUP PLAN If you're putting together an outdoor wedding or other event, always take into account the possibility of rain. Talk to your local equipment-rental or party-supply store about reserving a tent that's large enough for your event. Then keep an eye on the weather on the days leading up to the big day. If it looks like rain, go ahead and have the tent set up. If you wind up not using it, you should be able to get your deposit back.

If you're planning an event in a courtyard or other outdoor area at a large hotel, the establishment often will provide some sort of banquet room in case of rain. Since these rooms often are not very glamorous, watch the weather and have a plan in place to spruce up the room if you do need to move indoors.

Going to your backup plan fast can save a special occasion when Mother Nature wants to rain on your parade.

■ UNEXPECTED EVENTS

Fourteen people showed up at a party for twelve

KEEP SMILING AND IMPROVISE One of the toughest situations you may face as a party host is accommodating guests who show up uninvited or come after not responding to an RSVP. To reduce the risk of this happening, about a week before the party, call up any guests who haven't RSVP'd to see whether they're planning to come. If surprise guests do show up, the polite thing to do is to overlook their impoliteness and make them feel welcome. If at all possible, rearrange the place settings to make room for the extra guests. If you're throwing a really big party, set up an extra table beforehand, just in case. And

Get a Head Start
Depending on how elaborate the party, start planning early. Here's a sample timeline:

• Six to eight weeks before: Plan party's theme, activities, and music; send invitations; hire any entertainer and/or caterer.

• Two to three weeks before: Order nonperishable supplies and decoration; hire helpers.

• One week before: Call guests who have not RSVP'd; confirm entertainer, caterer, and helpers.

• Two to three days before: Buy groceries; make any dishes that can be prepared and frozen; begin cleaning the house.

• The day before: Thaw frozen foods; finish housecleaning; decorate party space and set up party table(s) and utensils.

• Party day: Complete food preparation; do a final check of the party space, bar, and kitchen; give yourself plenty of time to get ready; take a deep breath and enjoy!

when you plan the menu and food amounts, count on feeding a few more people than are on your guest list. If you don't, you'll just have to discreetly reduce everyone else's portions (before you serve them) in order to provide for the unexpected guests.

The food ran out before the party was over

THINK SUPERMARKET DELI SECTION Experienced party planners keep extra hors d'oeuvres in the freezer for such moments. If that's not an option, have someone slip out to the nearest supermarket. Most stock trays of prepared vegetables, dips, cheeses, and cold cuts. If they don't, here is a shopping list for a dozen hungry grazers:

Amount	Item
1 pound (500 grams)	sliced Genoa salami
1 pound (500 grams)	sliced smoked ham or turkey
2 pounds (1 kilogram)	Swiss or American cheese
1 jar	spicy mustard
2 boxes	crackers
2 loaves	French bread or baguettes
1 jar	green olives
1 large bag	bite-size peeled carrots
2 small baskets	cherry or grape tomatoes
1 large bunch	grapes
1 pound (500 grams)	dried apricots

I'm having a get-together I didn't know I was having

MAKE DO WITH WHAT YOU'VE GOT The phone rings, and suddenly eight people will be showing up in your living room in an hour. Not to panic. Here's a formula for throwing an instant party:

• Set the mood: Light some candles and pick out a few background-music CDs.

• Take an inventory of what's in your refrigerator and pantry and let your ingenuity run wild. If you run out of inspiration, try a food Web site, such as epicurious.com. Don't get too fancy. If you've got some potatoes and toppings (cheese, bacon, chives, sour cream, etc.), you've got the makings of a fun party centerpiece—a mashed-potato bar.

• If the cupboard (or liquor cabinet) is truly bare, you'll have to make a quick run to the supermarket (see previous problem), but let your guests pitch in, too. Turn the party into a participatory potluck affair by asking your guests to bring their own bottle or pick up a food item on the way to your place.

■ PROBLEM GUESTS

I need to make a wallflower blossom

MIX AND MATCH A frowning, uncomfortable guest is a danger to a relaxed, fun party and to your reputation as a host. If you see a guest sitting alone, corral someone who's a good talker or has something in common with the party pooper, and introduce them to each other. Have a three-way conversation for a few minutes and then excuse yourself.

The trick to getting a shy person to talk is to avoid questions that can be answered yes or no. Instead, try conversation starters that invite longer answers and follow-up questions: What travel have you done lately? What books are you reading—or what good movies have you seen?

One big mouth is monopolizing dozens of ears

DEFLECT ATTENTION You have dozens of people mingling in your home, but only one seems to be talking—the one standing in the middle of the room loudly braying jokes. Sometimes it's fine; a witty guest can keep the party rolling. But eventually the joking gets old, and you'd like to shift the spotlight. What should you do?

Often the situation resolves itself naturally. Guests will get up and move elsewhere, and the dynamics will change. Or you can wait for a particular anecdote, then step in and say something like, "Oh, that happened to Jenny, too. Jenny, tell us what happened." But sometimes, as the host, it becomes *your* responsibility to absorb the loudmouth's good cheer. Tell the big talker that you need a little help with a task, and ask him or her to assist you. By the time you return, others will have had a chance to start up conversations.

As party host, it's up to you to tame the talker. One fast way is to ask for his assistance in another room.

A tipsy guest is turning the party into unhappy hour

CALL A TIME OUT Loud, soused guests don't just put a strain on a good time; they can be a danger to themselves and others, and if they get into an accident on the way home from your party, you could be legally liable for it in some states. If a guest in your home is being loud and obnoxious, take the person aside and say discreetly that while you're glad he or she is having a good time, you'd like your guest to tone it down so everyone else can have a good time, too. If you don't know the guest very well, have one of the guest's friends try to calm him or her down. If the party is at a public venue, such as a country club or hotel ballroom, here are other ways of reining in overindulging guests:

- Have the bartender stop serving them drinks.
- Have the venue manager intervene.
- For true troublemakers, call security.

Caution: Do all you can to keep a guest from driving under the influence. Offer to call a cab for any guest who isn't sober enough to drive. If you know the person well enough, offer to let him or her sleep it off overnight on your couch or in the spare bedroom. Or discreetly slip out and give the person a ride home.

More light and less music quickly signal to your guests that it's time to head for the door.

Two friends are arguing loudly at my party

INTERVENE WITHOUT TAKING SIDES Here's a technique that will help you defuse the situation. Walk up to the two arguing people and say, "Is this a matter that you two can resolve? If not, I'm afraid I'll have to ask you to leave." This simple expression of question and consequence usually quashes the argument. It makes both arguing people accountable for their actions, regardless of who is in the right. And you, the host, are not forced to take sides.

My guests don't know when to call it a night

LIGHTS ON, MUSIC OFF The party is rolling along nicely: The guests are having a good time, the music is playing, and no one wants the evening to end. No one but you, that is. It's 1 A.M., and you just want the last remaining guests out of your house so you can go to sleep. Take your cue from entertainment professionals: A half hour before you know you'll want the guests gone, start telling them that the evening will soon be coming to a close. Start putting away the drinks and the food, turn on a few lights, and turn down the music. In a half hour, thank the stragglers for coming and help them to the door. Be polite, but firm.

I'm at a party with my enemy

KEEP CIRCULATING Maybe it's a coworker out for your job. Or the neighbor who keeps looking at your spouse the wrong way. Whatever the case, you're face-to-face in a social setting with someone you really dislike. The key here is to keep your animosity from ruining the party. At your first encounter, greet your nemesis as cordially as possible and move on. Parties are all about mingling and circulating, so there's no reason to linger with someone you dislike, much less air your grievances. If the party is a sit-down dinner and you know beforehand that this person is on the guest list, inform your hosts of the situation so that they can keep you well apart.

Some ears are more sensitive than others

USE A LITTLE CREATIVE DECEPTION It's inevitable: At wedding receptions or other parties with several generations of guests, the young people want the music cranked *up,* and the older people want it turned *down.* If you can't reach a happy medium, try this event planner's ploy: Simply tell your noise-sensitive guests that you've made note of their wishes and had the music turned down, but don't actually do it. This is a psychological trick that usually makes the listener think the music is indeed quieter.

◼ WEDDINGS

I'm afraid my wedding day will turn into chaos

APPOINT AN OVERSEER Having "too many cooks in the kitchen" all issuing orders on your wedding day can lead to confusion and chaos. If you're not using a professional wedding planner, select a "wedding marshal"—one person who'll be in charge when the day comes. Pick as your overseer a responsible friend or family member who will be at the wedding but who doesn't have a specific duty or isn't already deeply involved in the day. Don't choose the maid or matron of honor or the mother of the bride, as they already have enough to do. Give your wedding marshal a to-do list and specific instructions on how things should be done. The marshal will make sure the flowers are in

PROBLEM STOPPER

When Your House Smells Musty
Company's coming, and your house has a musty odor. You can cure this in no time if you have central heating and air conditioning. Just spray air freshener for a few seconds into the intake duct in your house. The furnace or air conditioner will distribute the nice clean scent throughout your house.

Most air fresheners do not contain alcohol, and you can spray them through the grate and wipe up any residue with a rag. If yours does contain alcohol (check the fine print), remove the screws on the grate with a screwdriver, pull the grate out of the way, and spray straight into the duct. Otherwise, the spray could damage the paint on the grate.

their proper spots, the chairs are set up in the right places, and all the caterers and helpers are where they need to be. Make sure to work with your wedding marshal well ahead of the event, rather than just handing him or her a list on the morning of the wedding.

I don't know how much to pay the person officiating at the wedding

WHEN IN DOUBT, ASK Officiant fees (or donations—the commonly used term when the officiant is a member of the clergy) vary a great deal depending on the officiant, his or her location, and the services he or she provides. Some officiants charge nothing or simply ask to be invited to the reception. Others suggest a donation to their religious order or house of worship. In most cases, however, there is a set fee/donation for performing a wedding ceremony, over and above the cost of hiring the church or other wedding venue. The officiant's fee, traditionally paid by the groom, can range from $75 to multiple hundreds. Traveling, customizing the ceremony, or attending a rehearsal typically adds to the cost. So don't be shy. If you're in doubt, ask the officiant what his or her fee/expected donation is, and what it includes.

I'm not sure how to thank our groomsmen and bridesmaids

THINK JEWELRY It's appropriate to give your wedding attendants a token of your appreciation and esteem. If it's within your budget, one gift your attendants will really appreciate is assistance with all or part of their wedding-day attire or accommodations costs. Less expensive alternatives include cufflinks, money clips, or bar sets for the groomsmen, and jewelry for the bridesmaids that can be worn on the day of the ceremony. Gift certificates for spa treatments are also a popular choice for bridesmaids.

I can't afford live music at the wedding

HIRE A MUSIC STUDENT You'd be surprised at the number of music students out there who'd jump at the chance to earn some money while practicing their art. Contact local music schools, private academies and instructors, and local performing-arts theaters. All may be able to recommend young, talented musicians who can provide beautiful music at a reasonable cost.

PROBLEM STOPPER

Wedding Day Toolbox
A smart bride, mother of the bride, or other person in charge of a wedding will keep a wedding day "emergency kit" ready to handle little last-minute incidents that can arise.

The kit should include scissors, needle, thread, and safety pins to repair accidental rips and tears in the wedding gown, tuxedos, or bridesmaids' dresses. Toss in a little can of hair spray and a travel hair dryer, for hair emergencies, and a painkiller, such as Tylenol, and some bandages to treat headaches and the occasional cut or scrape.

Yet another good tool in the kit is a small bottle of laundry detergent. One event planner used the stuff to fix a panic-stricken bride's train after it was dropped on a dirty sidewalk during the prewedding photo shoot. A little detergent and water dabbed onto the spots fixed it right up, and the bride calmed down by ceremony time.

Manners and Social Obligations

■ AWKWARD SITUATIONS

Someone has a cartload of stuff in the express line ahead of me

TALK TO THE MANAGER The shopper who abuses the express line poses the kind of problem that really makes people steam in these high-speed times. Some of these shoppers, with their carts bulging, are just being rude. But others may be making an innocent mistake. It's not up to you to confront them or ask them to go to another line. It's the *store's* responsibility to enforce their 12-items-or-less rule. If you notice that this problem happens a lot, ask the manager if he or she can do anything to keep the express lines moving in an express manner. And be sure to check your own cart before you start glaring at others'. If you find yourself with an item or two over the limit, that's probably OK. But if you realize you are way over the express limit, graciously find another line.

If the express line is regularly misused, you'll get results faster if you talk to the manager.

I forgot the name of someone I know

ACKNOWLEDGE IT WITH A SMILE Don't be mortified when you forget the name of an acquaintance or coworker. These things happen to everyone. Just say, "Oops, I've forgotten your name" and lightheartedly promise to remember it next time. When the person reminds you of his or her name, repeat it aloud as a way of helping you remember it better.

I called someone the wrong name—the *really* wrong name

SAY YOU'RE SORRY AND LET IT GO What may be worse than not remembering someone's name is calling the person by the wrong

Keeping Guests Out of the Kitchen

Your kitchen is a mess of pots and pans, hot stove and oven, and dirty dishes. It's not a place where you want guests to congregate But asking them to stay out is awkward.

Keep them in the right part of the house by planning ahead, recommends Austin, Texas, party planner Lee Carnes. "Don't put anything in the kitchen—no food or beverages," she says. By keeping such items out of the kitchen, guests will be more likely to stay in other areas of the house.

If possible, also shut the door to the kitchen. People are reluctant to go through closed doors in other people's homes.

name. For instance, you're speaking to a friend's new husband and you call him by the *old* husband's name. Or you refer to your new boss by the ousted boss's name. Try to acknowledge your mistake with a little humor. Perhaps say, "Oh, I really know you're Mike and not Tom." Apologize for your slipup and let it drop. If your mistake obviously insulted a person of authority, such as your boss, who wasn't impressed with how you recovered from the error, you might want to send a quick note later, again apologizing for the lapse.

I really put my foot in my mouth

DON'T DENY, JUST APOLOGIZE PROFUSELY You wrote a nasty e-mail message about someone—and now you realize you accidentally sent it to him. Or you just mocked an acquaintance who, you discover too late, is standing nearby. Since the floor isn't going to open up and swallow you whole, much as you wish it would, you're going to have to deal with this. You *must* offer an apology, and it must be a good one. Don't say, "I didn't really mean it." You probably did mean it, and denying it will just compound the error. In other words, don't apologize for what you think, feel, or said about the person. Instead, apologize for the *effects* of what you said. Try something like this: "I cannot apologize enough for making those careless comments about you. It was heartless, it was dumb, and you don't deserve whatever embarrassment or irritation I caused you." Apologize profusely and sincerely and then be done with it. Don't stretch out the explanation or keep bringing up how sorry you are later.

I've bumped into a friend who didn't invite me to his wedding

FORGIVE AND FORGET Your circle of college buddies swore you'd be friends forever. So your feelings were hurt when, five years after graduation, one of the guys invited everyone *else* to his wedding but not you. You've just bumped into him at a class reunion, and you feel awkward. In this case, take the high road and don't mention not going to the wedding. Perhaps you lived far away from the ceremony, and your friend didn't want you to feel obligated to buy a plane ticket. Or maybe the other friends had stayed in closer touch with the groom than you had. Whatever the reason, don't make a big deal of it. When you see your friend, congratulate him on his marriage and wish him and his wife the best.

A stranger asked me a personal question

REPLY POLITELY BUT KEEP IT SHORT Perhaps you're pregnant. Or your child has a birthmark or disability. Or you've adopted a child of another race. You'd think these matters would be your business alone, but unfortunately there are a lot of overly curious people out there. Although such questions are undeniably rude, bluntly telling the questioner to mind his or her own business is not the way to go. People don't mean to be rude. Give them the benefit of the doubt. Have a few polite responses ready, but don't offer too much information. Say something like "Yes, I'm expecting" or "Yes, she's adopted." Continue with "I'm in a really big rush" and keep walking.

My buddy has bad breath

OFFER A MINT How do you tell your friend he or she has breath that would slay the devil? Here's an easy, roundabout way: Pop a mint or piece of gum into your own mouth and then offer one to your friend. This way, you won't be saying anything outright, and if he or she accepts your offer, everyone wins. If not? Well, it depends on how strong your friendship is. You either risk offending your friend with the truth or ignore the problem and excuse yourself to get a breath of fresh air.

Is Etiquette Your Cup of Tea?

Etiquette isn't just for stuffy Victorian tea drinkers or Gatsby-esque croquet players. It's intended to help make your life better, no matter the color of your collar or your station in life. Here are some insights on how good manners benefit everyone:

- "People say to me that etiquette is pretentious. It's not. Etiquette is about kindness, courtesy, and respect." —*Melenie Broyles, founder of Etiquette Saint Louis, an organization that conducts etiquette classes*

- "Etiquette is just a set of rules that evolve as our culture evolves. We have travel etiquette, death etiquette, phone etiquette, and Internet etiquette. There are rules for everything." —*Lisa Mirza Grotts, San Francisco-based government protocol expert and founder of an etiquette consulting firm called the AML Group*

- "Etiquette helps smooth the way through different situations. It's about being considerate and respectful and honest and kind. It's based on consideration and respect—being able to empathize with how other people might want to be treated. A lot of it is common sense, and a lot of it depends on the situation." —*Peggy Post, author, columnist, and great-granddaughter-in-law of etiquette pioneer Emily Post*

**PROBLEM
STOPPER**

Peaceable Coexistence

If you have roommates or
close neighbors, odds are
that one of them will do
something at some point
that you'll find irritating.
Advance planning can
prevent many problems,
and the next-best solution
is to deal with the
problem immediately.
Here are some pointers
from Karen Mallett, of
In Good Company, an
etiquette-training firm
located in Winnipeg,
Manitoba, Canada:

Set ground rules right
up front with roommates.
Decide how often
boyfriends or girlfriends
can stay. Decide when
and how loudly everyone
can play music or watch
TV. Decide how the bills
and chores will be divided.
All are common hot-
button issues.

If your neighbors do
things that intrude on
your sense of calm, meet
with them as soon as pos-
sible to come up with a
solution. You'll save yourself a lot of pent-up
anxiety and hard feelings
over the issue.

■ PHONE ETIQUETTE

My telephone call just got cut off

CALLER REDIALS A disconnected phone call is a minor inconve-
nience, but the solution can be a major hassle. Which party should
redial and resume the conversation? If both people redial, both get
busy signals. If *neither* redials, thinking the other person will do it,
both people waste time staring at the phone. In general, the person
who instigated the call in the first place should do the redialing. But
if you know the disconnection was on your end—maybe you
bumped the "hang up" button on the phone—*you* call back.

I'm in public and my cell phone is ringing

BE DISCREET AND DON'T DISTURB OTHERS Improper cell-phone
usage is a major and mounting source of irritation these days. The
general rule is to avoid making or receiving cell-phone calls if you're
going to intrude on people around you. That includes settings such
as restaurants, movie theaters, libraries, public transportation, and
places where you should be interacting with others (on a date or at a
meeting, for instance). Don't disturb strangers with your conversation (especially if it involves intimate details), and don't make
friends and acquaintances feel second best when you take a call
during your time with them.

If you know you're going to be receiving an important call during
a meeting or get-together, tell your companions ahead of time that
you'll be called away at some point. Set your cell phone to vibrate
instead of ring, and head to a secluded area when you get the call. Of
course, if the call could be an emergency issue—say, it's from your
child's babysitter—you're forgiven for going ahead and taking it
where it would normally be impolite. Just be as discreet as possible.

■ SOCIAL COMMUNICATIONS

I'm never quite sure when
thank-you notes are required

WHEN IN DOUBT, WRITE Thank-you notes are on the endangered-
habits list. Etiquette experts plead for you to do your part to bring
them back from extinction. Write a thank-you note within a day or
two of receiving a gift. (After your wedding, you have six weeks to

send your thank-you notes, but sooner is always better.) Sit down with your children and see to it that they write thank-you notes for their gifts, as well. This is a habit that is best started when they're young. Steer clear of the prewritten cards that are becoming popular these days, which say something along the lines of "Thank you for the _____." They don't really convey much appreciation.

Gifts aren't the only reason to send notes, though. After you have dinner in someone's home, it's proper to thank your host in a call the next day, followed by a quick thank-you note. And *always* send thank-you notes to potential employers after an interview, thanking them for their time and interest. This habit is fading away nowadays, and a note will make you stand out from other candidates. If the employer will be making the decision very soon, an e-mailed thank-you is appropriate.

I'd like to offer my condolences to someone quickly

IT'S OK TO E-MAIL If someone you know suffers a tragedy or loss, you're expected to express your sympathy. Ideally, you should offer your condolences in person. If that's not possible, a written note should be your next choice. However, if you want to offer comfort immediately, e-mail is a good way to send the bereaved person a quick message. E-mails are preferable to phone calls, which might come at an inconvenient time and can't be dealt with later. Just be sure to follow up your e-mail with a visit or handwritten note later. E-mail should *complement* these methods, not replace them.

I need a card for someone who's terminally ill

TRY WRITING YOUR OWN You want to offer sympathy and support to a friend who's in a struggle that he or she is not likely to win. But what kind of card is the right one? Obviously, don't select "Get Well Soon." That message doesn't acknowledge the seriousness of your friend's problem, and it's a wish that probably won't come true. Go for a card with a message such as "My thoughts and prayers are with you." But send a card with a religious theme only if you know that the recipient shares those beliefs. Another option is simply to pick a pretty card that's blank on the inside, so you can express your own thoughts and best wishes.

PROBLEM STOPPER

The 10-Karat Tool
Maybe someday a scientist specializing in etiquette will invent a Rudeness Alarm that will go off when you're about to breach a rule of good manners. We're not there yet, but Melenie Broyles, an etiquette consultant also known as "St. Louis's First Lady of Manners," recommends this useful tool to help you behave appropriately in all circumstances:

Simply jot down the Golden Rule on an index card and slip it into your pocket. If you need a refresher course, the rule says: "Do to others as you would have them do to you." That is, if you wouldn't want someone else to do what you're about to do—whether it's double-dipping, cutting in line, or not thanking someone for a nice gift—don't do it to others. "I look at the Golden Rule as a tool," Broyles says. "Remembering that and always thinking of others first is the key to good manners."

I keep forgetting birthdays

KEEP TRACK MANUALLY OR DIGITALLY It's not that easy to remember everybody's birthdays and other special occasions. The basic strategy for keeping on top of such things is to compile a list of every date you need to remember, buy a calendar, and jot each one down. Of course, you're going to have to remember to check the calendar. Or better yet, have the calendar program in your PC or PDA (personal digital assistant) do the remembering and reminding for you.

What if you still keep finding yourself empty-handed on gift-giving occasions? Easy: Stock up on cards and gifts in advance. Go to a card shop and buy several cards appropriate for the occasions you observe, plus some tasteful-but-generic blank ones that will do for just about any occasion. Keep a laundry basket or cardboard box full of little gifts and wrapping paper. Visit a major discount store right after the holidays. You'll find plenty of handy gifts at discounted prices to stash away for those oh-gosh-I-forgot moments.

My holiday cards often go astray

DO AN E-MAIL ADDRESS CHECK We live in a mobile society, so keeping track of friends and acquaintances can be tricky. When it's time to send out holiday greeting cards, it's important to have everybody's contact information updated. To make sure your address book is accurate, send an e-mail to all your friends and family in October, asking them to e-mail you back with their updated contact information. (Give them yours as well.) Come December, you'll have everyone's addresses handy and won't have to scramble to get the address at the last minute.

■ DATING

My date's no fun, and I want to get out of here

DON'T BOLT Even if you're not having a good time, think twice before abruptly rushing away from a date who's not striking your fancy. First of all, it's rude. But there's another good reason to try to leave on a good note: You never know who you might meet through this person. Your date may be a dud, but that doesn't mean his or her brothers or friends are. Stay on good terms with the person, and you might be able to meet other people, one of whom might turn out to be a better match for you. This is particularly important for singles who have trouble meeting eligible dating candidates.

At the end of the date, just say, "It was nice meeting you," and leave it at that. If you feel like calling later, you will have set the stage for it. But if you don't call later, you never promised that you would.

Even if your date is not what you'd hoped for, leave on good terms. You never know who you might meet through this person.

I'm dating a high-powered woman executive and don't know how to act

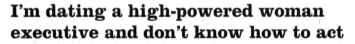

KEEP CHIVALRY ALIVE Treat her as you would any other woman. Chivalry may be dying, but it's still a great asset on a date, even if she has lots of zeros at the end of her annual salary. Open the door for her. Pull out her chair at the dinner table. And send flowers if you really like her. And if you're not sure about the longer term, a dozen and a half long-stemmed roses in a *variety* of colors says "like," not "love."

I have a first date—but not much money

KEEP IT SIMPLE AND ACTIVE Congratulations. You finally got up the nerve to ask her out. But your money's tight right now, and even if you had more cash, you're not sure what sort of activities she'd find fun. What should you do? First, don't get too worked up over making a first date a lavish event. Your only two goals are to discover whether you're remotely attracted to the other person and whether you enjoy being with this person. So don't get all tense and nervous, wondering whether you've finally found "the one."

Instead of spending $100 on dinner and a movie, keep the first date simple, aimed at just have a good time. Set the date for a Saturday afternoon. During the summer, go for a bike ride or a walk through a park. During the winter, go ice-skating and get some hot chocolate. If all goes well, the date can extend into the evening, and if not, you can say you have plans with friends later. If you both decide to continue the date, stick with the simple, low-key theme. Grab a bite at a café, for example, and save the fancier dinner for the second date.

■ GIFT GIVING

I've been invited to a dinner, but I don't know what to take

THINK WINE OR CHOCOLATES Your hosts have been kind enough to invite you into their home, and it's appropriate to return the kindness by bringing a small gift. A few rules apply. Unless you have the host's blessing in advance, never arrive bearing a dish of food, such as a casserole, that needs to be consumed right away. It might clash with the rest of the dinner. Nor should you bring a gift that requires immediate attention, such as fresh flowers that need to be cut and put in water. Your host already has enough to do. Bring a small potted plant, a bottle of wine, a box of chocolates, or some other small token of your appreciation. Don't expect to get a taste of that wine, though; the host isn't obligated to open it and serve it with dinner.

I'm not attending the wedding; I wonder if I should send a gift

YES, YOU SHOULD You received a wedding invitation, but the event is too far away to attend, or you have another obligation. Even so, sending a gift is the correct thing to do. The wedding gift isn't intended as repayment for partaking in the wedding ceremony and reception. It's a way of expressing your good wishes for the couple and responding to the regard they showed you by asking you to share in their big day. Just how much of a gift depends on how well you know the bride and/or groom. If the bride is a close niece, you'll obviously want to give a meaningful present. If the wedding involves the stepson of your former boss, it would be appropriate to send something more modest. Find out where the couple is registered for gifts. Odds are they registered for items with a wide range of prices.

TRICKS OF THE TRADE

Raise Your Wedding IQ

Before you head off to a wedding, here are a few tips to keep you in the couple's good graces:

• It's a myth that you have a year to send a gift. The gift should arrive by the wedding day.

• In general, don't take your gift to the wedding itself. In some cultures, it's appropriate to set the gift on a display table, where it's opened and displayed. Otherwise, send your gift before the wedding to the bride's house or the address specified on the gift registry.

• If you're a woman, never wear white to a wedding unless the bride has requested you to do so for some reason. When you wear white, it looks as if you're trying to compete with the bride, and other guests may think you seem jealous and petty.

• If you arrive late at the wedding, don't try to get up closer to family or friends—just slip quietly into the last pew.

I'm unsure whether to give a gift for an "encore" wedding

ENCORE WEDDINGS CALL FOR ENCORE GIFTS You gave your friend a fondue pot in 1980, a VCR in 1987, and microwaveable serving dishes in 1995. It's the new millennium, and your friend is getting married one more time. And yes, you do need to send another wedding gift. You always need to give *something,* but what, exactly, depends on the situation. If you just gave your friend an expensive wedding gift two years ago, it's appropriate to give more of a token gift this time around. If your friend's last wedding was 15 years ago, and the spouse has since died and your friend is finally remarrying, a more substantial gift to mark the event would be appropriate.

I didn't get a gift from someone who came to my wedding

IT'S OK TO CALL AND FIND OUT IF IT WAS LOST You're not sure why Aunt Ruthie didn't send you a gift even though you're very close. The proper response, you may be surprised to hear, is to call her up and ask if she intended to get you a gift. This may seem the *opposite* of polite manners, but here's the explanation given by etiquette experts: While it may seem as if you're pressuring her for a late gift or trying to make her feel guilty, you're really finding out whether her gift got lost in the mail or the order was misplaced at the store. If that's what happened, it would be inconsiderate to allow your friend or relative to spend money on a gift that you never got to enjoy. Discovering that the gift was lost can also prevent strain or awkwardness in your relationship.

I don't know what to give my letter carrier as a holiday gift

KEEP IT EDIBLE OR PRACTICAL It's proper to give a gratuity at the holidays to the service people who make your life easier, such as doormen, building maintenance staff, cleaning persons, dog walkers, newspaper deliverers, letter carriers, and others. Postal regulations prohibit mail carriers from accepting cash or cash equivalents (such as gift certificates), although unsolicited gifts worth up to $20 are permitted. The no-cash rule is often "forgotten" around the holidays, but if you do give your letter carrier a gift, make it something he or she can really use, such as a food item (cookies, candy, a food gift basket) or a scarf, rather than a seasonal trinket. A note with your gift saying, "No thank-you note needed" would also be appreciated.

■ FOOD ETIQUETTE

Yuk! Someone double-dipped into the salsa

ALERT THE HOST Taking a bite out of a chip and then dipping it into the salsa again is both inconsiderate and unsanitary. It also puts you, as the observer, in an awkward spot. It wouldn't be polite to confront the offender, but then it also wouldn't be right to say nothing and allow others to sink their chips into questionable dip. The solution is to discreetly tell the host or someone on the wait staff, "You may want to replace that dip." Don't go into detail, just say it's tainted and leave it at that.

I've just spilled my drink on a dining companion

ASSIST, BUT DON'T TOUCH, YOUR VICTIM Although your first instinct may be to grab a napkin and help dab away the beverage you just knocked over onto a dining companion, restrain yourself. No matter how helpful you intend to be, touching the spilled-on person intrudes on his or her personal space and might make the person feel even more uncomfortable. Discreetly gather napkins, seltzer water, or any other items that might be useful in cleaning up. Offer to pay the cleaning bill for the stained garment. But it's best to keep your hands to yourself.

Eating Styles: When in Rome...

American and Continental (i.e., European) styles are differentiated by how the knife and fork are held during a meal. In the American style, a person cuts food by holding the knife in the right hand while holding the fork, tines down, in the left hand. Once the person has cut a piece, the knife is placed on the plate (blade facing toward the eater), and the fork, with tines up, is switched to the right hand to convey the food to the mouth. In the somewhat more efficient Continental style, there's no switching of the fork. Food is taken to the mouth with the fork held tines down in the left hand, while the knife remains in the right. Both styles are acceptable, but what is never acceptable is to cut more than one piece of food at a time.

■ BUSINESS INTERACTIONS

I want to hand out my business cards at a friend's party

DO IT SPARINGLY AND CAREFULLY Business cards are a great way to share information about yourself, leave behind a little reminder of your presence, and encourage new business. But distributing them willy-nilly at a social engagement leaves a bad impression and devalues the card. Make sure that when you present your card, there's a certain amount of importance attached to it. That's not possible when you're wallpapering the room with them.

Not only should you be sparing with your cards, but you should also make sure you're handing them out at the right moment and to the right person. It's not appropriate, for instance, to thrust your business card at someone who's far higher up the corporate chain than you are. The best way to handle a situation like this is to ask for his or her card first, then ask if you may then return the favor. The exchange of business cards is almost like going on a first-name basis with someone; it should not be done lightly.

I'd like to introduce people properly

THINK RANK, NOT AGE OR GENDER Whether you're at a business or a social function, there's one basic rule you need to follow when introducing two people to each other. Don't worry about their gender or their age. Instead, always introduce the person of *lesser* authority to the person of *greater* authority. Thus, you should not say, "Joe Schmo, this is Ambassador Phineas Crabtree III," but rather, "Ambassador Phineas Crabtree III, may I present Mr. Schmo." Of course, if everyone is of the same rank, you may want to introduce the younger person to the older one.

There's a question on my voice mail that I don't have an answer for yet

CALL BACK WITH A PROGRESS REPORT If someone at work calls (or e-mails) you with a business-related question that will take a while to answer, you might be tempted to hold off responding until you know the answer. This is not a good idea. Instead, check in immediately with a progress report and say you'll come back with the requested information as soon as possible.

TRICKS OF THE TRADE

Elbows: The Fine Points
This may come as a surprise, but propping your elbows on the dinner table isn't a complete faux pas, says Lisa Mirza Grotts, a former government-protocol executive who currently works as an etiquette consultant.

As long as there's no food on the table, it's completely appropriate to rest your elbows on the table. This means you're cleared for landing before and after the meal and between courses. That's just your elbows, though. Keep good posture and don't sprawl your upper body on the table.

PART SEVEN

Everyday Life

First came cars, and not long after came the dented fender. With the invention of e-mail, spam was not far behind. When they invented cell phones, they also invented poor reception. Every innovation of modern life, it seems, creates a new universe of potential mishaps. For work, play, commuting, computers, travel, shopping, children, and more, we've got answers.

Modern Living

■ LOST, MISPLACED, AND STOLEN ITEMS

I left something in a taxi

NOTIFY THE CAB COMPANY AND HOPE FOR THE BEST It's a terrible feeling, watching a taxicab drive away with your stuff in it. Sadly, in today's world, many people keep what they find, especially if it has any value, or they simply don't bother to track down the owner. As soon as you become aware of a loss, contact the cab company, if possible, or the lost-and-found office of the local taxi commission or police department, and keep your fingers crossed. Here are some tips for improving your odds of recovering the lost item or avoiding a loss in the first place:

- Whenever you get into a cab, note the medallion number. This makes it a lot easier for the taxi company to at least identify the cab you were in.
- If you're already out of the cab, try to get the license plate number, for the same reason.
- Put your name, address, and phone number on really important items, such as briefcases, computers, and address books, along with a message offering a specific cash reward for the return of the item.
- Whenever you exit a cab, take note of everything on your person, especially your wallet and cell phone, two items that can easily slip out of your pockets.

I lost a contact lens on vacation

HAVE YOUR PRESCRIPTION FAXED The advent of disposable soft contact lenses and online vendors has made losing contacts much less of a problem than it once was. (When was the last time you saw someone on all fours looking for a tiny piece of clear plastic?) But if you are traveling and run out of your disposable lenses or lose one of your custom-fitted rigid lenses, you're going to be one unhappy camper. The most obvious solution is to travel with an ample supply of disposables or an emergency spare set of rigid lenses. But if you didn't think ahead and find yourself lensless, here's what to do: Contact an optometrist, optician, or ophthalmologist where you are and make sure that office accepts prescriptions by fax. If it does, simply call your hometown eye professional and have a copy of your prescription faxed. If you can't reach your eye professional, you'll have to start over and get examined for a new prescription.

I can't find my driver's license

REPORT IT TO YOUR LOCAL POLICE Your driver's license is the key to many transactions, from paying with a check to getting pulled over by the police. If you've lost your license, the first thing to do is to file a lost-property report at your local police station. Although you probably won't get your license back, at least you will have started a paper trail to show that you're working on getting another one. This will come in especially handy should you get pulled over. The police officer will be able to verify that you actually lost your license and are not just trying to put one over on him. The lost-property report will also be useful when you go to the Department of Motor Vehicles to get a new license. Each state has different rules for replacing lost licenses, so it pays to check your state's DMV Web site or call your local DMV office before you go there so you can bring all the required paperwork.

My purse was snatched!

CANCEL YOUR CREDIT CARDS RIGHT AWAY If your purse gets stolen, it's probably gone for good. Police do not recommend that you or a good Samaritan chase after the thief. What you should do is find a phone and cancel your credit cards immediately. If you don't have the credit card numbers handy, call home and ask someone there to dig up some old credit card receipts. (You do save them, right?) Tell your credit card company where and when your purse was stolen. If you report the loss before the thief uses the card, you won't be liable for any unauthorized charges. If the thief does run up charges before you call in, your liability is limited to $50. Follow up the initial call with a letter to the credit card company listing the account number, the time and place of the theft, and the date you reported the loss. And remember to keep checking your billing statements carefully, as you'll need to report each unauthorized charge to your credit card company in writing. Finally, be sure to file a police report. Not only might it help in apprehending your purse snatcher,

Don't run after that guy who just nabbed your purse—you'll be better off racing to the nearest phone.

but it will also come in handy if the credit card company questions your reported loss.

I can't find my wallet

HAVE OTHERS JOIN THE SEARCH Stop looking by yourself. You're just going to keep looking in the same places over and over again. Bring a fresh set of eyes into the equation. For instance, if you've lost your wallet around the house, enlist your neighbors' kids to look around your house and car. Whoever finds the wallet gets a $10 prize. It would be money well spent.

■ TAXES

I'm missing some of my tax paperwork

CHECK LAST YEAR'S RETURN Some 30 million people in the United States wait until the last minute to mail in their tax returns. If you're one of them, and you discover to your horror that you're missing some paperwork with information you need, here's what you can do:

- Find last year's tax return. Most people's tax returns do not deviate much from year to year, so last year's return should be a good indicator of the documentation you're missing this year.
- If you're looking for deductions, pull out old bank statements and credit card bills. If you can't find all of them, call your banks and credit card companies and have them rush you a copy of your yearly transactions. Most charge a nominal fee.
- If you need verification of mileage, ask your mechanic, who will have jotted down mileage numbers when you had your car serviced. This will help you estimate the miles you can deduct.

I'll never make the tax deadline

FILE FOR AN EXTENSION In the United States, it's possible to apply for an extension to file your return, but you must do so by the tax due date. You can obtain the proper form—a 4868—by downloading it from www.irs.gov or by calling (800) TAX-FORM. When you get the form, fill it out and send it back with a check for what you estimate that you owe. You can also file and pay electronically on the IRS Web site. Whichever way you file the extension request, you still must estimate what you owe the IRS; figure no less than 90 percent of what you paid last year, assuming most of the numbers are the same. If you don't pay the required estimate when you file the extension request, you'll be charged interest on the amount due (check the IRS Web site for rates), plus a failure-to-pay penalty of ½ of 1 percent of your unpaid taxes for each month, or part of a month, after the due date that the tax is not paid. The penalty for failing to file your return or failing to request an extension by the due date is usually 5 percent for each month or part of a month that the return is late, not exceeding 25 percent.

In Canada, if you do not pay the taxes you owe by the due date of April 30, you'll be charged daily compound interest at a variable rate. (Check the Canada Revenue Agency Web site at www.cra-arc.gc.ca.) The penalty for failing to file your return on time is 5 percent of your balance due, plus 1 percent of the balance due for each full month that your tax return is late up to a maximum of 12 months. If you filed late because of circumstances beyond your control, you may be able to get a waiver of interest and penalties. Check the CRA Web site.

■ MONEY AND BUYING

I'm spending too much money at the grocery store

STICK TO YOUR LIST There are so many temptations in supermarkets these days. But you didn't come for foie gras, you came for breakfast cereal. Here are a few ways to keep costs down while shopping:

- Don't go shopping on an empty stomach.
- Shop with a list, and stick to it.
- Don't dawdle. The faster you shop, the less you'll spend.
- If possible, don't take the kids. But if you *must* take them, give them a task, such as picking the peanut butter and the bread, so they're not pulling down every confection on the shelves.
- Buy staples, such as rice, pasta, and flour, in bulk and keep your cupboard well stocked. Not only is buying in bulk cheaper, but it might also allow you to do without shopping for a few extra days, thereby saving you more money.
- Use coupons. There's no way you'll need everything that's in the coupon circular, but trading on the Internet for coupons that you actually do need is easy and fun. For an idea of what's out there, simply go to a search engine and type in "coupon exchange" or "coupon swap."

- Tuesdays are generally the slowest day of the week for food markets, which is why many stores offer one-day, unadvertised specials on Tuesdays. Patterns may differ from store to store, so it's a good idea to ask the manager what's the best day for discounts at his or her store.

My credit card won't swipe

TRY PLASTIC WRAP You're in a rush at the ATM, and it tells you that your card "cannot be processed. Please try again." Or your debit card won't register in your supermarket's card terminal. Chances are, the magnetic strip on the back of the card is scratched, preventing the machine from reading it properly. Try this: Take a thin piece of plastic—a grocery bag is perfect—and wrap it very tightly around the card. When you swipe it again with the plastic in place, it should work. The extra layer of plastic will fool the machine into thinking there are no scratches on the strip.

Card won't swipe? Wrapping plastic around it will quickly solve the problem.

I'm in the market for a mortgage

GET A "GOOD FAITH" ESTIMATE AND NEGOTIATE Buying a house may be exhilarating, but it's stressful, too. And no part of the process is as stressful as securing a mortgage for the right price. With all the hidden fees and rigmarole, how can you make sure you're not getting toasted? Here are a few guidelines:

- To avoid surprises later on, get a signed "good faith" estimate. This is a detailed accounting of what you should expect to pay in upfront costs and what your actual mortgage rate will be. If a vendor won't supply a signed good faith estimate, run.
- Everything is negotiable. A lot of the upfront costs, or "origination" fees, you may be quoted are going right into the pockets of the person selling you the mortgage. Don't be afraid to haggle.
- Make sure you lock in your rate for at least ten days past your expected closing date. A closing date is usually a best guess as to when you'll actually be closing. If your rate expires and rates have gone up, you could find yourself paying more.
- If you can't come up with 20 percent down and are told you will need private mortgage insurance (PMI), ask about ways

around that. Many mortgage vendors offer piggyback loans (basically, a second mortgage at a slightly higher rate to cover your down payment) or 3 percent down programs. Be sure to ask about all your options.

- Find out what happens to your rate if you need to extend your time frame, or if mortgage rates go lower—or higher.
- Ask what fees are refundable should your mortgage not get approved or if you pull out.

It's time to pay the restaurant bill, and I forgot my wallet

LEAVE YOUR WATCH WHILE YOU FETCH YOUR WALLET Don't panic. You can get out of this fix without having to wash dishes. Offering to leave behind something of value while you dash home for your wallet works in most cases. Explain your situation to the manager and offer to hand over your watch, cell phone, or briefcase. A better solution: Call your spouse to get your credit card number.

I'm getting too much unsolicited mail

TAKE YOUR NAME OFF NATIONAL MAILING LISTS Your poor mailbox is groaning with junk mail. How do you stop the flow? If you live in Canada, it's easy. Simply tell your postal carrier, or put a note in your mailbox, that you do not wish to receive mail that is not addressed to you or your family. In the United States, you can do the same thing, but the post office is not required by law to weed out unsolicited mail. It's assumed, however, that your postal carrier will honor your request out of common courtesy.

Another way to cut junk mail out of your life: Go directly to the source. The Direct Marketing Association says that if you wish, you can cut the amount of mail you receive from national companies by 70 to 80 percent. To sign up, send a letter requesting that you be taken off these national lists to the Direct Marketing Association Mail Preference Service, P.O. Box 643, Carmel, NY 10512. You can also register online at www.dmaconsumers.org. While this will stop mail from national companies, it will not stop mail from local merchants, professional associations, political candidates, and mail marked "Occupant" or "Resident." If you have a credit card, you've probably been besieged lately with offers for dozens more. To get yourself off credit card company lists, call the credit reporting industry's OPTOUT number, (888) 567-8688, for more information.

TRICKS OF THE TRADE

Argue Like an Umpire

When you get into discussions that lead to arguments, you're always right. The problem is in persuading others of your point of view. The challenge is even more pronounced for sports referees, officials, and umpires. Next time you find yourself in a conversational scrape, think like a person in stripes.

"We usually try to explain how we saw it," says lawyer Alan Goldberger, author of *Sports Officiating: A Legal Guide.* "If a coach is ranting and raving, I'll say something like, 'If it happened the way you saw it, then I'm wrong. But that's not how I saw it.'"

In other words, a little give-and-take can go a long way in getting your point across. "Ask questions and force your opponent to support his theories," Goldberger says. "One question that always works is, 'Did you see the whole thing, or do you *think* you saw the whole thing?'"

I keep forgetting my lines when I speak in public

AD-LIB AND USE AN OUTLINE You're not alone. If you keep forgetting your lines when speaking in public, experienced speakers advise that you throw away the script. It's hard to remember the words if you're trying to follow a script that is too detailed. Speaking without a script is the best way to ensure a smooth presentation, because it gives you more flexibility. Jot down the main points you want to make so that you'll have an outline to remind you. Put them in the sequence in which you want to bring them up.

I said something dumb in a meeting

MAKE A JOKE, IF YOU CAN; OTHERWISE, APOLOGIZE No matter who's at the meeting, once you've say something stupid or out of line, you have become the focus of attention. What to do? The really sharp-witted among us may be able to diffuse the situation with a joke. Not a bad idea, but only if you've come up with something truly funny that won't offend anyone and make matters worse. For the rest of us, the best way out is to apologize gracefully. Say something along the lines of, "I am very sorry. I really did not mean for that to come out the way it sounded. What I meant to say is …" Most people will let you off the hook at that point.

If you don't feel that what you did deserves a mea culpa, you can pin the blame on that business-world mainstay: brainstorming: "Hey! I was just thinking out loud—brainstorming!" As any mid-level manager will tell you, there are no stupid ideas during a brainstorming session.

I'm in a karaoke bar and have to sing

PRACTICE AND RELAX Public speaking is not the only thing everybody is afraid of; how about public singing? Here are some tips to help make your next karaoke experience less nerve-racking:

- Pick songs you like and that are easy for you to sing.
- Practice at home. Sing along with the original recording to make sure you can hit all the notes. Watch yourself in a mirror to make sure you're not making too many faces. Record yourself if possible.

- Even though you'll have the karaoke screen to prompt you, you'll feel more confident if you know the words by heart.
- Before going "onstage," take a drink of water to lubricate your throat and vocal cords.
- There's a microphone on, so don't shout. And don't forget to breathe.
- Remember, this isn't Carnegie Hall. Relax, smile (if it's a happy song), and have a good time. If you're having fun, so will your audience.

I feel guilty about ignoring panhandlers

GIVE A FOOD GIFT, NOT CASH You're actually doing the right thing, according to social workers, and you shouldn't feel guilty. Unfortunately, many panhandlers have substance abuse problems or are mentally ill. While giving them money may get rid of a nuisance, the donation is likely to feed a self-destructive behavior and wind up in the coffers of a tavern or drug dealer. Here's how to make a positive contribution: The next time you're in a fast-food restaurant, buy a few gift certificates. Hand one of them over the next time you're approached by a panhandler. You'll feel good knowing that you've provided a meal. Another way to help is to make a donation to a homeless shelter in your area.

Practice may not get you to Carnegie Hall, but it makes singing karaoke a lot less stressful.

The salesclerk is being very rude to me

COMPLAIN TO THE MANAGER—AFTERWARD All you really want to do is buy a pair of jeans, a few apples, or perhaps a giant wall-mounted plasma TV. Dealing with an obnoxious salesclerk is not on your agenda at all. What to do? Complaining to the manager may not get you very far, because unless managers actually witness gross misconduct, they often feel compelled to side with their clerks. The best time to complain to the manager is later, after you either make or don't make your purchase, not in the heat of battle. Here are some other strategies for dealing with a rude clerk:

- Turn around and walk away, especially if you're in a store where the sales staff works on commission.
- Kill the clerk with kindness. You won't win in a battle of who-can-be-the-rudest, so have a little fun. Be extra nice. The clerk will probably lose his mind.

- Keep calmly repeating your questions. This will surely make the clerk angry and might help attract the attention of a manager.

■ SPILLS

My overloaded grocery bag ripped

IMPROVISE A CARRIER Your oranges are rolling one way across the supermarket parking lot and the canned tomatoes are rolling the other direction. This is the last thing you need in the middle of a busy day, but if you're wearing a jacket, it won't be so bad. First, set down your other grocery bags and gather the contents of the split bag. Take off your jacket and spread it out on the asphalt. Place as many loose grocery items as possible inside the jacket, zip it up, and tie the arms of the jacket together to form a loop, folding the bottom of the jacket through the loop so your bananas won't spill out. Hoist the loop of your impromptu carrier over your shoulder and tuck any remaining loose items in the good bags.

I spilled a box of beads

TAPE UP YOUR HAND It's a handicrafter's nightmare: a bevy of beads scattered all over the kitchen floor. The easy answer is in your utility drawer—a roll of masking or cellophane tape. Hold one of your hands out flat, fingers pressed together. Wrap the tape, sticky side out, around your hand until the palm and fingers are covered. Then lightly press your taped-up hand against the beads, lifting up to 20 at a time. Brush them off the tape into a container and then go after more escapees until the job is done.

■ LOCK OUTS

I locked my keys in the car

REACH FOR A WIRE HANGER The worst-case scenario is having to call a locksmith or your auto dealer. Neither of these options is cheap, which is why it's a good idea to have AAA coverage or another roadside assistance plan. AAA's Emergency Road Service is included in the membership fee and covers just about any eventuality, from flat tires to, yes, being locked out of the car.

If you don't belong to an auto service, hope and pray that one of your windows is open, even a crack. Then find yourself a wire hanger. If your car has manual locks—and the old-style mushroom-shaped lock plungers—straighten out the hanger and bend the end into a little U shape. The goal is to get the U around the base of the plunger. Once you manage to get it around the base, slowly start pulling the hanger up in hopes of catching it on the wider nub at the top. Once you do that, slowly pull up again, and you're in your car.

If your car has power door locks, it's often easier to use the hanger to press the button on the side *opposite* the slightly open window. That is, if you can find a piece of rod or a hanger long enough for the job. Keep jimmying the hanger down until you find the button, give it a good press, and you're in.

If the windows aren't open at all, some vehicles (mostly SUVs) have secondary windows that latch open and shut. In most cases, you'll be able to bend back the rubber holding the window in place, which will allow you to move the window enough to squeeze in a hanger.

I'm locked out of my house

YOU MAY HAVE TO BREAK IN If you're locked out of your house, and no one else has a key, you're faced with two choices: Call a locksmith (expect to pay $65 to $100) or break a window. While breaking a window is not something we're exactly recommending, there is a right way to do it. Obviously, pick a window low to the ground and make sure you can fit through it before you start breaking in. Next, find a hefty rock you can fit in your hand. Hold it against the window using a piece of cloth (a shirt or jacket will do) to cover

WORLD-CLASS FIX

It's a Steal

In 1998, a man was stopped by a security guard as he was exiting a drugstore in Reno, Nevada. It seems he had secreted about his body a number of toiletry items, jewelry, and a bottle of cologne for which he had neglected to pay.

The guard sorted through the pilfered items and broke the bad news to his prisoner: The sum total of his haul was $254. Why was this bad news? Because in Nevada, the theft of goods worth more than $250 is considered a felony. The suspect looked over the list of items he was about to be charged with stealing, and he had a brainstorm. He remembered that the cologne was on sale, and he pointed this out to the guard. Sure enough, the discount brought his haul down to $248.16, which made the new charge petty larceny, a simple misdemeanor.

your hand and then, very carefully, start tapping the rock against the window, near the lock. Tap until the glass shatters, then use the jacket to clear away any hanging glass near the lock. Put your arm though the hole and open the lock.

Now, of course, you'll have to get your window fixed, which means you'll be interested in reading "My windowpane got broken," on page 91.

■ LEGAL PROBLEMS

I've been arrested

SAY NOTHING WITHOUT A LAWYER Here are some things to do—and not do—should you find yourself in the backseat of a squad car.

- Keep your mouth shut. Be cooperative and do what the police ask, but do not answer any questions and do not offer any information.
- Unless you're being arrested for a serious offense, you won't be calling a lawyer as soon as you get booked. Most often, if you get arrested in the evening, you're going to spend the night in the hoosegow before you get to call anyone. So again, don't say anything until you've spoken with your lawyer.
- Don't sign anything, short of a sign-in sheet. Sometimes police officers will ask you to give a statement and sign it. Don't do it.

I've been pulled over, and I've been drinking

BE POLITE AND COOPERATIVE You may not actually feel drunk or impaired, but with the legal limit of blood alcohol concentration at .08 in all 50 states and Canada, it doesn't take all that much to get you over the legal limit. Should you be pulled over on suspicion of drunk driving, here's how to make the best of things:

- Do not refuse the Breathalyzer test. In most states, the penalties for refusing the test are similar to those for driving under the influence. So take the test and hope for the best.
- If an officer asks if you were drinking, tell the truth. Police officers, as a general rule, do not like being lied to. If they can smell the alcohol on your breath and you deny drinking, you can bet that they will do whatever they can to prove that you are legally drunk.

- Be polite. Police officers have a tough enough job as it is, and being kind and orderly can go a long way toward getting out of a ticket.
- Finally, police officers have a "drunk driving checklist" that they will use should you pass your Breathalyzer test. There are boxes for being polite, apologetic, cooperative, and such. It pays to be all of those things and more.

■ PASTIMES

My golf game is going nowhere fast

LOWER EXPECTATIONS AND PRACTICE PUTTING The object of the game is to keep whacking that little ball until it falls into a hole some 400 yards away. Some days, that seems more like punishment than fun. Here are some secrets from the pros:

- Do not play with any expectations. Banish "I'm going to break 80" delusions from your head.
- Don't spend a lot of money on clubs. There are billions of dollars of golf equipment sitting unused in garages all over the world. So hit those garage sales, check out eBay, and find yourself a set of good clubs cheap. (Use inexpensive balls, too.)
- Play late in the day, when the "serious" golfers are off the course.
- Have you whacked the ball ten times on the hole without finishing? Time to pick up the ball and move to the next hole.
- Two shots to try to get out of the sand trap and you're still stuck? Toss the ball out.
- If you must practice, practice on the putting green, not the driving range. Putting is the way to cut the most off your score.
- Walk the course; don't use a cart. Not only is this good for your heart, it's also good for your game, as it gives you more time between shots.

Banishing delusions and practicing your putting are the fast ways to improve your game.

I'm going to a racetrack for the first time

LISTEN TO THE EXPERTS So you've never played the ponies? Here are some pointers from a gentleman who's been winning at the track for decades:

TRICKS OF THE TRADE

Making Use of Time Spent Waiting in Line
When you're stuck in a long line, relax and use the time productively, says professional story-teller Dennis Goza of Burbank, California. For instance, Goza carries with him flash cards he has made to help him learn Chinese characters. "I practice 'writing' the characters by tracing them in the air with my finger—which helps ensure that the other patrons don't crowd me too much," he says.

- Remember, the track doesn't care who wins the race. If a long shot wins or the favorite wins, the track still takes the same cut. Which means you should take a good look at the racetrack experts' analysis, located in the program. The experts are there every day and know what they're looking at. They are sincerely trying to help you win, because the more you win, the better the chance you'll come back.
- When betting, look at the times of the horses in their most recent races. The faster the times, the better the chances. If the horse's times are getting progressively faster, so much the better.
- Finally, if you really don't know which horse to bet on, take a look to see how many times each horse in the race has finished "in the money" (first, second, or third). Many horses have a nose for the money and should be bet on. Giddyap!

My fantasy football team is doing poorly

FOCUS ON YOUR RUNNING BACKS If you're one of the millions of people who play fantasy football each year, chances are you want to win. Badly. Especially if it's an office league, where boasting about your team is the main work getting done from September to December. (For the uninitiated, in fantasy football, fans get to put together and manage their own teams by "drafting" talent from actual NFL teams. Your team competes with 10 to 14 others in a league. Scoring is based on the actual game-day performance of the NFL players on your team. As owner/manager, you also get to release and sign on players and trade them with your fellow owners.)

Let's say your team isn't looking so good. You're the owner/manager. How do you improve it? Your best bet is to improve your running backs. If they're doing poorly, chances are your whole team is doing poorly. So don't hesitate to trade your superstar wide receiver for a running back who is less talented than the wide receiver but better than one of your current running backs. Chances are, your new running back and new wide receiver (the one you scraped off your bench to replace your departed star) will outscore your old wide receiver and poorly performing running back. Why? There's a premium on running backs. Most NFL teams use only one as the featured back, and at least a dozen of them are pretty lousy. This means that in any given season, there will be only 20 or so running backs worth their salt. You'll need to have at least two of them if you expect to be competitive.

Electronic Life

◼ TELEPHONE HASSLES

I can't get through to my wife because the phone lines are tied up

HAVE SOMEONE OUTSIDE YOUR AREA MAKE THE CALL It's not often that phone systems get overloaded, but when they do, it can cause serious problems. During times of great joy or tragedy affecting large numbers of people, many phone lines serving the geographic area you're in are likely to be busy. If you can't get a call through to your wife, kids, or whomever you need to contact, try calling someone outside your area and asking him or her to call the person you're trying to reach. Sometimes, because of the way circuits are set up, you'll be able to get through to someone outside your area, who in turn will be able to get your message through to the person you are trying to call.

I can't get through to an 800 number

TRY CHANGING THE LAST DIGIT Most companies have toll-free 800 numbers these days, but what good are they if you can't get through because the line is busy, or because the "wait time" is 20 minutes or more? Here's a trick that sometimes works:

Change the last number or two of the phone number you're calling and dial again. Say, for instance, that the 800 number you're trying to reach is (800) 555-7000, and it's busy, busy, busy. Try calling (800) 555-7001, 7002, or 7003. Sometimes you'll get a totally different company. But other times you'll get an open line into the business you were intending to call.

Recorded phone menus drive me crazy

DIAL 0 RIGHT AWAY If your call gets through and you want to talk to an operator instead of going though endless menus, hit 0 repeatedly. Forget all that "Press 1 to hear more computer-speak" or "Press 2 to keep waiting." Just keep banging that 0 until you get a human on the line.

PROBLEM STOPPER

Sign Up for Silence
When you sign up for the National Do Not Call Registry, the calls you get from telemarketers will be reduced to a trickle within three months. To get on the list, call toll-free (888) 382-1222 or visit www.donotcall.gov. You can also file a complaint at that Web site.

You will still get calls from political organizations, charities, surveyors, and companies you do business with. Your number will stay on the registry for five years. By law, if you ask a telemarketer to take you off its list, the telemarketer must honor your request.

In Canada, a telemarketer must give you a registration number when you ask to be put on its do-not-call list. If the marketer persists, you can use the number as proof when you file a complaint.

I can't get good cell phone reception inside this building

HEAD FOR A WINDOW You can improve the reception of any indoor antenna—cell phone, TV, or radio—by moving it close to a window. Broadcast signals penetrate buildings most readily through window glass. So that's the best place to position the antenna for your FM radio tuner or the rabbit ears for your TV, and it's the best place to stand when talking on your cell phone.

If your cell phone is breaking up, simply moving near a window can quickly restore the signal.

Telemarketers keep wasting my time

FOLLOW YOUR OWN SCRIPT You think hanging up on telemarketers is rude. But that doesn't mean you need to listen to them. Follow this script, and you'll be off the phone in 20 seconds:

1. Cut the person short as soon as you realize it's a sales pitch.
2. Say that you have a strict policy of not doing business with strangers over the phone; if they wish, they may send literature.
3. Ask to have your name removed from their calling list and say that you forbid them to rent it to other telemarketers.
4. Confirm that they heard what you said; then politely thank them and hang up.

Remember: You have no obligation to listen to telemarketers. They are intruding on your time, and a pleasant rebuff is fair and appropriate. Never say yes to a phone offer unless it's a company you know and have complete faith in. Scams are everywhere

I need to curtail long phone calls

"DOORBELL'S RINGING. GOTTA GO" Forget telemarketers—just try cutting off a long-winded relative. You don't mean to be rude, but sometimes there are just more important things to do. Try these strategies for ending a call without hurting poor anyone's feelings:

- Open your front door and ring the doorbell, thereby alerting your gabby caller that a guest has just arrived.
- Say the battery is dying on your cordless.
- If things get really desperate, disconnect in the middle of your own sentence. The person on the other end of the line will assume there was a problem with the phone. Leave the phone off the hook for a while in case your talkative relative calls back.

■ INTERNET PROBLEMS

Searching on the Internet is frustrating

LET GOOGLE, MSN, OR YAHOO HELP With today's powerful search engines, finding what you're looking for on the Internet has never been easier, which is why it's so maddening when you can't find something. Keep in mind, though, that even Google, the Web's king of search, is looking at only about 10 percent of all the Web pages out there. So if you're searching for something really esoteric, you'll find these tips that apply to most search engines handy:

- Let's say you're looking for information about the New York Mets baseball team. If you simply type *New York Mets* in the search box, you'll not only get Web pages containing references to the Mets, but also pages that refer to New York itself, and eventually, to sites containing just the word *new*. But put *New York Mets* in quotes—*"New York Mets"*—and only sites that refer to the entire phrase will pop up.
- Suppose you want to know all about Washington state, but nothing about Washington, D.C. If you simply type in *Washington*, you're going to get sites about each place. To weed out any sites about the U.S. capital, insert a minus sign before D.C.: *Washington –D.C* (don't forget the space before the minus sign).
- Most search engines ignore words such as *the* and *and*. If those words are important to your search, put a plus sign in front of them. So if you're searching for the musical *The King and I*, type in: *+The King +and +I* (or put the whole phrase in quotes).
- If you don't know how to spell something, don't fret: Type it in, and if it's close enough to a word in the dictionary, most search engines will ask you if that's what you actually meant.

I'm overwhelmed with junk e-mail

FILTER OUT, OPT OUT, FIGHT BACK "Junk," "spam," "garbage," "bulk," whatever you call it, there it is, taking up space in your e-mail account. Here are some ideas for stemming the flow:

- Use your e-mail's filter programs. Set them on high to weed out anything that looks like junk. In the beginning, you'll have to check the garbage folder regularly to make sure important stuff isn't getting blocked, but after a while, you'll need to check only occasionally.

TRICKS OF THE TRADE

Getting Specialized Information
To find really specific stuff, use a specialized directory. These directories will find sites on the Internet for almost any subject or interest. They will collect pages that the major directories might miss. Start by searching a directory that lists such directories, such as Directory Guide (www. directoryguide.com) and Go Gettem (www. gogettem.com).

- Use different e-mail accounts for different purposes. Have a business e-mail, a home e-mail, and an e-mail only for commercial uses.
- Opt out. When you're buying products online, many vendors will ask if you want to receive e-mailed updates or announcements. The answer is no.
- Go to the Web site of the Direct Marketing Association at www.dmaconsumers.org/offemaillist.html and sign up to have your address purged from lists. This won't eliminate all the junk, but it will help.
- Don't reply to spam. This confirms your e-mail address as real, and will result in more spam.
- Don't post your e-mail address online, or at least do it rarely. This is where e-mails are harvested.
- In the worst-case scenario, you're just going to have to ditch your old e-mail address and start a new one. Then follow the rules above!

Pop-up ads are driving me crazy

TRY SPYWARE OR A POP-UP BLOCKER Nothing can slow your Internet experience down more than pop-up ads. To stem that tide, try downloading some free programs to rid your computer of "trackers," little bugs that electronically attach themselves to your computer, allowing pop-ups to come flying in. The best way to do this is to go to a site that lets you download software free, such as download.com or cnet.com, type *spyware* in the search box, and then pick a program that is compatible with your computer and operating system, Windows in most cases.

Another way to try to rid yourself of pop-ups is to download a pop-up blocker. The Google and Yahoo search engines both offer this feature free, and both seem to work well. Go to their Web sites, type in *toolbar*, and then follow the simple directions for download. You can also search for "pop-up blocker" on a free-software site to obtain a program that stops pop-ups.

I'm afraid to give out personal information online

READ THE FINE PRINT FIRST Many unsuspecting consumers get their identification and credit card numbers stolen through a variety of nasty tricks. Here are some ways to protect yourself online:

- Do not disclose your information without understanding how it will be used. In other words, read the fine print. Most reputable Web sites will not give away your information, but some will. Avoid those that do not have a privacy notice or do not guarantee confidentiality in their privacy notice.
- Never use your main e-mail address when you order something online. E-mail addresses are available free from dozens of online vendors, and your own Internet service provider may offer you extra ones. If you set up a few e-mail addresses for making purchases and rotate your use of them, online thieves will have a harder time tracking you.

My Internet service keeps freezing up

CLEAR THE CACHE When your browser won't load, it's most often the fault of the Internet provider. First, make sure all your cables and connections are still plugged in. If that doesn't help, call your provider's 800 number to verify whether it's the provider's problem and, if it is, how long it will take to fix.

If your provider says all is running smoothly on its end, take a harder look at your own computer. More likely than not, the problem has to do with your cache. This is where your browser keeps the Internet pages you've recently visited so that you can get back to those pages quickly. A problem with one of those pages can wreak havoc with your entire cache and keep you from accessing the Internet. The solution is to clear the cache. Here's how to do it for some common browsers:

WORLD-CLASS GOOF

A Big Serving of Spam

In the fall of 2001, a supplier for a major computer maker sent an e-mail to about 2,900 customers who had ordered a software upgrade. Unfortunately, the sender entered the e-mail addresses in the To field, where all of them would be visible to each recipient. An unscrupulous spammer could have easily harvested those names and then filled the customers' In boxes with junk e-mail. One analyst likened the blunder to giving away a customer database. That's a painful reminder of how important it is to BCC all the recipients of a mass e-mail.

The surest way to avoid being "phished" (see next page) is to give your personal identification only to sites that you have gone to on your own, not sites you reached by clicking on an unsolicited e-mail.

- For Windows Internet Explorer: Quit all other programs. Open your browser, and assuming it's not working, hit the Stop button. Then go to the Tools menu and choose Internet Options. Click on the General tab, and you'll see something called Temporary Internet files. Click the Delete Files button, then hit OK. You should now be able to get online.
- For Explorer on a Macintosh: Quit all other programs and hit the Stop button on your browser. Then choose Preferences from either the Edit menu (OS 9) or the Explorer menu (OS X). Click on Advanced under Web Browser and then, under the header labeled Cache, click Empty Now. You should be able to get online.
- For Netscape on either type of computer: Hit the Preferences button, then the Advanced button, and then click on the little arrow. Look for Cache and click on that. Then hit Clear Cache and try to get online.

I've sent an embarrassing e-mail to the wrong person

RECALL IT, IF YOU CAN Beware the Reply All button. It makes it so easy to send things out to the wrong people. We've all heard stories of poor souls who sent out embarrassing e-mails, only to end up fired, divorced, or worse. So what if that happens to you?

If you're lucky enough to be on a closed (controlled access) e-mail system at a company or an institution—specifically, one that uses Microsoft Outlook for its mail server—it's possible to actually recall an e-mail message, as long as it hasn't been opened. To do that, follow these instructions. But remember: This probably won't work from your home computer.

1. Select View, and then select Folder List.
2. Click Sent Items.
3. Open the message you want to recall.
4. On the Actions menu, click Recall This Message.
5. To actually recall the message, click Delete Unread Copies of This Message.
6. Click OK. Outlook will attempt to recall the message.

If you didn't send your embarrassing e-mail on such a system, your options are limited. One idea: Call the recipients and ask them to delete the e-mail before they open it. Fat chance, huh? Well, here's another, more devious suggestion. Send another e-mail to everybody who got the problem message. In the subject header, type something like VIRUS ALERT!!! In the body of the e-mail, tell them that you think your system has been infected by a virus and that they should immediately delete any e-mails received from you recently. Cross your fingers and stay away from that Reply All button in the future.

■ COMPUTER PROBLEMS

My computer keeps crashing

THINK SOFTWARE RATHER THAN HARDWARE Life without Google or Yahoo or MSN? No thanks. When your computer keeps crashing, try some of these fixes before you take it to a $100-an-hour computer repair shop:

- Make sure there are no disks in either the floppy or CD drive. Sometimes a disk will interfere with the computer's operation.
- Turn everything off when you shut down the computer. This means printers, outside drives, monitors, everything. If you leave some components on, "bad" information can pass back and forth, corrupting the whole system. So shut everything down, unplug everything, and then start over.
- More often than not, the problem will be software-related. If one program in particular seems to be the culprit, try erasing it from the computer and reinstalling it using the CD that you bought originally.
- Finally, give the computer a good whack. Seriously. Many computers, especially those in an office environment, will collect dust inside the guts of the unit. So turn it on its side, to dislodge any dust, and then give it a good whack or two. Any dust that's interfering with the connections will clear out.

My mouse is misbehaving

CLEAN THE BALL AND ROLLERS Few things are more annoying than an out-of-control cursor caused by a dirty mouse. Fortunately, there's an easy cure. If you're using a mouse with a ball underneath, clean it out. Disconnect the mouse, turn it over, and, using both thumbs, twist the ring that holds the ball in place counterclockwise. When you get the ball out, use a cloth moistened only with water to wipe the ball clean. Then blow into the ball hole to get rid of any dust lying around. Inside, you'll see three rollers. Use a fingernail or

PROBLEM STOPPER

Avoiding Repetitive Stress Injury
Repetitive stress injury (RSI) is a painful condition that occurs when a tendon or muscle is overused while being forced into an unnatural position. If you use a PC keyboard and mouse regularly, minimize your risk:

• Sit up straight with feet on the floor and thighs and forearm parallel with the floor.

• Keep your wrists in a straight line with your arms; don't rest them on the desk or twist them at an awkward angle.

• Be gentle; don't hammer on the keyboard.

• Take frequent breaks from typing; don't work for long periods in the same position.

• Learn to use keyboard shortcuts so that you don't always have to move your hands to click with the mouse.

a pair of tweezers to scrape away any grime built up on the rollers. Once the ball is dry, pop it back in and then twist the cover back on.

If you're using a cloth mouse pad, throw it away and replace it with an easy-to-clean plastic or vinyl one. A cloth pad collects dirt, which will get back into your mouse.

If your mouse is of the optical variety and it's suffering from the same problems, check your desk surface. If it's glass or a solid color, the mouse might be having a tough time "reading" the surface. Try putting it on a patterned surface or even on a piece of paper.

Some of the keys on my keyboard are sticking

SHAKE AND BLAST If your computer keyboard gets a fair amount of use, some keys will probably start sticking eventually. Built-up dirt is usually the culprit. The most rudimentary way to clean a keyboard is to disconnect it, turn it upside down, and give it a good shake over a garbage can. You can also use a can of compressed air, sold at computer or camera stores, to blast debris out from under the keys.

If shaking and air-blasting don't work, stop by an electronics or office-supply store and buy some contact cleaner, a chemical solution that won't interfere with electrical connections. Spray the solution on the stuck keys, let them dry, and see what happens.

To save a flooded keyboard, unplug it immediately and take it to the sink.

If all else fails, unplug the keyboard and pry off the stuck key with a flat-head screwdriver. Clean off the key with some compressed air or even a hair dryer. Use contact cleaner to get rid of heavier gunk.

Caution: Don't take off the space bar, as it's nearly impossible to snap back on correctly.

Help! I spilled a drink on my keyboard

DISCONNECT IT IMMEDIATELY They do make waterproof keyboards. But, chances are, yours is not one of them, so you're going to have to act quickly if you do spill something on it. The first thing to do—right away—is either unplug the keyboard or turn the whole computer off. Do this within seconds of spilling the drink to limit the chances of permanently damaging the computer. Liquid in the keyboard can act as a conductor and cause a short circuit.

Once you've shut down the computer, take the unplugged keyboard over to the sink. If you spilled only a little water on it, turn it upside down and let it drain and dry out. If you spilled a lot of water or—worse—juice, sweet milky coffee, or a soft drink, you'll need to clean out the keyboard. Pour distilled water, which contains no minerals or other impurities that might conduct electricity when you plug the keyboard back in, over the spill. Use just enough water to do the job; don't splash the whole keyboard. Turn the keyboard upside down and let it drain. Once it's completely dry, plug it back in. If the spill caused no damage, you should be in business. If it did, then it's time for a visit to the repair shop and a possible replacement.

■ ELECTRONIC GEAR

A tape is stuck in my VCR

REMOVE THE VCR TOP AND LIFT OUT THE TAPE One minute you're watching some home movies, the next minute you're cursing your VCR. Tape's stuck. But all is not lost. Chances are, the tape is tangled and jammed. Do not try to force it out. Instead, unplug the VCR and unscrew the top. You'll find the screws either on the top or the sides of the VCR. Once you get the top off, you'll see the tangled tape. Untangle it manually and lift the cassette out of the VCR.

If the tape is not too badly mangled, you can thread it back into the cassette. However, if it's wrinkled, ripped, or otherwise damaged, you'll need to go to an audio/video supplies vendor (or to the Internet) and buy a splicer and splicing tape. The splicer, which can cost from $4 to $40, will expertly cut out the part of the tape that's damaged. Use the splicing tape ($6 to $14) to tape the two pieces back together. The better of these splicing machines do this job in one fell swoop. Don't worry. Even a few inches of tape contain just a second or so of lost memories.

My CD or DVD won't play

CHECK THE DISC FIRST Digital technology is great, except when it doesn't work. There are no gears to check or tape to untangle, so figuring out why something's not working is just about impossible. However, there are ways to get things moving again. Before junking your faulty CD or DVD player, try the following:

- Make sure the disc itself is not the problem. A dirty disc is a disc that's going to cause you problems. So check the back of

TRICKS OF THE TRADE

Keep Your Favorite CD from Skipping
If a CD is skipping, try cleaning it with auto wax. Car wax is more versatile than you might think. Apply the wax to a 100 percent cotton cloth and wipe it on the disc. Let the wax dry completely and then buff it with a clean cotton cloth, wiping in a straight line from the center circle to the outside edge. (Don't use a circular motion.)

PROBLEM STOPPER

Stop Feeding Your VCR

Here are a few ways to preserve your tapes and keep your VCR from eating them:

• Store tapes in their sleeves to keep dust out.

• Keep your tapes vertical. If a cassette is stored on its side, gravity forces the tape against the wall of the case, thereby damaging the tape edges.

• Rewind your tapes after each use to keep the tape tension even.

• Don't store tapes in hot, humid locations—or near electrical equipment and stereo speakers, which generate magnet fields that can degrade the recording.

• If you're storing tapes for long periods of time, play them about once a year to prevent sticking.

the disc for dirt. Place it upside down and wipe it with a damp cloth. (An old white cotton T-shirt is perfect.) Wipe it from the center outward, as this is how the information is stored. Clean it and give it a shot in the machine.

• If a disc still doesn't play after cleaning, check for scratches. Most are superficial and are easily removed—with toothpaste! Use regular toothpaste, not the gel kind. Apply to a clean old T-shirt and wipe from the center outward. Then rinse the disc under water. You can also try window cleaner with alcohol if the scratch is a little deeper.

• If the above methods don't yield a disc that works, your problem may be with the player and specifically, its counter-weight, which centers the CD/DVD in the machine. Unplug the player and turn it over a few times. This should rebalance the counterweight.

• If all else fails, it may be time to start taking things apart. Dust may have settled inside the machine. A CD that sounds stat-icky or a DVD that breaks up on the screen is a telltale sign of dust in the player. Unplug the machine and unscrew the top. Using a straw—or even better, a can of compressed air—blow on the inside of the player to rid it of dust. It's pretty delicate in there, so try not to touch anything or use any foreign objects.

I can't get the CD or DVD out

JIMMY OUT THE TRAY If your machine won't release a disc, you'll have to do it manually. Find a paper clip and turn it into a hook, place it over or under the tray, and pull the tray out just a little bit. From there, you should be able to pull the tray out with your fingers to release your disc from captivity.

I need some rugged protection for my CDs

LOOK FOR FREEBIES IN THE MAIL When you buy blank CDs 50 at a time for data storage or music, they don't come with protective cases. The solution is free, and it comes right to your door. How many times have you received promotional mailings from a large online business, begging you to pop the enclosed CD into your computer and sign up for two months of free Internet service? Next time, save the plastic casing from that mailing and use it to protect your own CDs.

Family Life

■ INTERACTIONS BETWEEN KIDS

My kids are fighting over toys

GUIDE THEM TO A NEGOTIATED SOLUTION Few things are as exasperating as listening to children fighting over a toy or anything else. While your first inclination may be to banish the toy from existence, there's a better way to restore peace. Take advantage of the situation to teach your kids how to negotiate. The goal is to have them share the toy, or whatever it is they are fighting over. Direct them toward a compromise, but let them work it out themselves. Suggest possible solutions, such as that Tommy gets the toy for the morning and Jack gets it for the afternoon. Teach them that every either/or situation can be turned into a "'Why not both?" agreement. And make sure they understand that sharing the toy does not mean losing it for good.

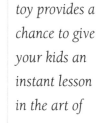

A fight over a toy provides a chance to give your kids an instant lesson in the art of negotiation.

My kids argue all the time

CALL A TIME OUT WHEN NEEDED Just because siblings are related doesn't mean they're necessarily compatible. Fighting and arguing are a normal part of growing up with brothers and sisters. Here are a few ways to keeping the bickering in check:

- Establish clear and firm limits on unacceptable behavior—no hitting, screaming, throwing things—and enforce them.
- Provide a distraction. Put on some music and tell the kids it's time to dance. Or invite a friend over for each of the squabbling siblings.
- Try not to get overly involved in the cause of the disagreement. Encourage the children to work it out themselves.
- If the arguing gets out of hand, call a time out for each child in separate places.
- Use positive reinforcement. Praise your kids when they're getting along.

My child shies away from group activities

GET THE CHILD INVOLVED INDIRECTLY Not all children adapt readily to group settings. So what to do if your child, or a child you're responsible for (such as a visiting playmate), refuses to participate in group games? One approach is to get the child involved without actually playing the game. If it's a sports game, for example, ask the child to help keep score, be the referee, or help decide disputes. This will give the child a stake in the outcome and may encourage him or her to give the game a try the next time.

A bully is tormenting my child

ENLIST A BUDDY'S SUPPORT Research shows that one of the best ways to deal with a bully is to have a buddy around. The buddy does not necessarily have to be big or trained in the martial arts. Just having someone be there often helps. Have your child stick with a friend on the school bus, on the playground, or wherever the bullying is occurring. When that's not possible, your child should be equipped with appropriate responses to disarm the bully. Here are several steps your child can take:

- Ignore the bully and walk away.
- In an assertive but not aggressive way, tell the bully to stop.
- Report the bullying to an adult.

Make it clear to your child that he or she could make matters worse by falling apart, crying, making a snide comeback, or letting the bully know that he or she is scared or upset. Make sure your child doesn't blame him- or herself for the bullying; the problem is with the bully, not with your child.

■ BEHAVIOR PROBLEMS

My child won't eat

MAKE FOOD FUN The threat is probably as old as civilization itself: "You're not leaving this table until you clean your plate." Thankfully, there are better ways to get children to eat their food. Here are some of them:

- Involve your kids in menu planning and food preparation.
- Offer your children foods cut into interesting shapes or that are otherwise visually appealing.

- Switch meals around: pancakes for dinner, a hamburger for breakfast. When meals are surprising and fun, children may eat more.
- Negotiate. No seconds of the favorite food—say, spaghetti—until your kids have tried some of the squash.
- Encourage your children at least to try a new or rejected food, but don't insist that they finish something they don't like. Watching you eat and enjoy a rejected food might get them interested in it.
- Take a relaxed approach and don't turn the dining table into a battleground. As long as your children are healthy, fluctuations in food intake are not a cause for alarm. Offer a variety of nutritious options and let your kids develop their own tastes and preferences.

I need to get my children to pick up after themselves

MAKE IT A REQUIRED CHORE Kids are very good at making a mess, less good at cleaning it up. Here are a few pointers:

- Every child's routine should include a regular household chore suited to his or her age and abilities. Make it clear to your children that putting away their toys, for example, is a requirement, not an option.
- Praise your kids when they do well; remind and cajole them when they don't.
- If your children still resist picking up after themselves, a good old threat now and then won't do permanent damage. Tell them that if they don't clean up right now, you're going to take three items lying around the floor and contribute them to Goodwill. (Be prepared to follow through.)
- If you have two or more kids, make a contest out of cleaning up. Whoever cleans the best or the fastest wins a prize.

Getting my kids to sleep is a challenge

STICK TO A BEDTIME ROUTINE Going to sleep can sometimes be the most trying part of a kid's day—for you, the parent. Here are some ways to help speed the process along:

- Establish a bedtime routine—with set times for bath, brushing teeth, slipping on pajamas, reading a story, and such—and stick to it. Give your kids a little notice so they can wrap up what they're doing before starting their bedtime preparation.

- This tactic works particularly well for babies, but is good for toddlers, too: Strap the child in the car, put on some calming classical music, and take a slow drive around the neighborhood. The movement of the car, the darkness of the night, and the soothing music will probably put the child to sleep.
- If the kids are acting hyper, it's next to impossible to get them to lie still. Turn this negative into a positive by playing a quick game of tag in the house. After ten or twenty minutes, everybody should be exhausted from running around.
- Children can be very creative when it comes to avoiding going to bed. Don't cave in. It's OK to insist that they stay in bed and go to sleep.

Going to the supermarket with my kids is an ordeal

KEEP THEM OCCUPIED AND INVOLVED Kids and shopping are often an unhappy combination. But there are ways to make the experience less exasperating for you.

- Try to avoid going shopping with your kids when they're tired, hungry, or not feeling well.
- Keep the kids occupied and distracted. Bring along toys and books, and make sure to interact with them.
- It can be frustrating for a child to watch you pick item after item from your list and have all his or her requests turned down. Instead of saying no each time your child asks for something, say instead, "Let's add it to the list." When you've finished shopping, read back the items on your child's list and let him or her pick one or two of those items.

My kids' whining is driving me crazy

THREE STRIKES AND IT'S TIME-OUT You've probably heard the old adage: "Your child knows your magic number." Your kids ask for something—candy in the supermarket checkout line, for instance, or an extra 30 minutes of TV—and you say no. Then they'll keep asking, over and over, until they hit the magic number of noes, when you either give in or lose your temper. Well, the old adage has been backed up by research. Here's the simple solution (also backed up by research): The next time your children ask for something, such as candy, and your answer is no, say no. If they whine or keep asking for the candy, wait five seconds and then give a warning, such as "If you ask me again, you'll get a time-out" (or whatever punishment is appropriate). The third time, follow through. Stick with this simple routine, and Mother's magic number will become 1.

My child had a bad day

LISTEN AND EMPATHIZE When children come home from school or the playground complaining about having had a bad day, because they got into a fight, for example, or lost a favorite toy, parents have a tendency to both downplay the incident and problem-solve. These responses can seem insensitive to children and may even keep them from confiding in you in the future. Chances are, what they really need is empathy. A good way to demonstrate empathy is through a technique called reflective listening, in which you gently repeat what your child is telling you. This makes your youngster feel that you're really listening and sharing his or her emotional experience.

Fear of the dark keeps my child awake

TURN ON A NIGHT-LIGHT AND COMFORT YOUR CHILD What child isn't afraid of the dark at some point? Night-lights or desk lamps help some of the time, but not always, especially not if your child is having vivid nightmares. Often after bad dreams, your child will want to sleep in your bed. For your child's benefit and yours, don't allow it. Walk your child back to his or her room and sit for a little while, if that helps, rubbing your child's back or singing a song. Create a calming ritual. But do not linger too long. You want your child to overcome his or her fears independently.

■ OTHER CHILDHOOD PROBLEMS

My kid's favorite toy is lost

IT'S NOT LOST—IT'S GONE ON AN ADVENTURE Losing a favorite stuffed animal or toy can be very upsetting for a child. To help dry the tears, try the "Toy Story" strategy: Tell your child the toy has gone off on an adventure, much like the toys in the movie. You can even take it to the next level by mailing letters or e-mails from the toy to your child. When the toy eventually turns up, arrange for your child to find it.

Teething pain is making my baby irritable

APPLY PRESSURE OR COLD There are many ways to help soothe teething pain, but the most effective methods involve pressure or cold. With a clean finger, gently massage your baby's gums. Or give the baby something cold to chew on—a wet washcloth chilled in the refrigerator or even a frozen bagel. Some mothers swear by frozen grapes, cut in half, or small pieces of frozen banana or cantaloupe. But make sure the pieces are cut small enough to eliminate any chance of choking and be extra vigilant when giving your baby food to teethe on.

The way to quiet teething pain quickly is with pressure and cold.

My middle child is asking me about Santa

'FESS UP Children younger than about 9 generally take Santa Claus, the Easter Bunny, and the Tooth Fairy at face value. After that age, they start questioning. Here's a good way to answer your child—and answer you must, because it's better to hear the truth from you than from the playground know-it-all. Tell your youngster that even if Santa is not exactly landing on roofs, the idea of Santa still exists, and that everyone has a little Santa in them. Explain that in addition to receiving gifts, your child will now be part of the gift-giving process and will be able to help pick out gifts for siblings and cousins. But make sure to tell your child not to tell other kids about Santa. That job is up to their mommies and daddies.

■ OUTSIDE CHILD CARE

I'm looking for a good day care program

OBSERVE, ASK QUESTIONS, DON'T SETTLE Try to find out as much as you can about local day care programs, and give yourself plenty of time to assess each one you're considering. Here are some issues to keep in mind when evaluating day care options:

- Make sure the center has an "open door" policy (i.e., you're allowed to visit whenever you want). Visit as often as you feel it necessary to make an informed decision.
- Leave your child at home for the first visit, but take him or her on subsequent visits—even if your offspring is still a baby—to meet with the caregivers and the children.

- Find out what the ratio of caregivers to children is, what training and education are required of them, and what type of educational program is offered.
- Assess the physical setting. Is the place clean, well organized, safe, and child-friendly? Is there enough play space and equipment? What kinds of meals are served?
- Spend time with the children at the center. Are they clean? Happy? Active?
- Ask about the rules on punishments and make sure you agree with them. Also find out what happens when a child gets sick.
- Interview the program director and the teacher whose class your son or daughter would be in.
- Trust your gut. If you have a bad feeling about a place, get out. It's not the place for your child.

I'm babysitting with my nieces and need to childproof my home

TAKE A CHILD'S POINT OF VIEW You have no kids. Translation: You don't have to worry about your windows being locked or your electrical outlets being covered. But if you're suddenly playing host to your young nieces for the weekend, you've got to kidproof the home, and quick. First, survey your home from a kid's-eye perspective. Then try to eliminate all the hazards you can. Here's how:

- If you have an older home, make sure the large heating ducts are securely shut. Many of these ducts are right on the floor, and little kids can get caught in them.
- Put furniture in front of your outlets or fit accessible outlets with safety caps.
- Get a childproof lock for the bathroom. These inexpensive plastic locks are impossible for a tiny hand to unlock, but easy enough for adults.
- Put razors, creams, and medicines out of reach of the kids, preferably in a locked cabinet
- Make sure all the windows are locked.
- If you're on an upper floor, move your furniture away from windows. Kids love to climb.
- Pull all of those dangerous cleaning substances out from underneath the kitchen sink and store them up high.
- Finally, take care of your personal stuff. If you value your CDs, move them to where the little tykes can't get to them.

TRICKS OF THE TRADE

Using an Allowance as a Teaching Tool
Giving children an allowance is a great way to help them learn how to handle money and make responsible decisions. How much to give depends on your financial circumstances. But don't give your child too much. Part of the lesson you want to teach is how to budget. Here are some other pointers:

• Set a regular allowance payday and keep to it.

• Establish guidelines for how the money is to be spent. Encourage your child to save and let him or her know what purchases are off-limits.

• Monitor your child's use of the allowance. Although a child is certain to make mistakes, let him or her learn from them. Resist the temptation to bail your youngster out each time.

• Don't use the allowance as a reward or bribe. Similarly, don't withhold it as a punishment.

I'm thinking of hiring a nanny

ASK QUESTIONS AND TRUST YOUR INSTINCTS A nanny or au pair will give your child individual attention in the secure setting of your home. When hiring a nanny, keep these points in mind:

- Be sure to check a prospective nanny's references and work history carefully.
- At the interview, don't be shy about asking all the questions you like. That's the only way to get to know her. Ask, for instance, why she went into this line of work and why she wants to care for your child in particular.
- Find out the candidate's approach to child rearing. Ask her what she would do in specific situations, such as an emergency, or when your child won't eat or won't stop crying.
- Make sure you give your children time to interact with the prospective nanny or au pair.
- Always hire on a trial basis. Personalities often clash, and a trial period makes it easier to fire the nanny should it come to that.
- As with a day care center, trust your instincts. Hire someone you and your children like and are comfortable with.

■ PARTIES AND TRAVEL

I'm throwing a party for a mob of kids

PLAN AHEAD AND KEEP IT SHORT Parties for children aren't just scaled-down versions of adult get-togethers. Keep these ideas in mind if you want all the guests at a birthday party to go home happy:

- Find out ahead of time if any of your little guests are allergic to anything. Some children face life-threatening reactions when they eat certain common foods, such as peanuts. If a parent says a child is allergic, make sure you know exactly what you can and can't serve the child. Even better, have the parent stay to chaperone the child.
- Make sure the venue—either your home or another location—is safe for children and that they won't be able to venture away from the party on their own.
- Get plenty of adults to help supervise the kids. The younger the children, the more adults you'll need.
- Keep the party short. Young children need only about 45 minutes to play, eat cake, and watch the presents being opened.

- Plan the entertainment carefully. Some kids are scared of clowns. Others are afraid to jump around on inflatable castle playgrounds that can be rented for parties. Make sure you have an attraction that most will like, and plan to have alternative activities available.

I'm going to a theme park with little kids

SET GROUND RULES AND A MEETING SPOT If there's nothing quite like the thrill of a roller coaster, there's also nothing quite like the dread of taking a bunch of little kids to a crowded, hot, expensive theme park. Here's how to maintain your sanity, and the kids', too.

- Before you go, make sure to call ahead and check the height restrictions for the rides. That way you'll avoid the unhappy spectacle of a child who can't go on any of the attractions.
- Also before you go, set the ground rules for crowded places. Tell the children that you will be watching out for them, but they also have to watch out for you and for each other.
- Make the kids easier to spot in a crowd by dressing them in the same brightly colored shirts.
- If you're going with a big group—say, from camp or church— do not put name tags on the kids. You don't want strangers calling out to them.
- Once you're there, designate a meeting spot in case anyone gets separated from the group. And point out the uniforms of the employees, so the kids will know who to go to should they get lost.
- Take a wagon or a stroller. While pushing a tired child around is not exactly fun, it beats dragging a youngster by the arms.
- The three most important rules for theme parks: sunscreen, sunscreen, sunscreen. And make sure to apply it often.
- Bring along some frozen juice boxes, so they will be cold when the kids get thirsty. Drinks are very expensive once you get inside the park.
- Bring a change of clothes for the children even if it's not a water park.
- Bring a big towel or a blanket. It's handy for naps, drying off, and relaxing in the shade.

TRICKS OF THE TRADE

Saving on Tickets for Big-name Theme Parks Prices for some theme parks are now running more than $50 per person (slightly less for children). Clearly, a family vacation can get pretty expensive. How to save money? Be on the lookout for packages and special offers, and buy your tickets in advance, either through the park or your travel agent. While one-day tickets will be the same price, multiday tickets bought ahead of time will be less expensive.

On the Road

■ CLOTHES AND PACKING

My clothes get jumbled up in my suitcase

PACK IN PLASTIC Self-sealing plastic bags are a veteran traveler's best friend. They're extremely lightweight, which is a plus when you have to haul your luggage through several miles of airport corridors. They're also transparent, of course, which makes baggage inspection go more easily and lets you find your possessions quickly in your hotel room. And they keep your clothes organized. Put all of your underwear and socks in quart- or gallon-size bags, for instance, and bulkier clothing in 2-gallon (7.4-liter) bags.

My shirts come out of the suitcase wrinkled

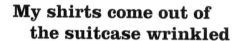

DRY-CLEANER BAGS TO THE RESCUE Nobody wants to look rumpled and disheveled while traveling. But who has time for touch-up ironing, even if your hotel provides an iron? The key is to pack your shirts and blouses so that they emerge from your suitcase wrinkle-free.

First, do a good job of folding your shirts or blouses. (If you pack them wrinkled—surprise!—they'll still be wrinkled when you arrive at your destination.) Then lay a dry-cleaner bag out on a flat surface and slide one of the folded shirts inside the bag, all the way to the top. Stack a second shirt on top of the first one, but outside of the bag. Fold the bottom of the dry-cleaner bag over the second shirt. Then slide a third shirt inside the open end of the bag and set it on top of the second shirt. Pack this stack of shirts snugly in your suitcase, using the interior straps if possible, so they cannot slide around. With each shirt sandwiched between slippery plastic, the fabric will not bunch up and wrinkle. This technique will work fine with only one or two shirts, of course. Just wrap the remaining plastic around them. If you need more than three shirts on your journey, lay out another plastic bag and start from the beginning.

To pack your clothes so that they emerge wrinkle-free, try using dry-cleaning bags.

The clothes I'm traveling with are grimy

WASH THEM IN YOUR HOTEL SINK What? You didn't schedule a stop at a self-service laundry in your tour of Paris? No matter. Fill the sink in your hotel room with water that's an appropriate temperature for your fabric. Pour in 2 tablespoons of shampoo. (Use regular shampoo that doesn't contain conditioner.) Drop your garment in and use your hand to agitate for three minutes. Let the water out of the sink, press the soapy water out of your garment, and refill the sink with fresh water. Rinse the garment and press the water out again (don't wring). To accelerate drying, spread a bath towel across your bed, lay the garment on it flat, and roll it up in the towel. After 15 minutes, either repeat with a fresh towel or hang the garment up to dry.

I'm traveling, and my jewelry looks dirty

RESTORE THE GLEAM WITH TOOTHPASTE Once again, the solution is right there in your hotel room. Just smear a little toothpaste on a tissue and rub your jewelry gently with it. The toothpaste's very mild abrasion will clean up jewelry in no time. Rinse under the faucet.

■ COPING AWAY FROM HOME

There's no way I'll find the hotel exits in an emergency

LET YOUR SHOES POINT THE WAY When the alarms are blaring and smoke is filling the building, you don't want to hesitate in your hotel room doorway dithering over which way to turn to get to the emergency exit. So on arrival in your hotel room, take a few minutes to study the fire-exit diagrams. Then, when you're ready for bed, leave your purse and shoes near your hotel room door. Point the shoes in the direction of the emergency exit in the corridor outside. If you ever have to evacuate in a hurry, you'll have a reminder of which direction to take to get to safety. And you can snatch up your shoes and purse on your way without wasting precious seconds.

I'm afraid of shaking hands and picking up a disease

RUB ON AN ANTIBIOTIC GEL Whether you're at home or abroad, shaking hands is an efficient way to transmit germs. When you're

TRICKS OF THE TRADE

The Successful Suitcase
Photographer Karen Kasmauski knows something about packing a suitcase. Her *National Geographic* assignments have taken her to more than 32 countries on six continents. Here's her plan for successful packing:

• First, place heavy, flat objects, such as books and papers, in the bottom of the suitcase.

• Next, pack the clothes that need to lie flat—pants, shirts, and such. Secure them with the suitcase's interior straps.

• Pack the shoes on top of that, wrapped in plastic grocery bags.

• Add your cosmetics case or toilet kit.

• Pack underwear in one self-closing plastic bag and your socks in another. Use these to fill holes in your suitcase's contents.

• Surround anything fragile with clothing for protection.

traveling, however, you may not always have access to a sink to wash your hands in. One solution would be to whip out an antibiotic hand wipe after a round of handshakes. But this approach would surely offend the people you're trying to be friendly with. A less conspicuous solution would be to carry a small bottle of antibiotic, "waterless" hand gel and discreetly rub a bit into your hands after you've been pressing the flesh.

Antibiotic wipes do have a place in a traveler's germ-fighting kit, however. Use them to clean your hands before a meal, for instance, or to wipe off a toilet seat.

I need to protect my camera from the rain

PUT IT IN A DISPOSABLE SHOWER CAP It would be a shame to let a good camera get ruined in the rain. On the other hand, it's a pity to miss photo opportunities because of a drizzle. Here's a quick and free solution. The next time you stay in a hotel, pick up one of the free, disposable shower caps provided in the bathroom. They often come in little boxes that fit easily in a camera bag. When it rains during a photo excursion, put the body of your camera in the shower cap, with the lens protruding through the circle of elastic. If the shower cap is clear, you'll be able to see through the camera's viewfinder. If not, make a small hole in the cap to give you access to the viewfinder. Pressing the shutter release is no problem through the thin plastic. And manual winding can be done through the plastic, too, if your camera doesn't have an automatic film advance mechanism.

There's no way to steady my camera

MAKE A BEANBAG On the deck of a swaying, vibrating boat or aboard a jiggling train, it's almost impossible to steady a camera, even on a tripod. Many photographers improvise a beanbag to stabilize their cameras. When traveling, they take along an empty cushion cover with a zipper closing on one side. (A pillowcase would work, too.) When they reach their destination, they head for a market to buy filling for the

bag, such as corn kernels, popcorn, lentils, or rice. The beanbag creates a platform for a camera on an uneven surface—a rock or a railing, for instance—and will cushion it on vibrating surfaces.

■ FLYING

I missed my flight!

BE EXTRA NICE AT THE CHECK-IN COUNTER Whether you're flying for business or pleasure, nothing is quite as dismaying as missing your flight. But while you're going to be late to your destination, there are some things you can do to soften the blow. For starters, most airlines allow a two-hour grace period. That is, if you arrive within the grace period, the airline will do its best to get you onto the next flight. This, by the way, is when it really pays to be polite to airline staff at the check-in counter.

Generally speaking, for domestic flights, there may be a $100 rebooking charge, although it's possible the airline will waive it. If you booked your flight through a full-service travel agency, call the agency's hotline. Your travel agent should be able to handle the work of finding you another flight—often for a lower cost than you could accomplish on your own.

My flight got canceled

CALL THE AIRLINE'S 800 NUMBER When a flight gets canceled, save yourself the aggravation of waiting in the line at the reservation counter. Calmly take out your cell phone and dial the airline's 800 number to find out what your options are—either a seat on the next flight or assistance in securing a hotel room for the evening.

If the problem is weather related, however, the 800 number is likely to be tied up, too, and you may be put on hold. If that happens, try both tactics simultaneously: Stay on hold while waiting in line with the rest of the crowd.

When you've missed your flight, it usually pays to be nice to the check-in staff.

I have only minutes to switch planes

BOOK A FRONT SEAT ON THE FIRST FLIGHT If you have to make a tight connection at an airport, make sure that your seat on your originating flight is as far forward in the plane as possible. Then you won't have to wait for as many passengers in front of you to get off the plane before you start your trans-airport sprint.

I hate checking my suitcase unlocked

SEAL THE LATCHES WITH DUCT TAPE If you check your luggage on a flight these days, you probably will be told to leave your bags unlocked for a security inspection. You then visualize the luggage handlers tossing your suitcase around, the latches popping open, and your underwear decorating the tarmac. Or, worse, someone groping through your baggage looking for valuables.

To curb your worries, try duct tape. Cover the unlocked latches of your suitcase with just enough duct tape to fit over the fastenings. This will prevent the latches from accidentally popping open but will

---

Making Last-Minute Travel Arrangements

Back in the old days (pre-21st century), making last-minute travel arrangements was costly. Airlines and hotels charged more, because they had you over a barrel. Today, with Internet travel sites, last-minute booking is not only less expensive than it used to be, but in some cases it's also cheaper than booking ahead! Here's a look at some top Internet travel sites and how they work:

- **Expedia, Travelocity, and Orbitz** These three top travel Web sites are easy to use. You type your travel dates and destination, and the sites come back with your choices and prices. Prices are generally comparable to travel agent prices, but they can vary wildly, from site to site and from moment to moment on one site. Always shop around before committing.

- **Hotwire** This site is tricky, but it can save you a lot of money. Here's how it works: You type your dates and destination, and Hotwire comes back with prices. If it's a hotel, you are given the star rating and a price. If it's a flight, you are given a selection of flight prices and whether there is more than one connection. But you aren't told the name of the hotel or the airline or what the exact flight times are, and you don't find out until you make your purchase. The prices, however, will often run from 20 to 50 percent below what you'll find at the Web sites mentioned above. (Surprisingly, though, Hotwire prices aren't always lower than those of the other sites, so it still pays to compare.) Generally speaking, the star ratings for Hotwire hotels match those for Expedia, Orbitz, and Travelocity hotels, so it's a matter of deciding whether the lower price is worth the gamble of booking without knowing where you are staying.

- **Priceline** The ultimate in travel roulette. Say you want a hotel in Philadelphia. You go to Priceline, pick the area of Philadelphia you want to stay in, pick the star rating of the hotel, and pick the price you are willing to pay. Within moments, you'll find out if your bid is successful. The same goes for airlines: You pick from the dates and destination, enter a price you're willing to pay, and roll the dice. Generally speaking, you can expect at least 40 percent off the prices you see on the Big Three travel sites, and about 20 percent off Hotwire prices. You can do some advance research on Priceline by visiting biddingfortravel.com. This is a giant message board for people to post their Priceline adventures. If you see that someone got a three-star hotel in Philadelphia for $44 on the same days you're traveling, you'll know that you won't have to bid much higher for your room.

Remember, Priceline and Hotwire bookings are nonrefundable. You bid it, you buy it, it's yours.

allow a security officer to inspect the bag by peeling back the tape. If you use tape that matches the color of your suitcase, the latches won't be as conspicuous to criminal eyes perusing a luggage-filled conveyor belt.

■ DRIVING PROBLEMS

I've hit a monster traffic jam

RELAX, DON'T STEW You're motoring along, and all of a sudden the traffic in your lane goes from maximum speed to zero. Accident, construction, rubber-necking, it doesn't matter; all you know is that you're stuck. Instead of stewing, take this as an opportunity to relax. Try some deep-breathing exercises: Inhale slowly and deeply through your nose, hold it for a moment, and then slowly release the air through your mouth.

Stuck in traffic? Make the most of it, to keep stress at bay.

When you're feeling relaxed, here are some ways to pass the time:

- Sing along with the radio.
- Use your cell phone to gossip with friends, assuming it's legal to use a cell phone while driving.
- Put the car in park and read a book.
- Roll down your window and chat with the other poor souls stuck in the same jam.
- Clean your car.

Above all, be thankful for this brief respite, during which no one can lean on you for anything.

I've lost control of my car

STEER WHERE YOU WANT TO GO So that you'll be prepared if you ever lose control of your car, here are some pointers on what to do. First, stay calm. Next, determine whether it's the front or the back wheels that have lost traction. If your car refuses to turn, it's the front wheels that are not gripping. If your car seems to be going into a spin, it's the rear wheels.

For a front wheel problem, do the following: Take your foot off both the accelerator and the brake and shift to neutral, but don't try

Deflating Experience

The moment you get a flat tire is no time to start pondering how you'll deal with the situation. Unless you're the handy type, it's a great idea to join AAA or another road assistance company. You place a call when you're having trouble; they come out, usually within a half-hour.

Another option is to keep in your trunk a can of emergency tire sealer/inflator, available at auto parts stores for less than $10. These cans come with a short hose that fits right into your tire valve, sending air and sealant into the tire. The fix, however, is only temporary. The air pressure in the tire will be significantly less than normal, and it won't last long. Basically, it should give you enough time to get to a service station. Remember that you're riding on a damaged tire, so put your hazard lights on and keep your speed under 40 mph (64 kph).

to steer right away. As the wheels skid sideways, they will slow the vehicle, and traction will return. As you gain traction, steer in the direction you want to go. Then put the transmission in drive, or release the clutch, and gradually accelerate.

The rear wheels are a little trickier: What you've always heard is correct—steer into the skid. In other words, steer in the direction that the rear wheels are going. If your rear wheels are sliding left, steer left. If they're sliding right, steer right. Execute a little turn if it's a little spin, a bigger turn if you're in a bigger spin. You should also add some acceleration, not for speed but to transfer weight to the back of the vehicle.

■ CAR CARE AND REPAIR

A rock chipped my windshield

BUY A WINDSHIELD REPAIR KIT A pebble tumbles out of a dump truck on the highway, your windshield smacks it at the maximum speed limit, and your day is ruined. Not necessarily—small chips and bull's-eye cracks are easy to repair. First, keep dust, mud, bird droppings, and such out of the crack, because they will interfere with the repair. So pull over and put some clear plastic tape over the windshield crack until you can make your permanent fix. Then tend to the crack as soon as possible. Changes in temperature and everyday vibration caused by driving can worsen the crack. Swing by an auto parts store and pick up a clear epoxy repair kit designed specifically for windshields. They cost less than $10. Apply the adhesive according to the package directions.

Do-it-yourself fixes won't work well for cracks larger than, say, 12 inches (30 centimeters). For those, you'll need to have the windshield replaced by a professional.

Someone scratched my car's finish

COVER THE SCRATCH WITH NAIL POLISH Rub your finger gently over the scratch. If you can't feel the indentation made by the scratch, you're in luck. Only the surface clear coat was marred, not the paint layer. Go to an auto parts store, pick up a polish (many feature scratch-removing properties), and follow the package directions.

If you can feel the scratch on the surface of your car's finish, buffing and polishing will not help. The only solution is to paint over the scratch to make it less noticeable. Browse through the fingernail polish available in your home, a drugstore, or a department store. When you find a shade that matches the color of your car, delicately paint over the scratch and let it dry. If you mess up the patch job, dab on a little nail polish remover with a cotton swab to clean it up, let it dry, and start over.

Auto parts stores also sell touch-up marking pens and colored polishes that will disguise a scratch temporarily.

I ripped the car seat

ANOTHER JOB FOR DUCT TAPE If you've cut a gash in your car's leather or vinyl upholstery, find duct tape that matches the color of the upholstery and cut a piece just large enough to cover the rip. Auto parts stores sell duct tape in a wide range of colors. The tape will mask the wound until you can get it permanently repaired at an upholstery repair shop. Auto parts stores also sell color-matching adhesive repair kits for leather and vinyl upholstery.

Duct tape and do-it-yourself repair kits don't work quite as well on fabric, however. For large fabric tears, you'll need the help of an auto upholstery shop.

I'm worried my child's car seat isn't secure

CHECK WITH YOUR LOCAL POLICE You never want to put your kids in harm's way. But an incorrectly installed car seat is doing just that. To find out if your car seat is up to snuff, take a quick ride to your local police station. Most police are trained to spot a faulty car seat and will be able to secure yours properly.

In addition, many libraries, doctor's offices, day care centers, and other places where kids congregate hold free car-seat checkups. Find out when the next one is scheduled.

My car has been dented

HAMMER OR SUCTION THE DENT OUT Here are two ways to fix a dent without taking your car to the shop:

- If the dent is on or near the wheel arch, you'll be able to tap it out with a hammer, but only after you unscrew the black plastic shields under the arch. To do this, first make sure the

PROBLEM STOPPER

Be Ready for Hazardous Roads
Most loss of driving control happens during the winter, when snow and ice make driving dangerous. Here are some preventive measures you can take:

• Make sure your car is in good running condition and is equipped with all-season or snow tires.

• Scrape all snow and ice off your car, including the roof, windows, and windshield wipers.

• Keep the headlights free of snow, ice, and mud.

• Brake carefully and gently on snow or ice.

emergency brake is in place. Next, using a small screwdriver, unscrew the four to six screws holding the shield in place. Depending on the size of the dent, use either your fingers or a hammer to knock out the dent. Of course, if the dent is on the plastic shield itself, there is no need to take it off. Just get underneath it and push out the plastic with your fingers.

- If the dent is on the side of your car, you'll need a little suction to repair it. Find anything with a suction cup attached. Many automatic pencil sharpeners, for instance, have them on their bases. Most auto supply stores sell suction cups for pulling out dents. They cost about $7. Take the cup, place it directly over the dent, and pull it off. That wonderful *pop* sound indicates you've pulled the body back into shape.

I got car wax on my bumper

WIPE IT OFF WITH WD-40 Until they make car wax that easily comes off plastic car components, thank goodness for WD-40. Spray a little of it on the wax and wipe it off with a rag or an old toothbrush. This also works for wax that gets into crevices.

I can't jump-start a dead car battery

POUR COLA ON THE TERMINALS You found a kind soul to help you cable up your reluctant car battery, but the engine still won't turn over. Don't despair. The good news is that a car battery might get really, really weak, but it's never completely dead.

If your jump-start isn't working and there's a lot of corrosion around the battery terminals where you attach the cables, pour a can of cola on the corroded area. The acid in the cola will dissolve the corrosion, improving your connection and increasing your odds of a successful jump-start. The cola also contains electrolytes, which will help improve the electrical flow. Once you get home, wash the battery with a little bit of water to get rid of the cola residue.

My car is specked with stubborn sap

DAB THE SAP WITH RUBBING ALCOHOL Soap and water won't remove sap stuck to the finish of your car. But there is a simple solution. Pour a drop of rubbing alcohol directly on the sap spot, rub with your fingertips, and watch the marks disappear. No need to rinse, either. The alcohol will evaporate.

■ BICYCLES

I bent my bicycle wheel

BANG THE WHEEL AGAINST A TREE Remove the wheel from your bike and smack it against a tree or some other hard object to bend it back into shape. Check your progress with each strike, so that you won't bend the wheel too far the *other* way. Replace the wheel on your bike and start pedaling. This is only a temporary fix; you'll need to get a new wheel.

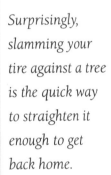

My bike tire is flat, and I don't have a repair kit

STUFF IT WITH LEAVES Pry one edge of the tire (the "bead") off the wheel rim of your bike. If you don't have a repair kit with you, you probably won't have bike tools to do this with, either, so try a pocketknife, some other piece of metal, or your bare hands. Once one edge of the tire is flopping outside the rim all the way around the wheel, gather a pile of leaves and moss and pack them tightly inside the deflated tire. Squeeze the edge of the tire back in place on the rim and start wheeling. The tire may not be as firm as you're accustomed to, but it will get you back.

Surprisingly, slamming your tire against a tree is the quick way to straighten it enough to get back home.

My bike tire got slashed off-road

LINE THE HOLE WITH A DOLLAR BILL A sharp rock has left a gash in your bike tire. Being a savvy cyclist, you know that when you patch the inner tube (or use your backup inner tube), it will pop through the hole in the tire and burst when you try to ride on it.

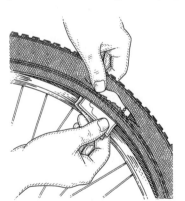

What you need is a strong but flexible material to place inside the tire against the hole. And paper money from your wallet is just the ticket. Pry one edge of the damaged tire off its rim. Pull out the inner tube and patch or replace it. Then place a bill from your wallet against the gash inside the tire. Press the tire back onto the rim and inflate the tire.

PART EIGHT

Health and Hygiene

If you have a serious medical problem, here's an important tip: Put this book down and call your doctor. Meanwhile, the rest of us are going to learn how to sneeze in public, how to cure a hangover, how to stop a nosebleed, how to avoid fainting, how to deal with a broken tooth, how to treat a sunburn, and much more.

Common Discomforts

■ PERSONAL ANNOYANCES

I've got the hiccups

CHANGE YOUR BREATHING PATTERN When you hiccup, your diaphragm tightens involuntarily. (Your diaphragm is a dome-shaped wall of muscle and connective tissue between your chest and abdominal cavity that contracts when you breathe in and relaxes when you breathe out.) There are several ways to trick your lungs and diaphragm to get back to their regular cycle. Try any or all, until your hiccups stop:

- Fill a glass with water, bend your head down, and take a long, slow sip from the back side of the glass.
- Take a deep breath and hold it as long as you can. The buildup of carbon dioxide in your lungs relaxes the diaphragm.
- Hold a paper bag against your mouth and inhale and exhale in it. Again, this causes a buildup of carbon dioxide.
- Take nine or ten quick sips in a row from a glass of water.
- Eat something shocking, like a slice of lemon or a teaspoon of cider vinegar.
- Eat a big teaspoon of peanut butter.
- Or the classic: Put a teaspoon of sugar or honey stirred in warm water on the back of your tongue and then swallow.

Breathing into a paper bag is one quick way to end hiccups.

I have bad breath

HAVE A DRINK, HAVE SOME PARSLEY Bad breath is generally caused by bacteria growing in the mouth, not the remnants of the lunch you just had. If you notice you have bad breath, swish water around your mouth and then drink up lots more. A dry mouth is a haven for bacteria. A sugar-free mint or some gum will give your mouth a perky, fresh flavor but does little for the underlying cause. Try a cola, seltzer, or iced tea to freshen the somewhat unpleasant taste that sometimes develops. They change the alkalinity of your mouth, which helps kill bacteria.

To keep your mouth more free of bacteria, brush your teeth at least twice a day and floss daily. Equally important, try brushing your tongue. The tongue is like a bacteria magnet. Brushing it removes bacteria and makes your mouth feel more comfortable.

A wonderful natural deodorant for your mouth is parsley. Try putting parsley, basil, or mint in your salads, because many dressings use garlic and other smelly spices as main ingredients. Also good for bad breath are fennel, dill, cardamom, and anise seeds.

If the problem is severe and won't go away, see your doctor. Sometimes it's a sign of other health problems.

I am sweating heavily under my arms

SOP UP THE MOISTURE AND APPLY AN ANTIPERSPIRANT There is a medical condition called hyperhidrosis—excessive perspiring—that hits 1 in 25 people. But for most of us, the sweat only pours out when we are tense, scared, or really hot. If the sweat is beginning to show through your shirt, excuse yourself, go to the bathroom, and towel down. Then apply an antiperspirant, NOT a deodorant. Antiperspirants contain aluminum chloride, which causes the pores that release perspiration to close up. If you sweat heavily, look for one with at least 12 percent aluminum chloride, the strongest non-prescription dose available. Next, if you have access to one, put on a T-shirt. Finally, drink some cold water to help cool your body down, and do what you can to calm yourself.

My feet stink

KEEP FEET CLEAN AND DRY Foot odor is caused by sweat. The sweat itself doesn't smell, but it breeds bacteria that give off foul odors. Charcoal shoe inserts work (they're available at shoe stores and pharmacies), but they can be expensive and are really only a temporary cure. If you are in a social situation in which foot odor is an issue, chances are it's because you have taken your shoes off; the odor is probably coming from them, not your feet. Either put the shoes back on or move them far away. Discreetly dry the insides of the shoes with paper towels; if necessary, stuff them with paper towels and leave them be. Chances are your socks have absorbed some of the odor, so put on dry, fresh ones, or take them off too and leave them with your shoes.

If you have a problem with chronic foot odor, here are some better things you can do:

PROBLEM STOPPER

Dampness a Problem? No Sweat

If sweating is a chronic problem for you, garment shields offer a solution, says Marcye Yorkman, a fashion stylist and image consultant at the Marcye Bodine Styling Company in Baltimore. These oblong, self-adhesive fabric guards are applied to the underarm of your sleeve to create a barrier between your underarm and your dress or your blouse. You can buy garment shields from any fabric store.

- Wash your feet with water several times a day. A couple of times a week, soak your feet in warm, soapy water. When you do, brush between your toes with a soft brush. Pour in a cup or two of white vinegar to help disinfect your feet. Dry them well after washing.
- Avoid nylon socks, which do not let feet breathe. Also avoid cotton socks, which absorb and hold sweat. Instead, wear wool/synthetic combination socks, which wick away odor-causing foot sweat. To kill bacteria, it's a good idea to wash your socks in hot, not warm, water.
- Avoid shoes that don't breathe, such as those with plastic or synthetic linings.

I'm too gassy

CHEW A HALF TEASPOON OF FENNEL SEEDS Fennel seeds, which have a licorice flavor, have been used for thousands of years to reduce gas and improve digestion. Caraway seeds have a similar effect. Of course, there are other quick remedies—the drugstore is full of antigas medicines that work. But for other home remedies, consider these:

- Make a cup of ginger tea by boiling slices of fresh gingerroot or steeping ¼ teaspoon of powdered ginger in hot water for five minutes or so.
- Make peppermint tea, but only if you don't have gastric reflux or heartburn, since peppermint can affect the flap between the esophagus and stomach. For most people with healthy digestion, though, peppermint tea works like a charm and can be consumed three or four times a day as needed.
- Go for a good long walk. And let the horn blow. Walking is a particularly good way to encourage gas dispersal.

Wax is blocking my ears

CLEAN WITH HYDROGEN PEROXIDE Earwax filters dust and other harmful particles out of the ear. Old wax is usually expelled by your chewing motions, which push the wax, along with dead skin cells and bacteria, out of the ear. But as people age and there is less moisture in their wax, it can build up in the ear, hardening and causing blockage and pain. Don't use a cotton swab to clean it out; the swab can lodge the wax deeper in the ear canal and damaging the eardrum. Instead, fill an eyedropper with hydrogen peroxide that is body temperature or a little warmer. Lie down or tilt your head so the blocked ear is pointing up. Drip the peroxide into the ear until it feels full. Wait three minutes before tilting your head the other way over a washbasin or towel to let the peroxide drain out. Then tilt your head again and gently squirt warm water into your ear. Let it settle, and then drain. Clean away the water and softened wax from your outer ear with a washcloth or cotton balls.

A few drops of baby oil or mineral oil can also do the trick. Let the oil work its way down into you ear. You can leave it in for up to one hour. Then squirt in some water to flush the oil out.

In either case, finish up by using a hair dryer to dry your ear. Use the coolest setting and don't bring it any closer than 12 inches (30 centimeters) from your ear.

■ SKIN PROBLEMS

My skin is dry and flaky

BATHE USING BATH OIL Normally, the body's natural oils, secreted from the skin glands, keep the skin moist. But seasonal changes, such as drier air in winter, along with showering every day, which many people do these days, can cause skin to dry

TRICKS OF THE TRADE

Moistening Your Hands
In winter when your skin tends to dry out, apply moisturizing cream to your hands while the skin is still moist. This helps trap moisture on the skin. Don't wait until your hands are dry; it will be that much harder to moisten the skin.

WORLD-CLASS FIX

Gas Masker

After Frank Lathrop of Houston developed chronic flatulence as a side effect of a diabetes medication, his employees became so tired of spraying air fresheners around the workplace that they gave Lathrop an ultimatum—either he build himself a private office in the back of his manufacturing plant, or they would quit. Lathrop's answer was the Flatulence Filter. It looks like a normal seat cushion, but the gray tweed chair cushion contains a superactivated carbon filter. Pass some gas while sitting on the cushion and, according to research published in 1998 in the British Medical Association's *Gut* journal of gastroenterology, the carbon filter will discreetly trap approximately 90 percent of the odor-causing gas. The filter seat, Lathrop claims, is great for sufferers of gas-producing illnesses such as irritable bowel syndrome and colitis, as well as for generally flatulent people. His company also makes a filter pad, which fits inside underwear.

out. And the soaps we use wash away our natural oils, leaving the skin dry, flaky, and irritated. The quick fix is to bathe less often, or at least cut back on the amount of soap you use and the scrubbing you do. In addition, instead of showering, take a bath and use a bath oil in the water. The oil will replace the natural oils lost in the bath. This will be easier and more effective than trying to rub down your whole body with expensive moisturizing lotion.

I have an ugly boil on my back

USE A WARM COMPRESS Boils are like massive pimples. Red, hot, painful, and sometimes oozing pus, they can arise almost anywhere on the skin, usually with a hair follicle as the place of birth. As with pimples, never squeeze a boil. You risk spreading infection to other parts of the skin or even to the blood. Don't poke it or prick it with a pin. Instead, place a warm, wet compress on it for ten minutes at a time, two to three times a day. These compresses will soothe the inflamed skin and possibly draw out the pus. You can use warm water, or warm thyme or chamomile tea, or a warm, moist teabag by itself. If you can't reach the boil, soak as long as you can in a hot bath. Another approach: Dry it out by applying an acne medication containing benzoyl peroxide twice a day. Or apply tea tree oil, which is a natural antiseptic.

I have warts on my hands

USE GARLIC TO BATTLE THE WART Commercial wart removers work fine and usually erase the wart in two weeks. But there are lots of effective home remedies that work too. For example, apply freshly crushed garlic directly to the wart and cover with a bandage. The caustic effect of the garlic will cause the wart to blister and fall off in as little as one week. Apply new garlic every day, avoiding contact with healthy skin. (Smear the area around the wart with petroleum jelly to protect it.) For added effect, eat raw garlic or take three garlic capsules a day to help the immune system fight the virus.

Another home remedy: Cover the wart with a small piece of duct tape and leave there for six days. When you take the tape off, soak the wart in water for a few minutes and then use a disposable emery board or pumice stone to file down the dead, thick skin. Leave uncovered overnight, then repeat the whole process. Other materials that people have used successfully to wither away a wart include vinegar, dandelion sap, ground vitamin C tablets, banana peel, and lemon peel.

I have a deeply embedded splinter

USE A WART REMOVAL DISK Squeezing and gouging is an ineffective way to remove a deep-seated splinter. Buy a wart removal disk containing salicylic acid, or other salicylic acid pads. (Some can be found for foot care.) Buy a single pad, because a pack will probably expire before you use them up. The pad measures about 3 inches by 2½ inches (7.6 by 6.4 centimeters). Use scissors to cut out a tinier pad, about ¼-inch (6.4 millimeters) square, and place the sticky side over the hole where the splinter entered the skin. Cover this with a plastic bandage and leave it for six hours (no more). The salicylic acid in the pad will supermoisturize the skin. As the acid draws bodily fluid to the wound, the splinter will also be drawn to the surface. When the six hours are up, remove the bandage and pad. The head of the splinter should be exposed. Remove the splinter with a pair of clean tweezers.

If you can't get a wart removal disk, and the sliver is made from wood, soak the area of skin where the splinter is buried in a cup of warm water to which you've added 1 tablespoon of baking soda. It should make the sliver swell up, making it much easier to remove. Repeat the soaking twice a day until the sliver emerges.

I have a pimple on my face

USE EYEDROPS AND MAKEUP Whatever you do, don't squeeze it. Squeezing pimples may cause an infection, create more inflammation, and even lead to scarring. Instead dab an over-the-counter product containing salicylic acid or benzoyl peroxide on the zit.

If the pimple pops up just before a social engagement, try this two-step approach for hiding it. First, apply some over-the-counter eyedrops (the kind meant to take the red out of eyes) to the zit. The liquid will enter the skin, constrict the swollen blood vessels surrounding the pimple, and reduce the redness. Then use makeup to cover the blemish. A green-tinted makeup will do the best job of hiding it, since green and red are on opposite sides of the color wheel. If the pimple is large or painful, call a dermatologist, who can treat the condition with a shot of cortisone, which will make it disappear without scarring.

Eyedrops are the quick way to "take the red out" of an embarrassing zit.

I have a cold sore

TREAT WITH ICE, ASPIRIN, AND LYSINE Cold sores can be painful, annoying and, when they erupt, rather unattractive. They are caused

**Preventing a
Poison Ivy Rash**
You've just blundered
through a patch of poison
ivy (or poison sumac or
poison oak), and your
heart is sinking down to
your knees. All is not lost,
though. Here's how a top
nurse says to prevent a
rash from breaking out:

As soon as you realize
you've been exposed, pour
a lot of rubbing alcohol
into a large bowl. Drop a
washcloth into the alcohol
and then wring it out so
that it's not dripping wet.
Scrub the skin that you
think has been affected.
Scrub long and hard, as if
you're scrubbing caked-on
mud. The alcohol will neutralize the proteins in the
poison ivy oil that's on
your skin. Make sure you
do this the moment that
you've been exposed,
because once the rash
develops, the rubbing
alcohol won't help.

by a herpes simplex virus and are contagious through skin-to-skin contact. Sometimes cold sores go away only to return months later in the same spot. That's because the virus hibernates under your skin in nerve cells. Different things, such as emotional or physical stress, cold wind, and sunshine, seem to trigger the reemergence of cold sores.

Apply ice directly to the sore. It will bring down the swelling, ease the pain temporarily, and if done early enough, keep the sore from growing larger. Also consider taking 125 milligrams of aspirin a day while you have a cold sore; studies show that that can cut the herpes infection's active time in half. If you have it on hand, the amino acid lysine is a top healer of cold sores. Take 3,000 milligrams daily until the sore goes away. You can also reduce the inflammation by dabbing the sore with the oil from a vitamin A or vitamin C capsule.

And if you want to go to a drugstore, you can use an over-the-counter antiviral cold sore cream. Apply the cream with a sterile cotton swab instead of your finger to avoid infecting the sore. Don't use alcohol-based disinfectants. Finally, be careful not to touch your eyes after touching the cold sore (yet another reason to avoid touching it altogether). The virus can cause an infection.

I have a strange rash

TREAT AN ITCH Skin rashes crop up for many reasons and can be frightening. Here's a rule of thumb: If it hurts, you should probably see a doctor. If it itches, you can probably treat it yourself. Two things can help stop the itching: spreading hydrocortisone anti-itch cream on the rash and putting cool compresses on the rash. If there's a chance that an itchy spot on your skin is a tick bite, the source of Lyme disease, see a doctor.

By the time my dermatologist saw me, my rash was gone

TAKE A SNAPSHOT You decide to see a doctor about a rash. Der-matologists, like all doctors, stay busy. And since most rashes, blemishes, and other skin conditions are not life-threatening emergencies, you might have to wait a few weeks before your appointment. By then, the condition has probably cleared up, making it harder for the doctor to suggest measures to prevent a reoccurrence. Solution: Take a photograph of the rash and show that to the doctor during your appointment.

◼ NOT FEELING WELL

My back is killing me

ICE FIRST, HEAT LATER We're assuming you don't have a chronic back condition, but rather muscle pain from overexertion, a sudden twist, or a really bad night of sleep. As a pain reliever, ice works great by blocking pain signals and reducing swelling. Several times a day, lay an ice pack wrapped in a towel on the painful area for up to 20 minutes. Or use a bag of frozen peas or corn. After 48 hours, switch to moist heat to stimulate blood flow and reduce spasms. Dip a towel in very warm water, wring it out, and lay it over the painful area. Cover the towel with plastic wrap and put a heating pad, set to medium, atop the plastic wrap. Leave it on for up to 20 minutes. You can repeat this three or four times a day for several days.

I feel like I'm going to throw up

SUCK A FRUIT POPSICLE There are many reasons you might feel nauseated. You have to judge how serious this symptom is. Generally speaking, though, you can settle your stomach by sipping on something cool and carbonated, such as ginger ale. Sometimes a fluid will coat the stomach and prevent the acidic secretions from causing discomfort. Drink too much too fast, however, and you might make things worse. Solution: Suck on a frozen fruit juice Popsicle, which is like taking little sips of juice.

I have bad diarrhea

DRINK WATER AND JUICES Depending on where you are and what you have recently eaten or drunk, you have probably ingested some sort of pathogen—a bacterium or virus, for instance. Most stomach bugs leave in two to three days. Assuming your diarrhea isn't bad enough to send you to the doctor, your main remedy is replacing lost fluids and electrolytes (body salts) by drinking lots of water and fruit juices. Black tea sweetened with sugar also is good; the tea contains astringent tannins that help reduce intestinal inflammation, and the sugar improves sodium absorption. Tannin-rich blackberries also have long been used for diarrhea. Make blackberry tea from tea bags made with real blackberry leaves. Raspberry tea may also be effective. Also consider capsules of the herb goldenseal, which appears to kill many of the bacteria that cause diarrhea. Over-the-counter diarrhea

PROBLEM STOPPER

Sleep Off the Pounds
Some research indicates that people who get too little sleep are more likely to overeat. Scientists theorize that the body's response to sleep deprivation is a craving for energy, in the form of food. The body reads the signal as a message to raid the refrigerator. At such low-energy moments, the body does not necessarily want a well-balanced meal. It craves a high-energy calorie boost—what you might get from munching a plate of fattening, carbohydrate-rich food. In addition, sleep deprivation creates a kind of stress. Cortisol, a stress hormone produced by the adrenal glands, was found to be higher in men deprived of sleep, according to one study. Cortisol triggers a release of insulin, a hormone that is believed to cause fat storage.

PROBLEM STOPPER

How to Prevent a Hangover

Here are three tips on how to avoid the dreaded hangover:

• **Avoid red wine.** Red wine contains congeners, natural chemicals that play a role in the taste of a wine. They're also believed to cause the next-morning headache. White wine also contains congeners, but in much smaller amounts.

• **Alternate nonalcoholic beverages with your booze.** This will not only cut your alcohol consumption in half but will also prevent dehydration, which contributes to your hangover. But avoid caffeine, a diuretic.

• **Eat foods cooked in grease before drinking.** Fatty foods go a long way toward lining the inside of your intestines, which will slow down alcohol absorption.

medicines containing bismuth subsalicylate can reduce the severity and dehydrating effects of diarrhea. Be sure to wash your hands frequently to prevent spreading the illness to others.

I woke up with a hangover

CONSUME MORE LIQUIDS AND EAT EGGS There is a bright side to hangovers. That dry-mouthed, head-throbbing, stomach-churning misery is enough to keep most people from drinking too much for their own good. Here's what you can do to feel better:

- **Drink lots of fluids.** Alcohol is a diuretic, causing frequent urination and, ultimately, dehydration. As the body gets low on fluids, it draws water from all over the body, including the brain's outer coating, or dura, causing pain and discomfort. By drinking lots of fluids, you'll both rid yourself of cotton mouth and rehydrate the rest of your body.
- **Make it a sports drink.** Part of dehydration is the loss of important electrolytes, such as potassium and sodium, which causes—you guessed it—pain and discomfort. Most sports drinks, such as Gatorade, contain potassium, sodium, and other electrolytes that are lost in heavy physical activity—or heavy drinking.
- **Eat eggs.** Eggs contain an amino acid known as cysteine, which helps in the body's detoxification process. This may be why you find eggs in many traditional hangover cures, including the bartender pick-me-up known as the Prairie Oyster (raw egg, brandy or vodka, olive oil, and Worcestershire sauce). But make sure the eggs *you* consume are cooked. (See "Licking *Salmonella*" on page 352.)
- **Eat honey.** Honey has a ton of fructose, a sugar that helps to work the alcohol out of your system. It also contains vitamin B6, which helps with hangover symptoms.
- **Try ibuprofen.** Ibuprofen, such as in Advil or Motrin, is going to be lighter on the stomach than aspirin. But be careful: Ibuprofen can upset the stomach, so use moderation. And ibuprofen and other over-the-counter pain relievers can cause serious side effects if a person consumes more than three drinks a day, health care advisers say.

■ UNSANITARY CONDITIONS

My doctor's waiting room is filled with sick people

KEEP YOUR HANDS CLEAN Doctors' waiting rooms can be dens of communicable diseases. You may have come in with a bad back, but you could very well leave with a bad back and a cold. Just remember: It isn't very likely you'll catch something floating in the air. Instead, it'll come from a germ getting on your hands and then entering your body when you touch your face. So:

- **Be careful with your hands.** While waiting, don't touch your mucus membranes—eyes, nose, or mouth—after touching magazines, chair arms, doorknobs, or anything else a sick person might have touched.

You're less likely to catch a germ floating in the air than one you pick up on your hands.

- **Wash up.** The minute you've left the room, wash your hands well. Regular soap will do just fine, as long as you're thorough, scrubbing for at least 15 seconds and rinsing well.
- **Carry antibacterial wipes or gel.** Alcohol-based wipes and gels are effective immediately against both bacteria and viruses (whereas other antibacterial agents often are not). Keep these handy in your purse or pocket. Use them to wipe off any surfaces you must touch, such as doorknobs. They also make a handy hand-washing alternative, in case you can't get to soap and water.
- **Avoid sneezes.** Although even respiratory viruses are spread more often by transfer from hands to mucus membranes, sneeze droplets are airborne germ bombs. Be aware, and do what you can to avoid them.
- **Check your own germs.** If you're sick, take precautions so that you won't spread your own germs in the waiting room. Wash your hands after blowing your nose or sneezing. Use alcohol wipes to clean anything after you have touched it. If everyone were more conscientious, the risk of catching something in a doctor's waiting room would be lessened.

I've got to sneeze, and I'm in public without a tissue

USE THE BEND IN YOUR ELBOW Sneeze or cough into the crook of your elbow, a part of the body that likely won't spread the germs to others through contact. Contrary to your instincts, covering your mouth with your hands is not hygienic. If you're sick, you will end up with infectious microbes on your hands and can make others sick by touching doorknobs or shaking hands.

My 5-year-old doesn't wash his hands long enough

SING A SONG The simplest and most effective way to prevent the spread of infectious diseases, such as colds, flu, and even hepatitis, is to wash your hands regularly before meals, after using the bathroom, and after sneezing or blowing the nose. But you have to wash your hands properly, soaping them and scrubbing for at least 15 seconds, to wash away harmful microbes.

Get your children into the habit of singing a song—"I've Been Working on the Railroad," for instance. The rule is that they're not finished scrubbing until the song is over. This makes washing more fun and more effective.

The locker-room floor at the pool is always wet

WEAR WATER SHOES OR SANDALS When you're in the gym locker room or in a public shower at the pool, wear water shoes or sandals. Flip-flops work particularly well because they are cheap, waterproof, lightweight, and easy to slip on and off. This will help you avoid two common skin conditions, athlete's foot and plantar warts.

Eek! My child has head lice

WASH CLOTHES AND BEDDING, SHAMPOO HAIR Lice only happen to other people's children—until they happen to yours. A case of head lice does not necessarily mean you've been a neglectful parent or that you're lacking in the hygiene department. It simply means that your child—at school, camp, or dance class—came into contact with someone with lice.

Here's how to stop the problem. Wash all of the child's clothing, pajamas, and bed linens in hot water (at least 130° F or 55° C). Dry on your dryer's hottest setting for at least 20 minutes. Vacuum carpets, upholstered furniture, and the child's mattress to suck up any traces of lice, including their eggs. Fortunately, lice—unlike those

PROBLEM STOPPER

Licking *Salmonella*

Salmonella bacteria used to be found only on the outside of eggshells. But in recent decades the bacteria have found their way into the egg yolks. The stomach acid of people with mature and healthy immune systems usually kills *Salmonella* bacteria. But in young children, the elderly, and sick people, *Salmonella* can thrive. That's why you should avoid raw eggs, which in turn means no more batter licking for kids.

You should also avoid eating these foods if they are homemade: eggnog, soft-boiled eggs, mousse, mayonnaise, Hollandaise sauce, Caesar salad dressing, ice cream, and raw cookie dough. (According to the Centers for Disease Control and Prevention, however, commercially manufactured mayonnaise, ice cream, and eggnog have not been linked to *Salmonella* infection, because they are made with pasteurized eggs.)

hearty survivalists, fleas—can survive for only about a day without a human host, so anything you miss should soon die. Pick up an over-the-counter pesticide-free lice removal kit at your local pharmacy. These kits usually include a removal shampoo and a fine-tooth comb for removing lice and their eggs, known as nits. Follow the directions carefully. For two weeks, inspect all family members daily for any traces of lice or nits. During these two weeks, have all family members avoid close contact with the infested child.

■ MEDICATIONS

I'm going on vacation and want to keep my medications straight

PLAN AHEAD AND BRING YOUR BOTTLES Traveling takes us out of our routines, so taking regular medications requires some planning. Here are some ideas for keeping it all straight while you're on the road:

- Keep a handy list of the prescription and nonprescription medicines and dietary supplements you take. If you're flying, keep the list on you, not in your checked luggage.
- Before departing, review dosage schedules and how travel across time zones will affect when you take your meds.
- Pack enough medicine to last the duration of the trip, plus at least an extra day's worth.
- If you use a pill dispenser, don't fill it until you arrive at your destination. Medicine containers have important information like medicine name, dosage, instructions, and warnings. They

also assure customs inspectors that you are not smuggling illegal drugs.

- Never pack medicines in luggage that will be checked on an airplane. Keep it in your carry-on bag.
- Be careful where you keep your medicines as you travel. Heat and humidity can damage them, so never store medications in car glove compartments, trunks, or beach bags.

My medicine cabinet is a mess

GET RID OF OLD AND UNUSED MEDICATIONS A messy medicine cabinet is a safety issue, since old or unidentifiable medicines can be dangerous. Furthermore, if you don't stay current with what's in your cabinet, you'll be unaware of missing medicines—prescription and over-the-counter—that you may one day need. Here's a step-by-step strategy for keeping your medicine cabinet safe and up to date:

1. At least once a year, clean out your medicine cabinet, checking bottle labels for expiration dates.
2. Get rid of out-of-date meds, meds your doctor has told you not to take, meds that have changed in smell or color, and meds with missing or illegible labels.
3. Dispose of dangerous meds safely. Don't throw them in the trash, where children can pick them out. Flush the pills or syrups down the toilet or wash them down the sink before tossing the bottles.
4. Make sure medicine bottles have child-resistant caps and that the caps still work.

Minor Health Emergencies

■ URGENT SITUATIONS

I scorched my finger on a pot

APPLY COLD, THEN ALOE We're assuming that you have a first-degree burn, meaning there is damage only to the top layer of skin, leaving it red and painful. More serious burns require more serious treatment. But if the momentary touch to something hot caused your burn, rinse the burned area in cold water for five to ten minutes to ease the pain. Then apply cool, moist cloths or a towel-wrapped ice pack. Over-the-counter pain relievers can help. Aloe-based moisturizers will soothe the skin. First-degree burns do not usually require medical attention and should heal in a week or less.

I gave myself a nasty paper cut

CLEAN AND COVER They hurt, but small cuts are rarely a problem unless they get infected. So wash the area thoroughly, apply an antibiotic salve, and then cover with an adhesive bandage. Cover it even if it isn't bleeding, because you still need to protect the exposed flesh from germs. In fact, the antibiotic salve should be reapplied three times a day for maximum protection. The cut should heal within a few days.

I bit my tongue and it hurts

RINSE WITH MOUTHWASH We all do it, and we all feel foolish about it. There's not much you can do to speed up the healing of a tongue bite. Gargling with a germ-killing mouthwash will help keep it from getting infected, and applying an oral analgesic ointment, if you have it, will reduce the pain. After that, your job is to keep yourself from biting your tongue again. Because your tongue is swollen, be mindful when chewing. Doctors recommend switching to soft foods until the swelling recedes. As with any cut, the swelling should go down within a few days, and the tongue completely healed within a few weeks.

A paper cut may hurt a lot, but all it needs is a little antibiotic salve and a bandage.

My child is crying because I have to remove an adhesive bandage

SOAK IT FIRST WITH BABY OIL If ripping off bandages sends shivers down your or your child's spine, there's a less painful way. Soak a cotton ball in baby oil and gently rub it over the bandage until it falls off. If you don't have baby oil handy, any cooking oil or bath oil will work just as well.

I just ripped the top of my fingernail off

TRIM IT AND LEAVE IT If the rip is in the top half of the nail, and the base of the nail remains securely in place, there is probably no damage to the skin underneath, so you can tend to it yourself. Otherwise, see a doctor. To fix a torn fingernail, take a nail trimmer and smooth out the edge to prevent it from catching on something and ripping further. Wash your hands and then leave the nail alone. Putting a bandage on it won't help; in fact, that will lock in moisture, which will soften the nail and make infection more likely. Rather, keep the nail dry. Let the nail grow back at its own pace.

My husband has a nosebleed

PINCH THE NOSE Nosebleeds happen to many people for all sorts of benign reasons. If the person is elderly or has a serious health condition, such as heart disease, diabetes, high blood pressure, or a blood coagulation problem, call a doctor when a nosebleed occurs. Otherwise, chances are that the nosebleed is not serious. There is a simple method that doctors recommend for stopping the blood flow: Pinch the soft part of the nose firmly. Direct pressure should halt the bleeding within minutes. If after 30 minutes the flow hasn't stopped, call a doctor.

■ EYE INJURIES

I got hit in the eye

USE AN ICE PACK To reduce swelling and pain, put an ice pack or cold cloth over the eye. Keep it there for 15 minutes. If the eye continues to hurt or turns red, or if you have blurred vision, double vision, or a lot of new floaters (small specks floating across your field of vision), go to an emergency room or see a doctor right away.

A Good First-Aid Kit

A first-aid kit should prepare you for almost any health emergency, from poison ivy to a blood-spurting cut. The Council on Family Health, a U.S.-based nonprofit organization, recommends the items listed below. Keep them in a waterproof box in an easy-to-find location.

- sterile adhesive bandages in assorted sizes
- sterile gauze pads, 2 inches and 4 inches (5 and 10 centimeters)
- cotton swabs
- anti-itch cream
- antibiotic ointment
- face mask
- clean towel
- eyedrops
- a roll of absorbent cotton
- at least three sterile roller bandages, 2 inches and 3 inches (5 and 7 centimeters)

- butterfly bandages and narrow adhesive strips
- emergency phone numbers (doctor, pharmacist, and poison control)
- a thermometer
- antiseptic ointment, spray, or towelettes
- bottled water
- latex gloves
- chemical ice packs
- a first-aid handbook
- hypoallergenic adhesive tape

There's a speck in my eye

WASH IT OUT Your tendency will be to rub your eye. Don't. You might scratch the cornea. Instead, try this: Gently lift the upper eyelid over the lower lid. Chances are the lower eyelashes will brush the speck off the inside of the upper eyelid. Blink several times to try to wash the speck out. If that doesn't work, flush it out with clean water using one of these methods: Either hold your head under a faucet and let the water irrigate your open eye, or submerge your head in a basin full of water and blink rapidly. If these methods fail, keep the eye closed and go to an emergency room or to your doctor. Left in place, a speck of dirt can scratch the cornea.

Chemicals splashed in my husband's eyes

FLUSH THE EYES WITH CLEAN WATER Whatever the chemicals, acting fast is very important. You need to rinse the eyes with lots of clean water. If you're able, hold your husband's head under a faucet and let the water flush the chemical from the eyes. Or bend his head and have someone pour clean water from a clean container into his eyes. Have your husband use his fingers to hold the eyelids as far open as possible. Have him roll his eyeballs during the rinsing. Rinse for at least 15 minutes. Once the chemical has been flushed away as much as possible, fill a clean sink, dip his whole face in the water,

PROBLEM STOPPER

How to Beat the Heat
Quick: Name the single "weather killer" of more people in North America than hurricanes, lightning, tornadoes, floods, and earthquakes combined. Would you believe it is excessive heat? But heat-related death can be prevented. Follow this advice the next time summer really cooks:

• **Find an air conditioner**. If you don't have one in your home, during the hottest parts of the day, seek out cool public spaces, such as malls, movie theaters, and libraries.

• **Stay hydrated**. Drink lots of water and other nonalcoholic beverages.

• **Dress the part**. Wear lightweight, light-colored, loose-fitting clothes.

• **Take it easy**. Limit strenuous activity to the cooler parts of the day.

and have him blink rapidly. If his eyes continue to hurt, go immediately to your eye doctor or to an emergency room. Do not bandage the eyes.

■ LIGHTHEADNESS AND HEAD INJURIES

I feel as if I'm going to faint

LIE DOWN Fainting is a common occurrence. Many different stimuli trigger fainting in susceptible people. Some people pass out when their hands get really cold. Others pass out when they see blood. Generally, fainting is brought on when blood vessels dilate, reducing blood pressure and cutting down oxygen flow to the brain. Before they actually faint, people often turn pale, begin sweating, and generally feel terrible. An instant antidote is to lie down. You want your heart and brain at the same level, so that oxygen-rich blood can get to the brain more easily. By lying down the minute you feel faint, you will likely remain conscious. If you don't lie down, you risk fainting and falling and possibly injuring your head.

I feel dizzy

LIE DOWN If you've been exercising and you feel dizzy, seek emergency medical help right away. Dizziness during any kind of physical workout can be a sign of cardiac trouble. Otherwise, feeling dizzy, like fainting, is fairly common. (If it happens more than once, however, see a doctor.) As with fainting, you should lie down, so that blood floods to your brain. If you're with someone, explain what you're doing, so that your companion can get help if the situation turns into an emergency. Take calming breaths and stay prone until you feel completely normal.

My child got hit in the head

STOP THE BLEEDING AND APPLY ICE Apply an ice pack directly to the wound to reduce swelling and alleviate the pain. If the wound is bleeding, direct pressure with a clean cloth should stop the flow. Signs that a head injury has damaged the brain include seizures, loss of consciousness, nausea, strange behavior, and memory loss. If your child shows these symptoms, get him or her to an emergency room right away.

My child is screaming on an airplane

USE STEAM FROM HOT TOWELS IN A CUP If you've tried everything—peekaboo, story time, bubbles—and your child still won't calm down, he or she is probably suffering from ear pain, caused by pressure changes in the ascending or descending airplane. If you've ever experienced ear canal pressure, you know how much this can hurt. Don't bother trying to get your youngster to yawn or swallow or do whatever it is you do to equalize pressure in your own ears. Instead, try this: Soak two paper towels in hot water. Place each in a plastic cup and carefully cover the child's ears with the cups. The steam should loosen things up, relieving the pressure and stopping the pain—and wailing.

For instant relief from an air-pressure earache, cover the ears with plastic cups containing hot, wet paper towels.

■ HOT WEATHER PROBLEMS

I'm overheated and cramping

SIT STILL AND DRINK JUICE If it's hot out, and you're sweating a lot from strenuous activity, your muscles, usually in the abdomen, arms, and legs, may begin to spasm, which can mean you are having heat cramps. Heat cramps are caused by low salt and moisture levels in the body. They can be a symptom of heatstroke (see page 244), which can be serious. If you think you might have heatstroke, or if you have heart problems or are on a low-sodium diet, seek medical attention right away for heat cramps. Otherwise, here's what you can do to make the cramps go away:

1. Stop what you're doing and sit quietly in a cool place.
2. Drink clear juice or a sports beverage.
3. Don't go back to the strenuous activity for a few hours.
4. If the cramps aren't gone in one hour, seek medical attention.

I've got a bad sunburn

APPLY COLD COMPRESSES Despite slathering on SPF 45 and sitting under umbrellas, occasionally we still get burned. Sometimes overexposure to sun even leads to second-degree burns. If sunburn causes fever, fluid-filled blisters, or severe pain, or if the burn affects an infant under the age of 1, call a doctor. A doctor can treat the burn and prescribe medicines to prevent infections or scarring from

Staying Safe When Lightning Is Popping

A thunderstorm can be deadly. If you can hear thunder within five seconds of seeing lightning, you are in a lightning zone. Keep in mind that lightning is attracted to metal and water and strikes tall things, such as trees and radio towers. Here's how to stay safe in a lightning storm.

If you are outside:

- Get out of the water.

- Avoid fields, golf fairways, and other wide open areas.

- Either wait in a car with the windows up or get to the lowest ground you can find and, instead of sitting, kneel or squat to minimize contact with the ground. Stay off hilltops.

- Stand at least 7 feet (2 meters) from trees, gazebos, poles, or anything else that's tall.

- Avoid metal objects such as golf carts, lawn equipment, and gates. Remove golf shoes or steel-toe boots.

- Wait at least 30 minutes after the last thunderclap or lightning strike before resuming your outdoor activity.

If you are inside:

- Stay away from windows and doors.

- Disconnect computers, stereos, televisions, and other electronic gear. Avoid using the telephone, except in emergencies. Your home's wiring attracts lightning.

- Avoid using sinks, tubs, or showers, since lightning can course through a home's plumbing.

- If things get really bad, close the main gas valve.

the blisters. Otherwise, the pain should be over in a few days, and the skin should be fully healed in a week.

To alleviate sunburn pain, apply cold compresses or immerse the burned skin in cool water. Rub in moisturizing lotion or aloe gel but not salve, butter, or ointment. Do not pop blisters.

My child has a heat rash

FIND A SHADY SPOT Heat rash strikes on hot, humid days when a person, usually a young child, is sweating profusely. It appears as a red cluster of pimples, most likely on the neck and upper chest, in the groin, under the breasts, and in elbow creases. The simple fix for heat rash is to cool off. Find a less humid spot. You can sprinkle dusting powders on the rash to alleviate the discomfort, but avoid using ointments and creams, which can make the rash worse.

■ DENTAL EMERGENCIES

I broke a tooth

PROTECT THE TOOTH IN YOUR MOUTH If it's a sizeable chip, save it. Clean the injured area and apply an ice pack to it. Contact your dentist, who may be able to reattach the broken part. If you cannot get to the dentist right away, toss the chip. It will no longer be of use. But here's how you can protect the broken part still attached to your jaw from infection or other problems: Buy some orthodontic wax, the kind used by kids with braces and sold by drugstores. Clean your mouth by brushing your teeth and swishing around some antiseptic mouthwash. Roll a small piece of the wax into a ball and stick it on the tooth. The wax will protect the exposed roots. If you can't find orthodontic wax, use a small piece of sugarless chewing gum until you can get to a dentist.

A filling fell out of my tooth

USE ORTHODONTIC WAX OR CHEWING GUM Old fillings fall out, and when they do, they expose a tooth's roots to painful substances, such as sweets and cold drinks, and to infection-causing bacteria. Until you can get to a dentist, here's what to do: Rinse your mouth, brush your teeth, swish around a little antiseptic mouthwash,

WORLD-CLASS FIX

Do-It-Yourself Dentistry

During a photographic expedition in Antarctica, Pat Keough bit down on a pebble in his porridge and split a molar in his lower jaw. The Canadian photographer would not see civilization for another month and a half, so he was forced to take matters into his own hands. Like many a handy person, his mind turned to duct tape.

To make a dental cap, Keough first snipped out a piece of duct tape 1 inch long and ½ inch (2.5 by 1.25 centimeters) wide. He used tissues to dry his mouth out, so the tape would bind with his teeth. Then he placed the tape over the top of the broken tooth and used his fingers to mold it into a snug fit. For stability and extra padding, he cut another piece of tape—1 inch by 1 inch (2.5 centimeters square)—and placed it over the broken tooth and the two neighboring teeth as well. The result was not the most comfortable dental cap ever created, but it did prevent the broken tooth from cutting his tongue, and it kept air away from the exposed nerve, reducing his pain. He spent the next several weeks chewing on the other side of his mouth and had to rebuild the duct tape dental cap about five times.

and then plug the gap with a small ball of orthodontic wax or sugarless chewing gum to protect the exposed roots.

The crown fell off my tooth

ATTACH IT TEMPORARILY WITH DENTURE ADHESIVE First, find the crown. You'll want to visit a dentist as soon as possible. But in the meantime, here's a quick solution: Rinse the crown or cap in clean water and reattach it with denture adhesive, available at pharmacies and supermarkets. (Bonus tip: To save money and avoid waste, look for a travel-size container of the denture adhesive.) This will reestablish your smile temporarily until the dentist can do it permanently.

My gums are killing me

RINSE WITH SALT WATER Gum pain is usually tooth pain caused by receding gums or a foreign object wedged between the gum and tooth. What hurts is the tooth's nerve, which healthy gums cover and protect. For gum pain, you should see a dentist. In the meantime, however, try rinsing with a warm water solution of either salt or baking soda. This will soothe the exposed tooth nerves and dull the pain.

Cold and sweets hurt my teeth

USE TOOTHPASTE FOR SENSITIVE TEETH The cause is likely receding gums that expose the teeth's sensitive roots. When cold drinks, sweets, and other substances come into contact with these nerve-entwined roots, you get a jolt of pain. Try a toothpaste for sensitive teeth. These products contain ingredients that seal dental tubules, reducing the roots' exposure. A toothpaste for sensitive teeth does not work overnight. Give it a couple of weeks. If the pain continues, make an appointment with your dentist.

At the same time, switch to a soft or extra-soft toothbrush and don't brush hard, because that can contribute to gum loss. Your gums are important, not only in keeping out pain-causing substances, but also in keeping out caries and decay.

My child's tooth got knocked out

TAKE TOOTH AND CHILD TO THE DENTIST Young people are at especially great risk of losing teeth. (Each year millions of teeth are

TRICKS OF THE TRADE

Teeth-Whitening Tips

• **Chew sugarless gum after meals.** The gum and chewing action stimulate the flow of saliva, which removes staining bacteria.

• **Rinse with water after meals.** A quick rinse with clean water will flush stain-causing matter out of the mouth.

• **Use a straw.** The less contact that colored liquids—soft drinks, juices, and iced coffee, for instance—have with your teeth, the better. The rule of thumb is that if it will stain your shirt, it will stain your teeth.

• **Drink clear fluids.** Try white grape juice instead of purple. Drink a lemon-lime soft drink instead of a cola. Even better, stick to water.

knocked out while youngsters play sports.) If your child—or anyone else—loses a tooth, act fast. If you get to an oral surgeon soon enough (within 40 to 60 minutes), the tooth can most likely be reimplanted. (If it's a baby tooth, there is no need to replace it—just have your child's dentist make sure the permanent tooth underneath was not damaged.) Here's what to do: Locate the dislodged tooth. Hold it by the crown only. Do not touch the exposed roots. Rinse it with clean water, but do not rub it or touch the roots with anything. The best way to protect the tooth while traveling to the oral surgeon is to put it back in its socket, cover it with gauze, and have the owner bite down on it to hold it in place. Or you can store the tooth temporarily in cold milk, salt water, or between your cheek and gum. The point is not to let it dry out. To find an oral surgeon, call your family dentist or local hospital's emergency room.

Act fast. If you can get to an oral surgeon within an hour, the tooth can be reimplanted.

Index

A

Acetone, for countertop stains, 41
Acne, 272, 348, 349
Adhesive(s). *See also* Glue; Tape
    denture, for loose crown, 364
    removal, 34, 39
Aerator, faucet, 111
Aging. *See* Antiquing
Air conditioner filters, 35
Air travel, 335–37, 361
Alcohol. *See also* Beverages;
    Wine
    for clothing odors, 256–57
    hangovers, 352
    for parties, 280, 283–84
    rubbing. *See* Rubbing alcohol
Allowance, 329
Aloe vera, for burns, 193, 397
Aluminum foil, for silver tar-
    nish, 274
Ammonia
    for bleach spots, 267–68
    for brass antiquing, 154
    for kitchen odors, 190–91
    for windows, 35
Amusement parks, 331
Animals. *See also* Pets
    attacks, 248–51
    pests, 131, 238–42
Antibiotic gel/wipes, 333–34,
    353
Antihistamines, for insect
    stings, 247
Antiperspirants, 345
Antiquing
    brass, 154
    furniture, 154
Antiscald devices, 122
Ants, 127–28, 237–38
Aphids, 234–35
Apologies, 287–88, 306
Appearance, 270–73. *See also*
    Clothing
    hair problems, 271–72
Apples, as squirrel bait, 241
Appliances, power outages,
    124. *See also specific types*
Arguments

between children, 323
between guests, 284
persuasive, 306
Armadillos, 240
Arrest, 310
Artwork, displaying, 146–47,
    152. *See also* Pictures/pic-
    ture frames
Aspirin, for cold sores, 350
Attic
    ice dams, 210
    insulation, 210
    vents, 116, 210
Attire. *See* Clothing
Auto-body filler, for sanding, 57
Automatic water shutoff valve,
    122
Automobiles. *See* Car/driving
Awkward social situations,
    287–88
Awning tears, 205

B

Baby oil. *See* Mineral oil
Babysitters, 328–30
Baby spit up, on carpets, 44–45
Baby wipes, 265
Back pain, 351
Bad breath, 289, 344–45
Bags
    emergency, 308
    grocery, 308
    laundry, 158
    plastic. *See also* Trash bags
        dry cleaner, 332
        grocery, 308
        for overshoes, 258–59
        storage, 165, 200
        for suitcase, 332
    shopping, 308
    vacuum seal, for clothing, 164
Bait
    for animal pests, 240–41
    for cutworms, 234
    for earwigs, 234
    for insect pests, 236, 238
    for snails, 234
Baking powder, homemade, 176

Baking soda, 176
    for aging roof shingles, 205
    for brass cleaning, 39
    for countertop burns, 40
    in homemade baking powder,
        176
    for laundry odors, 39, 268
    for mineral buildup, 38–39
    for refrigerator odors, 191, 192
    for shoe odors, 276
    for silver tarnish, 274
    for skunk odor, 248
    for sore gums, 364
    for toilet cleaning, 43
Ball cock, 115–16
Balloons, for skunk control,
    238–39
Balusters, repair/replacement,
    85–86
Bandages
    for paper cuts, 357
    removal, 358
Barbecue grills, 215–16
Baseboard heaters, cleaning, 34
Basement
    cracked walls, 207
    fans, 57
    water in, 207
    window wells, 207
Baskets. *See* Containers
Bathroom
    bathtubs, 113, 119
    carpet, 89
    cleaning, 37–40, 43, 159
    exhaust fans, 108, 158
    grounded outlets, 108–9
    locks, 103
    organizing/storage, 156–58
    toilets, 113–16
    tub overflow, 119
Bathtubs
    chipped, 113
    overflowing, 119
Bats, in house, 133
Batteries
    car, 340
    for keyless entry, 101
BCC (e-mail), 316, 317

lost filling, 363–64
sensitive teeth, 364
sore gums, 364
stained teeth, 364
teething, 328
Dents
car, 339–40
floors, 79–80
furniture, 58
metal doors, 99
Denture adhesive, for loose
crown, 364
Denture-cleaning tablets, for
toilet, 37
Desserts, 185–86
Detergent
for scorch marks, 269
for skunk odor, 248
for vinyl siding, 204–5
for yellow jackets, 236–37
Diarrhea, 351–52
Dimmer switches, 145
Dimples, in drywall, 68–69
Discomforts, common, 344–56.
See also Health problems
Dishes
mismatched, 181
storage, 161, 201
Dishwasher, 112–13
Dishwasher detergent, for
scorch marks, 269
Dishwashing liquid. See Deter-
gent
Dizziness, 360
Dogs. See also Pets
repellents for, 239
threatening, 248–49
Do-not-call list, 313
Doorbell, 109
Doormats, 148–49
Doors, 97–105
cleaning, 34
dents in, 99
fireplace, 72

garage, 104–5
holes in, 99–100
locks and latches, 100–104
loose hinges, 97–98
painting, 75–76, 99
self-closing, 98
stuck, 75–76, 98
weather stripping, 99, 100
Doorstops, loose, 98–99
Double constrictor knot, 135
Downspouts, 207, 209–10
Drain, jewelry removal, 275
Drainage, around house, 207
Drapes. See Curtains and
drapes
Drawers
dividers, 155
liners, for cushions, 149–50
loose knobs, 67
sticking, 64, 65
utensil, 200
Dress shields, 345
Drills, 52, 53, 54. See also Tools
and workshop
bit holder, 54
carpet damage, 87
drilling guide, 52
dust, 57, 73–74
pilot hole, 48
reverse switch, 53
Drinks. See Alcohol; Beverages
Drivers license, lost/stolen, 301
Driveway
cracks, 212–13
oil stains, 213
Driving. See Car/driving
Dropcloths, 78
Drugs. See Medications
Dry cleaner bags, 332
Dryers, 108, 109, 110
ducts, 265
wrinkle removal, 256
Dryer sheets
for buttonhole repair, 260
for static cling, 255
Dry skin, 347–48
Drywall. See Wall(s)
Ducts, dryer, 265
Duct tape
for awning tears, 205
for changing light bulbs, 106–7
for cuts, 246–47
for eyeglasses repair, 275
for torn car seats, 339
Durham's Rock Hard Water
Putty. See Water putty

Dust
fan filter for, 57
plaster, 73–74
from sanding, 56–57
Dusting. See Cleaning
DVDs, 321–22

E

Earrings, 273. See also Jewelry
Ear wax, 346–47
Earwigs, 234
Efflorescence, 208
Eggs, for hangovers, 352
Eggshells, for tomato plants,
227–28
Egg white, for facial mask, 272
800 numbers, 313, 335
Elastic waistband, 255
Electrical cords, 56
Electrical problems, 106–10
clothes dryers, 108, 109
doorbells, 109
exhaust fans, 108
grounded outlets, 108–9
hair dryers, 108–9
lighting, 106–8. See also
Lights/lighting
phones, 109
power outage, 123–24
refrigerators, 110
surge protectors, 122
Electrical tape, 245
Electric igniter, 215–16
Electronics, 313–22
CDs, 321–22
computers, 315–21
DVDs, 321–22
telephones. See Telephones
VCRs, 321
E-mail. See Internet
Emery board, 273
Entertaining, 285–86
alcohol/beverages, 183–85, 280
bad weather, 281
children's parties, 330–31
cleanup, 41–42
dessert disasters, 185–86
food, 280–81, 282
hostess gifts, 294
karaoke bar, 306–7
mismatched china, 181
planning, 280–81, 282
problem guests, 283–85
spills on dining companions,

Travel, 332–41. *See also*
    Car/driving
    bicycling, 341
    disease prevention, 333–34
    emergency exits, 333
    emergency supplies, 334
    flying, 335–37, 361
    last-minute arrangements, 336
    medications, 355–56
    packing, 332, 333
    photography, 334–35
    Web sites, 336
Trees
    broken branches, 229
    deer protection, 241
    pruning, 228–29
Tree sap, on car, 340
Trim screws, 48
Trisodium phosphate, for vinyl
    siding, 204
Trousers. *See* Clothing; Pants
T-shirts
    memory quilt, 155
    slip substitute, 256
Tubs. *See* Bathtubs
Tupperware. *See* Containers
Turkey, quick-cooking, 179
Turpetine, for marker stains, 44

U

Umbrella, for cold protection,
    244
Underarm stains, 264, 345. *See
    also* Perspiration
Upholstery. *See also* Furniture
    burns, 62
    cleaning, 122–23
    stains, 43–44
    torn automobile, 339
Urine
    for animal control, 239
    stains, 46–47
Utensils, organizing, 192

V

Vacuum seal bags, for clothing,
    164
Vacuums/vacuuming
    fleas, 128–29
    HEPA filter for, 121
    shop, 56
    soot cleanup, 121
Valve(s)
    automatic water shutoff, 122
    dishwasher, 112–13
    excess flow, for gas line, 122
    toilet
        refill, 115–16
        shutoff, 119
Varnish
    mixing, 80–81
    for scratched floors, 79
VCRs, 321
Vegetables
    composting, 222
    cooking, 169, 170, 174
    growing. *See* Gardening
Vegetarian guests, 182
Vehicles. *See* Car/driving
Veneer, loose/blistered, 62–64
Venetian blinds, cleaning, 36
Ventilation
    attic, 116, 210
    fans, 108, 158
Vermouth, 177
Videocassette recorders, 321
Vinaigrette, sun-dried tomato
    basil, 184
Vinegar
    for bathroom floor, 37
    for brass tarnish, 274
    for clothing wrinkles, 269
    cooking wine substitute, 177
    for mildew, 37
    for mineral deposits, 38–39,
        40, 111
    for outdoor furniture, 214
    for pots and pans cleanup, 188
    for salt marks on shoes, 277
    for smoke odor, 191
    for sour milk, 175
    for veneer repair, 63
Vinyl floors, 82–84. *See also*
    Floors; Tile
Vinyl siding, cleaning, 204–5
Vodka, for clothing odors,
    256–57
Voice mail, 297
Volcanoes, 245
Vomit, on carpets, 44–45

W

Wall(s)
    blisters, 71
    cleaning, 188–89
    cracks, 69–70
    dimples/bumps, 68–69, 71
    holes, 68, 70
    painting. *See* Paint/painting
    picture hangers, 74
    plaster dust, 73–74
    stains and marks, 44, 45, 72
    stud finding, 72–73
Wallet
    forgotten, 305
    lost/stolen, 300, 301–2
Wallpaper, cleaning, 188–89
Warts, 348
Washing. *See also* Cleaning;
    Laundry/laundry room
    hands, 333–34, 353, 354
Washing machine. *See also*
    Laundry/laundry room
    maintenance, 120
    odors, 268
Waste Paint Hardener, 78
Water-clarifying plants, 228
Water Crystals, 224
Watering
    lawn, 231
    plants, 223, 224
Water putty, 71
    for broken picture frames, 67
    for concrete block wall holes,
        70
    for loose doorstops, 98–99
    for loose knobs, 67
    for sanding block, 57
Water rings, 59, 60
Water shutoff valves. *See*
    Valve(s)
WaterSmart Crystals, 224
Water spots, on clothing,
    266–67
Water supply
    during blackouts, 124
    for lost persons, 245–46
Wax, 63
    automobile
        on bumper, 340
        for CD scratches, 40
        for countertop scratches, 40
    for butcher blocks, 65
    candle, 32–33, 44, 62
    ear, 346–47
    furniture, 58, 59, 60